I10700314

TO DETER AND PUNISH

To Deter and Punish

GLOBAL COLLABORATION AGAINST TERRORISM
IN THE 1970s

Silke Zoller

Columbia University Press
New York

Columbia University Press
Publishers Since 1893
New York   Chichester, West Sussex
cup.columbia.edu

Copyright © 2021 Columbia University Press
All rights reserved

Library of Congress Cataloging-in-Publication Data
Names: Zoller, Silke, author.
Title: To deter and punish : global collaboration against terrorism in the 1970s / Silke Zoller.
Description: New York : Columbia University Press, [2021] | Includes bibliographical references and index.
Identifiers: LCCN 2020055427 (print) | LCCN 2020055428 (ebook) | ISBN 9780231195461 (hardback) | ISBN 9780231195478 (trade paperback) | ISBN 9780231551342 (ebook)
Subjects: LCSH: Terrorism—History—20th century. | Terrorism—Prevention—History—20th century.
Classification: LCC HV6431 .Z648 2021 (print) | LCC HV6431 (ebook) | DDC 363.325/1709047—dc23
LC record available at https://lccn.loc.gov/2020055427
LC ebook record available at https://lccn.loc.gov/2020055428

Columbia University Press books are printed on permanent and durable acid-free paper.
Printed in the United States of America

Cover design: Milenda Nan Ok Lee
Cover image: History and Art Collection © Alamy

To Dane

CONTENTS

ACKNOWLEDGMENTS

It takes a village to help a history PhD succeed. Many people contributed their time and skills to help me improve this book, and my research is all the better for their effort. Any errors left in the book are my own.

Richard Immerman is an exceptional adviser. He empowered me to make my own finds and claims yet brought me back to earth when my head was figuratively spinning in the stars. He has always had my back each step of the way. I am deeply grateful for his support. My dissertation committee worked hard to help me see not just the trees but also the forest. Thank you to Petra Goedde, David Farber, Orfeo Fioretos, and Paul Thomas Chamberlin for bringing their distinct perspectives to my big-picture argument. In Tübingen, Germany, Georg Schild, my undergraduate and MA adviser, first nurtured my interest in the 1970s.

I was fortunate to receive research grants from the Society for Historians of American Foreign Relations, the Center for the Study of Force and Diplomacy, the Center for the Humanities at Temple, Temple University's Global Studies Program, and the Gerald R. Ford Presidential Foundation. I could not have conducted my research without the help of the archivists at the National Archives at College Park, the Presidential Libraries of Richard Nixon, Gerald Ford, and Jimmy Carter, the Library of Congress, the German Federal Archives, the Political Archive of the German Foreign Office, the National Archives Kew, and the Hoover Institution Archives. Thank you for guiding me through many (de)classified records with patience and grace.

The Clements Center for National Security and the John Sloan Dickey Center for International Understanding provided me with the time and resources I needed to transform my dissertation into a book manuscript. Will Inboden kindly brought me to the Clements Center, and Mark Lawrence helped me settle into its rich academic community. The Clements Center sponsored my manuscript workshop, and I thank Jeremi Suri, Alan McPherson, Katherine Unterman, deRaismes Combes, as well as Aaron O'Connell, for providing nuanced feedback on my research and argument. At the Dickey Center, Edward Miller helped me conceptualize how my dissertation would function as an academic book. So did Udi Greenberg and Jennifer M. Miller. Lydia Walker was a great support in navigating the early stages of being a PhD.

I benefited greatly from the community of scholars who engaged with my project. Tim Naftali, Bernhard Blumenau, Tobias Hof, Adrian Hänni, and Tim Geiger offered strong advice on how to improve my concepts and framing at early stages of my project. Alex Hobson and Mary Barton kindly discussed their own research results. I had a supportive community of graduate students at Temple University. My thanks to Carly Goodman, Sarah Robey, Thomas A. Reinstein, Manna Duah, Paul Braff, Tyler Bamford, Matt Fay, and Steven Elliott. Thank you also to Jay Lockenour, Jayita Sakar, Kyle Burke, Thomas Jamison, Jaehan Park, Theo Milonopolous, and Agnès Dubler for many engaging conversations.

The anonymous reviewers at Columbia University Press provided concise, on-point feedback to strengthen my work. My editor, Caelyn Cobb, has been a constant advocate for my research. Many thanks also to Mark Feldman and Frank Loy, who kindly shared their time and experience and saved me from a number of mistakes.

My family and friends have offered nothing but encouragement. As first-generation college students, my parents were not sure what having a daughter in academia would entail. But they always believed in me, had my back, and have eagerly engaged with my work. Spock the Shetland Sheepdog herded me outside for walks and fresh air. Finally, Dane has held me up (sometimes literally) and accompanied me down every step of this path. I love you.

ABBREVIATIONS

ALPA	Air Line Pilots Association
ARA	Bureau of Inter-American Affairs, U.S. State Department
BFV	Bundesamt für Verfassungsschutz (Federal Office for the Protection of the Constitution, FRG)
BSO	Black September Organization
CCCT	Cabinet Committee to Combat Terrorism, United States
CIA	Central Intelligence Agency, United States
CPD	Committee on the Present Danger, United States
EC	European Community
EPC	European Political Cooperation
FAA	Federal Aviation Administration, United States
FBI	Federal Bureau of Investigation, United States
FRG	Federal Republic of Germany
FRUS	Foreign Relations of the United States series
GSG9	Grenzschutzgruppe 9 (Border Security Group 9), FRG
IAEA	International Atomic Energy Agency
IATA	International Air Transport Association
ICAO	International Civil Aviation Organization
IDF	Israel Defense Forces
ILC	International Law Commission
IRA	Provisional Irish Republican Army

ABBREVIATIONS

NEA	Bureau of Near Eastern and South Asian Affairs, U.S. State Department
NSC	National Security Council, United States
OAS	Organization of American States
OLA	Office of the Legal Adviser, U.S. State Department
OPEC	Organization of the Petroleum Exporting Countries
PFL	Palestine Liberation Front
PFLP	Popular Front for the Liberation of Palestine
PFLP-EO	Popular Front for the Liberation of Palestine—External Operations
PFLP-GC	Popular Front for the Liberation of Palestine—General Command
RAF	Red Army Faction
SAS	Special Air Service, UK
SNIE	Special National Intelligence Estimate
TREVI	European Community states' domestic security network, founded in 1976
UN	United Nations
UNGA	United Nations General Assembly

TO DETER AND PUNISH

INTRODUCTION

Carlos the Jackal was the most infamous international terrorist of the mid-1970s. His real name was Ilich Ramírez Sánchez. Venezuelan by birth, Ramírez joined the Palestinian national liberation extremist organization Popular Front for the Liberation of Palestine (PFLP) in 1970. Working with leader Wadie Haddad, Ramírez went on to commit a string of attacks across Europe. In September 1974, he threw grenades into a Parisian café, killed two people, and wounded thirty-four others. The attack was part of a coordinated strategy to pressure the French government into conceding to PFLP-allied Japanese leftist extremists who had taken over the French embassy in The Hague. In January 1975, Ramírez headed two attacks at Paris's Orly Airport. He and PFLP associates fired rocket-propelled grenades at planes on the tarmac, injuring approximately twenty-five people. On December 21, 1975, Ramírez struck again in Vienna, Austria. With a team of Palestinians and West Germans, he seized the Organization of the Petroleum Exporting Countries (OPEC) headquarters. Ramírez and his team killed three people and took ninety-six hostages, including the oil ministers of Saudi Arabia, Iran, and Venezuela. The attackers eventually left Austria with forty-two eminent hostages. They flew to several capitals around the Middle East before vanishing into Algeria, possibly with a ransom worth millions of dollars from an undisclosed source. In subsequent years, the international press speculated fearfully on new attacks Ramírez

FIGURE 0.1. Carlos the Jackal, international terrorist.
Ilich Ramírez Sánchez became infamous in the 1970s for his attacks in Europe under his codename, Carlos.
Heritage Image Partnership Ltd / Alamy Stock Photo.

might be planning. European heads of state discussed Ramírez's where-abouts; his presence in several Eastern European states caused diplomatic tensions between them and their Western European counterparts in the late 1970s. Further attacks followed in the 1980s. Ramírez's luck finally ran out in 1994. Sudanese authorities turned him over to French intelligence agents in an extraordinary rendition coordinated with the U.S. Central Intelligence Agency (CIA). He currently remains incarcerated in France.

Ramírez positioned himself as a participant in a decades-long tradition of national liberation insurgency. Since 1945, dozens of new countries had gained independence from colonial control. Some decolonization processes were peaceful, but many of these countries underwent decolonization with significant internal violence and insurgencies. In some cases, former colo-nizers and authoritarian-leaning governments attempted to retain control with brutal counterinsurgent tactics.[1] In states such as Algeria, North Viet-nam, and Cuba, violent actors seized control and established their own

governments. These states inspired other self-proclaimed national liberation movements around the world by showcasing that violent actors could
overthrow existing governments to establish their own revolutionary states.
Algerian and Cuban officials facilitated a transnational revolutionary network.[2] Members claimed to be advancing the self-determination of their
populations.

In the 1960s, South Vietnamese and Palestinian violent actors became
the key groups within this transnational revolutionary network.[3] They committed significant acts of violence, including illegal attacks such as assassinations and bombings. So did violent actors throughout Latin America,
driven by local economic and political conditions as well as Cuban sponsorship.[4] Affected countries, usually within the Global South, established
repressive counter-programs that oftentimes violated their citizens' civil
rights—in many instances with U.S. assistance.[5] Most of these conflicts had
Cold War dimensions. Many anticolonial actors relied on leftist, Marxist, and Maoist ideology to facilitate more equitable economic conditions.
Meanwhile, affected states and right-wing violent actors used anticommunist and reactionary justifications for their countermeasures.[6] In the 1960s,
though, revolutionary anticolonial actors calculated that they had a real
chance of successfully creating their own states.

Yet Ramírez was also representative of a new type of transnational violent actor who emerged beginning in the late 1960s. After 1968, the extremist Palestinian Fedayeen ("those who sacrifice themselves") exported their
ostensibly anticolonial violence from their contested areas into the former colonial metropoles—the industrialized states of the Global North.
Through hijackings, mail bombs, and later embassy takeovers, attacks on
diplomats, rockets fired at airports, and similar acts, Fedayeen emphasized
that ostensibly anticolonial violence was no longer limited to former colonies or the Global South. After a brutal attack on the Israeli team at the
1972 Munich Olympic Games, contemporaries began consistently labeling
such attacks as "international terrorism," though they did not define what
that term meant. Somewhat rare beforehand, the term *terrorism* became
widely used. International terrorists were cosmopolitan, traveling and
attacking throughout Europe and the Middle East. They also cultivated
transnational contacts and soon became more diverse in terms of national
origin. Ramírez hailed from Venezuela, for example, but he was associated

with a radical Palestinian group and broke the law alongside West German citizens. And as his work with Haddad suggested, he claimed to advance the cause of the Palestinian national liberation movement and other self-determination actors. But the attackers' ideological convictions could not erase the brutality of such attacks. And publics in the Global North focused primarily on the fact that these actors were criminals who broke the law, hurt innocents, and created an ominous new security threat in homes previously untouched by decolonizing violence.

Throughout the 1970s, a pattern emerged: extremists committed a cross-border international terrorism attack, and target states responded with new policies and initiatives but lost traction until the next big attack. Most Global North governments passed new laws, strengthened the capacity of local and federal law enforcement agencies, adjusted judicial procedures, increased intelligence surveillance, or instituted militarized emergency responses.[7] But domestic antiterrorism initiatives stopped at national borders. So Global North officials collaborated to pass extradition agreements that would criminalize attackers around the world, cut off their safe havens, and ensure their criminal prosecution. In the 1970s international organizations adopted extradition conventions that covered hijackings, attacks on civil aviation facilities, attacks on diplomats, hostage-taking, and (in one regional European case) terrorism. Officials in the United States, West Germany, and the United Kingdom worked hard to enforce these conventions around the world and to sponsor related policies and practices.[8] As Global North states developed antiterrorism capacities, extremists found their attacks more challenging to implement. They responded with new and more brutal attacks. In 1970, 651 terrorist attacks occurred worldwide with 174 fatalities, while in 1980, 2661 attacks happened, with 238 fatalities in January alone.[9]

By the early 1980s, Global North states normatively handled international terrorism as a crime but found that corresponding law enforcement and extradition-based measures took time and were limited and contentious in scope. To address international terrorism and transnational violence more effectively, the administration of Ronald Reagan in particular began relying first on militarized rhetoric and then on military units and tactics.[10] This militarized approach was similar to 1950s and 1960s counterinsurgent practices. It delivered faster and more immediate results than bureaucratic and cumbersome law enforcement initiatives that spanned multiple borders and jurisdictions. Yet the earlier conceptions of international terrorism still remained. Contemporaries focused on the criminal aspects of attacks and downplayed local political contexts (though they retained large-scale Cold War views). Both criminal aspects and militarized practices fed into the later Global War on Terror.

The first major international antiterrorism initiatives in recent postwar history began during the 1970s. Notable is U.S., European, and other Global North officials' adherence to international law and crime-focused responses when they collaborated against this new transnational violence. In earlier decades, European and American officials had framed efforts against nonstate political violence within Cold War, anticolonial, insurgency, and definitely political contexts, and U.S. officials from the 1980s also emphasized Cold War and other political frameworks for cross-border terrorism. Why were 1970s initiatives different? Why did Global North contemporaries focus so much on crime and extradition responses in the decade when international terrorism established itself as a serious global threat? And how did 1970s antiterrorism collaboration affect later counterterrorism? To answer that question, this book analyzes U.S., European, and allied states' collaboration against international terrorism. It focuses on the period from 1968, when Palestinian hijackings began, to approximately 1984, when the Reagan administration introduced militarized U.S. counterterrorism policies.

With great controversy and limited success, U.S. and European officials regulated international terrorism as a nonstate criminal threat through multilateral agreements during the long 1970s. Their goal was to criminalize transnational violent actors and pressure all states to convict (but not support) such extremists. Lawyers in the U.S. State Department, West German Interior and Justice Ministry bureaucrats, and British Home and Foreign and Commonwealth officials led the way. Each set of officials had their own national context and aims. But to limit this new transnational threat, the U.S., European, and allied governments could not rely on domestic measures that stopped at national borders. Bureaucrats turned to another border-spanning tool: international law. If countries could agree on common definitions and practices concerning international terrorism, the advantage of nonstate attackers could be minimized. Global North officials needed shared rules and processes that all states would use—even the Global South states that the attackers most often came from. Thus, Global

North officials sought solutions to facilitate the identification, arrest, criminal prosecution, and extradition of border-crossing attackers. Most of the multilateral agreements Western officials drafted against such attackers in the 1970s were in fact extradition agreements.

European and U.S. officials insisted that international terrorists were first and foremost criminals and needed to be handled as such. They doggedly pursued this criminalizing approach over militarized strategies such as Israel's military interventions against Palestinians and neighboring states. Their international law initiatives were controversial and almost impossible to enforce. They infringed on states' sovereign control of their legal systems and on their conceptions of what constituted legitimate political (and especially national liberation) violence. But Global North officials insisted that international terrorists should be defined by the brutal and inacceptable violence they committed against these officials' populaces. Attackers were criminals. These efforts resulted in a substantive normative change in the Global North and the establishment of a weak corresponding international law regime. Officials in the United States and Europe, along with their allies, began conceiving of international terrorists primarily though their violent acts, significantly downplaying their political context.

The goal that the United States and other countries pursued was to get as many other states to sign these crime-focused agreements as possible in order to cut off safe havens for attackers and deter future attacks. Officials defined a wide variety of violent nonstate actions, from Palestinian hijackings to Latin American attacks on diplomats, as exclusively criminal, thus stripping the actions of political meaning. Strong opposition surfaced from recently independent states such as Algeria and Cuba, the nonaligned movement of states, national liberation groups, and anticolonial activists. They all insisted that anticolonial national liberation movements should not be held responsible for the violent international terrorist attacks committed by radicals on their margins—or for the colonial violence that incited victimized populations to terrorism in the first place. Hence, the global debate on international terrorism during the 1970s was about far more than just terrorism. It covered nonstate actors who sought sovereignty and statehood, and it raised the complex question of what sort of political violence such actors could legitimately pursue within international relations. The Global North delegitimized border-crossing, anticolonial actors by branding their violence as criminal "terrorism." European, U.S., and allied officials undermined the strong objections by adding loopholes to their extradition agreements and regulating only one type of attack at a time, in a piecemeal fashion, instead of going after the umbrella category of international terrorism. The controversy remained, however. And these agreements' loopholes and unenforceability meant that they were too weak to actually prevent or capture terrorists. The multilateral antiterrorism agreements of the 1970s created strong normative understandings in the Global North about terrorism being first and foremost a crime. But to resolve terrorism crises and achieve practical antiterrorism successes meant that, by the 1980s, the United States in particular turned to more militarized approaches.

Though Global North officials claimed to be addressing a criminal problem, international terrorism attackers viewed themselves as intrinsically political actors. By criminalizing border-crossing terrorist acts within international law, U.S. and European officials downplayed the global context and politics of decolonization. The result was that they politicized the regulation of crime—at home and in the world.

Since many new tools of the 1970s for addressing international terrorism were based on diplomatic and state-to-state collaboration, this book puts diplomats and bureaucrats at the center of the story. As an international history, this book traces state officials' approaches in various countries to issues of political violence and terrorism within international relations. It homes in on mid-level bureaucrats who conducted negotiations in international organizations and oftentimes shaped the policy results. At center stage are diplomats from the U.S. State Department's International Organization Affairs, Inter-American Affairs, and Legal Adviser offices, as well as bureaucrats from the Foreign Office and Interior and Justice Ministries of the Federal Republic of Germany (FRG). Acting with different national and bureaucratic priorities, these officials took the lead in negotiating the agreements and collaboration that shaped Global North positions on terrorism and political violence. They regulated international terrorism yet actively sought to avoid engaging with the nonstate actors who perpetrated it. The book also incorporates nonstate actors' voices, tracing how terrorists themselves, as well as civil rights activists, academics, airline executives, and aviation worker unions, supported or contested Global North officials' criminalization of terrorism. These nonstate actors pursued their own political interests and called attention to state actors' blind spots and prejudices. Sources are in English, German, French, Dutch, and Italian and from the United States and across Europe. Most documents hail from government archives, in particular the U.S., British, and German national archives, the Presidential Libraries of Richard Nixon, Gerald Ford, and Jimmy Carter, and the Political Archive of the West German Foreign Office. Pilot union records, newspaper publications, terrorists' manifestos, and antiterrorism experts and journalists' papers from the Hoover Institution complement this research.

In the 1970s, Global North states rejected counterinsurgency practices developed in the decolonizing world in favor of international organizations and international law instruments to control the transnational violence of the decade. The 1970s were a transformative era of economic uncertainty in which Western states could no longer definitively shape the politics and norms of the international sphere.[11] Processes of globalization brought people, goods, and ideas into ever-increasing contact with one another. The rapidly spreading aviation industry facilitated this exchange.[12] Like other travelers, violent anticolonial extremists also moved from the Global South into Global North venues. Yet the United States, the United Kingdom, and others generally did not foster on a global scale the repressive and counterinsurgent practices they had disseminated in former colonies and the developing world. Instead they turned to processes of state-to-state interdependence and multilateralism. International organizations served as venues and sponsors of negotiations, even though they had significant limitations in their capacity to regulate controversial issues and enforce compliance with the resulting agreements. Through antiterrorism cooperation and extradition agreements, Western officials did create a new international law regime and international norms surrounding border-crossing political violence.[13] They operated in line with the values of global interdependence prevalent in the international order of the 1970s.

In fact, Global North states utilized antiterrorism agreements during the 1970s as a means to retrench their global authority in response to the upheaving processes of decolonization and globalization. Through antiterrorism agreements and regulations, Global North states sought to control international norms, exclude nonstate actors from politics, and dictate terms to new states with revolutionary foreign policy agendas that upset the global status quo. Within international relations, recently independent states and anticolonial transnational movements demonstrated an increasing ability to assert their own interests by the 1970s. The United Nations (UN) was a useful forum for emergent states because its General Assembly (UNGA) gave each one a seat. African, Arab, and Southeast Asian delegations aggregated their numbers and successfully challenged highly industrialized states on issues of self-determination, civil and human rights, and more equitable economic systems.[14] Officials in many recently independent states thought that international terrorism attacks against Global North locations and citizens were a logical result of those states' support of repressive colonial and neo-imperial regimes in Israel, South Africa, and elsewhere. To counter these revolutionary perceptions and exclude nonstate extremists from participation in global politics, U.S. and European officials framed their antiterrorism initiatives as statist, sovereignty-building measures. They argued that recently independent states should support these initiatives to strengthen their (at times fragile) state institutions. Thus, debates about terrorism were also debates about state sovereignty.[15] By rejecting violent extremists' claims to self-determination, Global North officials argued, recently independent states reasserted their own sovereignty. The efforts of U.S. and European officials to delineate terrorism and counterterrorism during the 1970s were meant to secure the international authority and sovereignty of their states from the challenge of nonstate and revolutionary actors.

To achieve these aims, Global North officials worked hard to codify their initiatives as criminal issues, using a technical and apolitical framing that consequently denied violent attackers and their revolutionary-minded state supporters political legitimacy. Especially after the Munich Olympic Games attack in 1972, Western antiterrorism officials and their superiors defended their actions by "securitizing" international terrorism. They positioned their antiterrorism activities as a response to a particularly serious security threat that was unsolvable by ordinary measures.[16] In reaction, U.S., West German, and other states' expert bureaucrats built connections to foreign counterparts with similar legal and security competencies. Officials in the resulting communities and networks specialized in their limited security competencies and did not have the knowledge, jurisdiction, or inclination to address the large-scale political questions related to international terrorism that were implicit in their work.[17] These officials did not engage in or support attackers' and recently independent states' claims that terrorism was a national liberation issue. They instead addressed it exclusively around criminal law and extradition agreements.

Even if terrorists conducted successful terroristic attacks or drew public attention to their political grievances, Global North officials saw them first and foremost as criminals and worked to deny them their desired seat at the table in international relations. Many nonstate extremists framed their attacks as legitimate self-determination actions under the provisions of the Geneva Conventions and international humanitarian law. The Geneva Conventions provided mechanisms for individuals to legally commit violence (as combatants), gain specific protections (as prisoners of war), and have their organization recognized as a proto-sovereign actor (as long as it could reciprocally fulfill the requirements of the Geneva Conventions and its protocols).[18] Attackers made these claims even if their deeds violated the laws of war. Meanwhile, Global North officials had no interest in addressing violent extremists through these mechanisms that reinforced extremists' political outlook. Global North officials ignored or downplayed references to the laws of war. In public, they also disregarded any Cold War or ideological context in favor of (ostensibly apolitical) crime-focused approaches. Instead, U.S. and European officials turned to an extradition mechanism, *aut dedere aut judicare* (to extradite or to prosecute), and focused on the technical implementation of international law.[19] Only criminals were subject to processes of extradition between states, after all.

Major antiterrorism collaboration in international law reached the limits of its practical use quickly, however, because it abridged national sovereignty in practice even as it strengthened it in theory. The international law approach required states to arrest, prosecute, and generally handle politically motivated violent actors in specific, similar ways. Such shared approaches required cuts into states' sovereign legal traditions, judicial systems, criminal law codes, and policies concerning asylum and political dissidents. These cuts into sovereignty ran counter to many states' domestic and foreign policy considerations, as well as public pressure. The divides between Global North states and Global South states were most prominent. But even Global North states were oftentimes unable to compromise among themselves concerning how to collectively regulate political violence. States that faced significant transnational terroristic violence, such as West Germany and Italy, wanted practical antiterrorism solutions that branded terrorists as criminals and made it easy to prosecute them. In contrast, countries such as the United States and France sought to improve their geopolitical and foreign policy interests through antiterrorism initiatives. These differences made antiterrorism a challenging field for multilateralism, transatlantic cooperation, and European integration.[20]

Limits and checks on international law collaboration gradually motivated counterterrorism practitioners to prioritize other antiterrorism practices. During the 1970s, many U.S., European, and allied officials created antiterrorism policies and structures that corresponded with their crime-focused international law approach. They increased airport security, visa restrictions, and identity controls at national borders. These officials adapted their states' security institutions to globalization by fostering new domestic and national security measures that policed the ever-increasing movement of people, goods, and ideas around the world.[21] As a result, attackers turned to increasingly violent tactics to compensate and the number of overall casualties increased.[22] The crime-focused approaches of the 1970s took time, however, and required significant collaboration with other jurisdictions to successfully deter and curtail international terrorists. Global North officials eventually realized that military responses (along Israeli lines) were faster, required less international collaboration, and resolved many crises. In particular, special forces and similar antiterrorism tactical units could be deployed rapidly and effectively.[23] Most Global North states founded such units in the 1970s. Though their spectacular cross-border rescues made the front news in the late 1970s, most times such units were deployed at home within national borders. Finally, by the 1980s the United States in particular shifted toward a militarized counterterrorism that was easier to direct, deploy, and implement.

The majority of studies on historical counterterrorism are national in scope and, as a consequence, undervalue key international factors that shape officials' counterterrorism approaches, including foreign policy considerations, bilateral and multilateral agreements, and international norms. Recent research has focused on European states such as the United Kingdom, FRG, France, and Italy.[24] The small emergent historiography on counterterrorism collaboration sponsored by the German Institute of Contemporary History focuses strongly on European actors.[25] Related works examine the historical development of policing and police collaboration.[26] Fewer historical studies exist on U.S. counterterrorism.[27] American-focused historians tend to assume that the U.S. federal government hegemonically controlled the international parameters for counterterrorism at least in the post–World War II era.[28] By tracing cross-border interconnections, this book clarifies the international development of counterterrorism in the past and adds significant value to our modern understanding of this key security field.

Tracing how historical contemporaries understood and worked with the term *terrorism* casts new light on broad issues of political violence in the past and present. Historians analyze war, insurgencies, revolutions, violent self-determination movements, crime, and other occurrences. For the 1970s, historians have emphasized processes of détente, globalization, human rights, and hyper-individualism. Terrorism affected and shaped these large-scale developments.

While the international law agreements of the 1970s facilitated some actual antiterrorism practices, they had a more significant impact on international norms then and now. Both U.S. and European officials deployed parameters of (counter)terrorism to keep authority over state-building and sovereignty in their own hands and away from rival factions and nonstate actors. They delineated terrorism as an individual, nonstate, and criminal offense, a practice that diminished all kinds of revolutionary actors and strengthened their own authority, which they portrayed in contrast as rational and legal. According to this conception, states did not commit terrorism; nonstate actors did. And any state or actor who sought to gain power through cross-border political violence delegitimized themselves as either a state sponsor of terrorism or as a terrorist. Officials from former colonial metropoles and highly industrialized countries thus collaborated on norms that undercut so-called "rogue" states, nonstate insurgents, and related ideology. This practice began in the 1970s but continues in today's world of small wars and long-running insurgencies.

The body of scholarship on terrorism is huge, but it contains little on how terrorism and counterterrorism are conceptualized over time. Significant research on terrorism began in the 1970s, largely in response to the current transnational attacks.[29] Since then, most terrorism analyses have appeared in the field of political science. The number of publications has ballooned since the September 11, 2001, attacks. The field focuses on root causes of terrorism, especially ideology and radicalization processes, as well as on overviews of terrorist aims, tactics, and group dynamics.[30] The interrelated literature on counterterrorism has grown concurrently. Counterterrorism studies generally seek to showcase best practices of the field, such as deradicalization, to both educate practitioners and disseminate their experiences.[31] Works on international counterterrorism cooperation follow this trend and highlight strengths and weaknesses in collaborative structures.[32] Overall, much of the research on terrorism and counterterrorism tends to be informative and proscriptive. Reacting to this descriptive body of work, the interdisciplinary field of critical terrorism studies developed in the late 2000s.[33] Critical terrorism studies literature assumes that terrorism is a changing, politically charged term that many people have used across diverse contexts to describe a broad spectrum of violent actors.[34]

As a highly politicized term that has changed over time in meaning, terrorism holds powerful modern associations. Using it can seduce readers to overlay past developments with presentist understandings. Modern academia, the media, and military and law enforcement agencies around the world lack a consensus definition—in significant part due to the controversies identified in this book.[35] Relying on archival research, this book examines how historical actors utilized specific conceptions of terrorism and resulting counterterrorism approaches at a particular moment in time to advance their own political goals. This work thus situates itself within the field of critical terrorism studies. It does not offer proscriptive definitions of terrorism nor does it attempt to definitively categorize terrorism in relation to associated terms such as insurgency or guerilla warfare. Policymakers and academics associate insurgent and guerilla groups with additional factors such as operating in the open instead of clandestinely, holding militarized structures, or seeking territorial control. But in practice, insurgent, guerilla, and terrorist groups frequently overlap, and categorizing many violent groups into one or the other categories is tricky at best.[36] Instead, this book highlights the ideas and terminology that historical actors used to describe their actions and what they saw, including the terms *terrorism* and *insurgency*. The book empirically shows how this historical usage changed over time.

Yet the book cannot avoid utilizing the term *terrorism* in analytical segments. In such cases, it uses a simple definition that is not too general in its simplicity. I define terrorism as significant acts of illegal violence or the threat thereof for a political end and whose intended audience is larger than the actual target. By illegal, I mean acts that violate domestic criminal laws or the international laws of war. This simple definition covers key aspects of terrorism, including its political nature, reliance on fear, theatrical and performative aspects, oftentimes targeting of civilians, and its victimization of people not directly associated with the political goals in question.

As the term *terrorist* is controversial and oftentimes not an accurate reflection of historical contemporaries' views and thinking, I use the label *extremists* when discussing the nonstate violent actors in this book. Related nouns such as *terrorist, insurgent, guerilla,* and *radical* have similar meanings but carry deep ideological and political connotations. An extremist, on the other hand, signifies a person with harsh political views willing to commit brutal acts of violence without implying specific political alignments, ideology, or connotations.

Before 1968, states developed a series of evolving definitions of terrorism and of tactics to oppose it. By this time, the term *terrorism* had been in use as a political concept for almost two hundred years. The concept had policy baggage as well as ideological implications. By highlighting earlier associations with the label, I aim to contextualize the developments of that pivotal year and set the stage for an analysis of the changes that were to occur during the 1970s.

The term *terrorism* first emerged as a nuanced concept during the French Revolution. Previously, historical actors used the term *terroristic violence* literally. It described attacks such as targeted assassinations that were tailored to generate sensations of horror and terror, often to offset an asymmetric balance of power. Groups that practiced such attacks included the Sicarii, members of the Zealots, a Jewish religious sect operating against Roman rule in Judea before 73 AD, and the Assassins, a Shia Islamic sect in Persia around 1100.[37] From 1793 to 1794, French Jacobins reconceptualized the term *terrorism* more abstractly to brand their acts of destruction (such as mass executions) as virtuous steps to strengthen their new state. They named this period "The Great Terror." After the downfall of the Jacobin regime during the Thermidorian Reaction in 1794, terrorism lost its virtuous connotations, however, and became associated with criminal, unvirtuous, and illegitimate behavior.[38]

The next major group to adopt the label *terrorism* were members of the Russian revolutionary movement in the 1870s and 1880s. Groups such as Narodnaya Volna (The People's Will) assumed terrorism as an identity and a mechanism to overthrow the Russian monarchy. They used the term to emphasize the political motivation behind their violence, which included assassinations and bombings. Their greatest success was the assassination of Tsar Alexander II. The Russian state responded with brutal repressive measures. Despite this suppression, revolutionaries continued to perpetrate terrorism in the lead-up to the Russian Revolution in 1917.[39] In the twentieth century, contemporaries found it easy to associate the label *terrorism* with Russian and Soviet actors.

At the same time, violent anarchists operated increasingly throughout Europe and North America and became the antecedents of modern transnational terrorists. The terms *anarchist* and *terrorist* became interchangeable. Anarchists used bombings and political assassinations to undermine their modernizing societies. Due to the invention of the steam engine and the spread of railroads, they could travel easily between states and evolved into a transnational security threat. Examples of anarchist attacks included the assassinations of French president Sadi Carnot in 1894, Austrian empress Elisabeth in 1898, and U.S. president William McKinley in 1901. States reacted to anarchists with criminalizing measures and the first systematic law enforcement collaboration. European states began sharing information on suspects, and on police best practices. Authorities in the United States strengthened immigration regulations, especially through the Immigration Act of 1903 (also called the Anarchist Exclusion Act).[40] Overall, the criminal law reforms, immigration restrictions, and multilateral information-sharing methods laid the groundwork for police collaboration in the twentieth century.[41]

In the first decades of the twentieth century, resistance movements developed on the peripheries of European colonial empires; European officials quickly applied the labels of *anarchism* and *terrorism* to a range of anticolonial nationalist movements. This terminology associated such anticolonial actors with violent lawbreakers, delegitimized their political aims, and justified repressive responses in colonized spaces. In Ireland, nationalist resistance organizations against British rule developed from 1858 onward, causing the British government to institute the first police unit specifically to prevent terrorism, the Special Irish Branch of the Metropolitan Police.[42] Irish nationalist violence escalated into the 1916 Easter Rebellion and the 1919–1921 Irish War of Independence. This development inspired anticolonial and nationalist movements around the world. Similarly, Polish nationalists committed violence in Russian Poland in the first years of the twentieth century.[43] Another prominent example was ethnic nationalists from the Balkans. The Serbian Black Hand group triggered World War I through its assassination of Austro-Hungarian archduke Franz Ferdinand. Colonial powers responded with both civil rights reforms and military, law enforcement, and judicial repression.[44] Meanwhile, the Russian revolution stimulated communist, socialist, and leftist activists around the world. The U.S. federal government drew upon existing antiterrorist/anarchist terminology and practices to create anticommunist policies, considering these activists intellectual and economic extremists.[45] In the early twentieth century, anticommunist, colonizing, and antiterrorist policies overlapped in many empire-holding states.

Despite repression, however, violent anticolonial and leftist groups continued to operate. In 1934, Croatian nationalists assassinated King Alexander I of Yugoslavia. In response, the League of Nations attempted to revive the crime-focused international collaboration of the early twentieth century. It adopted the first multilateral convention against terrorism, the 1937 Convention for the Prevention and Punishment of Terrorism.[46] This convention foreshadowed many later antiterrorism agreements, emphasizing that states needed to pass criminal laws against terrorist acts and apply them uniformly to deter offenders and cut off safe havens for attackers abroad.[47] The convention was never ratified and faded into obscurity alongside the League of Nations in World War II. Yet it showcased that contemporaries relied on police collaboration and international law to deter and punish border-crossing extremists in particular.

Two major global developments, decolonization and the Cold War, shaped terrorism from the end of World War II onward. Multiple violent movements practiced sabotage, bombings, and assassinations against colonial regimes. Well-known examples include Jewish Zionists in Mandate Palestine, the Front de libération nationale and the opposing Organisation armée secrète in Algeria, the Viet Minh in Vietnam, the Malayan National Liberation Army in Malaysia, and the Kenya Land and Freedom Army (Mau Mau) in Kenya. Meanwhile, the Geneva Conventions of 1949 stated that "all measures of intimidation or of terrorism are prohibited" in warfare.[48] The United Kingdom and France responded to violent challenges to their empires with far-reaching programs under the label of "counterinsurgency." In Algeria, Vietnam, Malaysia, and Kenya, they adapted colonial strategies to repress violent actors and control the population. Among other measures, they instituted martial law, introduced new repressive legislation, criminal codes, and judicial practices, gave police competencies to military units, deployed special forces teams in targeted operations, employed spies and denunciators, resettled civilians to break up violent actors' support bases, and restricted travel and communications within contested areas.[49] The goal of these policies was to divide the population and remove popular support for violent actors in order to secure the colonial regime (or at least facilitate transitions to independence under the colonizer's oversight). European, and later U.S., counterinsurgency practitioners at times labeled particularly violent actors as terrorists. This unsystematic use of the terrorism label denounced attackers' brutal violence but still acknowledged their deep political aims and context.

Counterinsurgency practitioners integrated Cold War anticommunist conceptions into their practices. Soviet and Chinese ideologues inspired many anticolonial movements to seek socialist economic and political structures. These were ostensibly more equitable than the exploitative economies and political systems of colonial states. The clearest example is the Malayan National Liberation Army, but most anticolonial movements contained Marxist, Maoist, or socialist segments. Colonial leaders, local officials, and counterinsurgency experts in turn justified their repressive measures within the ideological framework of anticommunism. Associating anticolonial violent actors with communist sponsors and ideology made it easier for counterinsurgency officials to critique these groups' political claims and grievances.[50] In this period, information about Stalin's purges in the Soviet Union in the 1930s also spread. As a result, contemporary actors used the term *terrorism* to describe the state repression within the Soviet Union.[51] These anticolonial and anticommunist understandings were mutually reinforcing.

By the 1960s, dozens of former colonies throughout the Global South had become independent states. In countries such as Algeria and Cuba, former anticolonial activists became state officials. They were highly sympathetic toward and sponsored the efforts of other anticolonial movements. Meanwhile, the establishment of the revolutionary Algerian and Cuban states showed anticolonial activists around the world that the violent overthrow of a colonial (or quasi-colonial) regime was possible.[52] A range of other groups, mainly from the Global South, sought to do the same.

The anticolonial movements of the 1960s exploited new patterns of transnational political engagement to amplify their demands and project political influence beyond national and regional boundaries. Alongside violent attacks, they looked for international support—bolstered by officials in Algeria and Cuba. Anticolonial groups built transnational contacts with like-minded actors and advocated for their self-determination cause to global audiences. While contemporaries assumed that North Vietnam (the Democratic Republic of Vietnam) controlled the South Vietnamese National Liberation Front (the NLF, pejoratively labeled the "Viet Cong" by the United States), recent archival studies have shown that the NLF acted with substantial material and tactical independence.[53] In the Middle East, various violent Palestinian groups joined together to create the Palestine Liberation Organization (PLO) in 1964. The PLO's members sought to destroy the state of Israel in order to establish a Palestinian homeland. The most well-known of these groups was Fatah, led by the charismatic engineer Yasser Arafat.[54] Meanwhile, in Latin America, sharp economic inequality generated radical leftist groups, such as Uruguay's Movimiento de Liberación Nacional-Tupamaros, which were driven by local political conditions as well as national liberation ideology.[55] Inspired by Carlos Marighella's *Miniman-ual of the Urban Guerilla*, these groups sought to pressure states into taking repressive countermeasures that, the groups believed, would diminish the state's legitimacy in the eyes of the broader population. Anti-imperial groups increased their transnational propaganda efforts, diplomatic campaigns, and fame in the late 1960s. They became the stars of a global protest movement.

The states affected by such anticolonial violence during the 1960s adopted repressive military, law enforcement, and legal policies against violent extremists, which stemmed from practices of colonial and counterinsurgent control. These predominantly Global South countries were oftentimes former colonies or, in Latin America, under the influence of the hegemonic United States. Like the United Kingdom and France, affected states often framed their responses as antiterrorism measures. They saw terrorism as a political tactic in which deeply political nonstate groups or socialist states who had no legitimate means of exercising power committed illegal violence against civilians in order to expand their influence.[56] Policymakers continued to use the term *terrorism* primarily to refer to ideologically leftist actors, especially those with Soviet, Cuban, or Chinese sponsorship.[57] Israel and the United States reacted to Palestinian and communist challengers in the Levant and South Vietnam, respectively, with the use of asymmetric military force. In Latin America, U.S. policymakers trained security officials at the School of the Americas and sent counter-insurgency teams to advise local law enforcement and militaries. Overall, affected states such as Guatemala, Uruguay, South Vietnam, and South Africa frequently ignored the rule of law, incarcerating their citizens without trial and torturing prisoners. Examples included Uruguay, whose government incarcerated the Tupamaros, and South Africa, which created a series of "antiterrorist" policies and legislation targeting black dissidents.[58] These policies built upon preexisting anticommunist fears to undermine popular and worldwide support for anticolonial movements.

Global North states encountered a wave of local violent acts associated with the global student and worker protest movements of the late 1960s. But except for France and the United Kingdom, the societies of Europe, Canada, and the United States had not been directly exposed to the anticolonial and counterinsurgent violence surrounding decolonization. That was about to change. By 1968, certain Palestinian groups began targeting the Global North in an attempt to expand their self-determination struggles onto a global scale and gain publicity and leverage over former colonizing states. Global North officials faced an influx of border-crossing, ostensibly anticolonial attacks—principally by Global South actors. The book's narrative begins in this moment.

While the book covers a relatively concise timespan from 1968 to approximately 1984, it studies complex and oftentimes simultaneous negotiations to delineate and regulate terrorism. Its goal is to identify the numerous actors and political developments involved, highlighting origins, negotiation, adoption, and aftermath of each initiative. This approach is not well served with a purely chronological or geographic (U.S. side, European side) chapter structure. Instead, each chapter examines one process by which U.S. and European officials created an international agreement, or several entangled agreements, to delineate terrorism and counterterrorism. This approach provides in-depth study and clarification of each initiative while ensuring that the reader appreciates the overall cumulative development of the various international processes to delineate, regulate, and punish terrorism. Such initiatives oftentimes supported but did not always perfectly coincide with domestic antiterrorism policies. They built upon key developments within the international system of the 1970s, including the rising prominence of the Global South in international organizations and the oil market as well as the progression of European integration.

Chapter 1 traces how U.S. officials began conceptualizing certain attacks as a border-crossing crime issue—instead of as the political act attackers envisioned. State Department legal experts negotiated three international conventions to protect airplanes and diplomats from violent attacks between 1968 and 1971. Though the initial U.S. targets were Cubans and Latin American leftists, the conventions wound up significantly covering the actions of Palestinian Fedayeen extremists. These conventions required states to prosecute or extradite attackers as ordinary criminals. The United States secured early victories in creating shared norms concerning extremist violence that crossed national borders and jurisdictions.

Chapter 2 examines the U.S. State Department's initiative to criminalize international terrorism globally through the UNGA and analyzes how these efforts set off heated debates about the rights, limitations, and legitimacy of national liberation movements. The State Department pursued a UN convention to criminalize all acts of border-crossing nonstate violence under the umbrella term *international terrorism* after the 1972 Munich Olympic Games attack. Instead, though, recently independent states passed resolutions in favor of national liberation movements and their legal right to commit some (not all) forms of politically motivated violence against neo-imperialist targets worldwide. A U.S.-backed convention against attacks on diplomats succeeded, however, because of its far narrower scope. From the start, antiterrorism negotiations at the United Nations were really about whether national liberation actors had the right to commit politically motivated violence beyond their contested territory. Attempts by the United States to institute a global criminalizing international law regime against international terrorism encountered insurmountable opposition from recently independent states.

Led by the FRG, European security and law enforcement officials responded to the failure of the 1972 U.S. antiterrorism initiative in the UNGA by collaborating on their own to find, arrest, and convict transnational extremists. Specifically, chapter 3 identifies two networks they created in order to share information and develop common antiterrorism measures, processes, and technologies. One was the TREVI network. The other was the founding and increased collaboration of antiterrorism tactical units based on preexisting British and Israeli special forces teams. The basis for these collaborative networks was the idea that terrorism was not only a criminal threat but also one that affected everyone with extraordinary urgency. Recently independent states had no influence in these regional European networks. Officials also did not take into account the complex interrelated context of national liberation politics, which were outside their scope of competency. Most states worldwide implemented practical domestic security measures against international terrorism after 1972. But having failed to generate acceptable UNGA norms, European security officials also collaborated to improve their domestic and national security against terrorists.

In chapter 4, European judicial officials negotiated regional antiterrorism agreements as part of the process of European integration. Inspired by their countries' security networks against terrorism, justice officials collaborated on antiterrorism extradition conventions in the Council of Europe and the European Community. However, they vigorously contested the extent to which they should respect the agency of politically motivated actors. While officials from states facing high levels of domestic and transnational terrorism demanded that such violence be codified as an extraditable crime (FRG, United Kingdom), others with less at stake (France) prioritized their foreign relations with recently independent states and endorsed the right of anticolonial activists to commit (some) acts of political violence. FRG officials convinced the Council of Europe member states to pass and ratify the first multilateral convention that branded terrorism itself as a common crime. Yet the negotiations stretched out over years and finally soured most officials on international collaboration against terrorism. Even major European collaboration against international terrorism reached its limits over questions of national sovereignty.

Chapter 5 analyzes how Western officials consolidated their crime-based antiterrorism approach in the late 1970s but also began to shift their focus to the military solutions that dominate today's counterterrorism practices. At the end of the 1970s, European states reinforced their criminal conception of international terrorism alongside U.S., Canadian, and Japanese officials. They passed additional multilateral agreements in the UN, International Atomic Energy Agency, and the Group of 7. Yet Western officials tired of the complex and controversial negotiations and decreed that they had achieved what was possible at the time to advance a multilateral international law regime and corresponding policies against terrorism. Meanwhile, Israeli antiterrorism experts led by the future Prime Minister Benjamin Netanyahu reached out to Global North conservatives.

Emphasizing an ostensible ideological convergence between communism and terrorism, Netanyahu argued that international terrorism was an existential threat to Western democratic states. This view became popular especially among American conservative politicians and journalists, who began to emphasize that the Soviet Union and other U.S. enemies supported terrorists as proxies against the United States. This grave threat required the use of military countermeasures. Many adherents of this "terror network" theory joined the Reagan administration in 1981. Reagan and his key advisers continued to support the U.S. handling of terrorism as a crime. However, they also promulgated the idea that the terrorism was such a massive threat that it required military counterterrorism solutions. International law agreements against terroristic violence remained active and were gradually widely ratified. But as the 1980s progressed, U.S. officials in particular increasingly prioritized military over international law responses.

This book highlights that historical actors have been wrestling with the question of what terrorism is and how to handle it since the 1970s. Today's terrorism threat thus has a long history. This book interrogates why historical actors in the 1970s focused so much on crime- and extradition-based responses and what the ramifications of that choice were. The 1970s represent a time when most Global North states sponsored a specific nonmilitary approach within the international community. This multilateral approach emphasized the criminal and brutal aspects of terrorism, creating strong international norms that such attacks were illegitimate political steps. Yet addressing international terrorism outside of the context of war also had significant limitations, as debates over the limits of political dissent, national liberation activity, and national sovereignty did not provide fast and practical measures to respond to attacks. These limitations laid the groundwork for later militarized counterterrorism and the global war on terror.

Final disclaimers also seem appropriate to clarify my own position on the research of (counter)terrorism. Many of the attacks I analyze were already regulated as crimes in the domestic criminal law of the United States and European countries. When I discuss the criminalization of these attacks, I do not mean to imply that they had not been regulated as crimes beforehand. I also do not want to defend the commission of potentially lethal violence in pursuit of political aims. My goal is to place these attacks in historical context and highlight how contemporaries understood them—hopefully without relativizing the brutality of the attacks.

Chapter One

FROM ANTICOLONIAL TO CRIMINAL ACTS

Hijackings, Attacks on Diplomats, and Extradition
Conventions, 1968–1971

On June 17, 1969, former Black Panther Party member William Lee Brent hijacked a Trans World Airlines (TWA) flight from Oakland to New York City, diverting the plane at gunpoint to Havana, Cuba. His goal was to escape U.S. authorities. In November 1968, Brent had shot a policeman during a gas station robbery; Eldridge Cleaver subsequently expelled him from the Black Panther Party. By the time of the hijacking, Brent was out on bail pending his trial. Cuban authorities arrested Brent upon his arrival but eventually released him and allowed him to build a new life on the island. Meanwhile, on August 29, 1969, Leila Khaled stepped onto a TWA flight from Rome to Tel Aviv. Khaled was a member of the extremist group Popular Front for the Liberation of Palestine (PFLP). Alongside another PFLP member, Khaled hijacked the flight to Damascus. Her goal was to carry the Palestinian national liberation struggle beyond the territorial boundaries of Israel. Syrian authorities arrested her but released her in October 1969 without charges. A year later, Khaled participated in the series of hijackings that led to the Dawson's Field crisis. She attempted to hijack an Israeli El Al plane but failed when an air marshal shot her cohijacker. Landing in London, British authorities arrested Khaled but released her just a month later in exchange for PFLP-held British hostages.

Brent and Khaled had few commonalities, yet they were among a rising number of people who hijacked airplanes after 1968. And both justified their actions in the terminology of national liberation and self-determination. Brent claimed to be fleeing the racialized persecution of the U.S. government while Khaled targeted citizens of the Israeli state in the name of Palestinian self-determination. And both got away with it. Neither U.S. nor Israeli authorities ever managed to prosecute them for these hijackings, though both states very much wanted to do so.

Brent and Khaled were not aberrations in the history of the late 1960s. They were participants in a new wave of transnational, ostensibly anticolonial violence that increasingly affected industrialized Global North states. In the two decades before 1968, anticolonial violence tended to concentrate in the colonial peripheries, the Global South. But by the late 1960s, travel and communication were easier than ever due to processes of globalization and the growing aviation industry, so anticolonial extremists increasingly targeted the Global North. In particular, they hijacked large civilian airplanes with Global North passengers and attacked diplomats representing such states in Latin America. Pursuing its own geopolitical interests, the United States paved the way for an international response to these hijackings and attacks on diplomats with long-term repercussions. This chapter shows that modern antiterrorism norms and practices evolved as responses to anticolonial extremists' cross-border activity in 1968.

The U.S. State Department led early multilateral efforts to address acts of anticolonial violence against Global North targets in the late 1960s. Initially focusing on U.S. interests in Cuba and Latin America, U.S. officials created a normative framework in international law, which codified acts of nonstate violence as primarily criminal and not political. In 1968, the State Department sought to prevent two emergent forms of transnational violence: hijackings to and from Cuba and attacks on U.S., European, and Japanese diplomats throughout Latin America. Palestinian hijackings subsequently joined this set of cross-border problems. Alongside conservative Latin American allies such as Brazil and Argentina, U.S. diplomats generated two multilateral conventions in the International Civil Aviation Organization (ICAO) and one in the Organization of American States (OAS) in response. These conventions codified hijackers and people who attacked diplomats as ordinary criminals. Due to the complexity of the politics involved, the conventions were not as efficient as U.S. officials intended to deter attackers. However, the conventions undermined attackers' political legitimacy and made it harder for states to condone or support these forms of anticolonial violence. These conventions normalized the extradition of extremists as ordinary criminals, devalued political context, and precipitated a major change in contemporaries' conception and handling of terrorism.

Officials at the U.S. State Department did not address attackers' demands to be identified as anticolonial actors with legitimate claims to state-building and participation in international relations. Many of the U.S. diplomats tasked with creating a response to this transnational threat were legal specialists, which shaped their focus and priorities. These officials created what they considered technical legal solutions to border-crossing crimes. Focusing on international law in general and extradition regulations in particular, U.S. officials promoted an understanding of these border-crossing attacks as crimes and not as self-determination or national liberation acts. Officials in the United States used the format of multilateral extradition conventions to push other jurisdictions to adhere to this conception. Only criminals were susceptible to extradition, after all. Officials argued that a state's sovereignty was linked to its ability to prosecute and extradite non-state extremists. They worked with foreign counterpart officials and did not pay serious attention to attackers' political grievances. Young states with recent national liberation histories contested this framing, as did anticolonial activists and the attackers themselves. The extradition conventions also contained loopholes and were, for all intents and purposes, unenforceable. Nevertheless, this crime-focused framework became the foundational basis for subsequent negotiations about international terrorism. Discussions about terrorism in the 1970s thus always contained far larger questions concerning self-determination and the international community's limits on acceptable political violence. Furthermore, this legal approach would substantially shape how global publics and many governments understood the broader category of terrorism—as a criminal act regardless of political context—in subsequent decades.

The development of this crime-focused framework was not teleological or necessarily driven by a motivation to stop terrorism. In 1968, *terrorism* was a rare term used to describe violent attacks against civilians in anticolonial and Global South conflicts. It described nonstate attackers and sometimes state officials—the important thing was that political considerations drove the violence they perpetrated in specific political settings. But U.S. officials did not want to consider the political context of the new cross-border attacks. Hijackers frequently rerouted American flights to Cuba and later to the Middle East, complicating U.S. policies concerning both regions. In Latin America, attacks on diplomats threatened to undermine normal diplomatic relations. The State Department's main concern was to find expedient solutions to both problems. They turned to a technical regulation of these attacks as crimes within international law. The following chapters examine how U.S. and European officials applied the same extradition and crime-focused approach to more and more nonstate actors and violent acts. Modern understandings of terrorism did not drive negotiations concerning hijacking and attacks on diplomats; in contrast, these negotiations helped develop our modern understanding of terrorism as an offense committed by nonstate actors, which is always illegitimate regardless of political context.

Additionally, this chapter complicates the traditional narrative that U.S. antiterrorism policies developed in reaction to Palestinian attacks. Today's established wisdom is that U.S. antiterrorism initiatives were a direct response to Palestinian hijackings, as well as to the attack at the 1972 Munich Olympic Games.[1] In chapter 2, I argue that the Munich attack was indeed a watershed moment in the history of terrorism. As this chapter will show, though, the first multilateral U.S. initiatives against hijacking and attacks on diplomats came out of U.S. domestic turmoil, U.S.-Cuban relations, and U.S.-Latin American diplomacy. American foreign policy institutions responsible for the Arab-Israeli conflict, including the National Security Council (NSC) and the State Department's Bureau of Near Eastern Affairs (NEA), were not substantially involved in the ICAO and OAS negotiations. Though Palestinian attacks soon grew to dominate the focus of U.S. policymakers, the origins of the United States' international initiatives against nonstate political violence are more complex than the straightforward narrative of many terrorism histories suggests.

HIJACKING

In the late 1960s, the U.S. State Department spearheaded a multilateral initiative to address the burgeoning problem of hijacking through new international legal standards. It attempted to pressure all states to prosecute hijackers as criminals and not protect them as political dissidents. Officials also sought to deter hijackers by delegitimizing all political reasons for their crime. Both aims hailed from a slew of U.S. hijackings to Cuba.

The number of hijackings slowly rose in the 1950s and 1960s as political dissidents used the growing availability of commercial flights to escape oppressive regimes and garner public attention. In 1949 and 1950, for example, citizens of various Eastern European states hijacked eight airplanes to reach the Federal Republic of Germany (FRG) and other Western European countries.[2] Most frequently affected by far were the United States and Cuba, though. In the early 1960s, a few Cubans fleeing the Cuban Revolution used the tactic to reach the United States. Like their counterparts who traveled to Florida via boat, these hijackers requested (and received) political asylum when they landed in the United States. In addition, the U.S. federal government kept several of the hijacked airplanes to cover Cuban debts in the United States.[3]

Throughout the 1960s, the trend reversed as American citizens began hijacking domestic U.S. flights to reach the ostensible revolutionary haven of Havana.[4] The number of hijackings suddenly increased in 1968 in tandem with the turmoil of U.S. urban, race, antiwar, and student unrest. Controversies surrounding urban riots, the Vietnam War, and the presidential election split U.S. society that year. Violent domestic attacks within the United States skyrocketed. So did hijackings. Before 1968, twelve hijackings had occurred in the United States. In 1968 alone there were twenty-two. The trend continued with forty hijackings in 1969. Of the sixty-two U.S. hijackings in 1968–1969, fifty-six landed in Cuba.[5] Some U.S. hijackers were criminals evading the law. But many saw themselves as political dissidents escaping what they perceived as racial and political persecution from federal, state, and local governance in the United States. William Lee Brent was one such example. However, Cuban authorities only granted asylum in rare cases where hijackers could present a documented record of leftist political activity. Instead, Cuban judges sentenced most hijackers to lengthy prison sentences as criminals.[6]

Before 1968, few in the United States considered these hijackings a serious enough danger to warrant an active response. Passengers and crew rarely suffered injuries. The Kennedy and Johnson administrations were not interested in expending political capital on this low-key issue. The mainstream media generally ignored hijackings to Cuba until the number of occurrences skyrocketed in 1968. Journalists even portrayed

FIGURE 1.1. Passengers of a hijacked Delta Airlines plane at the Havana airport, March 3, 1968.
Before the summer of 1968, most Americans considered hijackings to Cuba an unavoidable nuisance.
Keystone Press / Alamy Stock Photo.

such hijackings as tropical adventures.[7] Meanwhile, airlines had few formal protocols about hijacking.[8] They considered security measures such as passenger and baggage screening prohibitively expensive and were more willing to pay potential ransom demands than to institute such practices. Hijacking was also an issue that fell between the cracks of federal bureaucracies. The FBI was responsible for cross-state hijackings, but it had no jurisdiction abroad, and FBI agents received no specific training for hijacking situations. The U.S. Armed Forces, which directed counterinsurgency efforts in Vietnam, were not involved in civil aviation security. The Federal Aviation Administration (FAA) was responsible for developing aviation security technologies and practice but delivered few results in the 1960s.[9]

While the FAA handled technical antihijacking innovations, the State Department was formally responsible for managing the political aspects and problems caused by hijackings. Throughout most of the 1960s, the State Department's main interest in hijacking was not as a security threat but as a complication for U.S. asylum policies. Cuban citizens hijacked a few flights to the United States in the early 1960s to escape their new revolutionary state. These hijackers received asylum, much to the chagrin of the Castro regime. Though intermediaries and public statements, Cuban authorities asked that the United States deny asylum to any Cubans who had fled via boat or aircraft. Refusing to acknowledge the new Cuban state, the Kennedy and Johnson administrations ignored these requests.[10]

However, the Johnson administration found itself in a predicament when, in turn, the number of U.S. hijackings to Cuba increased. Now in the opposite position, the administration wanted to prevent Cuba from giving asylum to U.S. citizens. Additionally, U.S. authorities wanted the planes involved in such incidents—high-value assets for U.S. airline companies—returned immediately. The Cubans, in turn, quickly became annoyed in 1968 by the rising number of arriving flights. On March 14, 1968, Fidel Castro threatened that Cuba might keep future hijacked aircraft if they kept coming.[11] This threat set off a wave of frenzy in the State Department's Bureau of Inter-American Affairs (ARA) and its subordinate Office of the Coordinator of Cuban Affairs. American officials would have to convince their Cuban counterparts to reject hijackers' asylum claims and return the hijacked aircraft, while they themselves had done the opposite on both accounts. Complicating the issue further, any change in U.S. policy to address this situation would in all likelihood affect U.S. asylum policies for the Eastern Bloc and other Cold War refugees. For assistance, Robert Sayre, the ARA's acting assistant secretary of state, turned to the State Department's aviation expert.

At State, Frank Loy was the key official working on aviation issues. A Harvard-trained lawyer, Loy had started at a private firm specializing in corporate law, transferred into federal service as special assistant to the FAA's administrator and then director of the FAA's Office of Policy Development, and finally joined the State Department.[12] From 1965 to 1970, Loy's portfolio as deputy assistant secretary for economic and business affairs included shipping, telecommunications, and aviation. The bulk of his aviation-related initiatives concerned flight route and airline access agreements with other states. Governed by bilateral and multilateral agreements, international aviation was a field that required significant cross-border collaboration to institute even the smallest policy change. Loy quickly became responsible for implementing the complex multilateral diplomacy surrounding aviation security and hijacking.

Sayre and Loy's priority was to gain physical custody of American air-planes and hijackers and demonstrate that Cuba was not beyond the reach of U.S. law; they had to find solutions without undermining the United States' overall Cold War asylum policies or acknowledging Cuba as a sovereign state. By March 1968, the ARA had set up an informal contact with the Cuban government through the Swiss embassy in Havana. Cuban authorities allowed hijacked aircraft and passengers to depart quickly upon Swiss request. However, they refused to hand over hijackers, imprisoning or deporting most.[13] This system maintained the U.S. diplomatic boycott of Cuba but did not address the asylum issue in any meaningful way for either country.

While Sayre and Loy considered hijacking in light of U.S.-Cuban relations, certain Palestinian Fedayeen groups began using it in 1968 as an anticolonial insurgent tactic, and in the process expanded their national liberation struggle from the Global South to the Global North. This new wave of hijackings extended the physical locations where many hijackings occurred from the Caribbean to anywhere in the world. These hijackings began after the Fedayeen defeat at al-Karameh. On March 21, 1968, the Israeli Defense Forces (IDF) entered the Palestinian al-Karameh refugee camp to destroy an installation of the Palestine Liberation Organization (PLO), a large Fedayeen umbrella group. The PLO lost the ensuring fight, but both sides incurred heavy losses. The group in turn celebrated al-Karameh as a propaganda victory and as ostensible proof of its ability to prevent the IDF from operating at will. The most radical of its members wanted to seize the moment and further pressure the Israeli state; leading them was the PFLP head and former doctor George Habash. The PFLP was smaller and more Maoist than larger Fedayeen groups, such as Yasser Arafat's Fatah. Its members' goal became to attack Israeli citizens and civilian institutions beyond the territorial boundaries of the Arab-Israeli conflict.[14]

Led by Habash, the PFLP targeted the Israeli airline El Al. On July 23, 1968, four PFLP members hijacked El Al Flight 426 on its way from London to Tel Aviv and took fifty-eight people hostage on the mid-sized Boeing 707. Landing in Algeria, the hijackers successfully negotiated, over forty days, for the release of sixteen Israeli prisoners of Palestinian origin. Israeli authorities almost immediately responded by placing armed guards on El Al planes. However, this hijacking initially appeared to be a resounding success. The PFLP had achieved the release of the prisoners and the hijacking and the PFLP received global media coverage. Israel could not deploy a military force in distant states where PFLP hijackers boarded planes or where hijacked planes landed. Through the seizure of aircraft and the taking of hostages, PFLP members extended their insurgency to new spaces, both literally and figuratively.

In the summer of 1968, however, Loy and the U.S. State Department continued to view hijacking primarily as a Cuban issue. As such, Loy had few policy options. He asked the Swiss and Mexican governments to reach out to the Cubans with no results.[15] Because Loy was ostensibly dealing with U.S.-Cuban question, he did not access the resources dedicated to the Arab-Israeli conflict or U.S. agencies with counterinsurgency experience. The military was not an option either. Using military units to rescue a hijacked aircraft outside of U.S. territory would draw unwelcome public attention to any high-level official authorizing this show of force. In addition, such actions would anger other states, including Cuba, the Soviet Union, Algeria, and others in the Middle East. It increased the risk of casualties and the danger of drawing the United States into an armed conflict.

Loy then reached out to nonstate contacts. Since he often coordinated with airline companies, trade organizations, and aviation worker unions, his transnational network stretched from the International Air Transport Association (IATA), which represented the trade interests of airlines worldwide, to the Air Line Pilots Association (ALPA), a union of U.S. airline pilots. These contacts were professionally invested in the safe and orderly conduct of air travel. Loy's most determined ally was the director of the IATA, Knut Hammarskjöld. He was the nephew of Dag Hammarskjöld, the former UN secretary general who in 1961 had died in a plane crash in Africa under mysterious circumstances. Hammarskjöld was deeply concerned about hijackers' potential to endanger and disrupt orderly airline travel. He frequently traveled to mediate in hijacking situations and advocate for improved aviation security. Loy was Hammarskjöld's primary contact in the State Department. During the spring of 1968, Hammarskjöld volunteered to advocate on Loy's behalf with the Castro regime to request the extradition of American hijackers.[16] In July Loy took him up on the offer.[17]

Hammarskjöld and Loy agreed to seek all possible solutions to the problem of hijacking, including multilateral outreach. In a meeting on August 1, 1968, Hammarskjöld recommended that IATA and the United States work with other states to influence the Cubans. Many bilateral agreements and a few multilateral ones governed state-to-state relations concerning civil aviation. Bilateral diplomacy with the Cubans was not possible. But a multilateral approach could create norms and obligations for all states to handle hijackers in specific ways congruent with U.S. interests. Such norms could pressure the Cuban government into returning hijackers and planes. Under U.S. law, only bilateral extradition treaties could serve as the basis for formal extradition requests.[18] The United States' extradition treaty with Cuba hailed from the overthrown Batista regime. Its status was in question and it did not cover hijacking. Loy was clear, however, that he did not need formal extradition mechanisms. He just needed the Cubans to hand over the planes and hijackers, who were criminals after all, without creating a reciprocal U.S. obligation to return political refugees to Cuba. Any multilateral antihijacking regulation would require significant international collaboration with Loy's counterpart officials in other states. Loy and Hammarskjöld agreed, though, that this effort might be worth it. Loy pointed out that the PFLP's hijacking two weeks earlier was causing internal tensions in the Algerian government. Thus, other states might be interested in a comprehensive antihijacking solution.[19]

To arrange a multilateral response, Hammarskjöld turned to a highly specialized international organization, the ICAO. Founded in Chicago in 1944, the ICAO quickly joined the UN agency system. Its mission was to regulate civil aviation worldwide.[20] Membership and adherence to its standards were voluntary. In its first decades, the organization was dominated by the United States and the United Kingdom, the countries that cornered the greatest share of the civil aviation market.[21] However, new members joined during the 1950s and 1960s. These new states, many from the Global South, pushed their own agendas and undermined British and U.S. influence. Nevertheless, the organization was the logical choice for any multilateral civil aviation collaboration. In addition, Hammarskjöld knew that his position at IATA carried weight there. When the ICAO's General Assembly met in September 1968, Hammarskjöld, with robust U.S. backing, asked the ICAO to take up the issue of hijacking. The Assembly agreed, adopting a resolution to study acts of "unlawful interference with aircraft."[22] The ICAO would focus on technical innovations to prevent hijackings, such as passenger screening technology, as well as legal steps concerning who had the right to prosecute border-crossing hijackers. While the FAA representatives on the U.S. delegation focused on the ICAO's technical deliberations, Loy's principal interest lay in the legal negotiations.

The ICAO had previously passed one legal agreement concerning civil aviation security, but the issue had ranked low on its list of priorities. The ICAO's main concern had been which state should have jurisdiction to prosecute a crime that occurred on board an aircraft in flight. On domestic routes or if an airplane was on the ground, the national laws of the state in question applied. However, international flights were trickier to regulate. An airplane could start, pass over, and land in various states whose criminal laws (and interpretations about who had jurisdiction over the crime) might differ substantially. Since 1953, the ICAO maintained a legal subcommittee to discuss this issue. The Cuban Revolution and subsequent hijackings to the United States motivated the ICAO to complete the 1963 "Convention on Offences and Certain Other Acts Committed on Board Aircraft," widely known as the "Tokyo Convention."[23] It was the first multilateral agreement on civil aviation security.

The Tokyo Convention focused on the issue of jurisdiction—specifically, who had the right to prosecute a crime committed on an international flight. The convention's solution was broad. It decreed that the country under which the airplane in question was registered had the legal responsibility to prosecute the crime. In addition, any country whose citizens, interests, or national security were threatened could demand jurisdiction, even if the offense had occurred beyond that state's territorial boundaries or airspace.[24] Potential threats went undefined. This formulation gave states significant leeway. In legal terms, the idea is called universal jurisdiction.[25] It allows any state to introduce criminal proceedings against a person who committed a crime onboard a civilian international flight—as long as that crime harmed the state's (vaguely defined) interests. While the convention gave states broad rights to prosecute offenders, it was much stricter about how states should treat the other people and property caught up in a hijacking. Signatory states to the Tokyo Convention were obligated to allow any passengers, crew, airplane, and cargo from a hijacking situation to leave their territory and return home as quickly as possible.[26]

Loy and Hammarskjöld did not consider the Tokyo Convention an ideal tool to address the issue of hijacking, however, because it had several serious shortcomings. The convention did nothing to prevent hijackings. It simply regulated who could prosecute after the fact. Even then, the convention contained no enforcement mechanisms to ensure that states actually did prosecute hijackers. It also ignored the issue of extradition, as well as attacks on airports or grounded airplanes. This focus left a gap in its coverage because not all hijackings occurred in flight.[27] Finally, ICAO members did not prioritize the Tokyo Convention and only slowly ratified it. The convention was not yet in effect. Neither Cuba nor the United States had ratified it.[28]

For help with the legal details, Loy turned to the State Department's Office of the Legal Adviser (OLA). Like Loy, the elite-trained lawyers there had experience in the business world and various branches of government service, and oftentimes they alternated between them. They were not traditional career diplomats. Richard Frank, the assistant legal adviser for Economic Affairs, was familiar with aviation industry law and regulations. So was Franklin Willis, an assistant legal adviser for Transportation and Telecommunications, who joined the State Department in 1969. Mark Feldman, an assistant legal adviser for Intra-American Affairs, focused on creating a legal framework that would address both U.S.-Cuban extradition and asylum issues. Knute (Gene) Malmborg, the assistant legal adviser for Security and Consular Affairs, was responsible for international law and legal aspects concerning the security of U.S. citizens abroad. They collaborated with the U.S. ICAO representative, Robert Boyle, who like Loy was a Harvard Law School graduate and former FAA bureaucrat. Loy also drew technical support from the Department of Transportation and the FAA.

By the end of 1968, when nineteen flights had gone to Cuba, the situation increasingly alarmed Inter-American Affairs' assistant secretary of state, Covey Oliver. Loy took the lead on ICAO, but multilateral negotiations would take time. Cuban authorities rebuffed Hammarskjöld's outreach efforts.[29] Oliver suggested approaching the Cuban government directly (through the mediation of the Swiss embassy in Havana) to discuss "the alarming increase in frequency of hijackings." Oliver and Feldman were unhappy about this option, saying that "if we do so we must be prepared to offer reciprocity by returning to Cuba hijackers of Cuban commercial planes even though they ask for political asylum."[30] Yet they were willing to at least consider all U.S. options to prevent a further increase in hijackings. Oliver thought a favorable Cuban response unlikely but was no longer willing to wait for ICAO reactions. The secretary of state, Dean Rusk approved, as did the assistant attorney general, Fred Vinson. But when the Johnson administration ended just weeks later, the incoming Nixon administration did not initially pursue this bilateral option. Unlike members of the Johnson administration, Nixon was genuinely interested in the problem of hijacking and its potential solutions. However, Henry Kissinger, Nixon's new national security adviser, was worried that Nixon would suffer in the polls during hijacking crises if he could not distance himself from this issue in advance. Kissinger and William Rogers, the incoming secretary of state, hindered Nixon from making public statements or initiating new antihijacking policies.[31] As a result, the task of addressing hijackings remained with Loy at the middling levels of the State Department.

Loy's multilateral ICAO initiative against hijacking thus needed to address several U.S. problems at once. On the one hand, it had to ease the potential strain to U.S. asylum policy. The U.S. federal government was unwilling to return Cuban boat refugees. But ICAO regulations covered only air travel, not political refugees arriving by boat. By stigmatizing hijacking as an extraditable crime, ICAO regulations could also potentially deter future Cuban refugee hijackers. On the other hand, ICAO action could generate pressure on Cuban authorities to return American hijackers and planes back to the United States. Any agreement reached would be the creation of the ICAO and would place the weight of the international community on Cuba's shoulders. These were the U.S. aims for the ICAO negotiations in early 1969.

"TO EXTRADITE OR TO PROSECUTE"

In late 1968, various ICAO committees began to discuss aviation security. Strong U.S. lobbying led to the creation of a new ICAO body, the Committee on Unlawful Interference with Aircraft. This committee intended to coordinate all ICAO technical security deliberations, covering technology such as metal detectors and practices such as passenger screenings. But in practice it achieved little because its members refused to broach "political" issues, especially hijackings.[32] Meanwhile, the ICAO's Legal Committee, the focus of Loy's attention, formed a new subcommittee to draft an agreement against hijackers in December 1968.

In contrast to the U.S. focus on Cuba, the other ICAO delegations concentrated on Palestinian and Arab-Israeli politics as they started their deliberations. On December 26, 1968, two PFLP members attacked El Al Flight

253 in Athens, killing one passenger before being overwhelmed by Greek police. All subsequent hijacking attempts of El Al planes would also fail due to significant Israeli security precautions. Two days later, the IDF raided the Beirut airport. Targeting the Lebanese government for permitting the PLO and PFLP to operate within its borders, the IDF destroyed fourteen aircraft belonging to various Arab-owned airlines. Infuriated, Arab states protested in the UN Security Council and sought to exclude Israel from the ICAO.

Yet Habash's targeting of border-crossing aircraft appeared successful, as his PFLP was able to influence international affairs and Israel's state-to-state relations even as a nonstate actor. Habash's group undermined the Israeli strategy to use military pressure against the PLO and its Arab state supporters. The Beirut attack was widely condemned in the UN. The U.S. had supported Israel significantly since 1967, but not even the U.S. ambassador to the UN was able to condone or justify the attack.[33]

However, the costs of this tactic were high. Hijacking threatened the PLO's carefully cultivated self-portrayal as national liberation actors, revolutionary combatants, and a proto-state organization. The Fedayeen hijackings hit airports and aircraft far outside of the territorial boundaries of Israel or even the Middle East and affected civilians unassociated with the Israeli state. Such targets were unacceptable both in normal (nonwarfare) international relations and under international humanitarian law. The international locations and victims of the PFLP thus threatened the PLO's self-determination claims. The PLO chairman, Arafat, opposed Habash's strategy, arguing that hijacking undermined the Fedayeen's image. By targeting civilians unassociated with the Israeli state, the PLO also risked forfeiting any claim to be a sovereign proto-state organization bound by norms of state-to-state relations. Yet Arafat could not prevent Habash's actions.[34]

The Arab delegates' attempt to exclude Israel from the ICAO and the hijacking subcommittee failed, but tensions remained high; Arab-Israeli politics were on all delegations' minds.[35] The ICAO legal subcommittee on hijacking met for the first time from February 10 to 23, 1969. On February 18, 1969, four PFLP members tried to hijack El Al Flight 432 at the Zurich airport. They fatally wounded a crew member but were stopped by an armed undercover Israeli agent on board. PFLP attacks thus shaped discussions in the ICAO subcommittee from the outset.

Meanwhile, the U.S. State Department maintained the position that hijacking was a criminal issue, not a political one. Loy was more concerned by American hijackings to Cuba, an established socialist state, than he was about the PFLP, a self-proclaimed insurgent group seeking statehood and sovereignty. Palestinians usually fell under the purview of the NEA at the State Department, and Loy's main goal was to utilize the climate of fear that the PFLP had generated to create an agreement that would place pressure on Cuba. The U.S. delegation also tried to undercut Arab complaints against Israel in the ICAO. Both aims could be achieved with the same approach: by addressing hijacking as a crime-based issue and not as a political one. The State Department thus adopted a "non-political crime" approach to hijacking for very political reasons rooted in the Cold War and U.S.-Cuban relations.

During the subcommittee negotiations, the State Department focused on a multilateral solution that would codify hijacking as criminal around the world and ignored any political, military, or insurgent context.[36] Castro's regime did not want to deal with the large number of arriving hijacked flights. However, Cuban authorities also utilized the hijackings as a propaganda tool. They accused the United States of persecuting racial minorities and other political dissidents until such actors had no other option but to escape via airplane to Cuba.[37] Loy's goals were to undermine these claims, motivate Cuban authorities to extradite U.S. citizens, and continue to return the valuable hijacked airplanes themselves.[38] Bilateral treaties were the only formal means under U.S. law of requesting extradition for hijacking-related charges such as kidnapping and weapons possession. But the U.S.-Cuban bilateral extradition treaty stemmed from pre-Castro times and did not cover hijacking. Cuba was a founding ICAO member, however, and Loy's group speculated that a multilateral ICAO agreement could influence Cuba when his other contacts had not. Headed by Gene Malmborg, the U.S. delegation's objective at the February 1969 ICAO subcommittee meeting was therefore to secure a multilateral agreement that required states to return aircraft and extradite hijackers for criminal prosecution.

While a requirement to return airplanes posed no problem for the ICAO delegates, Malmborg faced a procedural issue concerning the extradition of hijackers; extradition agreements generally contained a standard clause that protected political dissidents. This clause, called the political offense exception, allowed states to acknowledge an offender's political motivations. An offender had to demonstrate that they had committed their actions out of sincere political motivation or that a state wanted them extradited in

order to persecute them politically. If the judicial officials of the arresting country accepted these claims, they could invoke the political offense
exception to refuse the offender's extradition. Many American hijackers in
Cuba claimed a political motivation. These men (rarely women) habitually
used Black nationalism, civil rights, and national liberation terminology
to portray the United States as a racist and imperialist state from which
Cuba was their only refuge. Cuban authorities almost never accepted these
claims or granted political asylum to hijackers. But the Cubans exploited
such claims rampantly for anti-American propaganda purposes. The U.S.
delegation thus had to convince the other ICAO delegates that the act of
hijacking was never politically motivated and should always be considered
a common crime. Ambitiously, the U.S. goal was to override the political
offense exception and create a foolproof mechanism that obligated states to
extradite hijackers upon request.[39]

Most other subcommittee delegates rejected the U.S. position, though.
The committee included specific geographic quotas to ensure representation from around the world. Thirteen states participated, including the
United States, Canada, and Colombia from the Americas, four European
states (the United Kingdom., Denmark, Switzerland, and France), as well
as Algeria, Tunisia, and Nigeria from Africa and Israel, India, and Japan
from Asia. The committee members collectively agreed that hijacking was
a violent criminal act and that the threat of extradition was a plausible
method to deter offenders. However, most members wanted the ICAO to
simply recommend that states add hijacking to existing extradition treaties without touching the political offense exception. They recognized that
their actions could address broader questions about political violence in
general and anticolonial insurgencies in particular. In addition, the two
Arab delegates from Tunisia and Algeria were particularly sensitive about
any agreement that might require them to extradite anticolonial actors and
especially Palestinian Fedayeen to Israel, the United States, or former European colonizers. Such a requirement, they argued, would undermine their
states' sovereign control of their legal systems.[40] These delegates maintained
that states should be able to refuse extradition if they considered the hijackers politically motivated. Furthermore, they insisted that an antihijacking
extradition agreement should never override any national laws or interests.
Only the Colombian delegate supported Malmborg's proposal to ignore the
political offense exception. Arguing that the American proposals impinged

on states' sovereignty, inhibited compromise, and would end antihijacking negotiations before they even began, even close American allies such as the United Kingdom or France rejected the U.S. proposals. In his concluding report, Malmborg wrote that "the other states represented in the subcommittee represent a sufficient cross-section of the international civil aviation community so that their uniform opposition to the original United States protocol would seem to put that proposal to rest."[41]

The subcommittee therefore focused on how states should respond to hijacking without creating any mandatory extradition obligations. The most prudent course of action, the delegates agreed, was to recommend that the ICAO members add the offense of hijacking to their existing bilateral and multilateral extradition treaties and retain the political offense exception.

Unhappy with these suggestions, Malmborg introduced a potential compromise. He proposed a new approach based on an old legal principle called *aut dedere aut judicare* ("to extradite or to prosecute"). Created in the seventeenth century by one of the main developers of international law, Hugo Grotius, the principle ensures that violent offenders do not escape criminal prosecution for their act just because they are in a country that does not extradite them.[42] It requires that a state start prosecuting an offender through its domestic judicial system if that state's officials refuse to extradite him or her. International agreements, such as treaties and conventions, specify the offenses covered under "extradite or prosecute." In 1969, the concept was relatively rare. Most prominently, the 1949 Geneva Conventions contained a version for individuals who committed war crimes.[43] An ICAO "extradite or prosecute" convention would specify that states had to criminalize hijacking and when possible arrest hijackers. The arresting states' authorities then had a choice whether to prosecute the hijackers at home or extradite them. The Tokyo Convention's universal jurisdiction meant that all interested states could criminally prosecute a hijacker, even if the hijacking itself occurred outside of their territory.

This "extradite or prosecute" principle could not compel extradition, but it did force states to create domestic criminal laws against hijacking and to apply those laws uniformly and consistently. States could, at least initially, still use the political offense exception, though they had to arrest and handle hijackers under domestic criminal law. For Loy and the OLA, this principle was attractive because the United States could publicly criticize and shame noncompliant states, creating a potential lever to use against Cuba.

The other delegates were lukewarm on this U.S. proposal, with Malmborg noting "that a major effort would have to be made to persuade governments in general to follow the approach described as the United States compromise proposal, and even then such an effort may well be unsuccessful."[44] From February 1969 onward, Loy and his coworkers made the effort. Their goals were to secure an "extradite or prosecute" agreement and limit the political offense exception within it as much as possible.

At the ICAO, Loy, Boyle, Malmborg, Frank, and Feldman sought to gain custody of U.S. citizens in Cuba, but their efforts held far larger implications. The "extradite or prosecute" principle mandated that all hijackings be tried as domestic criminal cases, either in the courts of the arresting state or a state that had filed for the hijackers' extradition. Crucially, the laws of war and international humanitarian law would not apply. Hijackers would not be able to claim that they represented a proto-state organization or self-determination movement. Hijackers could also not demand the rights and benefits that went with such associations in international humanitarian law, such as the right to participate in diplomatic and state-to-state relations, combatant status (which protected violent actors from criminal repercussions), or prisoner-of-war status (which gave captured combatants rights not held by criminal prisoners). As a result, the U.S. proposals for an ICAO antihijacking agreement broadly devalued the actions of the PLFP. Anticolonial insurgents who dared to move beyond their contested territories to target Global North states, such as the PFLP, were to be tried as criminals. Though the political offense exception still provided a loophole, on average hijackings were no longer to be treated as legitimate acts of anticolonial political violence, or even as political at all.[45] They were a crime.

State Department officials still preferred an option with mandatory extradition. But because even the U.S. "extradite or prosecute" compromise position had so little backing from other states, Loy turned to his industry contacts to help him lobby in the ICAO. The U.S. delegation's chief allies were nonstate groups that represented frequent victims of hijacking, including IATA, ALPA, and the International Federation of Air Line Pilots' Association (IFALPA), an international pilot union. Led by Hammarskjöld, these actors emphasized the physical and economic danger to their persons and livelihoods. They lobbied ICAO delegates in favor of preventive security measures and stringent antihijacking extradition regulations that excluded the political offense exception. Their influence was limited, however. ICAO delegates on the hijacking subcommittee focused on the political questions raised by PFLP hijackings and did not substantively engage with aviation industry nonstate actors.[46] Hammarskjöld and other industry representatives continued to collaborate with the FAA and Loy but it was principally on technical security measures.[47]

In August 1969, another hijacking in the Middle East brought the PFLP to Nixon and Kissinger's attention, boosted discussions on aviation security in the ICAO and the UN, and highlighted the Fedayeen's ability to influence state-to-state relations to the detriment of U.S. and Israeli interests in the Middle East. Because attacks on El Al kept failing, the PFLP branched out to the airlines of Israeli allies, especially the United States. On August 29, PFLP members Leila Khaled and Salim Issawi hijacked TWA Flight 840 to Damascus, Syria.[48] That was the first time the PFLP had attacked a U.S. airline. The 1967 war and Israel's occupation of the Golan Heights were still fresh in Palestinians' minds. So was the military technology that Lyndon Johnson had provided the Israelis. The U.S. assistance to Israel was far more circumscribed than it would be several years later. Yet it motivated the PFLP to target the two U.S. airlines operating in the region, Pan American World Airways (Pan Am) and TWA.

In Damascus, Syrian authorities imprisoned the TWA 840 hijackers and released all hostages except for two male Israeli citizens the Syrians claimed were Israeli spies. One passenger had previously served in Israeli intelligence, though Israeli and U.S. officials kept this knowledge secret. The other was as professor of medicine in Jerusalem.[49] Syria's vice minister of defense, General Akil, stated that the two Israeli passengers would only be released through a formal prisoner-of-war exchange for two Syrian Air Force pilots. Israeli authorities had arrested these Syrian pilots as enemy combatants after they underwent an emergency landing in Israel.[50] The Syrians insisted that their pilots had been on a nonhostile training mission although no evidence supported this claim.[51] Arguing that the Israeli arrest of their pilots was a wartime act of aggression, the Syrians refused to release the two civilian Israeli passengers outside of a formal prisoner-of-war exchange with Israel.

Israeli authorities and the State Department were furious that the Syrian government was asking for an exchange instead of treating the two passengers as innocent victims of a border-crossing crime. The Syrian pilots were military personnel and the Israeli government refused to trade them for civilians.[52] But the Nixon administration was ill-equipped to address the situation. A military response against a Soviet-friendly state was out of the question. Complicating the situation, the United States did not even have diplomatic representation of its own in Damascus.

For six weeks, the NEA lobbied the Syrian government through the Italian embassy, TWA representatives on the ground, the UN, and the International Committee of the Red Cross. Loy also communicated with TWA and the ICAO. Officials relied on the Tokyo Convention to make their case that the Israeli civilians needed to be released. On September 5, the United States became the twelfth state to ratify the Tokyo Convention, which was the last requirement that the convention needed to enter into force in December 1969. The convention's signatory states committed themselves to allowing the passengers of a hijacking to return home without hindrance. Though Syria had not ratified the convention, the State Department argued in September 1969 that the Tokyo Convention now dictated civil aviation norms and created a customary obligation to release the Israeli civilians.[53] American officials sought to reach the Syrians; they did not reach out to the PFLP or PLO. Nixon, Rogers, and Kissinger viewed U.S. diplomacy in the Middle East as state-to-state relations. They were not interested in diplomatic overtures to nonstate Palestinian Fedayeen.

To complement the NEA's work, the State Department also sought to pressure Syria through Loy's ICAO antihijacking initiative. Nixon, Rogers, and Kissinger wanted to avoid a military prisoner-of-war exchange between Israel and Syria that would boost Syria's prestige in the region and undermine U.S. influence. Yet by mid-September 1969, none of their initial steps were working. Due to the TWA 840 hijacking, Loy and the OLA lawyers gained additional support from Nixon and Kissinger to create an ICAO convention that criminalized hijackers, disavowed any political context (such as the Arab-Israeli conflict), and, ideally, required the mandatory extradition of hijackers upon request. Nixon and Kissinger were also very interested in mechanisms that would allow them to punish states that did not comply with these requirements—like Syria.

Concurrent developments in Cuba motivated Loy and ARA officials. On September 19, 1969, the Cuban government published an antihijacking law, no. 1226. The law allowed for the extradition of hijackers from Cuba but solely in cases where Cuba had bilateral extradition agreements. It specifically rejected multilateral agreements such as the ICAO draft.[54]

Yet the State Department, NSC, FAA, and Department of Transportation agreed that the Cubans were responding to the U.S. engagement in ICAO. The Cuban law appeared only four days before the ICAO legal antihijacking subcommittee was to meet again. Cuba's new antihijacking legislation raised what John Volpe, the secretary of transportation, labeled "guarded optimism" that Cuban authorities might enter into further discussions about the extradition of hijackers.[55]

Driven by Cuban and particularly Syrian developments, U.S. representatives again petitioned the ICAO delegates on the antihijacking subcommittee, as legal specialists, to address the specific *criminal* problem of hijacking. The ICAO antihijacking subcommittee met for the second time from September 23 to October 3, 1969, and continued its work on an antihijacking agreement. On behalf of the United States, Gene Malmborg referenced the TWA 840 case and pointed out that hijacking was an increasingly urgent problem. He argued again in favor of abolishing the political offense exception.

The delegates on the subcommittee considered the broad political implications of the U.S. suggestions and drew the same conclusions as before. They did not want harsh, mandatory, or uncompromising formulations. But the subcommittee agreed that the TWA 840 hijacking was a problematic situation where further regulations would be helpful. Its delegates adopted the "extradite or prosecute" compromise. They agreed to create an antihijacking extradition convention that provided states with a range of options in hijacking situations. In any case, signatory states would pledge to arrest hijackers. Such states then had several choices, though. State officials could submit the case to their domestic judicial authorities for prosecution according to national criminal law. However, delegates agreed that the case only needed to be submitted for the purpose of prosecution. National judicial authorities were under no obligation to actually go to trial against a hijacker. If they found insufficient evidence for domestic criminal proceedings, officials could drop the charges at any time. Officials could also extradite a hijacker. Yet the rest of the committee rejected all U.S. proposals to delete or narrow the political offense exception. This outcome was acceptable to the Tunisian and Indian delegates (the Algerian delegate was absent). These two representatives of recently independent states were adamantly opposed to regulations that might restrict their states' national sovereignty to decide who merited protection on the basis of political motivation.

Malmborg and his superiors realized the narrow limits that the other delegates were comfortable with and supported the "extradite or prosecute" compromise in order to achieve at least something in the ICAO. The sub-committee's convention draft did not force states to extradite hijackers, which had been the original U.S. goal.[56] Instead, it adopted the compromise idea that Malmborg had floated earlier that year. The convention draft contained several ways in which states could react to hijackings, still permitted states to acknowledge hijackers' political motivations, and (like the Tokyo Convention) included no enforcement mechanisms to punish states that treated hijackings as insurgent or wartime occurrences instead of as criminal situations without political context.

As the committee deliberated, State Department officials began conceding that they had reached the limits of what they could do to resolve the TWA 840 case. Moshe Raviv, a counselor at the Israeli embassy, explained that a "Department officer expressed [a] personal view that we have virtually exhausted our numerous efforts through third parties to secure passengers' release and it becoming [sic] increasingly clear that Syrians will not . . . agree to their release without face-saving quid pro quo."[57] Nothing short of a prisoner-of-war exchange would do. Adding insult to injury from the American and Israeli perspectives, in October Syrian authorities released Issawi and Khaled. Khaled became a female icon of the global national liberation movement. Efforts to influence the Syrians stalled, and Malmborg had only limited success in the ICAO legal subcommittee. Yet the Nixon administration remained focused on the idea of punishing states that did not return passengers (or extradite hijackers). In November 1969, Loy and ARA pursued initiatives outside the ICAO to achieve the desired punishment options. Loy attempted to circumvent the ICAO and negotiate directly with friendly counterpart bureaucrats. In December 1969, Loy hosted representatives of fifteen major aviation countries, mostly U.S. allies, at a meeting in Washington, DC. Aviation was a rapidly expanding field in the late 1960s, and officials frequently met to re-negotiate routes, fares, and access to their respective countries. Loy tapped into the strong transgovernmental connections that already existed.

At that meeting, Loy and the new U.S. ICAO representative, Charles Butler, presented a controversial new idea. They demanded, for the first time, that the ICAO institute sanctions against countries that did not return a hijacked plane and passengers or who did not extradite hijackers. The

U.S. suggestion was that other states should stop all air travel to the state in question. These U.S.-proposed sanctions would cut off airline access to the sanctioned state and turn it into a pre-aviation travel and economic backwater. In an age of expanding globalization, these proposed sanctions were a harsh threat to the economy and relevance of the affected state. Such sanctions would require broad multilateral collaboration, though.[58]

Loy, Butler, and the other U.S. officials, however, were unable to gain support for this idea. The French and British delegates rejected the idea outright, as did the other delegations. All worried that the sanctions would undermine their own national sovereignty by forcing them to extradite someone who qualified for political asylum or did not merit criminal prosecution under their respective domestic laws. Another objection was that these sanctions would clash with preexisting bilateral extradition agreements.[59] Such sanctions could also undercut basic interaction within the ICAO. Membership in the ICAO was voluntary, as was the ratification of any ICAO convention. The meeting ended with the delegates' insistence on supporting the existing ICAO negotiations.

Meanwhile, Nixon approved a bilateral outreach to Cuban authorities via the Swiss embassy in Havana. Rogers, Kissinger, and Volpe considered the new Cuban antihijacking law an opening for the United States.[60] Directing the initiative were ARA's new assistant secretary, Charles Meyer, and his deputy, Robert Hurwitch. Meyer was a former Sears executive focusing on Latin America. A career foreign service officer, Hurwitch had significant experience with Cuba, having worked on the Bay of Pigs aftermath and the Cuban Missile Crisis. As an overture, Hurwitch sent a note to the Cuban foreign minister, Raúl Roa García, on November 28, 1969, via the Swiss ambassador to Cuba, Alfred Fischli. In the note, the State Department offered to return airplane hijackers to Cuba and asked for Cuban reciprocity in adherence with antihijacking law no. 1226.[61] The Cubans responded in December that they were "disposed to work out an agreement with the Government of the United States on hijackers of aircraft and other similar acts."[62] Yet Castro implied in subsequent speeches that his regime would only accept an agreement that also covered people who left Cuba on boats. Rogers was pessimistic about achieving a bilateral antihijacking extradition agreement. While the U.S. government was in theory prepared to return airplane hijackers (of which it had none at the moment), it would not return the many arriving boat refugees. Nevertheless, Rogers did not want

Cuba to claim that the United States was the one stalling negotiations. With Nixon and Kissinger's approval, Rogers ordered Hurwitch and the OLA to draft a potential bilateral agreement and follow up with Cuba.[63]

Yet U.S. progress appeared slow in comparison to developing events. In December 1969, the International Committee of the Red Cross conducted the Syrians' desired exchange. The two Syrian military pilots were included in an Egyptian-Israeli prisoner-of-war swap. Then the Syrians finally released the two Israeli TWA passengers. The PFLP hijacking had enabled Syrian officials to pressure Israel.

Meanwhile, the PFLP's actions were inspiring copycat hijackings around the world, underscoring that long-range international flights were now persistently under threat. In 1968, over thirty hijackings had occurred worldwide. In 1969 and 1970, that number increased to almost one hundred hijackings each year.[64] Some of these hijackers imitated the PFLP and used national liberation terminology to justify their behavior. On December 11, 1969, a North Korean citizen hijacked Korean Airlines Flight Y-11 from Seoul to North Korea. The North Korean government refused to return the crew and seven of the forty-six passengers.[65] On January 9, 1970, the French citizen Christian Belon hijacked TWA Flight 802 from Paris to Beirut. Belon had a criminal record in France but claimed that his hijacking was to draw attention to U.S. and Israeli aggression in the Middle East.[66] On March 31, 1970, nine members of the Japanese militant communist group Red Army Faction seized Japanese Airlines Flight 351 from Tokyo to Fukuoka. Taking 120 passengers and 9 crew members hostage, the hijackers redirected the aircraft to Pyongyang, where they hoped to secure transport to Havana. Their goal was to imitate U.S. and Latin American national liberation actors and gain sanctuary and guerilla training from Cuban authorities. The North Korean state granted the hijackers asylum but refused to let them leave the country. They were forced to settle in North Korea.[67] These hijackings gained global media attention.

Palestinian extremists also engaged in new forms of violence against civil aviation in the Global North. On February 21, 1970, a bomb (hidden in an airmail package) exploded in the hold of SwissAir Flight SR330 from Zurich to Hong Kong. The aircraft crashed soon after takeoff, killing all on board. That same day a bomb exploded in the cargo area of an Austrian Airlines flight from Frankfurt to Vienna, although in this case the pilot managed a safe landing. Assuming that the two attacks were related, Swiss prosecutors quickly linked them to a splinter organization of the PFLP, the PFLP–General Command (PFLP-GC), founded in 1968 by Ahmed Jibril. One of the original PFLP founders and a former Syrian army member, Jibril advocated more border-crossing insurgent acts and fewer propaganda efforts.[68] The PFLP-GC originally claimed credit for the Zurich attack but later rescinded its claim. Swiss and West German authorities never found enough evidence to prosecute anyone for the two bombings. In response to the attacks, Western European states petitioned the ICAO for speedy relief against nonstate extremists who endangered civilian passengers around the world.[69] Public awareness of the danger to civil aviation grew alongside these attacks.

As the ICAO came increasingly under pressure to act against hijacking, Malmborg and the U.S. ICAO delegation decided to utilize the forward momentum and acknowledged that the existing convention draft had the highest chance of approval. In February 1970, the ICAO Legal Committee met to review the antihijacking subcommittee's convention draft. The U.S. delegation dropped its emphasis on mandatory extradition and punitive measures against states. Instead, it threw its weight behind the existing "extradite or prosecute" formulation. Though the draft left the political offense exception untouched and did not contain sanctions, Malmborg supported it as the best option the United States could actually achieve.[70]

With U.S. support, the ICAO Legal Committee scheduled a diplomatic conference for December 1970 to adopt the existing convention draft. A diplomatic conference is a one-time meeting of experts dedicated to a certain subject, such as aviation security, who gather to pass a specific treaty or agreement. All experts present are familiar with technical, legal, and other specifications. This type of conference avoids unrelated issues or far-ranging political discussions that could more easily occur in a general body like the ICAO or UN.[71] Prompted by Western European states, the ICAO also decided to hold a previously unplanned General Assembly in July 1970 to discuss further security measures both in the technical and legal fields.

By early 1970, the U.S. diplomatic outreach against hijacking was slow, especially in the face of developing events. Further bilateral outreach to the Cubans was on the horizon. Yet Palestinian extremists' attacks on civil aviation also rose. Hijacking became a method through which Palestinian Fedayeen and states such as Syria could force not only the Israeli government but also powerful Global North countries such as the United States to face border-crossing acts of violence for which they were ill prepared. In turn, U.S. officials prompted the creation of a new ICAO antihijacking convention. But this "extradite or prosecute" convention was shaping up to include dedicated loopholes for self-declared political (read: national liberation) actors and their state supporters.

DIPLOMATS AS TARGETS IN LATIN AMERICA

Meanwhile, Robert Hurwitch at ARA faced a separate threat from Global South actors against Global North citizens and responded by copying Loy's antihijacking "extradite or prosecute" approach. In Latin America, leftist extremist groups attacked U.S. and other Global North diplomats. As the principal agents of state-to-state contact, diplomats traditionally enjoyed the right to conduct their duties irrespective of political or martial conditions in their host state. The UN's 1961 Vienna Convention on Diplomatic Relations specified that each sovereign state had the obligation to safeguard the diplomats on its territory.[72] Yet by 1969, many leftist Latin American groups realized that targeting diplomats was a means to achieve their political goals.

During the 1960s, Latin America was a hotbed of left-wing and right-wing violent activity. A convergence of large-scale developments facilitated the spread of violent groups, including systematic economic and racial oppression, U.S.-backed and U.S.-instituted dictatorial regimes such as in Guatemala, the Sino-Soviet split, and Cuban military, economic, and medical assistance to leftists in the wake of the Cuban Revolution.[73] Driven by Cold War considerations, the State Department focused on left-wing violence in the region. Though the State Department oftentimes grouped leftist insurgencies together as a single interrelated threat, groups varied widely in their organizational structure, ideological conviction, amount of violent actions, and level of collaboration with formal political parties, state governments, and foreign insurgent actors.[74] Most groups participated eagerly in the transnational exchange of national liberation literature and ideology of the 1960s. The most radical leftist Latin American groups with little chance of participation in ordinary political processes attacked military personnel, state officials, law enforcement, and businessmen—representatives of the capitalist and oftentimes dictatorial regimes they opposed.

Affected states turned to punitive military, law enforcement, and legal measures to suppress political dissidents. Many governments, including those of Brazil, Argentina, Uruguay, Guatemala, and Nicaragua, increasingly repressed their own populations. By the late 1960s and early 1970s, right-wing regimes in Latin America increasingly claimed that all political opponents were a subversive threat to the state. They adopted the so-called "National Security Doctrine," which was based on the idea that any person who criticized the conservative state could be a potential (or future) supporter of leftist insurgents. And such people needed to be policed.[75] Following American, French, and British practice, Latin American officials at times utilized the threat of terrorism to justify these actions. In the Latin American context, as in other Global South and formerly colonized areas, officials used the term *terrorist* to describe any person who could potentially join or assist leftist insurgents.[76] This definition was deeply linked to the political aims and ideology of the ostensible terrorist. Yet it was also vague enough that officials could apply it against a wide array of people— few were safe from terrorist allegations.

The U.S. government at times ignored, but more often enabled, such suppressive violence. Officials stabilized authoritarian regimes and undermined Latin American governments that did not fully cooperate with U.S. interests. For the U.S. government, right-leaning state and paramilitary violence in Latin America was a Cold War necessity against leftist threats. The United States eagerly assisted by providing military aid and counterinsurgency training to Latin American states. At the School of the Americas in the Panama Canal Zone, U.S. army instructors taught Latin American military and police officers counterinsurgency practices, including jungle warfare, intelligence operations, and interrogation (read: torture) techniques. Thousands of officers graduated per year, most from Latin America.[77] The U.S. government also provided on-site assistance. In 1967, for example, U.S. counterinsurgency training teams were deployed in Guatemala, El Salvador, Honduras, Nicaragua, Colombia, Argentina, Bolivia, Ecuador, Peru, Venezuela, and the Dominican Republic.[78] By the late 1960s, many Latin American countries conducted extensive campaigns to undermine political dissent.

As many Latin American states' repressive capacities increased, some leftist groups responded by targeting U.S. military advisers who trained local forces. In early 1968, the Guatemalan insurgent group Rebel Armed

Forces assassinated two U.S. military advisers, Colonel John Webber and Lieutenant Commander Ernest Munro.[79] When Guatemalan counterinsurgency responses led to mass repression and the arrest of most of the group's members, it decided to kidnap John Gordon Mein, the U.S. ambassador to Guatemala, in a desperate attempt to exchange him for Rebel Armed Forces prisoners. The kidnapping attempt on August 28, 1968, went awry; the attackers accidentally killed the resisting Mein. His death shocked the ARA and the State Department as its officials suddenly realized they were targets.[80] Mein's death was no singular incident, either. In its wake, other leftist extremist groups throughout Latin America responded to increased state repression by attacking U.S. and Global North diplomats.

From 1968 onward, leftist Latin American extremists kidnapped diplomats from the United States and other Global North countries to pressure their host governments into releasing captured prisoners; these attempts resulted in some notable successes. In September 1969, Brazil's 8th October Revolutionary Movement kidnapped U.S. ambassador Charles Elbrick and exchanged him for fifteen political prisoners. On March 16, 1970, Brazil's Popular Revolutionary Vanguard group kidnapped Japanese consul general Nobuo Okuchi in São Paulo and ransomed him for five political prisoners. A Dominican group named the Unitary Command against Re-Election kidnapped a military target, the U.S. Air Force attaché Lieutenant Colonel John Crowley, on March 25, 1970, and traded him for twenty-one prisoners.[81] On March 31, 1970, the Rebel Armed Forces struck again in Guatemala to kidnap West German ambassador Karl von Spreti; he was found dead on April 5. The FRG broke off diplomatic ties to Guatemala, blaming its government for failing to secure von Spreti's safe release. This murder sparked additional fear among diplomats stationed in the region. These attacks generated a severe security deficit for diplomats in Latin America and degraded state-to-state relations in and beyond the region.

Unsettled by the danger to their immediate colleagues, in early April 1970 Hurwitch and the ARA proposed new initiatives to protect U.S. diplomats in the future. In 1970 the State Department had no fixed policy about whether to concede to kidnappers' demands or refuse them. Officials decided how to react on an ad hoc basis.[82] Like Loy and antihijacking specialists, Hurwitch took a two-pronged approach. He sought technical innovations to prevent attacks before they happened. He also suggested legal initiatives to deter and punish attackers. William B. Macomber Jr., who was responsible for the budget and resource allocation of the State Department, advocated for Hurwitch's recommendations with high-ranking Nixon administration officials. On the technical side, Hurwitch recommended instituting standardized security protocols in all U.S. embassies and asked for additional security personnel and equipment for the Latin American embassies in particular.[83]

In their suggestions for legal responses against attacks on diplomats, Hurwitch and the OLA's Mark Feldman drew from the existing U.S. initiatives concerning hijacking. Hurwitch had turned to the OLA to consider means by which the State Department could "reduce the political benefits that politically-motivated kidnappers believe they derive from kidnapping U.S. officials abroad."[84] Hurwitch and the OLA lawyers saw the similarities between kidnapping diplomats and hijacking: both attacks targeted U.S. citizens, the attackers were leftist nonstate actors, and in each case Cuba seemed to incentivize further attacks.[85] Macomber, Hurwitch, and Feldman argued that in both cases, the United States needed to pressure other states to ensure the safe return of U.S. citizens, reduce public sympathy for the nonstate attackers, and also motivate the Cuban government to condemn the attacks. "There are indications that Cuba is experiencing political embarrassment as a result of hijacking, for hijacking as an undesirable event is associated in the minds of many Latin Americans as Cuban-inspired. Since some of the hijackers belong to left-extremist groups (as do the kidnappers), there is some reason to believe that their activities are an embarrassment to the Communist cause."[86] Because Macomber and Hurwitch stated that hijackings and the kidnapping of diplomats were similar situations, the U.S. legal response they suggested was the same.

Hurwitch and Feldman recommended a new multilateral convention that condemned the kidnapping of diplomats more than before through international law. As a creating organization, they suggested either the global United Nations or the regional OAS. Founded in 1948, the OAS was an international organization designed to foster hemispheric cooperation in the Americas. In 1970 it was undergoing extensive bureaucratic reorganization to become a more powerful regional political forum. Rogers approved Macomber, Hutwitch, and Feldman's recommendations on April 13, 1970.[87] Their description of hijacking and attacks on diplomats as comparable scenarios was the first step toward a cohesive U.S. policy against new forms of nonstate violence that directly affected U.S. (and other Global North) citizens.

That same day, on April 13, 1970, Nicanor Méndez, Argentina's foreign minister, proposed a multilateral convention in the OAS that fit Hurwitch and Feldman's purposes. After von Spreti's death earlier that month, the Argentinean government had reached out to other states on the American continent to find a solution for what it labeled terrorism. To reiterate, in 1970 the term *terrorism* was mainly associated with leftist and anticolonial insurgencies, and it described any actor committing violence against civilians in the context of this insurgency. Many conservative Latin American officials used it to describe political opponents that might possibly be connected to leftist insurgencies or possibly interested in using violence (even if they did not use it). In Argentina, leftist extremists attacked not only diplomats but also public luminaries and police officials. The attacks had become a significant internal security threat. Dismissive of civil rights, the de facto military Argentine government under Juan Carlos Organía countered by instituting repressive domestic policies that would later culminate in the "dirty war" against dissidents waged from 1974 to 1983.[88] To supplement domestic efforts with international ones, Méndez sought bilateral talks with neighboring states in early April on how to address the problem of leftist terrorists.[89]

The Argentinean initiative was a resounding success. Within days, Méndez discovered that many other Latin American governments with similar repressive inclinations, such as Brazil, Uruguay, and Guatemala, were interested in multilateral, not just bilateral, agreements against terrorism. Méndez brought his ideas to the OAS. On April 13, Méndez formally requested that the OAS act on the matter of diplomats' kidnappings by terrorists.[90] A week later, the OAS's judicial committee took up the matter, and decided to create a multilateral convention against terrorism.[91] This Argentinean initiative can thus be contextualized as a public antecedent to the later clandestine collaboration of South American states in Operation Condor, which caused the death of thousands of dissidents.

While Méndez broached an antiterrorism agreement with the OAS, developments within the United Nations rendered a diplomat-related convention there unlikely. In mid-April 1970, the Dutch government asked its allies if they would co-sponsor a UN Security Council initiative for the protection of diplomats. Many European states agreed.[92] But the Nixon administration resisted. In New York City, an extremist group named the Jewish Defense League had recently begun attacking the property of the

Soviet UN delegation to protest the lack of emigration options for Soviet Jews. Nixon was not interested in providing the Soviet Union with a Security Council platform to criticize the attacks in New York City. Thus, the Dutch ambassador was told that the United States wanted to focus on the OAS and regional politics. Nixon's UN Ambassador David Yost argued that a UN convention would have more potential for adoption if a regional OAS convention succeeded first.[93] The Dutch withdrew their initiative. Hurwitch and Feldman focused on passing a convention in the OAS.

However, disagreement developed between the Argentinean and U.S. delegations at the OAS about the scope of the convention. Méndez wanted an agreement that required states to criminally prosecute all forms of political violence under the label terrorism. His proposed agreement would allow states such as Argentina to convict and imprison alleged terrorists with far greater ease. Officials could then prosecute many diverse potential dissidents with vague terrorist accusations. The proposed agreement allowed Argentina and others to further disregard their citizens' political grievances. These states sought to use the convention as a tool to legitimate their domestic criminal prosecution of political dissidents. Such aims were in line with earlier Latin American and other periphery states' counterinsurgency programs.

In contrast, the State Department's goal was to protect U.S. diplomats in Latin America, who were not interested in being publicly associated with a Latin American initiative that facilitated repressive uses of criminal law. Hurwitch and Feldman wanted to enable Latin American states to do everything possible (including conceding to kidnappers' demands) in order to return kidnapped U.S. diplomats. Thus, the U.S. position in the OAS was that the new convention should focus only on attacks against diplomats. Implicit in the U.S. position was that states could more easily negotiate with criminal kidnappers if their political associations were delegitimized, thereby removing any stain on governments in case they had to give in to leftist extremists' demands. In addition, such a narrow protection-of-diplomats convention would be easier to achieve that one against the broad and vague term *terrorism*. Diplomats were already protected persons under international law. Hurwitch and Feldman also speculated that such a narrow convention could motivate Soviet and Cuban officials to restrain leftist radical groups. Such groups often sought to overthrow their governments and become state actors themselves. Hurwitch and Feldman hoped that leftist groups and their socialist state supporters would not want to be accused of violating a sovereign state's obligation to protect foreign diplomats.[94]

The main controversy in the OAS negotiations thus developed between Argentina and the United States over what violent acts the convention would actually cover. Argentina and its allies wanted the convention to declare terrorism and, relatedly, all political violence and alleged intent to commit such violence as criminal. The U.S. delegation intended to solve the concrete problem of protecting locally stationed U.S. diplomats.[95] For months, negotiations went back and forth between the Argentinean and U.S. OAS delegations about whether to create a broad convention criminalizing terrorism in general or a narrow convention that only criminalized attacks against diplomats.

Since he viewed hijacking and attacks on diplomats as comparable situations, Feldman used the "extradite or prosecute" principle from the ICAO negotiations to frame the U.S. position,[96] and the OAS judicial committee accepted it. Committee members decided that the new convention should require states to create domestic criminal laws against attackers and apply those laws uniformly. Signatory states would have to arrest offenders and then try or extradite them. And, unlike in the ICAO, the OAS delegates were willing to cut out the political offense exception. The exception was a protective measure for political dissidents that repressively minded regimes such as Argentina did not favor.[97] When the OAS General Assembly met in June and July of 1970, it approved the negotiations and instructed its legal branch to complete a final agreement. By September, the representatives there had a working draft and were negotiating details. Neither the public nor attackers themselves influenced these negotiations.

By applying the same "extradite or prosecute" concept to both Loy's anti-hijacking agreement at the ICAO and the ARA's protection-of-diplomats initiative in the OAS, Feldman and the OLA laid the foundation for a distinct U.S. foreign policy concerning transnational extremist violence that directly affected U.S. citizens. That policy addressed narrow U.S. interests in Cuba and Latin America but had far-reaching global implications. State Department officials worked within specialized international organizations and relied on counterpart bureaucrats and technical specialists in a process that excluded nonstate actors from influencing policymaking. Both organizations' convention drafts addressed acts committed by leftist extremists as common crimes. They required states to use domestic criminal law against attackers and strengthened states' ability to extradite offenders. Both drafts sought to fill jurisdictional gaps and enabled states to prosecute crimes in cases where the appropriate jurisdiction might not have existed before. The ICAO and the OAS were technical and regional organizations, respectively, and did not have the same global influence as the United Nations. Nevertheless, their specialized nature created an unanticipated space for the State Department to draft policies requiring other states to address anticolonial and revolutionary nonstate actors as criminals.

ADOPTING THE CONVENTIONS

As the OAS negotiations progressed throughout 1970, the legal and the technical initiatives to secure civil aviation at ICAO also accelerated. That summer, ICAO members sought to improve security in aviation facilities. Western European states drove this initiative. The wording of the Tokyo Convention and the new ICAO antihijacking convention draft was weak because it only covered situations aboard aircraft in flight. These agreements did not provide legal resolution or security measures for other situations, such as the bomb that destroyed SwissAir Flight SR330 in February 1970. After that bombing, Western European states had requested an extraordinary ICAO General Assembly to improve security within aviation facilities and on grounded airplanes. During this two-week meeting in June 1970, the ICAO General Assembly created two committees: one to confer about technical security measures and the other legal extradition options.

The technical committee discussed a range of technological security innovations for ICAO to sponsor and adopt as standard practice recommendations. These innovations included training more airport security personnel, regularly and systematically screening carry-on and checked baggage, introducing metal detectors, and reorganizing airports to create zones restricted to previously inspected passengers. A security manual explaining these innovations appeared in 1971. To follow up, the previously unresponsive ICAO Committee on Unlawful Interference, dedicated to technical security improvements, worked on integrating these innovations into existing ICAO regulations. In 1974, it added Annex 17 to ICAO's founding convention. Annex 17 consolidated these updated security practices and technologies as standard regulations for all ICAO members.

States' compliance with these regulations was consistently subpar, however, as they often required costly training and equipment.[98]

Concerning legal matters, the ICAO General Assembly agreed to create another multilateral convention. Again based on the "extradite or prosecute" principle, this second proposed convention would cover acts that endangered civil aviation on the ground. It defined all violent attacks against civil aviation as common crimes instead of insurgent acts. Increasingly engaged in aviation security since the SwissAir bombing, the British Home Office and Foreign and Commonwealth Office took much more initiative and considered this second convention a British-sponsored project.[99] The U.S. delegation again floated the idea of sanctioning noncompliant states, but the other ICAO members rejected it for a second time.

Loy left the State Department after the June 1970 ICAO meeting. Having served several years in the FAA and then at State, he took an opportunity to join Pan Am as a senior executive. Years later, he would return to State as assistant secretary of state for Population, Refugees, and Migration Affairs (1980–1981) and as under secretary of state for Civilian Security, Democracy, and Human Rights (1998–2001). Loy's successor at Economic Affairs, Bertram Rein, continued Loy's initiatives. Like Loy and the OLA lawyers, Rein moved in and out of government throughout his career as an international law expert. Rein also drove ICAO "extradite or prosecute" initiatives and supported Hurwitch's effort to achieve a U.S.-Cuban hijacking extradition agreement. In September 1970, however, a major PFLP-initiated hijacking crisis shifted the Nixon administration's full attention to the Palestinian national liberation group.

The Dawson's Field crisis in September 1970 pushed the Nixon administration to finally address hijacking more seriously because PFLP actors took U.S. citizens hostage and also directly threatened U.S. foreign policy interests in the Middle East. At stake were U.S. lives, the survival of Jordan as a Cold War ally, and whether the United States and Western European countries would have to acknowledge and negotiate with Palestinians as sovereign actors. Nixon and Kissinger held onto their policy not to formally negotiate with Palestinian nonstate actors. Meanwhile, the PFLP's goal was to display its control over Jordanian territory and "perform" its sovereignty claims.

The Dawson's Field crisis pitted the PFLP against Israel, the United States, several European countries, and King Hussein of Jordan, a staunch

FIGURE 1.2. Dawson's Field hijackings, September 1970.
Members of the Popular Front for the Liberation of Palestine (PFLP) hijacked four airplanes with hundreds
of U.S., European, and Israeli passengers, and landed three at a remote airstrip in Jordan. World History
Archive / Alamy Stock Photo.

U.S. ally whose governance was tenuous. In September 1970, a civil war
broke out between the Jordanian army and the PLO, which controlled
quasi-state structures in most Palestinian refugee camps in Jordan.[100] To
demonstrate that the PLO was exercising sovereign rights within Jordan,
PFLP cofounder Wadie Haddad planned to hijack multiple planes. A doctor and longtime friend of Habash, Haddad led the PFLP's more militant
enterprises. Haddad's premise was that he could demonstrate Palestinian
agency in a performative manner by hijacking several planes and bringing them to a PFLP-controlled space. Ideally, the hijackings would leave
Israel and other affected states with no choice but to acknowledge the PLO
as a sovereign negotiation partner and enter what the PFLP considered
wartime state-to-state prisoner-of-war exchanges. On September 6, 1970,
PFLP members hijacked two American (one Pan Am and one TWA) and
one Swiss (SwissAir) flights. Another attempt by Leila Khaled to seize an
Israeli El Al aircraft failed. An Israeli air marshal shot Khaled's Nicaraguan
cohijacker, and she herself was arrested when the plane landed in London.
The TWA and SwissAir planes flew to Dawson's Field, a PFLP-controlled

airstrip in Jordan. The Pan Am hijackers landed in Cairo because the plane was too large for their Jordanian destination. PFLP members seized another British plane and brought it to Dawson's Field, which they dubbed "Revolutionary Airport," three days later. In total, the PFLP had over three hundred hostages. Approximately half were U.S. citizens, while the rest hailed from Israel, the United Kingdom, the FRG, and Switzerland. For the first time, the PFLP held significant numbers of Americans hostage. The PFLP demanded that each of the other governments release incarcerated Palestinians in exchange for their hostage citizens.[101]

Haddad wanted to demonstrate that the PFLP was a proto-state organization, sovereign, and a legitimate actor in international politics. For this purpose, he was willing to accept the significant risk of targeting Israel and the major Global North countries. Holding not just Israeli but also U.S. and Western European citizens hostage had benefits for the PFLP. PFLP

FIGURE 1.3. PFLP press conference during the Dawson's Field hijackings, September 15, 1970.
The PFLP used the hijackings to emphasize Palestinian claims to sovereignty and self-determination.
History and Art Collection / Alamy Stock Photo.

leaders like Habash could speak to them and (hopefully) convince them of the righteousness of the Palestinian cause. The PFLP could also pressure Global North governments in new ways through threats to the hostages.

And at least initially, Haddad and the PFLP did achieve some success. The Nixon administration was vulnerable because no unilateral U.S. options were available. Nixon placed significant pressure on King Hussein to intervene militarily and threaten the PFLP with retaliation if anything happened to the hostages. Yet otherwise, Nixon's hands were tied. He did not want to deploy the U.S. military directly into the precarious political situation in the Middle East and risk the reprisal of the Soviet Union and its local friends such as Syria. In addition, direct U.S. action could undermine King Hussein's already tenuous hold on power and unseat a staunch U.S. ally in the region.[102] Nixon still refused to make concessions to the PFLP or even negotiate with it in public; he instructed the CIA to clandestinely back King Hussein and the Jordanian army.[103]

Besides the complex military situation, alone of the five affected countries, the United States held no imprisoned Fedayeen with whom to bargain. To secure the U.S. hostages, the State Department asked the United Kingdom, the FRG, and Switzerland to trade their few incarcerated Palestinian prisoners collectively for all hostages at once through the mediation of the International Committee of the Red Cross.[104] These multilateral negotiations were frustrating for U.S. diplomats. The other states stalled and were also clandestinely reaching out to Palestinian contacts behind the scenes to secure their respective citizens.[105] On September 12, the PFLP blew up the hijacked airplanes in front of gathered international media representatives. The group also released women and children and some men, declaring that it would only negotiate for the forty remaining hostages directly with individual states.

Yet Haddad, Habash, and the PFLP paid a steep price for their initiative. To protect the PLO from Jordanian reprisal, Arafat expelled the PFLP from the PLO. King Hussein's power was shaken. But he rallied in the face of Palestinians' demands for sovereignty. Starting on September 16, the Jordanian army mercilessly destroyed Palestinian refugee camps and PLO structures in Jordan in what Palestinians soon called their "Black September." Following the Jordanian army's military victories over the PLO, the PFLP gradually released the remaining hostages, completing the process on September 30, 1970. In turn, the United Kingdom, FRG, and Switzerland freed

Palestinian prisoners, including Khaled, thus fulfilling one of the PFLP's key demands.[106] For several weeks, the PFLP had asserted itself as an actor to be taken seriously in international relations, despite the unsustainably high cost in lives, influence, and territory, and despite the efforts of the highest-ranking men in the Nixon administration.

Frustrated, Nixon utilized his executive authority to avoid future situations in which a nonstate national liberation group held such leverage over the U.S. government. His first step was to institute unilateral aviation security measures. On September 10, Nixon announced that so-called sky marshals would secure random flights operated by U.S. air carriers.[107] The United States joined Israel in protecting its civilian aircraft with armed personnel.[108] The Treasury Department's Customs Bureau hired 1,270 sky marshals on short notice and kept them flying until 1974.[109] Nixon also asked the FAA to brainstorm plans for additional security measures at U.S. airports, including passenger screenings. But such planning would take years to develop.

Additionally, Nixon concluded that the United States needed to be more assertive in its multilateral efforts to regulate hijacking at the ICAO. Other ICAO delegates agreed that any antihijacking or aviation security convention needed to contain mechanisms that gave states the right to acknowledge the PFLP as political actors. To most, no other way to achieve a compromise and actually pass a convention existed. In contrast, the Nixon administration's new focus on PFLP hijackers only hardened the U.S. position. Nixon instructed the Departments of State and Transportation to increase their ICAO lobbying to criminalize hijackers unconditionally, without any reference to the political offense exception. He also revived the U.S. effort to sanction states that acknowledged (and in Nixon's view, supported) hijackers' political grievances. Nixon's goal was to ensure that other states did not give hijackers any political status.[110]

As the Nixon administration increasingly focused on Palestinian hijackers, its Cuban antihijacking initiatives shifted to uncertain bilateral contacts. Hurwitch, the ARA, and the OLA waited for contact from Cuban foreign minister Roa. In April 1970, the Cuban government sent a note to the State Department via the Swiss embassy, declaring a vague willingness to discuss hijacking. On September 29, 1970, another Cuban note reached State. Roa rejected a proposed U.S. draft for a bilateral antihijacking extradition agreement. He insisted that any extradition agreement would have to cover people fleeing Cuba on boats as well as on airplanes. This inclusion of boats was exactly what the U.S. side wanted to avoid. The State Department was willing to waive its asylum policies for Cuban hijackers because so few existed, yet to deny asylum to and extradite Cubans arriving by boat was politically unfeasible for the Nixon administration. Roa, in turn, claimed that the narrow U.S. inclusion of only airplane hijackers ignored the existing Cuban law and failed to meet standards of reciprocity between states.[111] Further contact with Cuba stalled, even as the State Department was coming in line with the rest of the world's focus on Palestinian hijackers.

Under pressure from Nixon to deliver results, the State Department also continued to lobby counterpart officials in allied governments outside the ICAO. In late September 1970, a U.S. delegation consisting of John Rhinelander, deputy legal adviser, Robert Boyle (now at the FAA), and Bertram Rein met in Paris with transportation and foreign ministry officials from eight allied North Atlantic states, including Canada, the United Kingdom, and the FRG. The U.S. officials again pushed their allies to support sanctions for states that harbored hijackers. The U.S. goal was to include such sanctions in the second ICAO draft for a broader civil aviation security convention.

Once again, however, the U.S. position proved untenable even for close allies. Only Canadian officials were willing to support it. French officials boycotted the meeting—in Paris—altogether. The other officials responded that the ICAO was a technical, not a political, organization. Sanctions were a highly political issue beyond the ICAO's scope. The Italian delegate pointed out that his country could not support any initiative in ICAO to influence the Middle East situation.[112] The other representatives worried that the United States was overly politicizing the negotiations precisely by insisting that questions about political matters were irrelevant.

These worries were well-founded. In October 1970, the ICAO's Legal Committee met in London to draft a second extradition convention covering attacks on grounded airplanes and aviation facilities. The work seemed simple. Committee members copied the "extradite or prosecute" language of the existing convention draft on hijacking and declared the draft for the second convention complete. However, U.S. representative, Charles Butler, persuaded the ICAO Council to adopt a resolution that required countries to act in hijacking cases. The resolution stated that noncompliant states might face sanctions, even though the ICAO had no way to enforce such sanctions.[113] Butler leveraged the resolution to demand that the Legal

Committee delegates include sanctions in the second convention draft. He called for the international community to sanction any state that did not convict or extradite an attacker. States should refuse to send their airlines to that country, or to let that country's airline land on their territory. Such a sanction would be a tough economic loss for the offending state.

Despite two additional weeks of exhausting detail-focused negotiations, the legal committee delegates did not take up the U.S. sanctions. They were unwilling to abridge each state's sovereign right to decide whether an offense was political or criminal or both, and which of the numerous accepted responses to pursue. A requirement to sanction nonextraditing states would have cut into this sovereignty. Additionally, the delegates feared that the introduction of sanctions could derail ICAO's entire purpose. Membership in the ICAO was voluntary, and sanctions would undercut basic interaction within the organization. The ICAO's voluntary membership also made sanctions unenforceable. The additional negotiations exhausted the delegates and further alienated them from the U.S. delegation.[114] The delegates agreed to discuss sanctions again—but only at some other time in the future.

Weary of the political landmines surrounding aviation security, ICAO delegates met on December 16, 1970, in The Hague, eager to adopt and be done with the first convention draft against hijackers. This draft became the "Convention for the Suppression of Unlawful Seizure of Aircraft," also known as the "Hague Convention." In progress since 1969, the Hague Convention codified the "extradite or prosecute" principle as ICAO policy on hijacking. It required all signatory states to initially treat hijackers as criminals. These states committed themselves to adopting domestic criminal laws against hijackers. They could then submit cases for prosecution or extradite the attackers. The convention gave broad jurisdiction to prosecute hijackings, allowing every state to build a case against a hijacker if its authorities wishes to. The convention contained the political offense exception. It did not force Cuba or any Arab state to extradite hijackers. The United States only extradited on the basis of bilateral extradition treaties, and thus could not use it as the reason for an extradition. However, the convention was a step in the right direction for the State Department. The Castro regime's claim that U.S. hijackers were political refugees was now less tenable. So were the PFLP's claims to political relevance. Hijackers themselves had no opportunities to shape the convention since it was a product of state-employed experts in a highly specialized international organization.

Because the ICAO's Hague Convention upheld the political offense exception and each state's sovereign right to treat a hijacking as a politically motivated offense, it was moderate enough for many states to accept and adopt. The Hague Convention required that hijackers' cases still be handed to domestic judicial authorities. There were no further stipulations, though. And overall, the convention was weak. A state only had to start proceedings against hijackers. But there was no requirement to actually go to trial. Authorities could simply release a hijacker, or give out very light sentences, without violating the convention.[115] The Hague Convention also contained no enforcement or supervision mechanisms. These loopholes made the convention acceptable to most Arab states. Cuban practices of trying U.S. hijackers domestically were compliant with the convention as well. The Hague Convention entered into force less than a year later, in October 1971, with ten ratifications, including the United States.

The State Department accepted the convention despite its weaknesses. Led by OLA's head, John Stevenson, the U.S. delegation at The Hague decided that a convention that generally criminalized hijacking, even if it left loopholes, was preferable to no convention at all. In addition, they retained the hope that they could abolish the political offense exception and include sanctions in a future ICAO agreement.

Indeed, the ICAO's Hague Convention set a significant precedent even though it was voluntary, originated in a small technical international organization, could not be enforced, contained significant loopholes, and gained relatively little publicity. The convention created regulations in international law that in turn shaped norms for how states were to treat hijackers. Normatively, officials needed to respond to hijackings with domestic criminal law and extradition. This approach stripped away the political validation that many nonstate hijackers sought through their acts. Most states delegated hijacking incidents to national criminal courts and less to institutions dealing with self-determination or warfare. Throughout the 1970s, even states that supported Palestinians, such as Lebanon (1973), Libya (1978), and Syria (1980), signed the convention. Within international law and international relations, hijacking became a predominantly criminal act instead of a political one.

The ICAO Hague Convention's widely accepted language became the foundation for similar multilateral agreements. Feldman had used the "extradite or prosecute" principle as a basis for the OAS negotiations. As the Hague Convention showed, a variety of states accepted this principle because it criminalized attacks while retaining the political offense exception. Additionally, the ICAO had negotiated the Hague Convention relatively quickly despite the complexity of the jurisdiction and political issues involved. The "extradite or prosecute" principle could thus serve the State Department's practical needs in the OAS. The wave of diplomat kidnappings in Latin America had not abated, and the West German and Swiss ambassadors to Brazil had both been kidnapped since von Spreti's death.[116] The State Department's goal was to pressure Latin American states to increase their protection of U.S. diplomats. Criminalizing attackers would make it easier for states to deter them (before an attack) or prosecute them (after an attack). In addition, the ARA hoped that it could leverage the convention to force Latin American states to negotiate with or even concede to attackers in cases where diplomats had been kidnapped. Such negotiations would not undercut or diminish the state's sovereignty because the convention ensured that attackers were branded as criminals, not as political agents.[117]

In January 1971, the OAS foreign ministers met in Washington, DC, to adopt their convention. Still open was the question of what political violence the convention would actually cover. The Argentinean and Brazilian delegations again pushed for a broad convention to criminalize all acts of political violence in the region. Their goal was to use a multilateral OAS agreement to criminalize insurgency and terrorism, enabling them to apply harsher criminal laws against potential political dissidents, deny similar actors from abroad asylum, and extradite them, all without facing backlash from the international community. The U.S. delegation, supported by Mexico and Venezuela, aimed for a narrowly defined convention to regulate only attacks against diplomats, without touching upon other violent actions.[118] The ARA and the OLA sought a more specialized convention, knowing that it would be easier to pass, implement, and sell to the public. With a narrowly defined convention, the United States could deny any negative publicity claiming that it was cooperating with repressive Latin American states on measures against political dissidents. State Department officials wanted to emphasize that they were cooperating only on protective measures for their own diplomats. After a week of contentious negotiations, six delegations that favored a broad convention, against all ostensibly terrorist attacks, walked out of the meeting.[119] The remaining thirteen delegations passed a narrowly focused convention in accordance with U.S. goals, reaching the required majority by a single vote.

The resulting OAS "Convention to Prevent and Punish the Acts of Terrorism Taking the Form of Crimes Against Persons and Related Extortion That Are of International Significance" (OAS Convention) never gained significant support among governments in the Americas.[120] But it bore striking similarities to the ICAO's Hague Convention. Feldman had copied the ICAO's "extradite or prosecute" language verbatim.[121] The convention covered a greater variety of attacks, particularly "kidnapping, murder, and other assaults against the life or physical integrity of" diplomatic representatives.[122] It labeled offenders who attacked diplomats as criminals and denied them political aims, grievances, or agency. The convention did not contain the political offense exception, including only the ambiguous formulation that it would not "impair the right of asylum."[123] This wording was weaker than the political offense exception. Overall, the OAS Convention extended the scope of "extradite or prosecute" for the United States. It increased the number of nonstate violent acts by Global South actors against U.S. citizens that the State Department addressed as a crime regardless of political context. The ARA and Feldman hoped that the convention would deter future attacks on diplomats in Latin America by reducing associated political benefits for attackers.

The OAS Convention was the first multilateral agreement in the post–World War II era that mentioned terrorism and attempted to regulate countermeasures; it diverged strongly from prevailing understandings, however, because it focused only on the criminal aspects of terrorism without considering any political or insurgent context. The convention retained the term *terrorism* from Méndez's original proposal. Yet it assumed that terrorists were criminal actors and described the offenses it covered in those terms. Previous conceptions of terrorism, especially in Latin America and former colonial territories, emphasized that terrorists were politically driven (and usually on the far left or communist). They sought to become state actors. These aspects separated the terrorist from the apolitical criminal. Now, the OAS Convention avoided any language connected to insurgency, warfare, or political violence.[124] Terrorism became a widespread term in subsequent years, but in 1971 few people were using it.[125] The OAS Convention laid the groundwork for later discussions because it emphatically linked the term *terrorism* to *crimes* committed by *nonstate actors* and ignored the political dimensions of these acts.

State Department officials used the Hague and OAS Conventions to lobby close U.S. allies; the goal was to recruit hesitant allies into sharing the

U.S. position at the ICAO and OAS. Feldman had hoped for European support to strengthen the U.S. negotiating position at the OAS because these states' diplomats were also frequent targets in Latin America.[126] To attract support, he cultivated an ally in an Italian counterpart, Marco Fortini, the director for Latin American Political Affairs at Italy's ministry of foreign affairs and international cooperation. Since 1969, the Italian government was facing escalating leftist student and labor protests that had already generated several acts of domestic violence.[127] The U.S. ambassador to Italy, Graham Martin, speculated that Fortini was especially worried about the potential of attacks in Rome, a major transportation hub between the East, West, and Global South, and was observing to see whether a similar agreement to the OAS negotiations could be implemented in Europe.[128] In August 1970, Fortini began lobbying the other European states to consider new international law regulations for the protection of diplomats.[129] France and the FRG were alienated from the OAS Convention by the tumultuous final negotiations in January 1971, which ended in six delegations walking out and a convention with minimal support.[130] Yet Fortini established connections to officials from Switzerland and the Baltic States who were interested in a new protection-of-diplomats agreement.[131] In early 1971 these contacts were not yet willing to commit themselves, hesitating due to strong French opposition. However, this network would provide valuable support for the United States and Italy when debates on diplomats and on terrorism shifted to the United Nations in 1972.[132]

Meanwhile, the OLA began collaborating with the Canadian government on civil aviation security. Canadian officials had shown interest in U.S. sanctions proposals in late September 1970. That October, Canada experienced a dramatic hostage crisis when the Front de libération du Québec, a separatist group, kidnapped Quebec's deputy premier, Pierre Laporte, and British diplomat James Cross. Canadian prime minister Pierre Trudeau instituted martial law and suspended civil liberties. Laporte was found dead in mid-October. To secure Cross's release in December 1970, his kidnappers received safe passage to Cuba. In the aftermath of the crisis, the Canadian government approached Roa to discuss options for a bilateral Canadian-Cuban antihijacking agreement.

Of broader significance, the Canadian government was now willing to support the U.S. idea of sanctions against any state that granted political asylum to hijackers. As previously mentioned, in October 1970, Charles

Butler had led two weeks of fruitless negotiations to add sanctions to the draft for the second ICAO convention on general aviation security. These negotiations failed. To placate the United States, however, the ICAO Legal Committee did agree to form a subcommittee to discuss sanctions further—at some other time. This subcommittee met in April 1971. Together, a U.S.-Canadian working group produced a working paper that served as the basis for discussion. Rein and the other State Department officials envisioned another new multilateral convention. This convention would institute sanctions against states that violated the Hague and Tokyo Conventions, supported hijackers, or granted them a safe haven.[133] Yet once again significant resistance arose against sanctions or any infringement on a state's right to recognize the political motivation of hijackers. French delegates insisted alongside a new ICAO member, the Soviet Union, that the ICAO was a technical organization; sanctions should best be left to the United Nations.[134] Their refusal undermined the U.S.-Canadian efforts. ICAO sanctions discussions stalled until the Munich Olympic Games attack the following year.[135]

Though the ICAO refused to approve sanctions, it did pass its convention draft, which covered all attacks against grounded planes and aviation facilities in general. In September 1971, the ICAO General Assembly adopted the "Convention for the Suppression of Unlawful Acts Against the Safety of Civil Aviation," or "Montreal Convention."[136] Mirroring the Hague Convention, it contained the principle of "extradite or prosecute," declared that states should handle all attacks against civil aviation as crimes, and gave any state with an attacker on its territory the jurisdiction to criminally prosecute that person. It criminalized attacks against grounded airplanes. It also identified the sabotage of airplanes or aviation facilities as a criminal offense. The Montreal Convention thus extended the list of violent actions that the international community pledged to generally handle as common crimes. It contained the political offense exception. But on average, it normatively removed these civil aviation attacks from recognition as acts of anticolonial protest or insurgency. Together, the Hague, OAS, and Montreal Conventions branded as criminal a variety of border-crossing attacks that American, Palestinian, and Latin American actors committed in the late 1960s.

Yet the new conventions did not achieve the State Department's original goal of ensuring that Cuba returned hijackers and planes. Roa refused to be

pressured into extradition through a multilateral agreement. Cuba only ratified the ICAO conventions in October 2001 after the September 11 attacks.

The State Department did reach an agreement with Cuba on hijacking
in 1973, but it was not prompted by the ICAO or OAS Conventions. In
November 1972 a particularly brutal hijacking to Havana with two casualties prompted Roa to reach out to the Swiss ambassador again.[137] Roa
may possibly also have been motivated by the media reports of Palestinian Fedayeen's attack on the Israeli Olympic team in Munich. He stated
that he was willing to negotiate a bilateral hijacking extradition agreement
with the United States that covered the hijacking of both aircraft and boats.
Crucially for the U.S. side, Roa dropped his insistence that the treaty apply
retroactively and cover all Cubans who had fled to the United States since
1961. He also agreed to include the right to asylum for all attackers who were
fleeing political persecution and had not caused physical injury or blackmailed anyone during their attack. This formulation was useful because
Cubans who left their country on boats oftentimes fit this description. The
State Department could thus still grant them asylum.[138] Charles Meyer
and the ARA moved quickly to conduct negotiations through the Swiss
embassy. William Rogers signed a bilateral memorandum of understanding with Cuba on February 15, 1973. This antihijacking agreement was not
a treaty between nation-states and retained U.S. practices not to acknowledge Cuban statehood.[139] Cuba renounced it in 1977 after right-wing Cuban
exiles in the United States bombed a Cubana Airlines plane and killed all
on board. Yet Cuban authorities continued to adhere to the premises of the
agreement after the fact.

The U.S. initiatives in ICAO and the OAS thus led to a U.S. policy to treat
hijackers and those who attacked diplomats as criminals, never as political
actors, and created international law to disseminate this view among other
states. However, these initiatives did not fulfill their original purpose—to
drive the U.S.-Cuban antihijacking agreement.

The OAS, Hague, and Montreal Conventions created a normative framework in international law that transformed hijackings and attacks on diplomats from potential insurgent acts into crimes that were to be adjudicated
only by each state's criminal law system. Signatory states agreed to institute
domestic criminal laws against the offenses covered by the conventions, to

arrest perpetrators inside their national borders, and to submit such cases to local prosecutors or extradite the offenders elsewhere. By regulating these acts of violence as common crimes, the three conventions worked to erase the political, insurgent, and martial background of such attacks. The political offense exception left a loophole for each state to accept an offender's political motivation, and this ambiguity made the conventions widely acceptable to most states. However, the conventions' criminal focus led leaders around the world to conceptualize hijackings and attacks on diplomats primarily within the framework of criminal law.

The conventions linked state sovereignty to the treatment of nonstate attackers as criminals. The three conventions gave the United States and other countries a legal basis in international law to deny attackers the political influence sought though hijacking and attacks on diplomats. The conventions were a reaction to self-declared anticolonial actors who had dared to directly target citizens, locations, and property belonging to the Global North. Since these groups were generally leftist, the conventions also provided another justification for the United States, its European allies, and Latin American states to reject the political aspirations of nonstate leftist, Maoist, and socialism-affiliated groups. At the same time, states could use their adherence to the conventions to argue that they were upholding and strengthening obligations available in international law only to sovereign states, not to nonstate actors. One such obligation was hosting and protecting diplomats. Another was to conduct prisoner exchanges only with other states—never with proto-state or nonstate agents. A third was retaining a monopoly on violence by arresting criminal nonstate offenders. Our modern understanding is that state responses to border-crossing terrorism began with Palestinian Fedayeen. But this chapter has shown that historical developments were more complex and that initial U.S. actions also need to be interpreted as a response to other nonstate actors in Cuba and Latin America.

Meanwhile, because the ICAO and the OAS were international institutions with specialized mandates, nonstate violent actors had few means of influencing the discussions other than by carrying out further attacks. In the ICAO, Arab and Global South states did defend the right of the PFLP and others to pursue anticolonial national liberation struggles. However, State Department officials were not interested in hearing or engaging with insurgents' political claims. As lawyers and legal specialists, their goal was to regulate violent acts so that other states also handled such acts as crimes. Since their initiatives occurred within specialized international organizations, anticolonial activists, national liberation groups, and terrorists had no direct contact with delegates and could not represent their own ideas to the contrary.

The controversies and negotiations around the Hague, Montreal, and OAS Conventions shaped how officials in the United States, but also elsewhere, thought about terrorism in the 1970s. The OAS Convention reduced the emphasis on political context when discussing terrorism. Rather than delineating terrorists as politically motivated actors (state and nonstate), the OAS Convention defined terrorists as nonstate actors who, while potentially claiming political motivation, were identifiable primarily through their criminal activity. Though the Hague and Montreal Conventions did not include references to terrorism, their similarities to the OAS Convention strengthened the connections between the term *terrorism* and a crime-focused international law approach to specific acts of nonstate violence. Consequently, policymakers especially in the Global North began highlighting the criminal aspects of such violence without stressing any anticolonial or insurgency context. This conception of terrorism solidified as further attacks occurred throughout the 1970s.

Chapter Two

WHAT IS INTERNATIONAL TERRORISM?

The 1972 Debates on Extremist Violence and National Liberation at the United Nations

Lufthansa Flight 615 was one of many airplanes hijacked in 1972. For several years, Palestinian, but also Japanese, U.S., and other nonstate actors had seized civil aircraft with increasing frequency; this hijacking was not even the first that the West German air carrier Lufthansa suffered that year. Flight 615 meant to travel from Damascus to Frankfurt on October 29, 1972. After a scheduled layover in Beirut, two passengers took its nineteen other occupants hostage. They identified themselves as members of the Palestinian extremist group Black September Organization (BSO) and demanded the release of three BSO members incarcerated in the Federal Republic of Germany (FRG). The West German government complied. Israel and European states had released prisoners before in exchange for hijacked planes and hostages. Yet the public attention and diplomatic fallout in this case were substantially stronger than in earlier cases. Israeli prime minister Golda Meir temporarily recalled the Israeli ambassador to Bonn. Why? The three released prisoners were the surviving attackers of the deadly 1972 Munich Olympic Games massacre. Garnering worldwide attention and outrage, the Munich attack and subsequent acts of transnational extremist violence, like the Lufthansa 615 hijacking, appeared to U.S. and European politicians, pundits, and audiences as a more ominous threat than in the past.

During the late 1960s and early 1970s, Palestinian Fedayeen and other self-styled anticolonial actors from the Global South created new insurgent spaces by exporting their guerilla violence to target the citizens (and territory) of European and other Global North states. Yet U.S. officials in particular viewed such attacks predominantly as crimes and not as anticolonial activity. Chapter 1 showed how the United States formulated a multilateral response to deny political legitimacy to extremist attackers and incentivize states to handle attacks as criminal, not political, issues. Within the International Civil Aviation Organization (ICAO) and Organization of American States (OAS), U.S. officials negotiated multilateral conventions to facilitate criminal prosecution and extradition for nonstate extremists who attacked international civil aviation and diplomats in 1970 and 1971. These conventions ignored extremists' political motivations and depoliticized their actions. Yet ostensibly anticolonial attacks on Global North targets continued and increased in violence. In question was how the international community of states would respond to such attacks (increasingly collected under the umbrella term *international terrorism*) in the future.

The 1972 UN debates surrounding international terrorism revealed the limits of the United States' multilateral legal approach against nonstate extremists. Reacting to increasingly violent attacks, the Nixon administration sought another extradition convention against the newly branded danger of international terrorism in the global venue of the United Nations General Assembly (UNGA). The major turning point for the State Department was the 1972 BSO attack at the Munich Olympic Games. In response, the United States and its Latin American and European allies attempted to frame international terrorism as an urgent and predominantly criminal threat. They pursued a UN convention that required states to apply domestic criminal law against nonstate international terrorists. But states with recent revolutionary pasts such as Algeria dominated discussions and ensured that their characterization of international terrorism became UNGA policy instead. Arab policymakers, backed by African and other nonaligned leaders, countered that international terrorism should not be misused as an umbrella label for transnationally active anticolonial insurgents. They argued that this term was a neo-imperialist tool that allowed metropole states to dismiss and devalue national liberation movements. Nonaligned leaders and UNGA delegates emphasized that it was crucial to contextualize these attacks and consider political factors. Officials in the United States thus contested fundamental limits of national liberation movements' agency with Arab, African, and other nonaligned delegates. The U.S. initiative to create a global crime-focused consensus and convention against international terrorism failed, driving Western states to a future splintered approach of piecemeal, unilateral, and regional efforts against border-crossing violent extremists.

The UNGA debate was the first global attempt to define who and what fell under the label of terrorism in the post-1945 world. Since the 1940s, Western policymakers, journalists, and academics had used that label unsystematically to describe (predominantly leftist) insurgent and state violence. In 1972, however, the concept of "international terrorism" became useful for the U.S. State Department and allied officials. It allowed them to consider recent attacks on their territories and citizens as one interconnected security issue. Their aim was to brand all of these attacks as completely illegitimate criminal activities worldwide, irrespective of factors such as attackers' national origin, political orientation or aims, race, or religion. But stripping the political origins from international terrorism crimes was itself a highly political and controversial strategy. Delegates from recently independent Global South states safeguarded the political agency of ostensibly anticolonial actors. While denouncing the most lethal terrorist attacks, they supported acts of political violence in general as acceptable national liberation and self-determination activity under the Geneva Conventions and international humanitarian law—even if these acts occurred outside of a contested territorial space. As the two sides fought over how to define international terrorism in the UNGA's Sixth Committee on legal issues, each was staking out larger perimeters concerning what sort of revolutionary, violent, or insurgent activity was acceptable to the international community (or not). Due to these fundamental questions, the effort to create an international consensus on the definition of terrorism failed.

The terrorism debate also highlighted the limits of U.S. authority in the UNGA, especially in contrast to recently independent states' revolutionary agendas and increasing assertiveness on decolonization issues.[1] For the State Department bureaucrats leading the negotiations, international terrorism was a present but second-tier security issue. They worried that unilateral U.S. measures against terrorism or actions in the UN Security Council would quickly spill over to influence larger U.S. foreign policy initiatives such as the Middle East peace process.[2] Those officials considered the UNGA the only venue where they could create broad diplomatic consensus against international terrorism; they needed this consensus to commit other states to specific antiterrorism actions without alienating these countries from the Nixon administration's key foreign policy endeavors. Yet State Department officials were not able to convince the other UNGA delegates of their position on terrorism. The U.S. international law response denied any claim that nonstate extremists deserved agency in state-to-state relations or protection under the laws of war. This broad devaluation made the U.S.-led efforts against international terrorism unacceptable to many states around the world, including not only recently independent Arab and African countries but also nonaligned states and the Soviet bloc. These states collaborated and ensured that their own views on terrorism became UNGA policy instead. On second-tier foreign policy issues, U.S. officials struggled against the increasing confidence of recently decolonized states. The resistance at the UNGA pushed both the United States and its European allies to develop unilateral and regional antiterrorism measures quarantined from Global South influence.[3]

This chapter is divided into four segments. First, the State Department expanded its existing multilateral initiatives against extremist violence from the specialized international organizations OAS and ICAO into the far larger UNGA. In 1971, the State Department leveraged contacts to European and Latin American counterpart officials to begin low-key negotiations for a "protection-of-diplomats" convention in the UNGA. Second, the Munich Olympic Games attack in 1972 forced U.S. and European officials to acknowledge Palestinian extremists' violence as an immediate threat to not just their foreign policy but also their domestic security. To delineate and describe this threat, officials began classifying all border-crossing nonstate extremists as one common security problem named international terrorism. Third, U.S. diplomats sought to discredit international terrorism as a revolutionary tactic in the UNGA by passing an extradition convention that codified it as a criminal offense. They modeled their effort on their earlier ICAO and OAS Conventions against more specific types of violent attacks. Many Arab and African states successfully collaborated to prevent this criminal approach, however, and instead shaped UN policy to support national liberation insurgents. Finally, the United States responded to its UNGA loss by returning to a piecemeal regulation of individual attacks and by prioritizing unilateral measures.

A GLOBAL PROTECTION-OF-DIPLOMATS INITIATIVE

The State Department's Economic Affairs Bureau, Inter-American Affairs Bureau, and the Office of the Legal Adviser (OLA) developed a U.S. multilateral response to extremist violence in Latin America and international civil aviation from 1968 to 1971. In particular, U.S. representatives successfully negotiated the Montreal, Hague, and OAS Conventions.[4] These multilateral conventions regulated the criminal prosecution of attacks on civilian airplanes and diplomats, which often spanned several national jurisdictions by the late 1960s. Signatory states agreed to create domestic criminal laws against these specific attacks and then either extradite or prosecute the offenders (using the judicial concept *aut dedere aut judicare*, "extradite or prosecute"). These requirements closed off safe havens and political refuges for attackers. The conventions specified that states had to treat transnationally active extremists as criminals, not as revolutionary or national liberation agents. These conventions did not have immediate practical ramifications, as they rarely served as the basis for extradition requests. But they did signal a shift in international norms. Officials used the "extradite or prosecute" conventions to pressure any state that treated hijackers and those who attacked diplomats as political agents. International law and norms now assumed that states would criminally prosecute but not support or politically legitimize such transnationally operating extremists.

These steps to depoliticize hijackings and attacks on diplomats were themselves highly contentious and required the United States to concede to a number of loopholes to get both Global North and Global South states to the signing table. The loopholes permitted states to acknowledge attackers' political grievances and support their national liberation claims. The conventions did not require taking an offender to trial—they just specified that the case had to be passed on to responsible authorities who could technically institute trial proceedings. A signatory state could refuse to try offenders or hand out only very light sentences. Additionally, a mechanism called the political offense exception allowed state officials to refuse extradition requests if they decided that an offender was a politically motivated actor. This mechanism was an important Cold War tool to protect socialist state asylum seekers in the United States and Europe. However, the exception also provided loopholes for states to acknowledge and treat members of self-proclaimed national liberation movements such as the Popular

Front for the Liberation of Palestine (PFLP) as revolutionary political actors. For example, in 1969 the Syrian Arab Republic arrested and then freed the hijackers of TWA Flight 840, PFLP members Leila Khaled and Salim Issawi, instead of placing them on trial for kidnapping and destruction of property.[5]

The State Department officials knew of the conventions' loopholes and sought enforcement mechanisms that forced states to extradite attackers, or at least adhere to the "extradite or prosecute" formula. In particular, U.S. representatives futilely attempted to introduce sanctions in the ICAO against states that did not extradite or prosecute hijackers.[6] However, even U.S. allies rejected the idea and correctly argued that such sanctions undercut states' sovereign control of their domestic legal systems.

Despite these controversies, the Nixon administration continued to pursue multilateral conventions against extremist violence. The president and his advisers instructed the State Department to create another protection-of-diplomats agreement, mainly to resolve an embarrassing and potentially expensive domestic situation with strong foreign policy implications. In the spring of 1970, the Jewish Defense League, an extremist Zionist organization founded by Rabbi Meir Kahane, began small-scale attacks on the Soviet UN delegation in New York City. Over the following months and years the group increasingly escalated its violence against Soviet representatives to protest the lack of emigration options for Soviet Jews.[7] In April 1971, a Soviet trade agency in New York was bombed and authorities attributed the attack to the Jewish Defense League.[8] Meanwhile, the Soviet ambassador to the U.S., Anatoly Dobrynin, vehemently complained about the United States' lack of security for the Soviet UN delegation. Soviet officials in Moscow threatened the U.S. embassy with reduced collaboration in the future.[9] These events occurred while the Nixon administration pursued its large-scale policy of détente.

Nixon, his White House counsels, Charles Colson and John Dean, his secretary of state, William Rogers, and John Stevenson, legal adviser from the State Department, had no interest in high-level U.S. responses that would draw significant international attention to the Soviets' grievances. The administration began work on a bill to make any violent attack on diplomats a federal offense and enable federal prosecution, but this legislation would take time to pass through Congress. Nixon also had no intention of draining the federal budget of the millions of dollars necessary to hire more policemen or security forces in New York City on a regular basis.[10] Yet the administration did not want to unnecessarily antagonize Dobrynin in the middle of Nixon and Kissinger's sensitive détente negotiations. New York City's mayor, John Lindsay, refused to increase his municipal security spending, however, and insisted on federal aid.[11] Worse, further State Department inquiries at the UN revealed that many delegations shared the Soviets' worries and felt generally insecure in New York City.[12] Due to the stalemate between New York City and the federal government over spending, the Nixon administration had no immediate domestic political response that it could sell to Dobrynin.

However, a foreign policy solution was still available: the option to pursue a UN convention that increased its member states' obligation to protect diplomats on their territory. Such a multilateral agreement could signal the willingness of the U.S. government to protect diplomats in theory, without requiring the Nixon administration to pass new criminal legislation or increase its actual security spending right away. The Soviet Union had a veto power and significant authority in the UN Security Council, and an agreement there could generate publicity for the Soviets to condemn the security situation in New York City. To suit U.S. aims, the agreement would have to pass in the UNGA, where the Soviet voice was diluted among many other actors. The State Department even had a template for a protection-of-diplomats agreement, the recently adopted OAS Convention. The Nixon administration's goal was to use the U.S. effort on this multilateral UNGA agreement to placate Dobrynin and other Soviet bureaucrats.

A team of mid-level officials from the State Department's International Organizations Bureau began pursuing such a UNGA agreement with OLA assistance on legal details and specific formulations. Ronald Bettauer, the assistant legal adviser for United Nations Affairs, performed most of the formulation and fine-tuning work on the OLA side. Mark Feldman, the Assistant Legal Advisor for Inter-American Affairs, had drafted the OAS Convention, worked on the two ICAO conventions, and helped with his significant experience. Once again, mid-tier bureaucrats with professional legal training performed most of the work and brought about the compromises necessary to get the initiative passed. These officials' aim was to generate a UNGA convention that obligated states to "extradite or prosecute" attackers. They viewed their work as expanding states' existing obligations to protect diplomats.

To begin the UNGA process for a protection-of-diplomats convention, Feldman, Bettauer, and the others turned to their colleague Richard Kearney. He was an experienced diplomat and had been deputy legal adviser from 1962 to 1967. Since then, Kearney was the U.S. representative to the International Law Commission (ILC), a body of twenty-five legal experts from around the world elected by the UN General Assembly to codify and develop international law. The ILC reported to and took its orders from the General Assembly's Sixth Committee, which handled legal matters and in which all UN members were represented. Any UNGA "extradite or prosecute" convention was likely to be drafted in the ILC. The involved U.S. officials advocated for their protection-of-diplomats convention here in order to decrease potential resistance from potentially hostile states.

Officials in the United States focused on the ILC because the UNGA posed significant political risks. Its large membership of recently independent states affirmed national liberation movements' right to commit certain acts of political violence. This group of states represented wide swaths of the Global South, including most of the African continent as well as South and Southeast Asia. Many of these states had national liberation movements and activism in their immediate past. The most famous examples were Algeria and Cuba, where revolutionary actors had violently created a new state and now filled its bureaucracies. On average, the delegates of recently independent states pursued foreign relations and UN policies sympathetic to the claims of national liberation movements.[13] This support remained and even increased if self-declared national liberation actors committed violence in the Global North—the former colonial metropoles. Recently independent states routinely accused former colonizers and the Cold War superpower the United States of first fostering repressive policies abroad and then decrying the violent fallout from these policies.[14] In addition, the protection-of-diplomats effort could disrupt other American initiatives in the UN, especially those concerning détente or the Middle East peace process. Such initiatives had the day-to-day interest of high-level U.S. policymakers, which the Bureau of International Organization Affairs, Bettauer, and Feldman did not. To succeed, they would have to avoid ruffling feathers—both at the UNGA and in the higher echelons of the State Department.

To circumvent recently independent states' critiques that the State Department was simply pursuing U.S. unilateral interests via new paths,

Kearney, Bettauer, Feldman, and their colleagues ensured that their protection-of-diplomats initiative went through appropriate legal channels with
as much multilateral support as possible. Instead of introducing the issue
to the entire UNGA assembly or even the Sixth Committee, they began by
attempting to win over the twenty-five legal experts in the ILC. In April
1971, Kearney proposed to the ILC that it add the issue of diplomats' protection to its agenda. The other ILC representatives did not agree, but their
annual report asked the UNGA plenary if the ILC should consider the issue
in 1972.[15] This setup allowed Kearney to lobby for an ILC protection-of-diplomats effort without emphasizing the U.S. origins of the initiative. Kearney
thus avoided recriminations that he was seeking unilateral U.S. interests.

In the fall of 1971, Kearney and the U.S. representatives at the UN
worked hard behind the scenes to convince other states to approve the ILC
initiative, and their lobbying won over most Latin American and European states. Conservative Latin American officials had initiated the OAS
Convention in order to be able to criminally prosecute political acts. They
were eager to introduce a global agreement at the UNGA.[16] The Uruguayan
delegation even circulated a convention draft based on the OAS Convention.[17] Meanwhile, the Italians helped advocate among other European
states. Marco Fortini, director for Latin American Political Affairs at the
Italian Ministry of Foreign Affairs and International Cooperation, had
collaborated with Feldman in 1970 to lobby for a regional protection-of-
diplomats convention in Europe.[18] Though their efforts failed, Fortini built
a network of connections to other European officials generally interested in
the topic.[19] This network now paid off. The Italians engaged the Baltic and
Central European states to favor the ILC initiative.[20] Meanwhile, extensive
U.S. lobbying convinced London that the issue was "urgent," gaining British
support that the ICAO and OAS Conventions had lacked.[21] Only France
remained a holdout, maintaining the position that new international conventions were a bureaucratic burden and unnecessary for the safe operation of diplomatic relations.[22]

With broad European and Latin American backing, Kearney and the
American representatives stressed to many Global South and recently inde-
pendent states that the ILC protection-of-diplomats initiative was a widely
popular endeavor to strengthen the mechanisms of diplomatic relations.
In early November 1971, the U.S. and Italian UN delegations approached
Middle Eastern, South Asian, African, and other Global South delegates

in informal corridor negotiations. Many represented young, recently independent states. Avoiding any mention of national liberation groups or political violence, the U.S. delegation emphasized that an ILC-drafted convention could strengthen states' sovereignty by improving their ability to conduct diplomatic relations with other states and international organizations.[23] This effort paid off. On November 8, 1971, the UNGA voted to have the ILC work on a protection-of-diplomats convention in 1972. The goal was to regulate all violent acts against diplomats as crimes within international law, signaling that the international community would not consider such acts legitimate for revolutionary actors or protostate organizations to pursue.

Collective agreement on such a convention was far from assured. Despite all U.S. efforts to downplay local conditions, the security situation on the ground in New York City also influenced UNGA delegates. The Jewish Defense League continued its attacks in New York City. Alongside the Soviets, other UN representations felt insufficiently protected.[24] Three days after the ILC decision, Cuban and other UNGA delegates scheduled debates in its Sixth Committee to complain about the high levels of attacks in New York City.

From the U.S. perspective, however, the 1971 preliminary negotiations at the ILC fulfilled expectations. In the past years, the State Department had negotiated multilateral conventions against violent Global South extremists who attacked U.S. and Global North citizens. These conventions had been passed in smaller technical (ICAO) and regional (OAS) international organizations. Now, the American initiative to extradite and criminalize violent cross-border extremists appeared to be viable on a global scale in the UNGA as well—despite the contentious nature of politics there.

MUNICH 1972 AND THE CONCEPT OF INTERNATIONAL TERRORISM

State Department and other Global North officials reassessed the scope of the problem that they faced more broadly in 1972. Up to that time the United States had sought multilateral legal conventions against specific acts of violence, namely hijackings, attacks on civil aviation facilities, and attacks on diplomats. Further ostensible anticolonial attacks targeted citizens and locales in the industrialized Global North, however, particularly on the European continent. And incidents such as a mass shooting at Tel Aviv's airport pointed to increased transnational collaboration between violent extremists. Overall, more people were getting hurt. After a Palestinian attack at that year's Olympic Games in Munich, Global North officials, journalists, and publics started conflating violent acts against themselves by Global South actors into a single umbrella category, which they called *international terrorism*. This term collated an array of violent acts—hijacking, attacks on diplomats, hostage-taking, bombings, and attacks on airports—into one interconnected security threat. In turn, U.S. policymakers started seeking multilateral ways to deter international terrorism attackers and, once more, get other states on board with handling them as criminals.

From 1970 onward, Palestinian Fedayeen faced new constrictions on their capacity to operate. The Palestine Liberation Organization (PLO) lost its power base in Jordan after 1970's "Black September," when the Jordanian army drove the PLO out of the country with significant civilian casualties.[25] Afterward, dissatisfied Fedayeen from Yasser Arafat's Fatah, the PFLP, and other groups formed the BSO. They dedicated themselves to attacking Israeli targets as well as any state that supported the existence of Israel. Like the PFLP, BSO members committed ostensible insurgent acts in transnational spaces. Yet increasingly sophisticated Israeli countertactics also made targeting civil aviation more difficult. Israeli sky marshals began protecting El Al flights. On May 8, 1972, four BSO members hijacked Belgium's Sabena Flight 571. Israeli Special Forces freed the plane at Tel Aviv's Lod Airport, however, in the first successful rescue of its kind. The Sabena operation signaled to BSO leaders that hijackings would be increasingly difficult in the future.

Other national liberation groups were also struggling. South Vietnamese insurgents, under North Vietnamese direction, had suffered devastating losses in the 1968 Tet Offensive, which took years to rebuild. By 1972, North Vietnamese leaders faced strong Chinese and Soviet pressure to negotiate a peace agreement with the Nixon administration. This pressure was a key result of Nixon's détente policies. South Vietnamese attacks in the Easter Offensive that year did not alleviate the pressure from the United States or from the communist sponsors.[26] Meanwhile, white supremacy governments in South Africa and Rhodesia brutally suppressed nonwhite populations.[27] The apartheid South African government arrested and imprisoned members of national liberation groups such as the uMkhonto we Sizwe, the armed branch of the African National Congress, under legislation such as the 1967 Terrorism Act. This law permitted the apartheid regime to criminally prosecute all political dissidents. It defined terrorism incredibly widely as any act that endangered law and order. This definition of terrorism fit into similar Latin American conceptions—widely defining terrorism in order to be able to prosecute as many political dissenters as possible.

In Latin America, similar state repression had undermined and destroyed many violent leftist groups. In Uruguay, for example, harsh civil liberties infractions undercut the Movimiento de Liberación Nacional-Tupamaros and similar violent groups by the early 1970s.[28] Conservative Latin American regimes repressed all forms of political dissent, though they targeted leftist anti-imperialist and anticapitalist actors with alleged Cuban sponsorship. Their repressive policies were the foundations for the Latin American "dirty wars," disappearances, and the Operation Condor intelligence program of the 1970s.

Yet national liberation and anti-imperialist groups still commanded significant transnational cultural and ideological influence, especially in the leftist networks of the late 1960s. Such groups' writing on national liberation and insurgent violence circled freely. This literature, and at times personal contact, generated support principally from students and leftist activists. Especially influential was Carlos Marighella's 1969 *Minimanual of the Urban Guerilla*, which advocated the use of political violence to push the state to delegitimize itself with repressive countermeasures. Marighella was a Brazilian whose group, Ação Libertadora Nacional, kidnapped U.S. ambassador Charles Elbrick in 1969. Widely disseminated, the manual influenced others to adopt a campaign of politically motivated violence in the aftermath of the 1968 global protest movements.

By the early 1970s, the national liberation movements and anti-imperialist activists of the Global South inspired other violent groups around the world. In 1968, student, worker, and activist protests had rocked societies around the world and particularly in the Global North. However, such protest movements decelerated in the next years as states not only met protesters' demands for civil rights but also improved their policing responses. French police developed antiriot practices and legislation.[29] In the United States, Nixon developed "law and order" strategies. The FRG passed so-called "federal emergency laws" that gave the government the right to act in crisis situations.[30]

As the protest movements lost traction, their most extreme leftist members increasingly radicalized and adopted violent guerilla-type tactics. Leftist extremists cited Marighella and the Palestinian and Vietnamese national liberation movements as inspiration. Such self-declared "armed resistance" or socio-revolutionary groups included Italy's Red Brigades, the United States' Weather Underground, Japan's Red Army, and the FRG's Red Army Faction (RAF). Their goal was to destabilize their established states and provoke repressive state reactions in order to elicit revolutionary change in domestic populations. Alongside socio-revolutionary groups, separatist groups such as the Provisional Irish Republican Army (IRA) in Northern Ireland, the Front de libération du Québec in Canada, and the Euskadi Ta Askatasuna in Spain sought independent states for specific regions and populations. Right-wing exiles from Yugoslavia and Cuba also attacked their states' embassies and representatives. The number of leftist or nationalist groups that committed terroristic violence within the Global North increased. So did public perceptions of the threat of nonstate political violence.

And overall, many states saw such actors as a domestic security threat and reacted. The U.S. Federal Bureau of Investigation (FBI) intensively pursued the Weather Underground.[31] In the FRG, the federal investigative service, the Bundeskriminalamt, tripled its size and introduced computer-based data mining to target the Red Army Faction.[32] In other cases, military force came into play. The United Kingdom deployed its military in Northern Ireland, suspended the Northern Irish parliament, and interred suspected IRA extremists without trial. When the Front de libération du Québec kidnapped the deputy premier, Pierre Laporte, and British diplomat James Cross, Canadian prime minister Pierre Trudeau declared martial law until the kidnappers released Cross and found sanctuary in Cuba. Laporte had been murdered. Socio-revolutionary and separatist groups in the Global North thus had the capacity to provoke strong state reactions.

Like their national liberation counterparts, leftist socio-revolutionary and separatist groups oftentimes claimed to be engaging in asymmetrical guerilla warfare against an illegitimate state. These groups often argued that they were legitimate political actors with protostate rights. For example, members the IRA and RAF demanded rights accorded to violent statist actors under the Geneva Conventions and international humanitarian law. In particular, they claimed prisoner-of-war status for themselves upon arrest—or at the very least the status of political prisoners, which would elevate them from criminals to perpetrators of legal violence. For example, in September 1971 the IRA announced, "Republicans have died on hunger strike in the past to obtain political treatment in 26 County prisons and we the leadership of the Republican Movement have no intention of permitting the 26 County prison authorities to impose criminal status on our comrades in prison."[33] The demand for such labels was part of extremists' strategy to validate their political claims and activity as legitimate state-seeking actions.[34]

In contrast, affected officials generally described the actions of socio-revolutionary groups with a range of terms that disassociated extremists from political status, including crimes, thuggery, sabotage, and anarchism. An exception was the United Kingdom, where officials described Northern Irish leftist extremists as terrorists. Northern Ireland was a former British colony, and officials' use of the term *terrorism* fit in with earlier uses of the term to describe leftist insurgents in other decolonizing settings, such as in Malaysia and Kenya.

Many of the left-oriented socio-revolutionary and separatist groups of the early 1970s operated principally within their national borders, but in their transnational contacts they went beyond such boundaries. They frequently read the same literature, shared similar ideological concepts, and they even met and supported one another. The Vietnamese National Liberation Front, Latin American groups, and the PLO fostered relations with leftist students and activists in the late 1960s. As a few of these leftists radicalized, their Palestinian connections, in particular, intensified. For example, in the summer of 1970, the core members of the new West German RAF traveled to a Palestinian refugee camp in Jordan to train with Fatah.[35] Subsequently, they committed a string of bombings at U.S. military installations in the FRG in May 1972. They justified their actions as insurgent national liberation warfare on behalf of the Vietnamese National Liberation Front and the PLO. A RAF declaration read that "U.S. imperialists . . . must know that their crimes against the Vietnamese people have created new bitter enemies, that there will be no place left for them in the world in which they can be safe from the attacks of revolutionary guerilla units."[36]

As Palestinian extremists' violent capacities seemed to be deteriorating, they adapted and took steps that relied on their ability to cross borders and form connections with like-minded actors. A shocking example of transnational cooperation, as well as national policies' inability to resolve such situations, occurred in the state with the most advanced domestic antiterrorism programs—Israel. On May 30, 1972, three Japanese citizens, Kōzō Okamoto, Tsuyoshi Okudaira, and Yasuyuki Yasuda, smuggled assault rifles into Tel Aviv's Lod Airport. They opened fire and killed twenty-six people, including a candidate in the upcoming Israeli presidential elections and seventeen U.S. Christian pilgrims from Puerto Rico. The three were members of the Japanese socio-revolutionary Red Army, and they had trained with the PFLP in a Palestinian refugee camp in Lebanon for the attack. Wadie Haddad had planned it. A founding member of the PFLP, after "Black September" Haddad thought that the PFLP leader, George Habash, was emphasizing propaganda over action. Haddad founded the PFLP-External Operations splinter group to carry out more violence outside of the PLO or PFLP's control. The three Japanese Red Army members combined PFLP national liberation with their own armed resistance ideology, seeing the two groups' purpose as intrinsically interlinked.[37] Israeli

FIGURE 2.1. Scene at the terminal at Lod Airport, Tel Aviv, May 31, 1972.
Three Japanese extremists opened fire with automatic rifles and hand grenades, killing twenty-six people and wounding many others. Keystone Press / Alamy Stock Photo.

security guards at the airport were unprepared for such actors; they were on the lookout for Palestinians. Only Okamoto survived. He received a lifetime prison sentence in Israel and was released in 1985.

The Lod Airport massacre shocked the international community due to its ostensibly secure and cosmopolitan location, large number of civilian deaths, and unexpected perpetrators. The attackers were Japanese, yet they had acted on behalf of Haddad and the PFLP-EO. State officials, activists, journalists, and citizens from around the world acknowledged that Palestinian national liberation extremists held increasing transnational contacts. Diplomats and the public alike questioned whether non-Palestinian attackers should be viewed as legitimate members of the Palestinian national liberation struggle. Most said no.[38] Public opinion also decried that the attack targeted a much-traveled transportation hub and random civilians who were mostly unaffiliated with the Israeli state. The American UN ambassador George H. W. Bush noted that even the UN delegation from the People's Republic of China, usually ardent supporters of national liberation groups, denounced "that [the] Lod attack was 'sheer terrorism which was not real battle and accomplished nothing.' "[39] Haddad's strategy of internationalizing his insurgency met with little sympathy from the international community in general.

Yet the Lod Airport attackers succeeded in provoking a major international response. The day after the attack, Israel and Lebanon circulated separate letters in the UN. Both states sought to strengthen their position in the Middle East peace process by accusing the other of illegally supporting or inciting (respectively) insurgent violence in their region.[40] Meanwhile, the State Department considered proposing a Security Council resolution condemning such violent actors. American officials rejected the idea, though, when the deputy chief of mission in Moscow, Boris Klosson, warned that the Soviet Union would make any Security Council resolution about the broader Arab-Israeli conflict.[41] The Lod Airport attackers thus pushed states engaged in the Middle East to reaffirm and defend their own political stakes.

In September 1972, global audiences further realized that Palestinian transnational violence was a major security issue due to a shocking attack at the Munich Olympic Games. The 1972 attack was a watershed event in the history of terrorism. It introduced the widespread use of the term *international terrorism*. Metropole officials and journalists chose this label to describe nonstate actors, mainly Palestinian in origin, who targeted their territory and citizens with ostensibly anticolonial violent acts. The attack also prompted contemporaries to conceptualize international terrorism as an immediate and border-crossing security problem. This focus has lasted to today.

The Munich attackers were BSO members devoted to continuing the Palestinian national liberation effort and spreading armed violence outside of the territorial boundaries of the Arab-Israeli conflict. The Sabena hijacking and Israel's successful use of Special Forces units to take the plane in May 1972 likely convinced BSO members to plan future attacks outside of Israeli borders and jurisdiction.[42] In the early morning of September 5, 1972, eight BSO members stealthily entered the athletes' housing at the ongoing summer Olympic Games in Munich. They accessed the Israeli team's apartments, killed two people, and took nine athletes and trainers hostage. The BSO attackers demanded the release of 234 prisoners from Israel and RAF leaders Andreas Baader and Ulrike Meinhof from the FRG. Israeli prime minister Golda Meir refused to negotiate. Meanwhile, the West German constitution did not permit its army to operate within the FRG. When the attackers attempted to leave the country with their hostages, the local Bavarian police conducted a poorly planned, last-minute rescue at the Fürstenfeldbruck airfield. The attackers turned automatic guns on their hostages and threw grenades into one of the helicopters containing the hostages. All the hostages died.[43] So did one police officer and five attackers. Bavarian authorities arrested the three surviving attackers. Global media outlets heavily covered the attack and had close access to the attackers and their hostages throughout the crisis.

People around the world were shocked at the location of the attack, the innocence of the hostages, and their violent deaths. The locale played a significant role. The Olympic Games were symbolic of peaceful state-based international competition, and athletes in particular represented this ideal. Most journalists agreed that athletes were not appropriate targets for an insurgency.[44] Worldwide support poured into Israel, dedicated both to the families of the hostages as well as to the Israeli state. Compounding this global shock was the sheer audacity of the attackers and their capability to procure and use deadly weapons in a foreign country. In addition, the West German and local Bavarian authorities had not been able to prevent or resolve the attack. The situation showcased brutally that domestic security

FIGURE 2.2. An attacker on the balcony of the Israeli team's quarters at the Munich Olympic Games, September 5, 1972.
All eleven Israeli hostages and five of the eight attackers died in the course of the hostage crisis and botched rescue. Bundesarchiv (German Federal Archives), Photo B 145 Bild-00006457 / Ludwig Wegmann.

measures were not enough to thwart transnational extremist attacks.[45] But while all contemporaries vocalized their horror at the brutality of the attack, regional discrepancies concerning its political implications quickly became apparent.

In the Arab Middle East, the Palestinian national liberation movement was generally popular, and public figures portrayed the attack as a horrible but understandable part of this self-determination struggle. They condemned the violence at Munich. But journalists and state officials strongly urged that the attack be viewed in its full political context. A Central Intelligence Agency (CIA) report summarized that "Arab League foreign ministers, meeting in Cairo this week, voiced a theme dominant in almost all Arab reaction. The ministers insisted on blaming the deaths of the Israelis at the Olympic Games on Israel's 'criminal' occupation of the Palestinian homeland."[46] Even leaders wary of Palestinian self-determination, such as the Saudis, felt unable to publicly oppose this popular sentiment. The only outlier was Jordan's King Hussein, a U.S. ally whose reign was almost overthrown by the PLO in 1970 and whose army had caused "Black September."

Meanwhile, in Algeria and neighboring Libya, popular support for Palestinian extremists' global campaign was strong, as was "gratification that the Palestinians have the capability to strike boldly and throw fear to the enemy."[47] In the spirit of Pan-Arabism, Arab media outlets argued, it was the duty of Arab states and publics to support these efforts even if attacks occurred outside of Israel's territorial boundaries.[48] Thus, any conversation about the Munich attack should be framed as a starting point, they claimed, for a longer debate on the Palestinian national liberation movement.[49]

In Western Europe and North America, however, the mainstream media rejected such an interpretation. Journalists and politicians emphasized that civilian targets far beyond the Middle East were not directly related to the Arab-Israeli conflict or Palestinian national liberation issues. The *New York Times* fumed that "by choosing the Olympic Games as the occasion for their bloody foray, the Arab terrorists made it plain that their real target was civilized conduct among nations, not merely Israel or the Israeli athletes captured and killed yesterday."[50] And to articulate this new and immediate threat, the Western mainstream media adopted the term *international terrorism*. This umbrella term covered all extremist violent attacks by Palestinians and nonstate associates targeting either Global North citizens, locations, or both. It included hijackings, attacks on diplomats, hostage-takings, bombings, and other attacks. Location-wise, the term particularly described attacks within Europe and on civilian airplanes.[51] Global North citizens increasingly realized that they were now vulnerable at home and also during air travel, an increasingly popular and affordable mode of transportation. For most international terrorism emerged as a new existential threat: a menace to every individual's body, home, and state. The future terrorism expert Walter Laqueur wrote bleakly, "The outlook, to put it mildly, is not promising: In all likelihood, the murder of innocent people will continue for years to come."[52]

In reaction to the Munich attack, leaders from Israel and the Global North instituted new security policies specifically tailored against the border-crossing threat of international terrorists. Israeli leaders continued their offensive-minded military approach. Israeli prime minister Golda Meir reaffirmed her dedication to counterinsurgency practices against Palestinian Fedayeen and preemptive military operations against Israel's Arab neighbors. Israel conducted air strikes on Fedayeen bases in Syria and Lebanon on September 8 and entered southern Lebanon in a brief military incursion on September 16. The attacks were meant to encourage Lebanon and Syria to move against Palestinian Fedayeen but did not have the desired effect; the UN Security Council instead voted to condemn the air strikes.[53] The Israeli foreign intelligence service Mossad began a program to assassinate the planners of the Munich attack. The program caused a public relations debacle when Israeli agents killed an innocent man in Norway.

In contrast, other states took defensive-minded measures that improved their law enforcement capacities and ability to police their territory and population. The shell-shocked FRG leadership instituted new visa requirements and immigration-screening policies for all Arab nationals and forbid several Palestinian and Arab student organizations. These steps made it considerably more difficult for Palestinians and any citizen of an Arab state to enter the FRG or organize politically there.[54] Chancellor Willy Brandt's cabinet also instituted domestic security reforms and reached out to neighboring states to discuss new joint ventures in that field. In one offensive-minded step, West German leaders announced that they would train a Special Forces–inspired unit for use in future crises; this unit would be located in the border police so that it could be deployed within the FRG.[55]

The Nixon administration likewise instituted new defensive-minded initiatives against international terrorism. Nixon had previously been restrained from engaging with issues of hijacking or similar violent acts by his advisers, who feared the potential political fallout if he proved unable to prevent a major attack against the United States. Now, Nixon became more active. On the one hand, he wanted to placate Israel and the Jewish voter population within the United States, who demanded U.S. action in the aftermath of the Munich attack. On the other hand, Nixon was genuinely fearful that the United States would become the next site of a major international terrorism attack.[56]

As before, most U.S. antiterrorism initiatives were carried out at middling bureaucratic ranks so that the president's advisers could still disassociate him and themselves in case of dramatic failures.[57] The CIA began compiling a weekly summary on the threat of international terrorism. On September 18, the Nixon administration began "Operation Boulder," a secret surveillance program to screen the citizens of Arab states who wanted to enter the United States. On September 25, Nixon founded the Cabinet Committee to Combat Terrorism (CCCT), which was mainly symbolic. The CCCT only met once, but it formed an interagency working group to develop new antiterrorist measures, monitor current events, and coordinate policy.[58] Chaired by the former foreign service officer Armin Meyer, this working group became a central hub for U.S. antiterrorism initiatives. It permitted representatives of the State Department, the Department of Transportation, and the FBI to coordinate with the Department of Defense, the CIA, and other intelligence agencies. Thus, the CCCT working group united experts with a wide range of experience and jurisdiction concerning domestic and national security, counterinsurgency, and law enforcement.

In addition to domestic measures, the Nixon administration pursued multilateral options. The State Department reached out to the International Criminal Police Organization (Interpol) and asked it to increase its efforts against international terrorism. In the North Atlantic Treaty Organization (NATO), U.S. officials asked for a round of meetings to discuss intelligence collaboration on this issue. The State Department renewed its efforts within ICAO to institute sanctions against states that harbored hijackers. Finally, Nixon turned his eyes to the UN, where dramatic and global action was possible.

Nixon ordered William Rogers to pursue a multilateral convention to condemn international terrorism as a criminal offense at the UNGA, building on the State Department's previous initiatives against hijackings and attacks on diplomats. Rogers had reservations about the assignment. Negotiations in the ICAO and OAS had been time-consuming and yielded at most ambiguous results in terms of overall U.S. interests. However, resentful that the State Department had cut out of the decision-making process for major policies on the Soviet Union, China, and more recently, the Middle East, Rogers saw an opportunity to exercise leadership over a new foreign policy initiative.[59]

Rogers turned to George H. W. Bush, along with Samuel De Palma, assistant secretary of state for International Organization Affairs, and the OLA, asking them to extend their earlier efforts and focus on international terrorism. Alongside the ILC's protection-of-diplomats initiative, they were to pursue a convention against the far broader, undefined, and difficult to delineate category of international terrorism. As before, the United States would pursue a convention with the "extradite or prosecute" principle. This legal principle required states to apply domestic criminal law when dealing with nonstate offenders—instead of the Geneva Conventions and related laws of war. It emphasized the criminal aspects of an attack over any political context or legitimation.

The State Department faced substantial difficulties at the UNGA, since Global North and South states already sharply disagreed on how to deal with violent nonstate actors and their political grievances. Many Arab, African, and nonaligned states at the UN had an established track record of supporting national liberation movements and political violence in search of self-determination.[60] But Rogers hoped that "while we recognize some Arab governments will continue to feel they cannot condemn terrorists publicly, we would hope they could at least disassociate themselves from the terrorists by denying latter means and opportunities of operating from territory of Arab states in question."[61] And Rogers, De Palma, and Bush had no better venue than the UNGA. The smaller Security Council was not an option for the United States, as the Soviet Union and the People's Republic of China were likely to favor the Arab bloc, vote against U.S. interests, and make the necessary majority for an antiterrorism convention impossible to achieve there from the outset.[62]

For this U.S. initiative, Rogers found a key ally in UN general secretary Kurt Waldheim. Waldheim had expressed concern about the threat of nonstate violence to civilians around the world after the Lod Airport massacre. Two days after the Munich attack, he asked the UNGA to place the issue of international terrorism on its agenda. Waldheim shared the U.S. view that international terrorism should be handled as a new stand-alone issue separate from decolonization, national liberation, or Arab-Israeli topics. This move, and the U.S. initiative, had no guarantee of success.

INTERNATIONAL TERRORISM AT THE UNITED NATIONS GENERAL ASSEMBLY

On September 11, 1972, Rogers initiated a worldwide State Department campaign to create an UN "extradite or prosecute" convention that would codify international terrorism as a crime. By doing so he put before the UNGA an issue that was, at its heart, deeply embedded in decolonization politics. Though the concept of international terrorism had spread in the five days following the Munich attack, no consensus existed about which violent acts or actors the term should cover.[63]

And immediately, even the basic question of whether to discuss international terrorism at all became highly contentious. Waldheim attempted from the outset to create a favorable negotiating framework for the United States. He entered a series of grueling negotiations with UN members about whether the UNGA should broach this subject—and how it should be handled. In general, Arab and African delegations initially opposed any debate that addressed international terrorism as a separate issue from the Arab-Israeli conflict.[64] Bush feared that they could undermine Nixon and Kissinger's Middle East peace process initiative.[65] After two weeks, the Egyptian, Chinese, and many African and nonaligned states' delegations reluctantly agreed to discuss the issue in the UNGA's Sixth Committee on legal matters, where they could bury it under legal technicalities.[66] Yet they dragged their feet. Delegates from Saudi Arabia, Syria, Libya, Sudan, Mauritania, and Guinea delayed the General Assembly vote to establish a separate international terrorism item in the Sixth Committee until

FIGURE 2.3. The UN General Committee recommends inclusion of terrorism item in the Assembly's agenda, September 22, 1972.
UN representatives George H. W. Bush (United States), Sir Colin Crowe (UK) and Louis de Guiringaud (France) confer as the UN General Assembly votes on whether to discuss the hotly contested subject of international terrorism. UN photo by Yukata Nagata.

September 23, 1972.[67] Algerian and other Arab delegates postponed further by placing international terrorism among the last items on the Sixth Committee's agenda, creating the risk that the committee might not even get to the issue at all that calendar year.[68] International terrorism was such a politicized issue that even basic procedural questions became points of contest. These early controversies in the days after Munich foreshadowed substantial conflict during the actual content-based discussions.

Despite the inauspicious start, the State Department worked hard to set and control the terms of the international terrorism discussions. On September 25, 1972, Rogers's speech during the General Assembly's opening session emphasized the UN's duty "to deter and punish international crimes" such as hijackings, attacks on diplomats, hostage-taking, letter bombs, and bombs placed aboard aircrafts. Rogers underscored the urgent need to act against this ostensibly novel global security threat and referred to the Munich and Lod attacks as prime examples of the new danger to civilians if the UN did not take action.[69] The next day, the State Department circulated a working paper on international terrorism, drafted by the OLA, to form the foundation of negotiations. It was based on the existing ICAO and OAS Conventions. The paper suggested similar conditions, namely that states pass domestic criminal laws and always apply them to "extradite or prosecute" international terrorists. The attacks had to cross national borders either physically or jurisdictionally, and the draft did not apply to military ventures enacted under the laws of war.[70]

However, the U.S. working paper was ambiguous enough to apply to basically all serious violent acts outside of formally declared wars. Previous conventions had included lists of specific crimes that they covered. The U.S. working paper, however, did not list every act that could fall under the broad category of international terrorism. It contained only a vague description of what constituted terrorism, namely "any person who unlawfully kills, causes serious bodily harm or kidnaps another person," as well as attempts or complicity thereof.[71] As U.S. officials moved to regulate international terrorism, the ambiguity in the working paper was also present in authoritarian states' repressive antiterrorism legislation. For example, South Africa's 1967 Terrorism Act defined terrorism as the commitment or conspiracy to commit any act "with intent to endanger the maintenance of law and order in the Republic or any portion thereof, in the Republic or elsewhere."[72] Such antiterrorism legislation could then be used by persecuting authorities to target a wide range of people. The working paper's similar vagueness caused massive problems for the State Department during subsequent negotiations.

In early October, the Sixth Committee discussed the ILC's protection-of-diplomats draft; these negotiations served as a trial run for the content and themes of the international terrorism debate. Based on Kearney's 1971 efforts, the ILC had completed its draft in time for the Sixth Committee's fall 1972 session. Diplomats were already protected persons under international law, but this convention draft reinforced their status. Similar to the ICAO and OAS Conventions as well as the U.S. terrorism working paper, the draft required states to adopt and apply criminal law against people who attacked diplomats, regardless of political context, thus "eliminating 'safe havens' for persons committing such crimes."[73]

Rogers, Bush, and other State officials considered the international terrorism and protection-of-diplomats initiatives intrinsically interconnected.[74] Both ostensibly regulated anticolonial extremists who attacked Global North citizens. Nevertheless, U.S. officials hoped to avert any linkages between the two agenda items by other delegates, since such connections could allow Algeria and similar recently independent states to more easily connect the U.S.-sought conventions to the Arab-Israeli conflict and other decolonization issues. In a worst-case scenario with such linkages, the protection-of-diplomats and terrorism debates could prompt results unfavorable to U.S. interests, such as a resolution like the recent Security Council vote after Munich condemning Israel for military aggression.

Ironically, the Israeli delegation and recently independent countries linked the ILC protection-of-diplomats convention to the Arab-Israeli conflict and refused to consider attacks on diplomats outside of their political context. The Sixth Committee discussed the protection-of-diplomats convention draft from October 7 to October 18, 1972. Most Arab delegations on the committee were uniformly hostile to the idea that attackers of diplomats were always ordinary criminals. So were African and Asian states that had gained their independence since World War II. The Nigerian, Tanzanian, Zambian, Pakistani, and Chinese delegates criticized the ILC draft for disregarding the political motivations of attackers and failing to stipulate protection mechanisms for national liberation movements.[75] They expressed their opposition to discussing such a convention separately from the Arab-Israeli conflict and the terrorism agenda item. The Israeli

ambassador to the UN, Yosef Tekoah, in turn demanded that the UN condone Israeli military and counterinsurgency tactics as a response to attacks
on diplomats. This linkage to insurgency and warfare conceptions was
exactly what the United States had wanted to avoid with its crime-focused
legalistic approach. Bush reached out to Tekoah and promised to collaborate fully on a bilateral level in return for a less public Israeli position in the
Sixth Committee.[76]

Realizing that other Sixth Committee delegates were mainly debating
Palestinian and other national liberation actors' right to commit violence,
Bush and De Palma tried to avoid further challenges to the protection-of-
diplomats convention draft by rushing its adoption as is. They called for an
urgent diplomatic conference of legal specialists to sign the convention. The
U.S. representative on the Sixth Committee was the veteran foreign service
officer and deputy UN representative W. Tapley Bennett. Bennett had been
the U.S. ambassador to the Dominican Republic during its civil war in 1965
and had facilitated a U.S. military intervention by exaggerating the threat
from ostensible communist extremists. Bennett had little personal regard for
nonstate revolutionary actors. He garnered support for a speedy diplomatic
conference from many U.S. allies recruited early by Kearney and Feldman in
1971, including the United Kingdom, Canada, Denmark, Austria, New Zealand, and Australia.[77] However, delegates from Kenya, Madagascar, Maure-
tania, and Pakistan countered by requesting that the draft be discussed by
the full UNGA plenary in its next meeting during the spring of 1973. This
delay would provide them with more opportunities to insert broad political
considerations such as the Arab-Israeli conflict and the agency of national
liberation actors into the protection-of-diplomats discussions.[78]

The recently independent delegates succeeded in delaying the passage
of the protection-of-diplomats convention and transferred it to the UNGA
Assembly. Several Latin American delegations backed them, such as Mexico and Chile under the democratic socialist president Salvador Allende.
In contrast to their more conservative neighbors, these Latin American
states wanted to build ties to the nonaligned movement and strengthen
political asylum for political dissidents. Bennett successfully prevented any
results that formally linked the protection-of-diplomats draft to international terrorism. But he could not deter the combined Arab, African, and
Latin American pressure from transferring the draft to the UNGA Assembly, thereby delaying its passage for a year and opening it to new political

discussions.[79] This delay was a setback for the State Department and boded ill for the upcoming terrorism negotiations.[80] Several days later, on October 24, the U.S. Congress passed legislation making attacks on diplomats a federal offense. The Nixon administration had begun work on this legislation in April 1971, also in response to the Jewish Defense League attacks in New York City.

In late October 1972 two incidents highlighted the different reactions of Global North and Global South officials to Palestinian extremists. On October 24 Dutch authorities arrested Ribhi Khalum, who held an Algerian diplomatic passport, with a suitcase full of explosive materials. They released Khalum the next day, before Israeli authorities identified him as a Palestinian Fatah member.[81] American diplomats urged the Algerians to stop issuing diplomatic passports to Palestinians, which enabled them to travel and transport dangerous weaponry. The Algerian leadership was not happy with the arrest. Yet vis-à-vis the United States, the Algerian ambassador to Lebanon, Muhammad Yazid, stated that the government of Algeria was only concerned with the fact that Khalum had been arrested, not with the fact that he intended to use the passport for violent anticolonial activities.[82] On October 29, BSO members hijacked Lufthansa Flight 615 and demanded that the West German government release the three surviving Munich attackers. Brandt complied, but Meir was furious and recalled the Israeli ambassador to the FRG. The Israel Defense Forces (IDF) bombed several Palestinian targets in Syria. But the Munich attackers were given a hero's welcome when they finally arrived in Libya and then disappeared unmolested.[83]

In the first week of November, the State Department attempted to improve its shaky negotiating position by convincing African delegations to support the U.S. terrorism working paper. Many African delegates voiced strong concerns that the United States was planning to create a new imperialist tool against insurgent freedom fighters in South Africa, Rhodesia, and elsewhere on the continent. These delegates were particularly unsettled by the vague definition of terrorism in the U.S. working paper. They worried that such a lack of clarity would further enable states such as South Africa to criminally prosecute every citizen with even the vaguest link to political protest. Their recent independence struggles, and the South African example, provided powerful case studies of such criminal prosecution of political dissent. Instead, African delegates strongly supported the Arab position that nonstate violence needed to be interpreted in the context of national liberation struggles. State Department officials offered to amend the U.S. working paper to address these concerns. On November 8, 1972, David Newsom, the assistant secretary of state for African Affairs, traveled to New York and individually met with delegates from Mauritius, Togo, Dahomey (now Benin), Mali, Sierra Leone, and Chad to pitch the latest changes to the U.S. working paper.

However, Newsom struggled to make his case because the amended U.S. paper still placed significant limits on the political agency of national liberation movements. He proposed to create a working group to discuss "causes" of international terrorism. He maintained that it would provide Arab, African, and other delegates a forum to discuss the political context of self-determination and national liberation. Meanwhile, another working group on "measures" to counter terrorism would work out an "extradite or prosecute" agreement to criminalize international terrorism. Newsom confirmed the right of national liberation movements to exist but denied them the right to use violence.[84] He failed to persuade the African delegates. He summarized that "all stressed common concern that African group fears must be satisfied that action contemplated would not harm southern African national liberation group activities."[85] In their responses, delegates pointed out that the United States was pursuing its own interests by relegating the national liberation context to a separate "causes" forum; this separation ensured that the United States could focus on its punitive and criminalizing goals in the "measures" working group. They added that the Americans' ambiguous definition of terrorism still let states such as South Africa or Israel label any kind of dissident, insurgent, or revolutionary act as a "terrorist" serious offense—even if the act was not particularly violent and no civilians were hurt. This terrorism label delegitimized such acts and enabled states to take whatever criminal countermeasures they chose. The U.S. suggestions thus still enabled neo-imperialist suppression of dissent.

The differing visions of national liberation coalesced as the central point of contention when the debate on "international terrorism" finally started in the Sixth Committee on November 9, 1972. The key issue was whether border-crossing extremist violence was an act of national liberation or a common crime.

Longtime Saudi UN ambassador Jamil Murad Baroody articulated the Global South position. It framed the issue at stake through (de)colonizing warfare and national liberation fighting. Together, many Arab, African, and nonaligned countries argued that politically motivated violence against former colonial and neo-imperialist targets was a key dimension of national liberation struggles. The Arab, African, and other delegates claimed that extremist violence was an aspect of national liberation organizations' state-building efforts and needed to be handled in that context. So did states' countermeasures. These delegates acknowledged that brutal acts of violence against "innocent" civilians were inexcusable. They insisted that true terrorists were rare outliers, however, and that overall, national liberation movements should not be delegitimized through the terrorism label. In any case, offenders' political motivations were crucial and needed to be considered in order to find a sustainable solution to this sort of violence. Baroody also stressed that states themselves engaged in terrorism as well. He denounced former colonizing states for committing terrorism within the warfare they waged against colonized peoples—now and in the past. He accused Israel, the United States, and other imperialist states of engaging in current state terrorism against civilian populations, particularly through their intelligence agencies. And he decried, as summarized by Bush, that the U.S. working paper "would not seem to protect civilians from war." Instead, it allowed colonial powers "to wreak havoc" in occupied territories.[86]

The contrasting Global North position maintained that international terrorism was a brutal crime without any political legitimacy. Representatives of this position included the United States and Canada, most Western European states, the Baltic states, Japan, and Australia. Bush summarized their opening position in a telegram to State. These delegates highlighted that the "term international terrorism is unfortunately ambiguous and emotive, but that acts to which it refers must be stopped."[87] Bennett and his allies insisted that extremists' violence against civilians invalidated any sort of political context or grievances. Such attacks were not an act of armed conflict. They were an urgent threat to global safety. The international community needed to create certainty that states would duly punish and not support nonstate attackers. A multilateral "prosecute or extradite" agreement was a solution that required states to generally treat attackers as criminals and created such certainty. The Global North delegates also vehemently denounced the idea that the convention should cover only "innocent" civilians because that terminology implied that state officials or military and law enforcement officers could be legitimate targets.

Meanwhile, a domestic U.S. hijacking on the second day of negotiations undermined the State Department. The hijacking prompted Nixon to shift his foreign policy priorities concerning international terrorism from multilateral agreements to hardline sanctions and unilateral measures he could more easily control. On November 10, 1972, three U.S. fugitives hijacked Southern Airways Flight 49 in Birmingham, Alabama, taking the airplane on a four-thousand-mile journey that ended in Havana. The hijackers threatened to crash the airplane into a nuclear reactor at Tennessee's Oak Ridge National Laboratory. Nixon demanded responses. On January 6, 1973, the Federal Aviation Administration (FAA) put into effect Regulation 107.4, which for the first time required screening 100 percent of passengers at all airports within the United States and on all flights operated by U.S. air carriers.[88] Congress appropriated funds for the FAA to purchase previously-tested metal detectors and other security equipment.[89] To cut management and maintenance costs, the FAA passed ownership of the equipment to U.S.-registered airlines.[90] By mid-1973, U.S. air carriers operated security detection equipment by themselves in U.S. and in foreign airports.

Nixon also insisted that the State Department create enforcement mechanisms for the existing ICAO and OAS and the upcoming UNGA Conventions. More precisely, he wanted the United States and the international community to be able to sanction states that harbored attackers. All of these conventions were voluntary. No means existed by which states could force other states to adhere to the conventions. During earlier ICAO negotiations, other states had almost unanimously rejected the idea of sanctions as politically unfeasible. Now, Nixon wanted such enforcement sanctions in the UN Convention against international terrorism as well. This demand made the U.S. negotiating position more untenable than before. In the ICAO, even U.S. allies had rejected these sanctions as an overly intrusive outside interference with states' sovereign legal systems.

Even as internal pressure mounted for the State Department to achieve an enforceable UN antiterrorism convention with sanctions, the department encountered obstacle after obstacle in the Sixth Committee. Baroody kept the negotiations focused on how to protect the agency of national liberation actors and not on how to abridge it. He emphasized that national liberation actors were simply adapting to a globalizing world. Baroody repeatedly stated that neo-imperial, metropole, and allied states had provoked national liberation-related violence through their imperialist oppressive behavior. They now had to face the results of their actions. African delegates from Senegal, Cameroon, Uganda, and Chad shared his opinion that the United States and its allies meant to use the current negotiations to discriminate against national liberation movements. The Cuban delegate supported his African and Arab colleagues and criticized the United States' imperialist actions. Yugoslavia and many other nonaligned states agreed that preventative measures against terrorism were needed but would do nothing to undermine the political agency of national liberation struggles.[91] After a week of discussions, the divide between the Global North and South positions was wider than ever.

In addition, Bennett experienced significant trouble with U.S. allies who openly discussed the political context of national liberation in the Sixth Committee. These allies were uncomfortable with and even sabotaged the American position. Tekoah feared that the United States might appease African delegates with language sympathetic to self-determination aspirations. He criticized that any such language played right into Arab and Palestinian rhetoric about the validity of Palestinian statehood.[92] On November 16, he delivered a long, passionate speech in front of the Sixth Committee. Bush summarized: "Detailing Nazi atrocities, he accused Arabs of similar desires and motivations. Acts purposely directed towards innocent civilians, he said, are leading the world toward barbarism. In light of Arab campaigns of violence against Jews, he said it [was] not surprising that Arab del[egate] s opposed discussion of terrorism and now press for delay in any [UN]GA action."[93] Tekoah also insisted that Israel would "take all necessary steps to combat acts of terrorism"—these steps referenced intelligence and IDF action. The speech incited many delegates, and the Iraqi, Egyptian, and Syrian delegates tore into Tekoah and scathingly criticized Israeli policies, claiming that (another Bush summary) the "history of Zionism both before and after [the] illegitimate birth of Israel gives examples of perfidy cruelty and terror."[94] Arab delegates received wide-ranging support from African, nonaligned, and East Bloc states as well as the Soviet Union. Meanwhile, the French delegate Guy de Lacharrière was attempting to slow the U.S. initiative by stating that states should first extensively research international terrorism. American inquiries at the French foreign ministry produced no answers beyond that the situation was politically complex. Bush was irritated, complaining that the French were a "wet blanket" and "apathetic and pathetic."[95]

Neither side was ultimately willing to compromise on their understanding of national liberation, conceptualization of international terrorism, and resulting proposed solutions. Thus, when the debate ended on November 27, both Global North and South submitted a draft resolution restating their position. The Sixth Committee's choice of resolutions would cement the outcome of the Sixth Committee negotiations. Each side raced to catch delegates' votes.

Acting as a surrogate for the United States, the Italian ambassador to the UN, Piero Vinci, spearheaded the drafting of a Global North resolution with other European and British Commonwealth countries.[96] Bush and De Palma hoped that Vinci's efforts would increase the draft's chances of approval by disassociating the United States from it.[97] They knew that the U.S. position on sanctions had no backing and had alienated neutral delegates.[98] The Italian draft called for the creation of a convention in the next UNGA term (in late 1973) against international terrorism in "countries not party to [the terrorists'] conflict."[99] The resolution draft thus restrained itself to violent acts committed in locations outside of the attackers' perceived political or national liberation struggle. Such acts could more easily be branded as politically illegitimate. The resolution draft also called for a separate committee to discuss the origins of international terrorism. The Italian draft thus adopted the U.S. strategy of separating the debate on terrorists' political motivations into a different venue from the negotiations about criminalizing and punishing attacks.

In contrast, the Global South resolution called for research into the situation of national liberation movements.[100] This draft recommended the establishment of an ad hoc committee to further discuss the self-determination origins of terrorist violence, specifically mentioned the right of national liberation movements to exist and pursue their goals, and solicited more state opinions on terrorism to brainstorm long-term solutions.[101] It did not recommend any regulations or immediate punitive actions to prevent terrorism. This resolution was exactly what Rogers, Bush and the other State Department officials did not want.

Arab, African, and nonaligned states won out and set priorities for the UN's handling of terrorism that subverted U.S. goals. The Sixth Committee adopted the Global South resolution on December 11, 1972, and undercut the U.S. initiative in favor of the Arab, African, and other nonaligned states' policy interests. The UN would focus on national liberation movements and their political context instead of working to criminalize international terrorism. The UNGA plenary adopted the nonaligned resolution on December 18, with the United States voting against, as Resolution 3034 (XXVII) "On Measures to Prevent International Terrorism." The resolution stated that the UNGA

> 3. Reaffirms the inalienable right to self-determination and independence of all peoples under colonial and racist régimes and other forms of alien domination and upholds the legitimacy of their struggle, in particular the struggle of national liberation movements . . . ;
>
> 4. Condemns the continuation of repressive and terrorist acts by colonial, racist, and alien régimes in denying peoples their legitimate right to self-determination and independence and other human rights and fundamental freedoms.[102]

Overall, the Sixth Committee terrorism debate and its results highlighted the increased influence of recently independent states and the concurrent decline of U.S. authority in the UNGA.

FIGURE 2.4. The UN General Assembly adopts resolutions on terrorism and other matters, December 18, 1972.
Against U.S. and European wishes, the resolution focused on the political context of national liberation movements instead of prioritizing the criminal extradition of terrorists. UN photo by Yukata Nagata.

This resolution allowed the Arab, African, and other nonaligned delegates to shape the parameters and content of the future UNGA ad hoc committee on terrorism while the U.S. delegation shifted to what it considered damage control. In a telegram dated December 11, 1972, Bush vented and blamed the African delegations for their collaboration with the Arab states, as well as Israel and France for their lack of support.[103] As a slight balm, a NATO meeting on December 13–14 showed that intelligence collaboration was progressing well between NATO members on the issue of international terrorism. But this NATO meeting could not denounce or regulate international terrorism throughout the world.[104] Compounding the U.S. disappointment, Interpol announced that it would not address international terrorism, as it considered the issue a political and not a purely criminal problem. The United States had failed to create a UN "extradite or prosecute" convention against terrorism following the 1972 Munich attack and to criminalize international terrorism in global politics. Recently independent states had used the UNGA to exert their own interests on national liberation. They stymied U.S. efforts to build a crime-focused consensus surrounding international terrorism.

The Nixon administration quickly adapted to prevent potential damages from the UNGA debate. On December 16, De Palma recommended that Bush participate in the ad hoc terrorism committee set up by the nonaligned resolution, even though "we are not sanguine that there is substantial possibility that committee will produce meaningful report or even that we will be able to have appreciable influence on its content."[105] The U.S. goal was to stop nonaligned delegates from passing resolutions through the committee that might damage U.S. interests, such as another condemnation of Israel or a declaration of support for the PLO.

FROM MULTILATERALISM TO UNILATERALISM

After the United States' plan for the UNGA initiative failed, the Nixon administration struggled throughout 1973 to represent its views in multilateral forums and keep the protection-of-diplomats convention draft and similar projects alive. These struggles increased the administration's weariness with multilateral steps, and Nixon increasingly prioritized unilateral efforts against international terrorism that the U.S. government could implement and control.

In the ICAO, new aviation security negotiations began just weeks after the UNGA debacle. Since 1969, U.S. officials wanted to impose sanctions on states that did not extradite or (at least) criminally prosecute hijackers. The Munich attack reignited the ICAO debate over sanctions, and its Council decided to move forward to discuss new proposals for sanctions or other civil aviation security mechanisms. A U.S.-Canadian convention draft formed the basis of discussions in January 1973.[106] The State Department also began renegotiating bilateral U.S. extradition treaties (the only basis under which U.S. courts considered extradition requests) to include the provisions of the ICAO Hague and Montreal Conventions.[107] Meanwhile, in February 1973 the United States finally signed the U.S.-Cuba Hijacking Agreement, which the State Department had sought since 1968. But these aviation discussions were soon mired in a new controversy. On February 21, 1973, Israeli fighter planes shot down Libyan Arab Airlines Flight 114 because the civilian aircraft strayed into airspace over the Israeli-controlled Sinai Peninsula.

Many Arab leaders again used the attack to condemn what they deemed Israeli neo-imperial overreach and advocate for Pan-Arab sympathy with the Palestinian national liberation cause. Libyan foreign minister Mansur Kikhia claimed that the shooting was criminal and stated, "We consider these victims as martyrs of the Israeli aggression. We are prepared to accept more sacrifices in the service of our cause of destiny."[108] The Lebanese ICAO delegation responded to the shooting with a petition to have Israel's ICAO membership revoked, signaling that the politics of the Arab-Israeli conflict were becoming an issue within the technically specialized ICAO.[109]

Ironically, the Israeli attack presented an opportunity for the United States to once again demand sanctions against the (mainly Arab) states harboring hijackers. The ICAO Council responded to the Israeli attack by announcing an extraordinary assembly and diplomatic conference to discuss aviation security in Rome from August 20 to September 21, 1973.[110] The State Department and the FAA calculated that Lebanon's call for Israel's punishment might open the doors for an ICAO convention that created and enforced sanctions against states violating ICAO regulations. Although none of the United States' allies favored such punishment mechanisms, they all seemed interested in passing new ICAO aviation security regulations. French, Swiss, and British officials even drafted a proposal to make adherence to the ICAO aviation security conventions obligatory for all members, not just signatory states.[111] The August ICAO conference thus provided a window of opportunity for the State Department to persuade the other ICAO members to consider the U.S.-desired sanctions.

Soon after, an attack on diplomats in Sudan directly and lethally exposed the State Department to the BSO. On March 1, 1973, eight BSO members charged into a reception at the Saudi embassy in Khartoum and took ten diplomats hostage, including the American ambassador, Cleo Noel Jr., and the deputy chief of mission, George Curtis Moore. The attackers demanded the release of multiple prisoners around the world, including Palestinians imprisoned in Israel, Red Army Faction members incarcerated in the FRG, and in the United States, Sirhan Sirhan, Robert Kennedy's assassin. The Nixon administration had previously pursued a case-by-case policy on whether or not to accede to demands in hostage and kidnapping scenarios involving diplomats. This hostage situation's location, timing, and perpetrators, in the wake of the Munich attack, hardened Nixon's resolve. On March 2, 1973, Nixon publicly stated that the United States would not give in to any demands. That same day, the attackers shot Noel and Moore, as well as Guy Eid, the Belgian charge d'affaires. Sudanese authorities arrested the BSO members and ended the crisis two days later. While worldwide condemnation followed the attack, most Arab leaders used their condolences to again explain that terrorism was a political act caused by the suppression of the Palestinian population and resulting national liberation struggle.

Just like the 1970 Dawson's Field hijackings, the Nixon administration had little leverage over the attackers or the Sudanese government. The Khartoum attack infuriated Nixon, but all military or economic reactions risked alienating larger Arab states and undermining the U.S. Middle East peace process. The Sudanese government cooperated with the United States during the crisis. After the attack, it chose to exercise its sovereign right to place the attackers on trial at home rather than extradite the offenders to the United States. Nixon and Rogers began a large-scale security update of U.S. embassies. They also continued the U.S. initiative to enact a UN protection-of-diplomats convention with the "extradite or prosecute" principle.[112] Their goal was to use the convention to pressure Sudan and ensure that the trial against the perpetrators fulfilled American expectations and delivered harsh sentences.[113] The OLA's Ronald Bettauer continued to formulate and disseminate the U.S. position on the protection-of-diplomats convention, aided by the CCCT's chairman, Armin Meyer, and his successor, Lewis Hoffacker.[114]

Still, Arab, African, and nonaligned states' conceptions of terrorism (as an aspect of national liberation) dominated all multilateral discussions in the summer of 1973. The UN Ad Hoc Committee on Terrorism met for the first time from July 16 to August 10, 1973. Most of the committee's time was spent condemning state violence and repression in Israel, South Africa, and Rhodesia.[115] The committee met again from 1976 to 1979 and always focused on national liberation issues. Meanwhile, the ICAO gathered in Rome from August 20 to September 21, 1973. Just days beforehand, on August 11, 1973, Israeli fighter planes diverted a Lebanese civilian airplane from Beirut and forced it to land in Israel, hoping to find the PFLP founder, George Habash, on board.[116] This move supercharged the atmosphere at the conference. The American delegation decided not to advocate for sanctions after all, judging it too risky that Arab states could gain a tool to use against Israel.[117] British delegates at the conference complained at home that the U.S. was too rigidly favoring Israel.[118] Though all parties agreed that aviation security was important they were unable to find workable compromises. Negotiations in the UN and ICAO revealed that the deep conceptual divide between the United States and many Global South states endured.

By the fall of 1973, little enthusiasm remained in the State Department for multilateral approaches against international terrorism, and its efforts increasingly shifted toward unilateral initiatives. The State Department requested millions of dollars for security procedures for U.S. diplomats and businessmen abroad.[119] Ironically, this funding did not extend to New York City, where the Jewish Defense League continued to remain somewhat active and still exists to the present day. Like his predecessor, President Gerald Ford would continue to veto increases in federal funds to protect New York City embassies except in extraordinary cases.[120] In the Middle East, the Yom Kippur War cemented U.S.-Israeli relations and shifted the geopolitical landscape in favor of more (publicly) moderate Palestinian leaders than Habash; in its aftermath the CIA began a clandestine dialogue with the PLO in order to (among other things) reduce its incentive to commit violence against the United States.[121] But in 1975, Ford publicly assured Israeli leaders that the United States would not recognize the PLO until the PLO recognized Israel's right to exist.

In the ICAO, U.S. representatives pushed to have U.S. civil aviation security standards adopted by other states.[122] The FAA began a training course for domestic and foreign civil aviation security officers in its Transportation Safety Institute in Oklahoma City.[123] Subjected to aggressive U.S. lobbying, the ICAO passed Annex 17 to its charter in 1974, which strengthened the ICAO's overall security requirements and created U.S.-drafted standards by which countries could assess the quality of one another's civil aviation security.[124]

With so many failures on the multilateral front, Nixon turned back to U.S. domestic law to increase his capacity to punish international terrorists and their (state) supporters. Congress adopted Public Law 93–366 on August 5, 1974. Formally, it was the legislation the United States needed to implement the ICAO Hague Convention. However, its first section, the "Anti-Hijacking Act of 1974," permitted the president to take punitive actions against any country that supported acts of hijacking, harbored hijackers, or maintained lax civil aviation security standards.[125] It gave the U.S. president the option of unilaterally placing sanctions on states that prioritized hijackers' political background. Nixon finally had a unilateral option to sanction states that did not treat hijackers as politically irrelevant criminals. The second section, the "Air Transportation Security Act of 1974," introduced more stringent requirements for security procedures. All air carriers operating to and from the United States were required to screen all passengers and their baggage.[126] The law thus required foreign airlines and foreign airports to uphold FAA security standards if an airline wanted to fly to the United States. Overall, Public Law 93–366 allowed the U.S. federal government to pursue unilateral measures against international terrorists and states that acknowledged them as political actors.

Two exceptions for the U.S. distaste of multilateral legal action remained. In 1974, the State Department began to discuss the security of nuclear materials with other nuclear-capable states. These discussions continued at the first 1975 conference for all parties to the Nuclear Nonproliferation Treaty; the conference's goal was to review the success and status of the treaty.[127] Under the auspices of the International Atomic Energy Agency (IAEA), its members in the late 1970s negotiated a U.S.-drafted convention to protect nuclear materials in transit between states. Though framed in most literature as a nonproliferation device, this convention also included "extradite or prosecute" requirements for offenders and mirrored the other antiterrorism conventions.[128] Members of the CCCT working group worried that international terrorists might gain access to nuclear weapons, and this worry likely drove U.S. investment in the IAEA negotiations.[129]

The State Department also engaged in the final negotiations for a UN protection-of-diplomats convention. In the fall of 1973, the American UN delegation worked with European and Latin American allies to pass the ILC's diplomats convention draft in the UNGA. Supporters of the convention draft used the Khartoum attack to illustrate that every country's diplomatic corps could become a target of nonstate violent actors. They claimed that states had to protect their sovereign ability to host and conduct diplomatic relations by safeguarding every diplomat.[130] This phrasing was tailored to appeal to all UN member states, including recently decolonized countries eager to foster their own sovereignty. The Soviet delegate backed this argument, likely due to the U.S. failure to adequately protect Moscow's New York City consulate from the Jewish Defense League.[131]

The Global South states that had principally opposed the international terrorism initiative accepted that the convention would help protect their own sovereignty but nevertheless nearly derailed negotiations by attempting to insert protections for national liberation groups into the draft. They insisted that the convention not cover any violent acts committed by populations engaged in self-determination or anti-imperialist struggles. This linkage to national liberation groups made the convention draft unacceptable to the United States, its European allies, and most Latin American states; they refused to accept the idea that violence against diplomats could be a politically legitimate act. Neither side backed down. Yet, after three weeks of negotiations the sides finessed the impasse by outsourcing the self-determination language to a resolution. This resolution would accompany the convention and promised that the convention would not impede upon any efforts to engage in self-determination.[132] Arab, African, nonaligned, and recently independent states' delegates were pleased that their national liberation ideas had gained traction. The United States and its allies were relieved that the convention itself would not contain this content.[133]

The United States' initial approach of addressing only one type of attack in a convention worked once more. Like the ICAO and OAS Conventions, the new UNGA convention covered a specific list of precisely delineated violent acts. On December 14, the UNGA voted to adopt the "Convention on the Prevention and Punishment of Crimes Against Internationally

FIGURE 2.5. Legal Committee considers amendments of draft convention on protection of diplomats, October 16, 1973.
The Diplomats Convention caused less controversy at the United Nations than terrorism discussions because it regulated a far narrower field of attacks. UN photo by Yukata Nagata.

Protected Persons, Including Diplomatic Agents" (Diplomats Convention). Like the OAS Convention before it, it listed its covered crimes, gave universal jurisdiction so that any interested state could indict offenders, and included the principle of "extradite or prosecute." Though the convention did not require signatory states to draft new criminal laws, it did stipulate that the signatories "shall make these crimes punishable by appropriate penalties which take into account their grave nature."[134] At the least, states had to submit such cases for criminal prosecution. They had to instigate criminal repercussions. Ideally, they would then extradite or try offenders.

This result was less than what the State Department intended—U.S. diplomats would have preferred some kind of mandatory extradition requirement. The convention also again included the political offense exception. However, it was the first UN convention in the vein of earlier conventions that denounced Global South extremists' violence against Global North citizens. The piecemeal approach of addressing specific violent acts as criminal worked where a blanket condemnation of international terrorism had failed. The United States ratified the Diplomats Convention alongside the OAS Convention in 1976.[135]

Aside from this piecemeal agreement, recently independent states continued to shape the UN discussions on international terrorism in subsequent years. The Arab and African-sponsored resolution kept the issue of national liberation movements and their agency tied to the issue of diplomats' security. Furthermore, by late 1973 the Nixon administration was embroiled in the Watergate scandal. As a result, neither Nixon nor Rogers was inclined to let the State Department expend more effort on multilateral antiterrorism. Turning inward, the administration no longer pursued the strategy of criminalizing international terrorism, leaving it to be picked up by other countries in the future.[136] Recently independent states and PLO supporters controlled debates in the UN on terrorism in subsequent years and used them to safeguard the political agency of national liberation movements.[137]

The failure of its UN terrorism initiative pushed the United States to take increasingly unilateral measures. In the years after 1973, the Nixon and subsequent Ford administrations did not seek multilateral "extradite or prosecute" conventions against international terrorism. Instead, U.S. officials focused on the enforcement and ratification of existing conventions and on unilateral security practices they could control.

The 1972 UNGA terrorism debate highlighted the power of recently independent states to set the agenda and pursue their own interests instead of catering to superpower and former colonial states. One of the nonaligned states' main interests was protecting protostate and nonstate actors who sought sovereignty for themselves by dismantling established imperial power structures. A major example of how recently independent states gave agency to these nonstate actors was Yasser Arafat's 1974 speech in front of the UN General Assembly. This interest shaped the recently independent states' policy position of handling international terrorism as one aspect of anticolonial violence.

Yet the 1972 debate also showcased how Global North states were slowly adapting to the increasing authority of recently independent states. Instead of regulating terrorism, which had faced substantial Arab, African, and nonaligned states' resistance, the United States and its European and Latin

American allies returned to their practice of regulating bits and pieces of this issue. They criminalized specific violent acts, which drew less overall resistance from recently independent states and would continue in the future. The 1972 UNGA terrorism debate thus showed the influence of recently independent states on issues of decolonization, but it also emphasized how Global North states could limit this influence by breaking issues into more technical subissues.

Meanwhile, the definition of "terrorism" remained wide open. Recently independent states ensured that in the UNGA terrorism continued to be associated with national liberation and insurgency. However, the United States and its European and Latin American allies had developed the position that terrorist acts were primarily crimes and that the political context of such acts should not be considered when arresting and prosecuting offenders. This idea of treating terrorists as criminals did not fade with the American withdrawal behind its own national borders. It continued to spread, especially in Europe. At the UN, the United States, together with its Italian allies, had assembled a wide coalition against border-crossing nonstate extremists. After the United States' failure to secure an antiterrorism convention at the UN, its European allies discussed such transnational extremists in local bureaucratic networks and international organizations. Led by the FRG, states instituted new antiterrorism measures within European regional forums where Global South states did not have a direct voice. International terrorism became a key segment of multilateral European domestic security policies during the mid to late 1970s.

Chapter Three

TACTICAL ANTITERRORISM COLLABORATION IN EUROPE AND THE GLOBAL NORTH

On February 27, 1975, members of the West German leftist extremist group 2 June Movement crashed a small car into the vehicle carrying a candidate in the West Berlin mayoral race, conservative politician Peter Lorenz. The attackers struggled to overpower Lorenz, but finally kidnapped and hid him in West Berlin. The 2 June Movement demanded the release of six convicted leftist extremists, ransom money, and a plane to fly out of the city. Meanwhile, the West German government under Chancellor Helmut Schmidt initiated large-scale data mining initiatives as well as identity control checkpoints and intensified border controls in West Berlin. Yet Schmidt, his cabinet, and members of Lorenz's opposition party were not able, throughout multiple crisis meetings, to figure out a solution that ensured Lorenz's safety and yet denied the kidnappers their demands. They gave in. One convicted terrorist, Red Army Faction (RAF) attorney Horst Mahler, declined to leave his prison sentence. The five remaining prisoners flew out of West Berlin on March 3, 1975, accompanied by former West Berlin mayor Pastor Heinrich Albertz as a hostage. The five vanished in South Yemen. Lorenz was released safely on March 5.[1] The Schmidt cabinet attempted to locate the released prisoners abroad with no luck. Within the next few years, four of the five released terrorists reappeared in the Federal Republic of Germany (FRG) and its neighboring countries to commit new violent acts. For the Schmidt cabinet, the Lorenz kidnapping and its

FIGURE 3.1. Pastor Heinrich Albertz, voluntary hostage of the group of extremists forced free by Peter Lorenz's kidnappers, alongside released extremist Gabriele Kröcher-Tiedemann on the plane that would take them to South Yemen, March 3, 1975.
Kröcher-Tiedemann and the other extremists would go on to commit further attacks throughout Europe.
dpa picture alliance / Alamy Stock Photo.

aftermath were a security threat along the same lines as the 1972 Munich Olympic Games attack. Both incidents highlighted that FRG domestic security structures were insufficient to identify, arrest, and prosecute violent extremists who had rampant transnational contacts and could flee to safe havens abroad. To improve its domestic security against such extremists, in the 1970s the FRG government became the principal advocate for security collaboration among its European neighbors.

By 1972, politically motivated violence was an escalating security threat for countries on the European continent. Many states faced homegrown violent actors, oftentimes separatists or people radicalized by the 1968 protests. Besides local groups, foreign actors comprised an increasing threat. In particular, Palestinian extremists targeted the former colonial metropoles of Europe to draw attention to their struggle and to dissuade European states from supporting Israel. Most dramatically, the 1972 Black September

Organization attack on the Israeli team at the Munich Olympic Games demonstrated that domestic border security controls, law enforcement procedures, and weapons possessions laws were insufficient to prevent brutal acts of transnational terroristic violence.

Before the Munich attack, the United States was the principal driver of international initiatives against transnationally active Palestinian and Latin American extremists. The Nixon administration viewed such violence as a foreign policy problem that inhibited the attainment of other, more important U.S. interests in Latin America and the Middle East. The State Department sought to prevent other states from supporting nonstate extremists through multilateral international law agreements that required all states to apply criminal law against such attackers. But this approach had limited success. International law agreements were voluntary and could not force states to criminally prosecute extremists. In addition, Algeria and other recently independent countries used the United Nations General Assembly (UNGA) to affirm that Palestinian extremists were political actors with legitimate grievances. A global approach based around international law and foreign policy could create norms that associated political violence with crime. But it could not prevent attacks. Antiterrorism efforts in the United States after 1973 focused more on unilateral initiatives. Europeans, however, began to cooperate more.

In subsequent years, European states collaborated on ways to find, arrest, and prosecute international terrorists. This chapter explains how European states created collaborative networks of law enforcement and security experts to increase their chances of tracing and capturing transnational extremists. Chapter 4 then examines how European domestic security exchanges opened a window of opportunity for these states to negotiate extradition, judicial collaboration, and regional norms concerning international terrorism.

After 1972, Western European security officials created bilateral and multilateral networks to exchange information and foster effective practices against international terrorism. These networks were not foreign policy initiatives but rather domestic security collaboration. But the U.S. antiterrorism initiatives motivated European officials. And European collaboration also advanced crime-focused and tactical responses to violent extremists in the Global North without really addressing political context. European governments had a wide range of policies against political violence in place, varying in their use of law enforcement, legislation, judicial systems, willingness to take extralegal steps, the military, and history with and acceptance of counterinsurgency-related practices. Driven by the FRG, however, the European Community (EC) states began collaborating with one another across national boundaries against the threat of transnational extremists. While high-level policymakers prompted negotiations, mid-level security experts set the content and focus of multilateral discussions. These security officials sought means to perform their antiterrorism tasks more efficiently. As a result, they pursued strategies that predominantly fell into their crime-fighting scope of competencies. Within new antiterrorism networks, European states began cooperating in the field of domestic security—an area where they had sparsely communicated before. And through this collaboration, European officials significantly normalized criminal conceptions of terrorism and related practices that addressed violence but not its political context.

European domestic security collaboration against international terrorism was a complex process containing significant tensions and paradoxes. The idea of collaborating on domestic security at all was unusual for European states. Law enforcement and domestic security are a key part of a state's sovereign control over its territory, and traditionally, politicians are averse to undermining their sovereignty by collaborating with other states. In the early twentieth century European states had shared information on anarchists, but such cooperation remained sparse.[2] In the 1950s and 1960s, political scientists strictly distinguished between "domestic" and "national" security, with one encompassing criminal threats within a state and the other military, statist, and foreign threats to a state.[3] However, like anarchists before them, transnational extremists in the 1970s blurred these boundaries. FRG and other European officials turned to bilateral and multilateral collaboration to improve their domestic security against what they perceived as an extraordinary (out-of-the-ordinary) new threat of international terrorism. In turn, they laid the groundwork for domestic security cooperation within European integration and, later, the European Union. International terrorism drove European collaboration in the field of domestic security, which historically was not an area of state-to-state cooperation.

Another tension was that these collaborative networks functioned as an echo chamber, reinforcing participating officials' claims that international terrorism needed to be treated as a normal criminal issue—despite all evidence and their own actions to the contrary. To discuss international terrorism and domestic security, specialized officials worked within communities of like-minded counterparts with similar competencies. Some participants were experts in law enforcement practices and technologies, while others specialized in more controversial intelligence, surveillance, and counterinsurgent practices. To prevent their discussions and solutions from leaking to terrorists, officials created a restricted environment where experts could focus on the tactics and criminal dimensions of international terrorism, not its more abstract political aspects. And unlike United Nations diplomats, security officials had little need to consider outside voices of terrorist actors, leftist and civil rights activists, public opinion (which could and was influenced by terrorist attacks), or Arab, African, and nonaligned states friendly to the Palestinian national liberation movement. Policymakers, especially the FRG officials who drove significant amounts of antiterrorism collaboration, worked hard to justify the results that did become public, portraying them as necessary means to preserve the rule of law. In their domestic security collaboration, European officials discussed what they considered necessary crime prevention measures against international terrorism. Yet their antiterrorism networks operated in secret behind security clearances, were unaccountable to the public, and often included legally ambiguous elements.

This chapter analyzes two distinct avenues of collaboration that brought together different communities of security experts. First, FRG interior ministry officials established connections to counterparts in other European states after the 1972 Olympic Games attack. They sought to extend the FRG's ongoing program of domestic security reform throughout the EC to address the unusual danger of international terrorism. The result was an informal structure of working groups known as TREVI, which was established in 1976. TREVI delegates shared intelligence, cooperated in police training, discussed innovative criminological technologies, and crafted border patrol regulations. It provided early avenues of European collaboration in domestic security and created the foundations for the European Union's Third Pillar, "Cooperation in Justice and Home Affairs."[4]

A second avenue of collaboration was the development of tactical units, comparable to and drawn from military Special Forces teams, which were dedicated to handling international terrorism among European states and their global allies. These units blended military and law enforcement competencies in ways that advanced Western states' militarization of antiterrorism even as they declared international terrorists to be nonmilitary targets. After the 1972 Munich attack, the FRG created an antiterrorism tactical unit, the Grenzschutzgruppe 9 (Border Security Group 9, or GSG 9), based on existing British and Israeli Special Forces teams. When the GSG 9 achieved a spectacular rescue at Mogadishu in 1977 that dazzled the media in the wake of a comparable Israeli operation at Entebbe, other states hastened to create similar units. These various units were scattered in national armies, law enforcement, and mixed institutions, such as gendarmeries. Officers in the United States, Israel, the UK, and the FRG became the center of a military and law enforcement training, equipment, and management network dedicated to fight international terrorism. FRG leaders in particular justified this development as a necessary means to uphold their rule of law against the extraordinary threat of international terrorism. Through their exchanges, antiterrorism tactical units advanced and normalized the inclusion of military gear and specialized practices within Western law enforcement and presented themselves as an attractive diplomatic and domestic security option for Western governments in crisis situations.

Within the TREVI and Special Forces networks, European security officials went beyond U.S. unilateral or international law initiatives to pursue collaborative domestic security measures against international terrorism. Individual states' antiterrorism policies and priorities differed. Tensions and paradoxes ran through their multilateral collaboration. Yet officials cooperated on practices and norms that addressed international terrorism as a criminal, politically irrelevant act. Among themselves and to the public, they stressed practical, at times extralegal, steps as necessary against such a transnational domestic security threat.

SETTING THE SCENE: THE FRG's RESPONSE TO THE 1972 MUNICH OLYMPIC GAMES ATTACK

FRG officials provided the main impetus for European collaboration against international terrorism in the mid-1970s—both in domestic security and (as shown in chapter 4) in international law. Shocked by the 1972 Olympic Games attack, the FRG interior ministry tapped into previously established bilateral and multilateral connections, especially from processes of European integration, to ensure that its neighboring states were just as meticulous as the FRG about preventing international terrorism.

In 1972, most European states had spent several years dealing with the political turmoil of the 1968 protest movements, as well as with extremists who had radicalized out of these movements. In the early 1970s, Western Europe became a hotbed for politically motivated acts of violence. The nonstate attackers included local actors as well as ones from outside the European continent. Domestic actors' motivation varied from leftist socio-revolutionary extremists, such as Italy's Red Brigades and West Germany's RAF, to separatist nationalists, such as the Provisional Irish Republican Army (IRA) in the United Kingdom and the Euskadi Ta Askatasuna (ETA) in Spain. Meanwhile, the spreading aviation industry facilitated easier access to the region for self-proclaimed national liberation and anticolonial extremists from the Global South. European states' responses to politically motivated violence at home varied as much as the labels they placed on the attackers.[5] These measures were heavily shaped by national context and legal tradition.

Relatively few acts of political violence marred post-1968 France. French armed forces and law enforcement had significant experience with coun-terinsurgency-related practices from the Algerian War, including control-ling the colonized territory as well as harsh domestic security regulations within metropole France.[6] During the 1968 protests, the French govern-ment responded with tough state action, including demonstration bans, the dissolution of leftist organizations, and new antiriot measures. Yet state responses generated a wave of public sympathy for the (mainly left-ist) protesters. During the 1970s, the French interior ministry and police authorities thus shifted to emphasize that they sought law and order, as well as measures that adhered to the rule of law.[7] A powerful leftist scene in France, meanwhile, watched public authorities and opposed measures that policed left-wing and anticolonial activity.[8] Political violence and relatedly, the appropriate terminology and reactions thereto, were highly controver-sial and fought over in 1970s French society.

In West Germany a minority of the leftists who had engaged in the 1968 protest movements radicalized into socio-revolutionary violent groups. The most prominent was the Maoist-inspired "city guerilla" group RAF, which the press at first described as "anarchists" or the "Baader-Meinhof Gang." Founded in 1970 by Andreas Baader and Ulrike Meinhof, the RAF's goal was to undermine FRG state structures and attack U.S. installations in the FRG.[9] It never gained popular appeal and only had 60–80 total members throughout its twenty-year existence.[10] Between 1970 and 1972, the RAF committed a series of bank robberies and bombings. Meinhof justified these actions by arguing that the FRG and the United States practiced repressive, imperialist policies both at home and in the world.[11]

In the early 1970s, FRG chancellor Willy Brandt introduced law enforcement reforms and new domestic security legislation, nested within a larger initiative to update the management and bureaucracy of the FRG state. Leaders argued that their reforms improved "internal security," a catchphrase comparable to the United States' "law and order."[12] These reforms were controversial. To prevent an erosion of FRG democratic institutions, law enforcement, intelligence services, and the military usually held strictly separate institutional competencies.[13] In 1968, policymakers introduced the German Emergency Acts, amending the FRG constitution to give the state emergency powers in nonmilitary situations. Subsequent controversies erupted in West German society about whether the state was repeating the same mistakes that had led to the downfall of the Weimar Republic and the rise of Nazism.[14] In response to RAF attacks, the FRG's Federal Criminal Police Office, the Bundeskriminalamt, dramatically expanded and introduced new investigative techniques, such as the use of computerized data mining. It became a centralized powerhouse in the otherwise heavily federated FRG police.[15] The FRG parliament, the Bundestag, passed a series of laws making extremist political beliefs of any kind prosecutable as a threat to the state.[16] After FRG authorities arrested Baader, Meinhof, and other RAF leaders in the spring of 1972, the domestic political situation seemed to calm down. Overall, FRG policymakers publicly sought to balance safety and civil liberties. They were careful to argue that their reforms protected FRG citizens from the RAF and yet legally (and normally) supported democratic institutions and civil liberties—instead of undermining them.

Italy meanwhile faced an explosion of left- and right-wing political violence, but the multiparty state was for a long time unable to address or stabilize the violence through the legal reforms it undertook. The Piazza Fontana bombing in December 1969, which killed seventeen people, began a decade known as the "years of lead" due to the large number of violent attacks. Left-wing violent groups such as the Brigade Rosso (Red Brigades) developed when the student and worker protest movements radicalized. In contrast, right-wing groups such as Ordine Nuovo (New Order) and Ordine Nero (Black Order) sought to reintroduce fascist and authoritarian principles. Spanning 1969 to the 1980s, the period included thousands of attacks with at least four hundred deaths and two thousand other casualties.[17] Italian officials labeled this violence as extremism and crime. By 1972, left-leaning politicians started labeling right-wing attacks as terrorism, and right-wing politicians did the same for left-wing attacks. Both sides used the term to delegitimize the opposite side's political aims by emphasizing their violence toward civilians. Heavily influenced by political affiliation, their usage of this term was still relatively unsystematic.[18]

Italian officials responded with slow steps to overhaul Italy's very outdated criminal laws. Somewhat counterintuitively, they sought to liberalize their criminal code, which had not been reformed since 1931, in order to undermine left- and right-wing critique of the Italian state.[19] In addition, Palestinian radicals frequently used the lax security at Rome's Leonardo da Vinci–Fiumicino Airport to board and hijack international flights. In December 1973, thirty-four people died in a major Palestinian attack and hijacking at the airport.[20] Italian officials were not able to address political violence at home effectively in the early 1970s, however. By the mid-1970s, the Italian state was slowly turning from liberalization to stricter laws and law enforcement reforms.

The United Kingdom also faced significant and continuous political violence related to its colonial history in Northern Ireland. In 1969, sectarian ethnic conflict broke out when the Northern Irish Catholic minority insisted that the Protestant majority and British officials ignored its civil rights. Prime Minister Harold Wilson deployed British troops to police and repress violent outbursts in Northern Ireland. These included the Special Air Services (SAS), a Special Forces unit with extensive experience in counterinsurgency operations in former British colonies such as Malaysia. Meanwhile, the Catholic separatist movement split. Its radical wing formed the IRA, a paramilitary group inspired by the anticolonial Irish Republican Army in the early twentieth century. The British government quickly branded the IRA and other Northern Irish separatists with the label *terrorism*, which in previous decades had been used mainly to delegitimize leftist anticolonial and insurgent fighters. The following thirty years became known as "The Troubles" as leftist and Catholic, but also police, military, and Protestant violence escalated in Northern Ireland. The IRA attacked targets throughout the United Kingdom as well, committing over 2,600 attacks by 1998.[21]

The British government had a long history of counterinsurgent practices in its former colonies, which it applied in Northern Ireland. In 1971, the new prime minister, Edward Heath, introduced internment without trial in Northern Ireland on the basis of the 1922 Civil Authorities Act. The following year, Heath suspended the Northern Irish Parliament and introduced direct rule from London. The Northern Ireland (Emergency Provisions) Act of 1973 established courts that tried Northern Irish separatist extremists without a jury. The Prevention of Terrorism Acts, renewed yearly from 1974 to 1989, gave British police forces significant powers, including the ability to arrest without a warrant and to proscribe organizations.[22] The British government's response to Northern Ireland's political violence in the early 1970s stemmed from its prior counterinsurgent and colonial experiences.

Most European states faced political violence in the early 1970s, and this violence could often be traced back to the 1968 global protest movements. However, violent acts played out in different national contexts and with differing state responses. Except for the United Kingdom, few contemporaries used the term *terrorism* systematically to describe what was happening.

Since European officials viewed political violence as a local domestic security issue, they were not substantially interested in collaborating against it the way they cooperated on a range of political, economic, social, and cultural issues. Since the 1950s, Western European states pursued an active program of European integration and unification. International organizations formally structured many of these initiatives. The EC facilitated economic, cultural, and social integration and trade.[23] Defense alliances such as the North Atlantic Treaty Organization (NATO) enabled military collaboration for national and regional security.[24] Organizations such as the Council of Europe advanced human rights, democracy, and the rule of law on the European continent.[25]

By the early 1970s, Western European policymakers and civil society leaders wanted to extend their collaboration. Most importantly, the EC member states (France, the FRG, Italy, Belgium, the Netherlands, and Luxembourg) began to collaborate informally on foreign policy. They harmonized their UN positions to a greater extent. The EC itself gained UN observer status in 1974.[26] The EC states also developed a system of ad hoc meetings and working groups between heads of state, foreign ministers, and relevant officials to coordinate foreign policy. They named this informal network the European Political Cooperation (EPC).[27] The EC states thus began to subordinate not just military or economic interests but also foreign policy planning to processes of European integration. But these collaborative initiatives rarely touched the domestic structures that in each state policed and controlled violence.

Domestic security was not an area of European integration in the early 1970s. A fundamental aspect of exercising sovereignty for any state is to maintain a monopoly over violence in its territory.[28] To protect their sovereignty, states rarely discuss or negotiate domestic security institutions or practices with other states. Europeans had engaged in domestic security collaboration against anarchists in the early twentieth century. They hosted a range of anti-anarchism conferences that led to the founding of the International Criminal Police Commission in 1923, which become the International Criminal Police Organization (Interpol) in 1956.[29] After World War II, European states shared information on suspected communist actors.

Rebuilding their institutions and sovereignty, postwar European states otherwise collaborated only rarely on domestic security. Their few instances of domestic security cooperation were ad hoc, nonbinding, and informal. An example was the Club de Berne, an informal intelligence-sharing network founded by Western European security officials in 1969—in some cases (Switzerland) without the approval or even the knowledge of their respective ministers.[30] Similarly, the EC states and United Kingdom created the Co-operation Group to Combat Drug Abuse and Illicit Trafficking in Drugs (Pompidou Group) in 1971 to share experiences related to the illegal drug trade.[31] These clandestine groups were unaccountable to the public to prevent knowledge of their actions from reaching intended targets. European leaders did not envision domestic security as a substantial field of cooperation in the early 1970s, even as they coordinated military, economic, and other issues in an ongoing process of European integration.

In September 1972, Europeans saw the Olympic Games attack as a landmark event that highlighted their vulnerability to Palestinian extremists and the new threat of international terrorism. Chapter 2 contained an in-depth analysis of the attack and the resulting shock for Global North policymakers and publics. European leaders ordered their law enforcement and intelligence agencies to be more vigilant against this threat.

The FRG leadership was especially active in response. It pursued unusual, fast, and comprehensive measures against what had previously been a foreign policy issue. Chancellor Willy Brandt had spent the previous years creating a careful balance between foreign relations with Israel and with the Arab states. Unlike his predecessors, Brandt did not emphasize a special relationship between the FRG and Israel. He also pursued new diplomatic relations with Arab states. For the first time, in 1969, West Germany abandoned its long-standing Hallstein Doctrine of refusing to acknowledge East Germany and pushing its allies to also not acknowledge that state. This reversal opened new diplomatic opportunities for Brandt in the Middle East, where he no longer had to pressure Arab states to not acknowledge East Germany. Brandt's foreign policy goals were to secure broad support for his détente policies, especially with East Germany. But now the FRG's monopoly on violence on its own territory had been dramatically breached. The victims were Israeli citizens, which was particularly problematic given Germany's Nazi past. Cabinet members were personally shell-shocked. The interior minister, Hans-Dietrich Genscher, retroactively described the Munich attack as "the most horrible day of my long tenure as a member of the federal government."[32] The West German public felt less safe and demanded firm action, as did the Israeli leadership.[33]

The combination of shock, transnational origins of the attackers, and a feeling of urgent threat drove Brandt and his cabinet to respond immediately and with steps they might not have pursued otherwise. While the FRG had previously considered Palestinian extremism as a foreign policy issue related to the Arab-Israeli conflict, Brandt now addressed it as a domestic security threat. On the day after the attack, Brandt increased visa requirements and border vetting for citizens of Arab states, physically restricting their movement into the FRG. The goal was to prevent Palestinians from using other Arab states' passports to enter the country. Many screening requirements were based on racial qualifications. Brandt's cabinet also banned FRG-based Palestinian student and worker organizations.[34] Three weeks later, Genscher created a border police unit, GSG 9, based on existing British and Israel Special Forces teams. As will be discussed later in this chapter, GSG 9 became a pioneering antiterrorism unit whose members helped train counterpart teams abroad in the late 1970s. Collectively labeled *Terrorismusbekämpfung* (combating terrorism), these steps were extraordinary and unusual measures for the FRG leadership. Other leaders took some comparable steps. For example, Richard Nixon introduced the surveillance program Operation Boulder to control Arab citizens entering and traveling within the United States. But in the West German context, where policymakers were careful to frame their actions as within the rules of law, these reactions were unusual.

Another unusual step that Brandt, Genscher, and the foreign minister, Walter Scheel, took was to ask neighboring states to collaborate in the sovereignty-laden field of domestic security. They sought to expand their existing "internal security" reforms to other states and in the process further address the extraordinary problem of international terrorism. The Brandt cabinet promoted the idea that domestic/internal security and related efforts against international terrorism should become a segment of European integration.

European states had collaborated against anarchists in the early twentieth century and begun sharing information on individual offenders and on national law enforcement processes. But that collaboration had been on a smaller scale. And FRG records show no documentation that this collaboration was on Brandt, Genscher, or Scheel's minds seventy years later. For all intents and purposes, for them this endeavor was new. It signaled a willingness to surrender a measure of sovereignty in pursuit of law enforcement and intelligence collaboration with FRG neighbors. European collaboration could also offset potential criticism that FRG leaders pursued authoritarian policies. Since the EC was an exclusively European forum, it also had the advantage that the Brandt cabinet would not have to address the Arab-Israeli conflict directly. Most Arab and African states demanded consideration of Palestinian and other national liberation movements in the wake of the Munich attack. European domestic security collaboration could secure the FRG against international terrorism without addressing the complex geopolitics of the Middle East.

THE TREVI NETWORK: MULTILATERAL COLLABORATION AGAINST INTERNATIONAL TERRORISM AND CRIME

Reacting to the Munich attack, the FRG interior ministry sought to address the issue of international terrorism with multilateral domestic security collaboration and in the process created large-scale exchanges between security officials in the EC. The resulting network of bureaucratic experts, named TREVI, did not produce the Europe-wide measures and regulations against international terrorism that FRG officials envisioned. However, TREVI laid the groundwork for a range of bilateral domestic security treaties and served as an information-sharing venue for the EC states. It created the foundation for the European Union's domestic security sector. And within their contacts to one another, EC governments prioritized crime-focused responses to international terrorism even if they favored other approaches domestically. The TREVI network reinforced among participating European officials a normative understanding of international terrorism as a criminal, not a political, problem.

The FRG's leaders wasted no time in reaching out to neighboring states after the Munich attack on September 5–6, 1972. Their goal was to address the extraordinary threat of international terrorism by disseminating the FRG's preexisting "internal security" reform program. The week after Munich, FRG foreign minister Walter Scheel brought up international terrorism at an EPC meeting with other EC foreign ministers in Frascati, Italy. In this informal setting, Scheel advocated for a range of measures to prevent international terrorism across the EC. He suggested more cooperation between EC states' national border patrols, law enforcement, and intelligence agencies. He recommended exchanging information on antiterrorism measures, outstanding warrants, and notable persons to observe at borders. Scheel also proposed that the EC states compare national criminal laws to find and resolve any loopholes that international terrorists could use, especially concerning extradition.[35] Foreign Office records clarify that Scheel was hinting at the creation of a new extradition convention comparable to the International Civil Aviation Organization (ICAO)'s Hague and Montreal Conventions.[36] These recommendations all cut into states' independent control of their domestic security and law enforcement institutions.

Scheel's initiative wound up being a big idea with few results. The five other foreign ministers agreed to form EPC working groups to discuss collaboration against international terrorism. It quickly became clear, though, that the other states were not interested in opening existing law enforcement and judicial systems to outside influence. The issue of political violence was controversial and almost impossible to legislate within France, so the French delegation threatened to withdraw immediately if these antiterrorism discussions became public knowledge.[37] The groups dawdled without results.[38] On January 1, 1973, the United Kingdom, Ireland, and Denmark joined the EC in its first expansion, further distracting officials.

The West Germans encountered similar hesitancy in other international organizations. NATO officials considered their preexisting intelligence cooperation sufficient.[39] The Council of Europe, a small international organization dedicated to strengthening the rule of law in Europe, began discussing extradition procedures for international terrorists. However, these discussions progressed slowly and showed little promise for immediate action. Meanwhile, Interpol had been founded in 1923 specifically to address border-crossing violent actors.[40] However, the organization contradicted the U.S. and FRG positions, announcing that international terrorism was a political act, which Interpol did not have the jurisdiction to investigate. It would adhere to that position for the next decade.[41] The UNGA condemned individual terrorist attacks but also adopted a December 1972 resolution stating that international terrorism was a national liberation issue. In subsequent years, the UNGA maintained that only the resolution of decolonization issues and Palestine would end such attacks. This result was a disappointment for the Nixon administration and also for European governments who had counted on the United States to shape global policies on international terrorism there.

Nevertheless, Genscher remained invested in the problem of international terrorism and in finding domestic security solutions with neighboring states. In January 1973, he instructed the FRG interior ministry's Department of Public Security to work on alternative multilateral options. One of the ministry's main sections, Public Security supervised federal law enforcement and intelligence agencies and handled the prevention of crime and (now) international terrorism. Directing the initiative were the department head, Werner Smoydzin, and his deputy, Gerhard von Löwenich. Like Loy and the State Department's legal advisers, they were trained as lawyers. Both had spent their careers in government service. Von Löwenich had worked since 1957 in various courts as well as the Bavarian and federal interior ministries. In 1956 Smoydzin had entered the FRG's domestic intelligence service Bundesamt für Verfassungsschutz (BfV), the Federal Office for the Protection of the Constitution. He was its vice president from 1970 to May 1972, when he joined Public Security. Smoydzin thus had extensive experience with the RAF and with extremist violence.

In subsequent months, Public Security recommended holding a multi-lateral conference attended by all EC ministries tasked with the prevention of local and transnational politically motivated violence. The conference would be unburdened by the politics of existing organizations such as the UNGA or Interpol. It would cover "internal security" and address how to implement practical measures for the arrest and prosecution of terrorists in far more detail than earlier UNGA, ICAO, and other initiatives.[42] Smoydzin and his subordinates suggested that they could directly approach counter-part domestic security bureaucrats in other EC states to get them involved and invested in such a conference. They also secured international organi-zation endorsement. With FRG lobbying, the Council of Europe recom-mended a domestic security conference to its broad membership, though Public Security really preferred to limit participation to the EC states (with their strong prior history of cooperation and integration).[43]

Public Security's first step on the road to its envisioned conference was to negotiate bilaterally with France. The goal was to exploit a tradition of Franco-West German cooperation in European integration and undermine potential French opposition. Initially, von Löwenich planned to broach the issue with all EC states. The Foreign Office strongly recommended recruit-ing the French government's support first, however.[44] Franco-West German collaboration had been critical to establish international and supranational European structures such as the EC. Public Security officials would be able to tap into existing bureaucratic collaboration practices and experiences. In addition, the biggest obstacle to FRG plans was France's known hostil-ity to multilateral efforts against international terrorism. French officials had waffled on the U.S.-desired UNGA antiterrorism convention and dis-approved of the similar ICAO conventions, arguing that such efforts cre-ated unnecessary bureaucratic regulation and political controversy. Von Löwenich recommended to Genscher that Public Security persuade the French interior ministry to support a multilateral domestic security confer-ence first. Then, they could present the conference as a Franco-West Ger-man bilateral project to the other EC states.[45]

Though the FRG Foreign Office voiced concerns about French hostil-ity, French officials proved to be genuinely interested in limited bilateral collaboration. In October 1973, Genscher wrote France's interior minis-ter, Raymond Marcellin, emphasizing his wish to discuss domestic secu-rity at the ministerial level.[46] On February 5, 1974, Smoydzin met several high-level French security officials—Jacques Lenoir, director general of the National Police, Jacques Solier, director of the National Police's criminal investigation division, and Guy Fougier, who was responsible for legislative questions in the French interior ministry—to discuss collaboration on domestic security issues.[47]

FRG and French officials began negotiations with different policy aims and priorities. Genscher and Smoydzin's primary goal was to create binding multilateral regulations that strengthened their own internal security reforms and demonstrated the FRG's adherence to the rule of law. Such cross-border regulations would also make it easier to find, arrest, and prosecute international terrorists, whom FRG officials considered an extraordinary threat requiring unusual responses. To achieve these somewhat contradictory goals, FRG officials were willing to sacrifice a sliver of their sovereignty and undisputed control over domestic security. Oberloskamp argues that this willingness probably hailed from the FRG's sovereignty being limited, in general, by postwar agreements with the allied states, as well as a federal state structure that weakened central authority.[48] Smoydzin sought to broach as many domestic security issues as possible, including "measures to combat and prevent politically motivated violence, illegal weapons and explosives smuggling, white collar crime, improving border controls at the exterior borders of the EC member states, immigration and alien registration laws," as well as civil aviation security and drug trafficking.[49] Many of the issues from this list were already covered in other forums, such as the ICAO. To sell this initiative, the West Germans emphasized to the French that these issues touched upon EC jurisdiction and would accelerate the process of European unification—a goal both states welcomed.

In contrast, the high-level French police and interior ministry officials wanted to improve only specialized antiterrorism capacities, without delving into broad, multilateral, or binding domestic security regulations. Due to the influence of a strong centralized government, French officials were less willing to sacrifice any sovereignty than their FRG counterparts.[50] They also feared the political fallout from public awareness of the negotiations. A strong leftist movement in France opposed any overt measure against left-wing or anticolonial political agitation.[51] French policymakers did not think that they would be able to sell most antiterrorism initiatives to the French public. In addition, the French foreign ministry was not willing to risk its relatively good foreign relations with many Arab states, especially after the 1973 oil crisis. It feared that these states would accuse France of targeting Palestinian national liberation actors.[52] The West Germans realized that French officials were only interested in secret, limited, and bilateral cooperation to share information on new law enforcement technology and intelligence on terrorist suspects.[53]

The two sides compromised. They started secret bilateral negotiations but did not exclude future multilateral steps. The officials created two working groups to discuss both civil aviation security and general domestic security issues. The working group on domestic security handled such broad issues as combating crime, intelligence services' coverage of terrorism, and antiterrorism border patrols. A third group, added in the summer of 1974, covered mutual assistance in catastrophes.[54] French participants were directors or high-level officials from the French police and intelligence services, while Public Security sent specialists from its offices, supported by law enforcement officers from the Bundeskriminalamt and intelligence officers from the BfV.[55] Both sides stressed that their primary goal was to improve each respective state's domestic security by beginning to share information. A secondary goal was to create "limited extraordinary measures" against the particular threat of international terrorism.[56] The FRG side emphasized also that such exchange should form the basis for further collaboration with the other EC states.

The three bilateral working groups began meeting in the summer and fall of 1974. In this time, several high-level personnel changes occurred in both countries, but these shakeups did not affect the discussions. The high- and mid-level bureaucrats on each side continued their work. New leaders continued their predecessors' support of the negotiations, including new heads of state: FRG chancellor Helmut Schmidt and French president Valéry Giscard d'Estaing, and new interior ministers, Werner Maihofer and Michel Poniatowski. They did not discuss the field of extradition, leaving it to the two states' justice ministries (who jealously defended their jurisdiction and control over this issue).[57]

The Franco-West German negotiations focused on highly specific issues, as favored by the French, instead of the extensive coverage hoped for by the West Germans. This framing matched French perceptions that the discussions were limited and specialized. The West Germans had wanted broad discussion of topics to show that these negotiations were long-term and comprehensive. But the key working group on domestic security proved too widely delineated. Its members found their discussions inefficient. They formed three subgroups on combating crime, terrorism and intelligence, and border patrols. The police and interior ministry specialists who staffed all groups rarely discussed their work with experts from other groups or subgroups, even though their competencies overlapped. They preferred to address the same questions and even repeat the same work instead of collaborating across groups.[58]

A subsequent series of attacks in the FRG and France motivated officials to continue their work. France had not encountered significant international terrorism attacks in the early 1970s. But in September 1974, the Japanese Red Army, whose members had committed the Lod Airport massacre on behalf of the Popular Front for the Liberation of Palestine (PFLP) in 1972, initiated a hostage takeover of the French embassy in The Hague. Three Japanese Red Army members stormed the embassy, took eleven hostages, and successfully negotiated the release of a fellow Red Army member incarcerated in France. The attackers were flown to Damascus and turned themselves over to the Palestine Liberation Organization.[59] During the hostage standoff, Ilich Ramírez Sánchez, a Venezuelan national and PFLP member, threw a grenade into a Parisian café and killed two people. Ramírez would soon become known as a prolific international terrorist under the codename "Carlos the Jackal." In January 1975, Ramírez led Palestinians and twice attempted to shoot down El Al planes at Paris's Orly Airport with a bazooka. While the first attack on January 13 only lightly injured bystanders, the second attack on January 19 led to a gun battle with French police and the taking of ten hostages. Ramírez fled while the other attackers released the hostages in return for a plane to Iraq.[60] These attacks showcased that France was also a site for international terrorism committed by Palestinians and their transnational collaborators.

Meanwhile, attacks by West Germans drew FRG officials' focus from Palestinians to home-grown extremists who engaged in similar violent transnational activity. Local West German RAF members and affiliated leftists operated across state lines, sought safe haven in certain Arab countries, claimed prisoner-of-war status, and expanded their transnational networks, mirroring the Palestinian extremists that FRG officials were so worried about. In November 1974, RAF member Holger Meins died in an FRG prison as a result of a hunger strike. His death created a wave of sympathy for the RAF in leftist audiences around the world, who blamed the

FRG state for creating the repressive penal conditions that led to Meins's death. The prominent French philosopher Jean-Paul Sartre, for example, called the incarceration terms "in contrast to the Rights of Man. . . . This system is specifically against the human person and destroys it."[61] The next day, members of the 2 June Movement, a socio-revolutionary group closely affiliated with the RAF, assassinated Günter von Drenkmann, chief justice of the highest city court in West Berlin. In February 1975, the 2 June Movement kidnapped Peter Lorenz and successfully blackmailed the Schmidt cabinet into trading him for several incarcerated 2 June Movement and RAF members. The entire group disappeared into South Yemen. Within the next years, four of the five released prisoners (Verena Becker, Gabriele Kröcher-Tiedemann, Ingrid Siepmann, and Rolf Heißler) reappeared to commit violent acts in the FRG, Austria, and Lebanon.[62]

West German extremists continued to increase their cross-border activity. In April 1975, RAF members took over the FRG embassy in Stockholm, Sweden. The group called itself "Commando Holger Meins," as RAF members imitated the Palestinian habit of naming operations after martyrs. They killed two FRG diplomats and demanded the release of twenty-six incarcerated RAF members, including leaders Baader and Meinhof. Unlike the Lorenz kidnapping, the Schmidt cabinet decided not to negotiate, and the Swedish police eventually apprehended the attackers. In May 1975, the trial against RAF leaders Baader, Meinhof, and two others began. Supported by leftists at home and abroad, the defendants portrayed themselves as political dissidents, demanded prisoner-of-war status, and accused the FRG of being an authoritarian state. They claimed that they were legitimate revolutionary combatants being subjected to a political show trial, emphasizing that the trial was "an empty façade" and that "in contrast to the hidden concept of these proceedings a fascist-military trial at least has the dignity of unambiguity."[63] These events reinforced the West German leadership's desire not only to demonstrate the FRG's adherence to its rule of law but also to develop the capacity to police Palestinian international terrorists and similar West German actors.[64]

Subsequently, the Franco-West German working groups quickly generated informal bilateral agreements. In August 1975, Maihofer and Poniatowski approved an informal civil aviation agreement. FRG and French officials promised to share security-related experiences, coordinate with one another during crisis situations, and begin to harmonize airport security measures so that the same standards applied in both countries.[65] The informal agreement rarely led to practical collaboration, but it was an expression of political goodwill. In the meantime, the domestic security group's subgroup on terrorism and intelligence designated one contact person in each state's intelligence services who would share terrorism-related information.[66] This contact system facilitated the transfer of information and personal connections. The working groups continued negotiating more formal agreements, as desired by the West Germans. And due to constant FRG pressure, by August 1975 Poniatowski grudgingly agreed to extend the Franco-German collaboration into a domestic security conference with the other EC members.[67]

Ironically, it was a new EC member, the United Kingdom, that introduced the concept of multilateral domestic security collaboration in the EC, not the well-prepared FRG and France. FRG officials were surprised when the United Kingdom, which had joined the EC only in 1973, seized the lead on the delicate, sovereign-laden issue of domestic security. Lord John Harris, the British minister of state for Home Affairs, began floating the idea of a domestic security conference in the summer of 1975. His Home Office had recommended the issue as an area of interest that Harris could pursue to demonstrate British dedication to the EC, especially in light of a range of foreign and economic policies where the United Kingdom deviated from EC policy.[68] Harris's goal was to demonstrate British commitment to European integration. Meanwhile, the British government shifted its Northern Ireland policies, prioritizing the so-called strategy of Ulsterization. Named after Nixon's "Vietnamization" strategy, the goal was to reduce political violence in Northern Ireland by handling Irish separatists as normal criminals and returning authority from British military forces to local police.[69] Harris planned to discuss only the potential for future domestic security and antiterrorism collaboration. In contrast, Maihofer wanted well-prepared experts to begin content-based discussions and create immediately adoptable results right away.[70] In December 1975, British prime minister Harold Wilson suggested a 1976 conference on domestic security to the other EC heads of state, leaving details vaguely open. The others agreed to Wilson's idea.[71] Public Security officials, though surprised, embraced the idea and sought to shape the conference's content, structure, and results to their intent.

Only days later, a hostage crisis at the Organization of Petroleum Exporting Countries (OPEC) headquarters in Vienna shook European leaders and demonstrated that a range of citizens from various states, not just Palestinians, practiced international terrorism. On December 21, 1975, six people calling themselves the "Arm of the Arab Revolution" stormed the OPEC headquarters, where a meeting of member states' oil ministers was taking place. Wadie Haddad, a PFLP founding member, had planned the attack, like he had plotted much of the PFLP's campaign to export the Palestinian national liberation struggle to the Global North via hijackings and similar attacks. Haddad began operating more independently after the 1972 Munich attack, when the PFLP became more moderate (at least in public). He founded the splinter group PFLP-External Operations (PFLP-EO) to conduct further attacks. The OPEC attackers were of mixed nationalities, however, and Ramírez led the group. This attack catapulted Ramírez to celebrity status; for the next two decades he would be infamous as "Carlos the Jackal." Another attacker was Lebanese. Two other attackers were West German, and one, Gabriele Kröcher-Tiedemann, had been released as part of the Lorenz exchange. The attackers killed three people and took ninety-six hostages, including the oil ministers of Saudi Arabia, Iran, and Venezuela. They released a communiqué demanding that Arab and Third World people have a greater control over their oil reserves.[72] The Austrian government allowed them to fly out with forty-two hostages, and after several stopovers the attackers released the last hostages in exchange for twenty million dollars as well as political asylum in Algeria.[73]

The OPEC takeover highlighted that Palestinian Fedayeen were collaborating with outside actors; it showcased how transnational contemporary international terrorism was. Europeans and North Americans realized that attackers were not limited to Palestinians. "An international terrorist network is operating globally with help from radical governments," mourned the *Chicago Tribune*. "Terrorism has a future so significant that some experts believe it may have a major long-range impact on the current system of international order."[74] Additionally, Arab leaders realized that they, too, could become targets of international terrorism. In the wake of the 1973 Arab-Israeli War, leaders of the Palestinian national liberation movement wanted to influence (and potentially join) peace negotiations. They engaged in diplomatic outreach. Yasser Arafat's speech before the UNGA in November 1974 was part of this trend. Meanwhile, the most extremist Palestinian Fedayeen sought to spoil the peace process and targeted not only Israelis, Americans, and Western Europeans but also those Arab leaders who did not (in their estimation) wholeheartedly support their cause.[75] Overall, international terrorism's attackers and victims appeared to be diversifying.

By the mid-1970s, academic interest in this new, distinct, and transnational security threat was also growing. Such research was from its outset transnational as well, bringing together U.S., European, and Israeli experts. It was deeply intertwined with Global North governments' initiatives to understand and address international terrorism. Academics such as Brian Jenkins, Walter Laqueur, Yonah Alexander, and Paul Wilkinson began publishing treatises on the subject.[76] Many of the U.S. and UK terrorism researchers were former counterinsurgency experts, and their research was often funded by government, affiliated, and other institutions interested in insurgency and strategy.[77] In the United States, the interagency Working Group of the Cabinet Committee to Combat Terrorism (CCCT) was responsible for planning and managing practices against international terrorism.[78] The CCCT commissioned several studies on how to police and stop international terrorists, including the "Mass Destruction Terrorism Study" and "Facing Tomorrow's Terrorism Incidents Today."[79] Meanwhile, conferences sponsored by the U.S. State Department and by academics on international terrorism proliferated, and organizers invited security officials from the United States, the UK, and other European countries in order to hear about practitioner experiences. Participating officials were limited in what they could say due to the security clearances involved in antiterrorism efforts.[80] Yet overall, contacts between academics and engaged state officials increased. In particular, such interactions provided collaboration between U.S., European, and Israeli academics and officials.

Several officials used their academic and government contacts to facilitate exchange and advance practical knowledge on how to address international terrorism. Strong examples of state officials who bridged government service and academic outreach were Robert Kupperman, chief scientist at the U.S. Arms Control and Disarmament Agency (ACDA), and Hans-Josef Horchem, head of the state-level intelligence agency Office for the Protection of the Constitution in the FRG state of Hamburg. Both formed extensive networks with academics and foreign officials to increase their knowledge of how to prevent international terrorism through intelligence and domestic security measures. For example, in May 1976 Kupperman led a U.S. delegation to discuss measures against international terrorism with the British Home and Foreign and Commonwealth Offices, the International Atomic Energy Agency, the Austrian minister of the interior, Public Security in the FRG interior ministry, and the Munich and West Berlin police.[81] Horchem published German books and English-language articles on the RAF and right-wing extremists in the FRG.[82] He also supported conferences and training initiatives that brought academics into contact with colleagues such as Kupperman.[83] In 1978, his Hamburg superiors deployed Horchem to Spain for four months to advise the Spanish police on antiterrorism practices.[84] Overall, academic research on terrorism provided officials with new contacts to one another, though secrecy classifications provided restraints to what they could or could not discuss.

As worldwide academic and government interest in international terrorism increased following the OPEC attack, the FRG took stock of its developing bi- and multilateral antiterrorism initiatives. The domestic security conference was in the works. Public Security also began reaching out bilaterally to the foreign officials it encountered during conference preparation. But the FRG interior ministry was not the only West German ministry active in antiterrorism collaboration. Genscher was now foreign minister. He still advocated for state-to-state antiterrorism cooperation. By January 1976, his Foreign Office was planning a new global initiative against hostage-taking in the UNGA. Meanwhile, the FRG justice ministry had turned to the Council of Europe to pass a "prosecute or extradite" convention against terrorism.[85] The three FRG initiatives, led by the Foreign Office, interior ministry, and justice ministry, remained separate, with the ministries ill-informed about one another's progress. Public Security officials hoped, though, that the three initiatives could eventually reinforce one another.[86] Their expectations were not unreasonable. In the United Kingdom, for example, officials discussed the domestic security conference and the Council of Europe convention as interrelated initiatives.[87]

In the first half of 1976, mid-level officials from all EC states met several times to hash out details concerning content and procedure for the domestic security conference.[88] These officials were domestic security experts instead of diplomats. Depending on national jurisdiction over domestic security, these officials worked within the interior/home (FRG, France, the United Kingdom) or justice (Luxembourg, the Netherlands) ministries. Foreign ministries supplied supporting personnel.[89] Smoydzin again led the FRG delegation. The French delegates prioritized secrecy. They easily convinced the others to keep their work secret and informal. This approach would prevent terrorists from learning about their efforts but also allowed the delegates to avoid public reactions to their work. And cooperation would be informal, comparable to the EPC with its ad hoc working group meetings.[90] This informal working group setup allowed officials to avoid sovereignty infringements as well as binding or formal agreements that might not align with their foreign and domestic interests.

Meanwhile, the well-prepared FRG officials from Public Security dominated the content-based discussions. Smoydzin, von Löwenich, and their subordinates preferred wide-ranging, formal, and binding treaties to extend the FRG's domestic security program, and they were unhappy that the meetings would generate informal nonbinding agreements at best.[91] Nevertheless, they submitted a working paper with wide-ranging content proposals that the other experts largely adopted. FRG proposals included that officials should build information-dissemination networks concerning international terrorism (both among law enforcement and intelligence agencies), share national antiterrorism policies and experiences, conduct police exchanges, integrate police training practices, secure civil aviation, protect nuclear facilities, cooperate in cases of natural or man-made catastrophes, and aid one another in concrete terrorist cases.[92]

The EC interior ministers (and ministers with similar responsibilities) finally met for the anticipated domestic security conference on June 29, 1976, where they agreed to institute a new system of multilateral collaboration— an informal network of working groups. It was comparable to the already existing system on foreign policy, the EPC. This time, though, discussions were about domestic security. The ministers stated that they aimed to "improve their collaboration against international organized criminality, and especially against terrorism." They would "develop practical and efficient means for the solution of the problems which make a collaboration that goes across national boundaries necessary."[93] These working groups were to meet regularly. European officials quickly began referring to their new domestic security network as TREVI.[94] The origin of this name is not entirely clear. Most sources state that it was a French-language abbreviation for the network's targets: terrorism, radicalism, extremism, international violence.[95] To facilitate information-sharing, the EC states labeled all TREVI correspondence "secret."[96] Few people knew details about TREVI, as its officials did not submit information to national parliaments. The sparse press communiqués published after the rare meetings of TREVI ministers highlighted that domestic security collaboration existed without going into detail.[97] Information and accountability moved only between the participating officials and their superiors.

While TREVI officials discussed a wide range of antiterrorism and domestic security measures, they did so in highly specialized groups. FRG officials wanted to discuss many issues. As preferred by France, though, each group covered only narrowly-defined topics. The main groups were dedicated to combating terrorism (group one) and police technology and training (group two). These main groups then parceled out competencies to subgroups. Other groups lasting only one or two years covered additional issues, namely civil aviation security (group three), nuclear security (group four), protection from catastrophes (group five), and fire protection (group six). In the meantime, higher-level bureaucrats (including Smoydzin) met biannually in their own working group to finalize results that could then be forwarded to the top level, the ministers, for adoption.

These specialized working groups brought together equally specialized bureaucrats. Mid-level experts from interior, justice, intelligence, and law enforcement institutions staffed them. Most delegates were highly qualified specialists in their specific fields.[98] Institutional and national boundaries barred them from one another. In TREVI, these bureaucrats had opportunities to exchange information with foreign counterparts. Ministers and high-level officials also maintained increased contact.[99] TREVI became an informal institution in which mid-level bureaucrats shared information on domestic security. In this space, officials could focus on their areas of expertise, discuss their practices against violent actors, and scope out foreign approaches.

Group one, on combating terrorism, generated formal and informal intelligence-sharing practices. The group met twice a year until 1980. Law enforcement and intelligence officers dominated the delegate lists. Four delegations were composed only of such officials (Ireland, Luxembourg, Italy, Denmark), and in six out of nine cases (including France and the Netherlands), these officials also led their respective national delegations.[100] As a regular and predictable meeting location, group one became a crucial spot for intelligence officers to share information face-to-face.[101] They also agreed to institute so-called "connection offices," situated in each state's intelligence services, to facilitate information-sharing on terrorist activity with one another.[102] Though the connection offices had severe time-lag issues, they became active during crises. For example, when the Italian Red Brigades kidnapped and later murdered former Italian prime minister Aldo Moro, FRG officials kept in touch and offered computer assistance to find the kidnappers.[103] Finally, group one hosted officials who had handled specific crises, including the RAF's Stockholm embassy takeover in April 1975. Also featured were British officials who had negotiated during the Balcombe Street siege in December 1975—a hostage standoff in London in which four IRA members took two civilians hostage for six days. These officials conducted seminars in which they walked the delegates through their decision-making processes.[104] Group one became an important information-sharing venue for antiterrorism intelligence.

Group one officials also discussed national policies and general practices related to international terrorism and political violence. Vast discrepancies existed, and delegates were keenly interested in their counterparts' approaches. FRG officials in particular valued these exchanges, arguing that they highlighted areas of mutual compatibility where future bilateral agreements might be possible. Topics under discussion included border control practices and potential cooperation at borders, the stationing of police observers in foreign law enforcement agencies, and protection mechanisms for visiting dignitaries. In 1978, group one took over civil aviation and nuclear security when groups three and four shut down. Later, delegates broached issues such as the media's handling of terrorist incidents and terrorists' use of non-EC diplomatic passports. By 1982, group one delegates considered their discussions on international terrorism comprehensively exhausted. For six years, they had shared practical-focused knowledge, intelligence, and experiences concerning international terrorism.

Meanwhile, delegates in group two (on domestic security in general) focused on police technologies and innovation. Participants in this group were highly specialized technical experts. There were subgroups on telecommunications, computer systems, law enforcement technology, equipment, weapons and explosives trade, and finally, training and professional development.[105] For example, group two experts organized training courses for foreign police officers at one another's police academies. They discussed fingerprinting machines and radio signaling. And they shared information on the latest computer systems as well as the data mining for suspects that one could achieve with them. The FRG's Bundeskriminalamt was a path-breaking leader in computer-based investigative methods and law enforcement data mining in the 1970s. FRG officials pushed the other TREVI delegations to develop their computer capacities. In addition, the TREVI states began sharing electronic data on terrorist suspects, notwithstanding the national privacy laws limiting this transfer.[106] The technology- and training-focused collaboration in group two continued throughout the 1980s.

Alongside these multilateral discussions, FRG officials used the contacts they gained in the lead-up to and during TREVI to foster bilateral collaboration with their neighbors. The Franco-West German working groups active since 1974 completed several agreements. On February 3, 1977, the two states signed two formal bilateral treaties. One pledged mutual assistance in cases of catastrophes. The other required border patrol units to collaborate if the other side sought criminals in Franco-West German border regions. In November 1977, France and the FRG signed a further protocol that enabled police officials to briefly pursue a terrorist into the other state's territory. In March 1978, Maihofer and new French interior minister Christian Bonnett agreed on shared principles to combat illegal immigration, pledging that they would coordinate border-screening measures and share information on entering or exiting citizens of other states.[107]

Similar relations developed between the FRG and Italy in 1976. By the late 1970s, political violence was still rising in Italy, and Italian authorities shifted from liberalizing to harsh reforms. Italian officials used the condemnatory term *terrorism* more frequently to describe leftist extremists, introduced new antiterrorism laws, upgraded police competencies, and reformed the legal system to ease the prosecution of violent actors.[108] Bilateral contact helped both Italy and the FRG strengthen domestic antiterrorism reforms. The two states agreed to institute regular working groups to collaborate on domestic security. In October 1976, Italy and the FRG agreed on fixed procedures to share information on terrorist suspects. In February 1977, the two adopted principles for collaboration in civil aviation security practices.[109] Meanwhile, British Home Office officials conducted bilateral discussions with France and with the FRG every now and again from 1975 onward to learn about these states' best practices in domestic security and brainstorm future efforts.[110]

Overall, the TREVI working groups led to the large-scale adoption of domestic security as an aspect of European integration. They facilitated significant exchange among European security officials, giving them access to one another's time and company in secure environments in unprecedented form. And terrorism attacks in Western Europe began dropping overall, going from a high point of 1,020 in 1979 to less than 600 a year for the rest of the 1980s.[111] After 1980, TREVI delegates decided that they had covered international terrorism exhaustively. The EC states reorganized the TREVI groups and emphasized new issues, including the illegal drug trade and organized crime. Adapting to states' interests, the TREVI network continued to share domestic security information, practices, and experiences until the foundation of the European Union with the Maastrich Treaty in 1992. Maastrich dissolved TREVI but integrated domestic security as a formal component of the European Union with permanently dedicated officials and resources. Renamed Justice and Home Affairs, domestic security became one of the three major pillars of collaboration within the European Union. Its subordinate institutions actively promoted multilateral counterterrorism practices after September 11, 2001.[112] TREVI thus laid the foundations for formalized domestic security collaboration within the European Union.

Through TREVI, European security officials networked and built contacts to discuss the practical steps associated with tracking and capturing terrorists. This network was staffed with government-employed specialists. Their interaction with foreign counterparts amplified participants' focus on the mechanisms of terrorism instead of its social or political context. The national representatives in TREVI were interior, justice, intelligence, and law enforcement officials. They were tasked with preventing terrorist attacks and with arresting terrorists after any attack. They discussed measures to efficiently facilitate their duties. Issues such as the Arab-Israel conflict, decolonization, imperialism, national liberation, and other political considerations never made the TREVI agenda. Extremists sought to draw attention to their political grievances, and the mainstream media debate on international terrorism dove into its social and political origins. But these media reports did not sway TREVI experts or shape their security-clearance level discussions. In fact, attacks and subsequent media output were more likely to alienate officials from both the attackers and a media that they perceived as overreporting during concrete crises.[113] In turn, officials' recommendations and policy suggestions to their superiors focused on ways to capture international terrorists. European Community states held differing antiterrorism policies at home, but in their relations to one another they emphasized the policing of international terrorism over any political context. In turn, when European policymakers, ministers, and heads of state met, they habitually and normatively discussed international terrorism as a mutual domestic security problem with tactical, not political, emphasis.

THE PROLIFERATION OF ANTITERRORISM TACTICAL UNITS DURING THE 1970S

A growing number of tactical units during the 1970s also reinforced militarized collaboration among security experts and policymakers against international terrorism. As high-profile attacks continued into the 1970s, more and more states began developing tactical units as a specific tool to resolve terrorist crises. The term *tactical unit* refers to a small team of highly trained officers who are trained to deploy in covert action and other situations outside of the scope of normal military or law enforcement settings. These units utilize military skills such as sniping and armed breaches. Yet they specialize in antiterrorism scenarios that officials oftentimes do not perceive as warfare or insurgent situations. Many tactical units are military Special Forces teams. Others are located within law enforcement. Successful missions, such as at Entebbe and Mogadishu, convinced the public and state officials in the Global North of their efficacy. They could resolve crises and rescue hostages with low casualty rates. States frequently relied on exchanges with foreign experts to build their own units and learn about training, gear, and tactics. And countries with training capacities for tactical units, both in the military and law enforcement, began hosting and sharing information on antiterrorism practices and technology with foreign officers in ways that mirrored military and police exchanges. The United Kingdom, United States, and the FRG were key in these exchanges.

During the 1970s, the number of tactical units dedicated to fight international terrorism rose rapidly around the world. While almost no states had such units in 1970, by the 1980s most Global North states fielded at least one, if not several. These units facilitated the use of military technology and tactics against international terrorists, even as they enabled policymakers to avoid deploying their regular armies against nonstate extremists. The tactical units were early examples of the militarization of antiterrorism responses.

These tactical units blended military practices with law enforcement competencies in ways strongly reminiscent of colonial policing and post-colonial counterinsurgent practices; at the same time, they ignored the political context of international terrorism and their own origins. They normalized this amalgamation as a domestic security option throughout the Global North. These tactical units were based on Special Forces teams such as the British SAS—developed to counter insurgents and control local populations in decolonizing British colonies. In the 1970s, however, policy-makers discussed these Special Forces skills in covert action, hostage nego-tiation, and explosives use as antiterrorist skills. This label hid the imperial and oftentimes counterinsurgent origins of these skills and teams. Military and law enforcement officers subsequently cooperated on such antiterror-ism skills across national, jurisdictional, and institutional lines. Officers frequently traveled to visit other units to learn how they functioned. States with established Special Forces units sent trainers abroad and made space for foreign officers in national training schools and seminars. This collabo-ration mirrored various other military exchanges between allied countries such as the NATO bloc. Due to this networking, both law enforcement and military personnel developed a shared set of terminology, practices, and tactics associated with international terrorism that hailed from colonial contexts and yet ignored that history.

When discussing their units, state officials prioritized the concrete details of an attack over political context. Policymakers with access to such units were able to avoid giving into international terrorists' demands. State officials stressed the units' successes and tactical approaches. Such units allowed officials to focus on the concrete details of an attack without having to emphasize or publicize the background of the attackers. The use of such units thus fed into establishing norms that international terrorists should be judged by their criminal actions and not by their political grievances.

The antiterrorism tactical units of the 1970s had their origins in ear-lier military Special Forces teams. During World War II, units such as the British SAS regiment developed to conduct secret missions in German-controlled areas. Later, British and French armed forces reconstituted such units and employed them in decolonizing conflicts in the 1950s and 1960s, including in Algeria, Malaysia, and Kenya.[114] Such units countered leftist and anticolonial insurgencies by policing populations, gathering intelli-gence, seizing targets of value, and enforcing martial law. Oftentimes civil and military institutions amalgamated in contested areas.[115] Skills practiced by such units included weapons and explosives expertise, operating in small teams, and deployment from air- and seaborne vehicles.

Special Forces units served in contested former colonies throughout the 1960s. American armed forces employed them in Vietnam. The fledgling Israeli state created a wide range of Special Forces units within its armed forces and intelligence services to operate against Palestinian guerillas and hostile neighboring Arab states.[116] In the late 1960s, the British government also deployed SAS within Northern Ireland.

In 1972, FRG leaders created a comparable tactical unit specifically to counter international terrorism. The contemporary FRG state had no institutional experience in anti-insurgent practices, and its efforts adopted Special Forces skills from Israeli and British teams while at the same time disassociating such practices from their colonial and anti-insurgent context. West German law enforcement held a federalized structure and was organized mainly at the state, not federal, level. Local Bavarian authorities and police were unprepared for the 1972 Munich Olympic Games attack, however. They made numerous errors, of which the most egregious were giving the media almost unrestricted access and engaging in an ill-planned last-minute rescue effort that led to the death of the Israeli hostages.[117] After this tragic end, the Brandt cabinet decided that it needed a specially trained team, situated at the federal level, which could be rapidly deployed to handle such situations. How to create such a team would be tricky. Other countries' Special Forces units were located within their armed forces. Yet the Brandt cabinet considered international terrorism a domestic security issue. The FRG constitution did now allow any blend of military and law enforcement competencies.[118] In addition, the FRG constitution forbid its armed forces from deploying within the FRG except in very rare declared cases of natural disaster or national emergency. A tactical unit dedicated to fight international terrorism would thus need to be nested within law enforcement. It could not be part of the armed forces, like in the United Kingdom.

Leaders found a compromise that blended a law enforcement venue with military tactics and legal status. On September 26, 1972, Hans-Dietrich Genscher announced the creation of a tactical unit within the border police. This agency had authority to operate throughout the FRG. Additionally, it held the legal status of military combatant, and would be able to utilize military tactics and equipment. Yet it was not part of the FRG armed forces. Genscher envisioned that the unit, named Grenzschutzgruppe 9 (Border Security Group 9, GSG 9) would include highly trained specialists, including "snipers, weapons and explosives experts, chemical and electric technicians, as well as communications and other technical specialists."[119] Since FRG police and armed forces held strictly separate roles, this team bridged institutional capacities between them in novel ways. Like earlier Special Forces units in British and French counterinsurgency programs, the GSG 9 blended military tactics with (ostensibly) civilian duties.

To develop the necessary skills, the unit relied on Israeli trainers at its outset. FRG armed forces had no comparable units or collated training. To lead his new tactical unit, Genscher picked Colonel Ulrich Wegener. Wegener entered the police service in 1952 and joined the FRG border police in 1958. By the time of the Munich attacks, he was the border police's liaison officer in the interior ministry. Genscher sent Wegener to participate in an Israeli armed forces training course titled "Combatting Arab Terrorists Through Special Forces Units." The course, which ran from October 30 to November 12, 1972, covered a broad range of skills, including information on Palestinian Fedayeen organizations' hierarchy, training, and actions, the deployment of Special Forces against terrorist bases and in hijacking scenarios, the protection of key persons and potential target locations, conducting manhunts, and the safe handling of explosive materials.[120] In contrast to the FRG, the Israeli training blended law enforcement, intelligence, and military areas, covering issues such as manhunts (law enforcement), intelligence-gathering (intelligence services), and commando deployment (armed forces). The GSG 9 adopted such skills. From its readiness for service in April 1973 onward, the GSG 9 combined tactics and skills usually distinct within the FRG security institutions.

Other European states also created similar units to improve their ability to respond to large-scale international terrorism attacks after Munich. In several states, gendarmeries (armed forces units with law enforcement duties) already combined military status with law enforcement work. Antiterrorism tactical units fit neatly into them. Belgium formed a gendarmerie unit named "Group Diane" in 1972 specifically against terrorism.[121] The Netherlands followed in January 1973 with a unit in the Dutch Marine Corps, the Bijzondere Bijstandseenheid Mariniers.[122] From 1974 onward, Italy experimented with small antiterrorism units in the national police and the carabineri, a gendarmerie police branch of the armed forces, but quickly reintegrated the members of these units into regular police structures.[123] In 1974, the French national gendarmerie, an armed forces police branch responsible for security in rural areas, founded its own tactical unit, the Groupe d'intervention de la Gendarmerie nationale.[124] That year, the Soviet Union created an antiterrorism Special Forces team named Spetsgruppa "A," or Alpha Group, within its intelligence service Komitet Gosudarstvennoy Bezopasnosti (KGB).[125] After a hostage standoff, botched rescue, and the massacre of twenty-one schoolchildren in the Israeli town of Ma'alot in May 1974, Israeli authorities created Yeḥida Merkazit Meyuḥedet (Yamam), or Centralized Special Unit. This tactical unit was located in the border police and specifically trained to prevent international terrorism attacks within Israel (Israeli military Special Forces teams [for example, Sayeret Matkal, the Special Reconnaissance Team of the General Staff] generally specialized in foreign operations). Like the GSG 9, these tactical units combined armed forces and combatant status with domestic security and law enforcement duties. They introduced to law enforcement more specialized violent tools and tactics.

The GSG 9 collaborated with such units to increase one another's necessary skills and training. So did the British armed forces. Having lost most of the British colonial holdings, in the 1970s British policing efforts focused inward on Northern Irish separatists such as the IRA. Meanwhile, SAS officials participated in the United Kingdom Military Training Assistance Scheme that delivered military training to former colonies and Commonwealth states. In the mid-1970s, the British cabinet discussed whether or not to deploy the SAS abroad in international terrorism incidents.[126] Though cabinet officials considered this option unlikely, by 1975 the SAS was interacting more with European law enforcement, gendarmerie, and military counterparts also responsible for international terrorism and political violence. In May 1975, Wegener participated in an antiterrorism conference hosted by the Royal Army and the British secret service, alongside military and law enforcement personnel from the United Kingdom, the FRG, the United States, Canada, Barbados, Italy, the Netherlands, Norway, Sweden, Denmark, and Switzerland.[127] In late 1975, the GSG 9 sent officers to the Netherlands to advise the Royal Netherlands Marechaussee, a Dutch armed forces gendarmerie with both military and civil police duties, on how to resolve two hostage situations.[128] Both sides benefited from the other's experience.

In 1976 and 1977, many more states became aware of the existence and utility of such antiterrorist tactical units. During the Entebbe and Mogadishu hijacking crises, Israeli and FRG units garnered spectacular media attention by showcasing their skill sets as well as their effectiveness at ending Palestinian-induced crises outside of their respective states. While Israel had deployed tactical units to rescue hijacked aircraft before, the media focus and level of attention on the teams in these crises was new.

The Entebbe operation was the first high-profile rescue and became an international media spectacle. On June 27, 1976, two Palestinians and two West Germans hijacked Air France Flight 139 from Tel Aviv to Paris, taking 260 hostages. Wadie Haddad again planned this attack. Two of the hijackers were members of his PFLP-EO. The other two were West German citizens and founding members of the Revolutionary Cells, a socio-revolutionary group with close ties to the RAF and 2 June Movement. The hijackers flew the plane to Entebbe, Uganda, where Ugandan president Idi Amin ordered his armed forces to guard the terminal and hostages. A staunch supporter of Palestinian national liberation, Amin spent the following days attempting to persuade Israel and France to give in to the hijackers' demands, pay ransom, and free fifty-three incarcerated Palestinians and their allies—including RAF and 2 June Movement members as well as Kōzō Okamoto, the only surviving attacker from the Lod Airport massacre. The hijackers released over a hundred hostages gradually but refused to let go of 106 Israeli citizens, ostensibly Jewish passengers, and the plane's staff. On July 4, 1976, the Israeli Special Forces unit Sayeret Matkal stormed the Entebbe Airport building, rescuing the hostages in the airport.[129] Three hostages, all the hostage-takers, and twenty Ugandan soldiers died, and an elderly hostage receiving treatment in a nearby hospital was murdered after the raid. On the Israeli side, the only casualty was the team's commander, Lieutenant Colonel Yonatan Netanyahu. His family, especially younger brother Benjamin Netanyahu, became very active in ensuring his legacy and promoting Special Forces and military responses to international terrorism. The operation brought global media attention.

Coverage of the rescue, hostages, and Sayeret Matkal was generally triumphant despite involving troublesome foreign policy implications. Western media reports of the Entebbe raid presumed that the attackers were not politically legitimate actors, that they had illegally targeted civilians, and that the unusual threat to the civilians' lives warranted this military response. In contrast, Amin protested that Israel had violated Ugandan sovereign territory in an act of war.[130] The Organization of African Unity, an international organization to foster integration and oppose imperialism on the African continent, gave him significant backing in the UNGA and Security Council.[131] Amin undermined his position, however, with his assistance of the hijackers, as well as the subsequent murder of Dora Bloch, the remaining elderly hostage, and of Kenyan citizens in Uganda in retaliation for Kenya's assistance to Israel during preparations for the raid. These acts violated the protections for civilians set up by the Geneva Conventions and other instruments of international law. Most Global North leaders and the mainstream media argued that the legality of the situation was complicated but that Israel had done what was needed to rescue kidnapped civilians. They celebrated the Israeli raid as a unique rescue operation.[132]

Besides drawing global attention, the Entebbe operation strengthened the collaboration between Western antiterrorism officers. The Schmidt cabinet feared that it would soon suffer worldwide accusations that FRG citizens were anti-Semitic fascists. Two hijackers at Entebbe were West German and media reports quickly spread that one, Wilfried Böse, had sorted the hostages into Israeli and non-Israeli citizens, bringing to mind the sorting of Jews during the Holocaust.[133] As a result of the Entebbe hijacking and the 1975 Stockholm embassy takeover, the Schmidt cabinet committed itself (privately) to a tough, no-negotiations position in future crises involving local and foreign terrorists.[134] To prepare for such eventualities, Schmidt and Maihofer supported the GSG 9's efforts to increase its skills and connections. Most notably, ties to the British armed forces intensified. During the Entebbe crisis, Wegener had joined British Special Forces officers in at an officer's club near Entebbe's airport to observe the situation.[135] In the following year, the number of exchanges between British and FRG institutions rose, with at least three visits between SAS, GSG9, and officials in the FRG interior ministry and the British Home Office. The officials exchanged information on training, tactics, equipment, and strategies, covering the entire scope of antiterrorism tactical activities.[136] Meanwhile, the SAS delivered tear gas and other equipment to the Netherlands and trained Dutch staff on its use.[137] The GSG 9 met with U.S. officials when Robert Kupperman brought over William Meinke and Jay Cochran, assistant directors at the FBI, to meet with various Israeli, British, and West

German police and military experts to discuss antiterrorism technology in January 1977.[138]

The Schmidt cabinet's support paid off when the GSG 9 successfully ended a hijacking in Mogadishu in October 1977 and undercut both RAF and PFLP-EO aims. From spring to fall of 1977, the RAF, 2 June Movement, and Revolutionary Cells conducted a wave of terrorist attacks throughout the FRG in an attempt to coerce the release of imprisoned RAF leaders. Arrested in 1972, Andreas Baader and three other RAF members were placed on trial in the FRG from 1975 to 1977 for multiple counts of murder, attempted murder, homicide, membership in a criminal organization, and violations of multiple laws concerning the regulation of guns and explosives.[139] The trial ended with guilty convictions in May 1977, and all defendants received long prison sentences in a specially constructed high-security incarceration facility at Stammheim. In turn, RAF members and their allies attempted to coerce the Schmidt cabinet into releasing the prisoners. From the spring to fall of 1977, they assassinated Siegfried Buback, the FRG attorney general, killed a prominent banker, Jürgen Ponto, in a botched kidnapping, and kidnapped the head of the Confederation of German Employers' Associations, Hanns Martin Schleyer. Buback's assassin was in all likelihood Verena Becker, who had been released as part of the Lorenz exchange. The 1977 attacks generated such public fear for the stability of FRG state and democratic institutions that contemporaries called the period the "German Autumn."[140]

Showcasing the transnational connections between Palestinian and West German extremists, Haddad's PFLP-EO supported the RAF by targeting Lufthansa, the FRG's national airline. On October 13, 1977, four PFLP-EO members hijacked Lufthansa Flight 181 from Mallorca to Frankfurt, taking ninety-one crew members and passengers hostage. The hijackers flew the aircraft around the Mediterranean and Middle East before landing in Mogadishu, Somalia. A plane carrying a GSG 9 team and two SAS observers trailed them clandestinely.[141] Unlike the Israelis at Entebbe, Helmut Schmidt negotiated permission to operate on Somali territory from President Siad Barre (in return for aid delivered at a later date).[142] Led by Wegener, the GSG 9 team seized the plane on October 18, 1977. The team killed three of the four hijackers without further casualties from hostages or rescuers.[143] Hearing of the operation, Baader and the other incarcerated RAF leaders at

FIGURE 3.2. Reception for the GSG9 and Lufthansa crew, October 1977.
West German chancellor Helmut Schmidt congratulates GSG9 commander Ulrich Wegener, who led the successful assault to free a hijacked Lufthansa airplane in Mogadishu, Somalia. Bundesarchiv (German Federal Archives), Photo B 145 Bild-00006950 / Engelbert Reineke.

Stammheim committed suicide and Schleyer's kidnappers murdered him. The three events effectively ended the "German Autumn."

The GSG 9 succeeded not only in resolving the hijacking but also in strengthening the FRG state narrative that international terrorism was primarily an illegitimate tactic to commit violence—without respectable political dimensions. Media outlets around the world celebrated the GSG 9 as well as the FRG government. In statements echoed by journalists, Schmidt and others emphasized that the FRG had defended its rule of law, restored its citizens from violence, and refused to cater to illegitimate political actors' demands. The media gushed that "Germans can be strong and humane."[144] Similar congratulations reached FRG diplomats in the United Nations and at the Conference on Security and Cooperation in Europe.[145] Meanwhile, media reports focused on play-by-play tactical narratives of the rescue and barely explored the attackers' political motivations or grievances. What was important was that they had kidnapped civilians and been stopped by means that did not violate FRG domestic law or Somali sovereignty. Since the FRG had negotiated with Barre first and received his permission to act on Somali soil, the operation was far less controversial than at Entebbe. Overall, the FRG leadership's strategy to pursue unusual tactical options against international terrorism seemed to be working without causing mainstream domestic or foreign audiences to doubt the FRG rule of law.

The Mogadishu operation generated great interest around the world in the GSG 9, and the FRG received a flood of inquiries from the media and other governments. The interior ministry wanted to keep terrorists unaware of its capacities and tactics and did not collaborate with media outlets.[146] However, it had no compunction about sharing information with allied governments. In the weeks after October 18, many of the officials who had been in prior contact with the GSG 9 visited to hear about the tactics and equipment used in the operation. On November 4, 1977, a British delegation from the Ministry of Defense, Home Office, Foreign and Commonwealth Office, the Metropolitan Police, the Security Service, and SAS met a GSG 9 representative at the FRG interior ministry. A Dutch delegation of foreign and justice ministry officials and police officers followed in late November.[147] An American delegation visited Schmidt's chancellery to hear from Wegener on December 8. It included William Odom, military assistant to Zbigniew Brzezinski, the national security adviser, a range of armed forces representatives, and public intellectuals such as the conservative William F. Buckley.[148] By January 1978, further inquiries arrived from many other countries. They asked for assistance to create their own antiterrorist tactical units and requested to collaborate with the GSG 9.[149] Governments around the world became interested in the option of a tactical unit dedicated to terrorism crises.

Units such as the GSG 9 and SAS fulfilled that interest. In 1978, their contact network grew exponentially. As shown by the Entebbe and Mogadishu operations, tactical units enabled policymakers to respond to international terrorists with a fast and high-success option that did not include sensitive political considerations or sacrifices. States across the globe sought to emulate this model, and they requested aid from established units to develop know-how and skills. The FRG records on GSG 9 provide a window onto the network of developing tactical units around the world. The records show a slew of informational requests from other European states and countries throughout North and Latin America, Africa, and Asia. These requests were more than the GSG 9, with a total of about four hundred personnel, could handle.[150] A smaller set of records from the British Foreign and Commonwealth Office shows that SAS developed a similar network in this time.

The GSG 9's close ties to British security forces, especially the SAS, deepened. In January 1978, the British Cabinet approved the potential use of the SAS in international terrorism incidents abroad.[151] Officers from each unit increased the frequency of their visits.[152] Gradually, the exchanges became more about training and tactical collaboration than about simple transfers of information. In the spring of 1979, GSG 9 and SAS began conducting joint training exercises.[153] By 1980, the exchange of trainers was common. GSG 9 sent officers to learn about bomb defusing from the British army.[154] Scotland Yard officials took sniper and munitions courses from GSG 9.[155] In May 1981, GSG 9 sent officers to train SAS on how to storm a Boeing 747—the largest commercial passenger aircraft available at the time.[156] Overall, this collaboration led to a diffusion of skills and contacts between the British army, police, and GSG 9.

Law enforcement and military agencies in the United States became crucial collaborators as well. Strong relations developed between U.S. and FRG specialists, generating a cooperative network between the U.S. army, the FBI and regional police agencies, and the GSG 9. These close relations started with information exchanges after the Mogadishu operation. Wegener received invitations to speak on Mogadishu from the U.S. Army War College as well as the FBI, and he traveled to the FBI training site in Quantico in April 1978.[157] As previously stated, U.S. officials also visited the GSG 9 in January and December 1977.

Contacts quickly deepened, and soon U.S. and FRG officers exchanged skill training. U.S. colonel Charles Beckwith, commandant of the U.S. Army Special Warfare School in Fort Bragg, North Carolina, had been working to create a Special Forces unit based on the SAS. He founded the 1st Special Forces Operational Detachment-Delta, often abbreviated as Delta Force, on November 17, 1977. Since Beckwith wanted Delta Force to be capable of resolving hostage situations, the U.S. army sought aid from the GSG 9. Wegener spent several weeks in Fort Bragg in July 1978 and November 1979, engaging in what his reports label "training activities."[158] In addition, GSG 9 sent shooting and explosives experts, as well as technical specialists, to Fort Bragg, and hosted Delta Force members at its FRG headquarters.[159] By 1979, FRG-U.S. collaboration had evolved to the point where Wegener was able to personally meet and discuss counterterrorism strategies with the directors of the CIA and FBI as well as senior representatives from the the Defense Intelligence Agency and the State Department's Office for Counterterrorism.[160] In December 1979, GSG 9 participated in joint Special Forces training exercises with the U.S. Army in the FRG.[161] Further invitations and joint training exercises followed, focusing on both "counterguerrilla" and "counterterrorism" scenarios.[162] The FBI and U.S. law enforcement also developed ties to GSG 9. The FBI extended frequent invitations for GSG 9 officers to participate in workshops at Quantico. GSG 9 members partook in a counterterrorism course in 1979 and a hostage negotiations course in 1981.[163] Representatives also had contact with U.S. state and city police agencies such as the Port Authority of New York.[164] By the early 1980s, the GSG 9 thus had deep links to not only SAS but also the U.S. law enforcement, intelligence, and military communities.

Meanwhile, the FRG's neighboring states adopted the model of a hybrid law enforcement and military antiterrorist tactical unit. In December 1977, Switzerland, whose police force was organized on the canton level, decided to institute a national antiterrorism police unit. GSG 9 had worked with the canton-level police, and the FRG interior ministry promised to continue the collaboration.[165] On January 1, 1978, the Austrian interior ministry elevated a previously existing border security police unit into a federal antiterrorism tactical unit, the Gendarmerieeinsatzkommando. It maintained working contacts to the GSG 9. This unit quickly garnered the nickname "Cobra," from a popular TV crime series.[166] After the kidnapping and murder of Aldo Moro in the spring of 1978, the Italian government founded two tactical units. The Nucleo Operativo Centrale di Sicurrezza was located in the national police, while the Gruppo d'Intervento Speciale was housed in the carabineri, an armed forces branch tasked with police duties. Both units were successfully deployed in domestic Italian terrorist crises in the early 1980s.[167] After 1977, a range of new contacts developed between tactical units from North America, the EC states, and the German-speaking Austria and Switzerland. This network disseminated tactical "antiterrorism" skills and accelerated European law enforcement's use of militarized practices and equipment.

The FRG interior ministry also used the GSG 9 to strengthen domestic security and antiterrorism collaboration with friendly, but not necessarily closely allied, states in Europe and around the world. In January 1978, Singapore offered the FRG a "special collaboration" against international terrorism. The details of this proposal are not yet accessible, but it was generous enough to convince the FRG to open communication lines.[168] In September 1978, the FRG struck a deal with Saudi Arabia, bolstering its relations to the major petroleum exporter. Five GSG 9 officers traveled to Saudi Arabia and trained thirty Saudi police officers in tactical antiterrorism skills. These Saudi officers could in turn teach these skills within the Saudi security agencies.[169] In Europe, the EC states in the late 1970s gradually improved their relations to Spain and Portugal. Run as authoritarian states since World War II, these two countries transitioned to new elected governments and began overcoming their pariah status within European integration in the mid to late 1970s. As part of this process, the FRG interior ministry agreed to share information regarding GSG 9 strategies and new computer technologies with Spain.[170] Horchem's visit was also part of the exchange. The Spanish government, meanwhile, created two antiterrorism tactical units. The Unidad Especial de Intervención was instituted within the Civil Guard, an armed forces gendarmerie, on June 3, 1978. The Grupo Especial de Operaciones within the National Police Corps began operating in January 1979. Similar exchanges occurred between the FRG and Portugal in early 1979.[171] In 1982, Portugal completed the organization of a police tactical unit, the Grupo de Operações Especiais. The tactical antiterrorism network thus stretched beyond its U.S. and EC core.

Since the FRG interior ministry considered international terrorism a domestic security issue instead of a counterinsurgency, foreign policy, or war-related problem, it was even (briefly) willing to cooperate with Cold War rivals, including the Soviet Union and Romania, to share a small amount of information on the GSG 9. In May 1979, newly instated FRG interior minister Gerhard Baum traveled to the Soviet Union to discuss security measures for the 1980 Moscow Olympic Games with Nikolai Shchelokov, the minister of Internal Affairs, who asked about the GSG 9 and especially its equipment.[172] After heated discussions between interior ministry bureaucrats, Bundeskriminalamt officials, and GSG 9 officers, the interior ministry decided to pass on nondetailed training guidelines, a schematic of the GSG 9's organization, clothing details, and manufacturing contacts. Soviet officials asked about a laser gun used by GSG 9, but since this weapon was a U.S. model, no information was transmitted.[173] That same month, a Romanian delegation visited the FRG interior ministry and Bundeskriminalamt to discuss potential antiterrorism collaboration. The Romanian officials were disappointed by the paltry information they learned from GSG 9, and few further contacts ensued.[174] However, the European (and U.S.) branding of terrorism as a criminal and domestic security issue allowed security officers from the FRG, Soviet Union, and Romania to briefly set aside Cold War differences to discuss a common threat—international terrorism.

Since the FRG interior ministry justified the GSG 9's existence and blend of military with law enforcement capacities by emphasizing that it was a tool to uphold the rule of law, it was wary of undermining this justification by collaborating with states that had especially poor civil and human rights records. It frequently turned down requests for training or information from non-European states that egregiously violated their citizens' civil liberties or ones where the interior ministry feared that the training would be applied in foreign interventions contrary to FRG interests. Collaboration requests turned down included those from states such as Zambia, Cameroon, Egypt, Lebanon, Pakistan, Afghanistan, Thailand, Columbia, and Uruguay.[175]

British authorities had slightly different priorities when scheduling SAS collaboration. Since the SAS was a military unit, they were absolutely unwilling to discuss it with the Soviet Union or similar states. Yet Defense, Home, and Foreign and Commonwealth officials had no issues with sending the SAS to states willing to pay for training or bringing officers from these states to the United Kingdom. Due to its long history and earlier colonial and anti-insurgent focus, the SAS had significant experience with training foreign officers. All EC states except for Ireland sent officers to the SAS center at Hereford. Contacts with the United States, Canada, and Australia intensified. The SAS also fielded questions from officials from such politically diverse places as Portugal, Brazil, Argentina, Greece, Israel, and Iran.[176] From 1978 to 1980, SAS training visits included Saudi Arabia, Kuwait, Jordan, and Bahrain.[177] British officials appear to have viewed Special Forces training as a sellable service more than their FRG counterparts did. A 1980 report on SAS training for Saudi Arabia lists France and the FRG as competitors in offering this service.[178] The Foreign and Commonwealth Office even considered offering tactical antiterrorism training as a new aid option in foreign relations but scrapped the plan due to austerity cuts in the late 1970s.[179] Yet overall, SAS trainers also extended their contact network significantly.

During the mid to late 1970s, an array of tactical units developed to address international terrorism. These units blended police and military practices to most efficiently resolve potential crises and undermine transnationally operating extremists. They ignored most political dimensions of international terrorism. Instead, they focused on it as a tactic to commit violence—one that could be successfully addressed through their hybrid military and law enforcement responses. Due to the high security clearance surrounding such units, the exact number of deployments is unknown. But when they fulfilled high-profile rescues, such as at Entebbe and Mogadishu, policymakers touted these achievements (without going into detail on the tactics themselves). Such units became attractive to Global North leaders as a fast and effective means to resolve terrorism crises.

The creation of such units was marked by international collaboration from the outset. Representatives from these units frequently observed one another's setup, training, and equipment, seeking information on how to organize and improve their own group. Relations between security institutions in the Global North states, especially the UK, United States, and the FRG, became strong enough that these states exchanged trainers and invited foreign officials to participate in domestic training seminars. For example, the GSG 9 trained over one hundred foreign officers in 1979 and 1980.[180]

Throughout this process, the FRG and other states normalized the use of small teams with military tactics and gear for ostensibly nonmilitary situations. Western states cultivated such units, at times in law enforcement, at times in military or mixed gendarmerie settings, yet denied any colonial or warfare context when deploying them. And these governments held such units in high regard and continued their interaction.[181] By the 1980s, for example, the new tactical antiterrorism units were firmly integrated into domestic security and military planning in the UK, the United States, and the FRG. The FRG, Italy, and Austria deployed their units against potential terrorist and domestic security threats during the early 1980s. When four Palestine Liberation Front members hijacked the cruise ship *Achille Lauro* in 1985, U.S. president Ronald Reagan sent Special Forces units to arrest the hijackers on their subsequent plane travel.[182] Contemporaries praised such operations as effective tactics against transnational extremists, while domestic and international law, foreign policy and armed intervention, and border-bound law enforcement could not resolve the situation. Due to their successes, these tactical units were harbingers of the later militarization of counterterrorism in the 1980s and 1990s.

After 1972, new networks among European security experts shaped antiterrorism policies on the continent and advanced the FRG's crime-focused and oftentimes unusual strategies against international terrorism. The FRG interior ministry became a principal advocate for multilateral collaboration on domestic security in general and against international terrorism in particular. Novel networks of security experts formed around TREVI and tactical units. They brought interior, justice, law enforcement, and military institutions in the EC, Western Europe, and the United States into ongoing conversation with one another. High-level politicians often initiated collaborative processes, and signed off on results, while mid-level officials dominated the actual discussions and set the content. Their communication, often held behind a wall of secret clearances, amplified specialists' focus on expertise and mechanisms against the tactic of international terrorism. By pursuing and discussing related practices, these networks significantly advanced the norm that international terrorists were first and foremost criminals and violent breakers of national and international laws.

Security experts' collaboration was complicated by tensions and paradoxes. FRG officials justified their steps against international terrorism by highlighting it as an unusual and extraordinary domestic security threat. This claim laid the foundations for European domestic security collaboration. Policymakers also used it to create tactical units to give themselves new response options other than negotiating or conceding to demands. Such tactical units ended attacks and rescued hostages. Yet at the same time, the involved officials strove to normalize what they were doing. Whether in public or private, policymakers emphasized that their steps were necessities to uphold domestic security. Overall, security officials juxtaposed an emphasis on normal practices, the rule of law, and the criminal nature of terrorism with a focus on its extraordinary danger and secret as well as militarized countermeasures.

Overall, the domestic security networks were successful in codifying for security officials that terrorism was a violent problem no matter its political context. Meanwhile, the FRG's pursuit of this domestic security collaboration laid the groundwork for other European antiterrorism initiatives. Further conventions and international law frameworks normatively criminalized and delegitimized terrorism within international law. By the mid-1970s, the FRG justice ministry and Foreign Office built on the interior ministry's efforts and pursued new conventions to extradite terrorists as criminals in the Council of Europe and the United Nations, respectively. These FRG initiatives raised earlier public and state-to-state controversies about whether to account for terrorists' political motivations—once again pitting the FRG, alongside the United States and the United Kingdom, against France, the Soviet Union, and the Arab world.

Chapter 4

SOVEREIGNTY-BASED LIMITS TO ANTITERRORISM IN EUROPEAN INTEGRATION, 1974–1980

On January 7, 1977, the main planner of the 1972 Munich attack entered France. Mohammad Daoud Oudeh, known as Abu Daoud, was a leader of the extremist Black September Organization. Under a false alias, he meant to attend the funeral of a recently assassinated Palestinian in Paris. On January 8, 1977, the West German interior ministry informed French authorities that the Bavarian state government had an outstanding arrest warrant for Daoud and was preparing an extradition request. French law enforcement officials arrested Daoud. Yet the administration of French president Valéry Giscard d'Estaing quickly deported him to Algeria instead of turning him over to the West Germans. French officials claimed that the FRG request was invalid on procedural grounds. France had not received a properly filed and dated extradition request through diplomatic as well as judicial channels.[1] The request also did not include Abu Daoud's false alias, and French officials suggested that the man's identity was not absolutely clear. The French position bewildered the West Germans, who were expecting the opportunity to prosecute Abu Daoud for his role in the Munich attack. (Meanwhile, the Israeli government had also learned of the arrest and was preparing its own extradition request. Israeli authorities were furious.)[2] The controversy around Daoud's arrest highlighted that European states varied greatly in their willingness to prosecute and extradite suspected international terrorists. In the second half of the 1970s, European judicial officials saw these discrepancies. In response, they conducted long-winded negotiations to try to streamline their judicial collaboration and develop a joint European political stance against international terrorism.

West Germans again facilitated this initiative. The FRG government became a driver of European antiterrorism efforts in the years after the 1972 Munich Olympic Games attack. The FRG interior ministry turned to regional collaboration to improve its domestic security against attacks like the one at Munich. It created new antiterrorism contacts among security officials from the European Community's (EC) member states, especially in the TREVI network and among antiterrorism tactical units. The FRG justice ministry built on the interior's initiative by pursuing its own European multilateral antiterrorism project. This chapter examines the results by tracing how European judicial officials built upon earlier processes of European integration to negotiate a joint antiterrorism extradition convention. It also highlights the limits of this endeavor.

Despite the EC's public pursuit of European integration, European judicial officials wound up sharply contesting joint antiterrorism regulations because they eroded national sovereignty to a degree that policymakers could not accept. From 1974 to 1980, the FRG justice ministry negotiated a multilateral antiterrorism extradition convention among European states, framing its efforts as part of the ongoing expansion of European integration. These negotiations were based on existing extradite-or-prosecute conventions. They focused on how to standardize European states' processes for collaborating with one another in judicial matters. But the negotiations faced two major issues. First, states held differing interests concerning how far to recognize and legitimate political violence. While states that faced significant violent attacks, such as the FRG, the UK, and Italy, claimed that international terrorism needed to be treated as a brute criminal act, other states with differing foreign policy interests focused on the danger of antiterrorism regulations to political dissidents' civil rights. By conceptualizing terrorism through the regulation of crime and criminal laws, European officials transformed these regulations into highly divisive political issues. Second, judicial integration related to antiterrorism required significant cuts into and adaptation of states' domestic criminal laws, judicial procedures, and even legal traditions. This abrogation of national sovereignty proved unacceptable, especially to smaller European states. Overall, negotiations surrounding the European antiterrorism convention reinforced normative Global North understandings of international terrorism as a crime. Yet judicial antiterrorism infringed too much on national interests and sovereignty to be an effective area of multilateral collaboration and European integration.

The FRG was able to pass its preferred antiterrorism convention, which became the first ratified multilateral agreement worldwide to broadly label (international) terrorism as a primarily criminal offense. The 1977 European Convention on the Suppression of Terrorism (European Convention) solidified the norm among Western European states that cross-border violent attacks should be handled as crimes first and foremost, irrespective of political context.[3] It was the first multilateral convention against terrorism (not just a specific terroristic attack) to be both adopted and ratified. The United States had fostered the conventions that European states used as precedents—the International Civil Aviation Organization (ICAO)'s Tokyo, Hague, and Montreal Conventions and the UN's Diplomats Convention.[4] Now, Western European states dedicated themselves to a broader convention that required them to "extradite or prosecute" all terrorist offenders as criminals. They normalized the Global North practice of regulating and addressing international terrorism as a principally criminal issue.

However, the FRG's multilateral antiterrorism efforts institutionalized international terrorism as a problem within European integration in a way that kept the problem intact and unresolved. By conceptualizing terrorism through the regulation of crime and criminal laws, European officials transformed these regulations into highly divisive political issues with sensitive implications for national sovereignty. The negotiations over the European Convention revealed that European states could not form a homogenous position on international terrorism and the legitimacy of political violence even among themselves. When deciding who was a terrorist and what types of politically motivated violence to outlaw, European states operated according to their own interests instead of reaching a common position. The result was a weak and divisive compromise. In addition, officials were exhausted by the long negotiations surrounding the European Convention, the process of acquiring a sufficient number of signatures, and its ultimate ratification. European judicial officials eventually achieved the consensus understanding that conventions against international terrorism were useful tools for symbolic normative change. Yet they required too much labor, political capital, and cuts into the sovereign control of national legal systems to function as commonplace terrorism prevention mechanisms or to advance political goals such as European integration.

THE FRG JUSTICE MINISTRY SEEKS AN ANTITERRORISM CONVENTION

After the 1972 Munich Olympic Games attack, the FRG leadership sought to create new mechanisms against international terrorism in collaboration with its European neighbors. This effort was spearheaded by Hans-Dietrich Genscher, the interior minister. To prevent further Palestinian attacks, in September 1972, Genscher and the foreign minister, Walter Scheel, advocated for European collaboration in domestic security practices, especially border patrols, law enforcement, and intelligence. Since FRG leaders were primarily interested in developing domestic security reforms alongside their neighboring states, they focused on regional initiatives close to home in Western Europe. The FRG also lacked full UN membership until 1973 and could not significantly contribute to the United States' global antiterrorism initiative there. Scheel inquired about Genscher's envisioned domestic security collaboration among the other EC states just days after the Munich attack. He also recommended that European states analyze and potentially revise their extradition regulations.[5]

In the FRG's Foreign Office, the Legal Department's International Law Division quickly laid out what the FRG would need to consider if it wanted to pursue the issue of extradition with its neighbors. Carl-August Fleischhauer headed this division. A longtime civil servant, Fleischhauer held a doctorate in international law. In September 1972, he emphasized that the FRG needed to pin down what it meant by terrorism. Earlier multilateral conventions before the 1970s had defined offenses such as piracy.[6] The ICAO's Tokyo, Hague, and Montreal Conventions had laid out what acts constituted hijacking or aviation sabotage. Fleischhauer wrote that the FRG could utilize these conventions and build upon their language to create a new antiterrorism extradition convention. However, officials would need to be precise about what it was they were regulating.[7] The term *terrorism* was too vague to be used otherwise.

Genscher and Scheel hoped that they could introduce domestic security measures, particularly ones against international terrorism, as a new avenue of European integration. Since 1954, European organizations such as the EC strengthened economic, social, and cultural links between Western European states.[8] By the 1970s, European leaders actively sought new ways to integrate. In 1970, EC heads of state agreed to coordinate their foreign policy and develop "European" foreign policy stances vis-à-vis the superpowers, nonaligned states, and Global South.[9] This coordination, named the European Political Cooperation (EPC), involved regular working group meetings between relevant officials on select foreign policy issues.[10]

The issue of human rights was another upcoming integrative field. The main venue here was the Conference on Security and Cooperation in Europe, as well as its successor, the Organization for Security and Cooperation in Europe.[11] An older international organization that addressed human rights as well as legal reforms was the Council of Europe.[12] Founded in 1949 by ten Western European states to harmonize rule of law and human rights issues among themselves, the Council of Europe had grown to eighteen members by the end of the 1970s, adding Scandinavian and Southern European countries. Its members had discussed hijacking and attacks on diplomats in the early 1970s. When the Italian foreign ministry official Marco Fortini attempted to sway other European states to create their own protection-of-diplomats convention in 1970, he pursued discussions in the Council of Europe, among other places,[13] since hijacking and attacks on diplomats were issues of interest there.

Before Munich, most Western European leaders did not see antiterrorism measures as a potential field of cooperation in their ongoing process of European integration. Each state had previously addressed terroristic violence (homegrown or committed by transnationally operating extremists) with various national policies based on local contexts and domestic legal traditions. Meanwhile, European collaboration on domestic security issues remained rare, informal, and ad hoc.[14] In addition, the UK Foreign and Commonwealth Office remembered (as might have others) that the one previously adopted multilateral convention against the broad term of terrorism—a 1937 League of Nations convention—had failed ratification and faded to obscurity.[15]

The FRG's first efforts to create domestic security collaboration and extradition revisions stalled in the EC. Following the Munich attack, Scheel urged the other foreign ministers to act together against international terrorism. They agreed to institute antiterrorism working groups, but these produced no sustained results.[16] Overall, the FRG's neighbors were wary of sacrificing any control over their domestic security arrangements and possibly infringing on their national sovereignty. A follow-up Belgian suggestion to create an antiterrorism extradition convention interested the West Germans, but all other EC members shot down the proposal.[17] In the next two years, the Belgians proposed a UN convention against the specific crime of hostage-taking but then withdrew the idea due to European recalcitrance and Arab, African, and nonaligned states' hostility. The FRG interior ministry increasingly shifted to the strategy of cultivating informal contacts among foreign security officials.

While the interior ministry turned to the alternative forms of collaboration described in chapter 3, the Foreign Office and justice ministry continued to seek antiterrorism extradition regulations in the Council of Europe. Interior ministry officials bemoaned that the EC would have been able to provide faster and more effective collaborative measures against international terrorism. In light of stagnation there, however, the Council of Europe at least had a precedent extradition agreement.[18] In 1957, its members had adopted the European Convention on Extradition. The convention regulated "the extradition between Parties of persons wanted for criminal proceedings or for the carrying out of a sentence."[19] Though the convention did not apply to "political or military offenses," Fleischhauer thought that a new convention could expand this preexisting agreement to cover international terrorism—if officials could manage to precisely define terrorism as a criminal offense without touching upon broader political contexts.[20] The Council of Europe had already discussed potentially creating a comparable (narrower) protection-of-diplomats convention in 1970, though without results. The Foreign Office was supported by the justice ministry, which held jurisdiction over FRG extradition matters. From 1972 to 1974, FRG delegates in the Council of Europe lobbied for a new extradition convention covering international terrorism offenses. Coordinating on the Council of Europe side was Heribert Golsong, the council's director of Legal Affairs. A West German doctor of law, Golsong had a long career serving in the legal branches of European organizations. He worked closely with FRG delegates.

The Council of Europe discussions on terrorism quickly mirrored earlier and ongoing debates in the UNGA, ICAO, and Organization of American States (OAS). Negotiations focused on how to define an act of international terrorism in order to be able to regulate it as an extraditable offense. This approach would reduce an attack to its criminal elements and strip away political context. In October 1972, the Council of Europe passed Resolution 684, which recommended forming a "joint European front to combat terrorism" and to dissuade all states from giving asylum to terrorists.[21] Golsong then pressed for the creation of an ad hoc committee to brainstorm legal aspects concerning international terrorism.[22] After lengthy discussions, the Council of Europe passed Recommendation 703 in May 1973, which called for member states to establish and enforce regulations against the (not defined) "international terrorism."[23]

But the Council of Europe faced the same problems encountered by other international organizations, namely that it was far easier to recommend action than to actually perform the work: to define and distinguish terrorism from violence that European officials considered driven by legitimate political grievances and to push states to agree on these matters. Progress lagged. Most delegates felt that convention initiatives on the global stage would be more efficient than regional efforts.[24] Yet the United States' global antiterrorism initiative in the UNGA showcased that terrorism was a broader concept and thus more difficult to regulate than specific acts of terrorist violence such as hijacking. Europeans' global focus remained throughout 1973 despite the lack of results in the ICAO and UNGA (the UNGA's protection-of-diplomats convention was an exception).

Even as its delegates pressed on, few seemed genuinely invested in action within the Council of Europe. In January 1974, the Council of Europe passed Resolution (74) 3 on International Terrorism, which called on member states to adopt an "extradite or prosecute" convention against international terrorism.[25] These conventions defined their respective crimes by listing violent acts that they covered. The "extradite or prosecute" formula required states to pass criminal laws against people who committed these specific violent acts, apply those laws uniformly, and to either submit cases for trial at home or to extradite offenders. Such conventions mandated that signatory states (at least initially) treat offenders as criminals. Under these conventions, a state could still acknowledge a nonstate actor as a politically motivated actor through a mechanism called the political offense exception. But such an acknowledgement was supposed to be the exception rather than the norm. The Italian delegate on the Council of Europe and UK officials in the Foreign and Commonwealth's Security Department wondered whether it was possible to define international terrorism or, relatedly, delineate a "politically motivated offense," at all.[26] Most European foreign ministries knew from their recent experiences in the ICAO and UNGA that an "extradite or prosecute" convention required substantial effort and the expenditure of political capital to negotiate. Since there had been no further Palestinian attacks on the perceived scale of the Munich attack within Europe, European leaders were unwilling to make that investment.[27] Few expected any major follow-up to Resolution (74) 3.

Meanwhile, after 1973 the FRG interior ministry decided to pursue domestic security and antiterrorism collaboration outside of formal international structures. In early 1974, its Public Security office opened domestic security discussions with the FRG's closest ally in the process of European integration, France. These negotiations would, over the course of several years, expand into the EC states' TREVI network.[28]

As the FRG interior ministry prepared for these negotiations with France in the fall of 1973, justice ministry officials felt that it was overstepping its competencies. The interior ministry's Public Security Office prepared a range of security and judicial issues to include in the negotiations, even though some fell under the institutional authority of the justice ministry. Specifically, the interior ministry included extradition and requests for mutual assistance in criminal matters on its list of issues to discuss with France. By precedent, the justice ministry had jurisdiction over both. Justice officials rightly felt that the interior ministry was intruding on their territory. In December 1973, the head of the justice ministry's International Criminal Law division, Paul-Günter Pötz, wrote Genscher on behalf of the justice minister, Gerhard Jahn, and requested that the two issues not be included in the interior ministry's forthcoming negotiations.[29] While the interior ministry dropped its focus on extradition, it continued to discuss mutual assistance in criminal matters with France and later other countries.

To display their institutional monopoly over these issues, in January 1974 justice ministry officials decided to also engage in international collaboration on extradition and international terrorism with their European neighbors.[30] Pötz was responsible for day-to-day work alongside Erich Corves, head of the new International Fight Against Terrorism division. The two offices were subordinate to the criminal law branch of the justice ministry. Pötz and Corves continued operating within the Council of Europe; this international organization had already called upon its members to draft an antiterrorism extradition convention and thus provided a venue and justification for negotiations.

The justice ministry's main goal was also a quick and decisive result. The FRG's ministries sought solutions that were easy to negotiate and to implement. Their goal was to remove safe havens for extremists throughout Europe and allow the FRG to more expeditiously file extradition requests. The goal was to seize custody of attackers but also (and maybe more importantly) to deter Palestinians and homegrown extremists likely to be hiding in neighboring states from even attempting attacks.[31] Like the U.S. State Department, for this deterrence purpose FRG justice officials preferred an agreement that would require states to extradite terrorists. But it pursued an "extradite or prosecute" convention because this format seemed to be the most achievable. The FRG justice ministry was now attempting what the U.S. State Department had failed to accomplish: the establishment of an "extradite or prosecute" convention against the broad category of nonstate, cross-border international terrorism. As the American UNGA initiative against international terrorism in the fall of 1972 had shown, such a broadly delineated term was more contentious and difficult to work with than the narrow offenses defined in earlier conventions in the ICAO and OAS.

To pass a Council of Europe convention, Pötz knew that the FRG would require French support. Like the interior ministry, the justice ministry prioritized reaching out to French counterparts. Along with the FRG, France was the largest power involved in the process of European integration. In addition, French opposition to any regulation concerning international terrorism had stalled earlier Italian and U.S. initiatives within the UNGA, ICAO, and other international organizations. The French argument had been that these conventions had too much bureaucratic hassle with no substantive payoff. Future resistance was to be expected. In early 1974, the FRG interior ministry approached the French interior ministry to discuss domestic security collaboration.[32] FRG justice officials piggybacked on this opportunity. They used the occasion of the visit to reach out to the French justice ministry.[33] Their plan was to get the French justice ministry to support a Council of Europe extradition convention, undermining future French resistance. Then, they could create a joint Franco-West German lobbying campaign in the Council of Europe, which would be more forceful than a sole FRG effort. Overall, the FRG ministries' two strategies in early 1974 were very similar—get France on board and then move to multilateral discussions. West German officials arranged a meeting between FRG justice minister Gerhard Jahn and French justice minister Jean Taittinger to discuss a Council of Europe convention in early 1974.

Taittinger showed interest in the FRG project, but other French governmental ministries warned that it could undermine French national interests. The French Ministry of Foreign Affairs voiced substantial opposition. While the FRG interior ministry broached collaboration with France in secret, the FRG justice ministry's extradition convention would be known to the public and recently independent states and national liberation movements would react to it. In 1974, France had better relations with the Middle East than most other Western industrialized states. The French foreign ministry worried that a convention against terrorism would undermine French economic and diplomatic relations with Arab states in the wake of the 1973 oil crisis.[34] The foreign ministry's priority was to protect French access to Middle Eastern oil. Meanwhile, French officials across the board warned that domestic support for a multilateral convention against international terrorism would be weak. A strong leftist scene in France supported the political motivations, if not always the actions, of left-leaning extremists. Leftists had the power to oppose and disrupt the domestic ratification of any antiterrorism convention in France. The French justice ministry thus faced significant domestic institutional opposition to its participation in the FRG Council of Europe initiative.

However, the FRG justice ministry's initiative also played to broader French foreign policy interests. It was an opportunity for France to shape European integration concerning judicial matters and procedures. The Gaullist political movement in France sought to create a strong, integrated Europe, inspired by France, which was independent of the United States and the Soviet Union in defense, security, and economic respects. After World War II, French president Charles de Gaulle had endeavored to offset U.S. and Soviet power in Europe by creating separate French defense capacities and strengthening European economic integration. French president Georges Pompidou and his successor, Valéry Giscard d'Estaing, were leading Gaullists or Gaullist allies, respectively.[35] Unlike the interior ministry's negotiations, any extradition or judicial convention would be a matter of public knowledge. French leaders likely thought that the FRG justice ministry's initiative might be a vehicle to increase French influence among the EC states. An agreement on judicial collaboration (in general) would also not specifically target Palestinian attackers and thus offend Arab states, French leftists, and other supporters of national liberation movements. The French justice ministry tentatively agreed to collaborate with the West Germans.

From the outset, French and FRG interests thus diverged. The FRG justice ministry sought to improve its domestic security by creating a multilateral European agreement to extradite transnationally operating extremists and cut off their potential safe havens. Jahn, Pötz, and Corves pursued practical and easy to implement measures. Meanwhile, the French justice ministry was interested in advancing the process of European integration—and the French influence within it. French officials cared less about short-term utility of any agreement and more about its potential long-term geopolitical impact. Like their respective interior ministries, both sides entered negotiations with differing political aims and hoped-for outcomes.

Yet FRG and French justice ministry officials saw enough potential benefits in a new Council of Europe convention to discuss collaboration options despite their divergence of interests. From the spring of 1974 to the spring of 1975, they held a series of discussions to align their policy positions. Though neither side convinced the other to share its priorities, they continued talking. Jahn and Taittinger passed their jobs on to successors, Hans-Jochen Vogel and Jean Lecanuet, who supported the continuing discussions, as did new FRG chancellor Helmut Schmidt.

During the course of these discussions, a series of terrorist attacks added to both states' interest in extradition options. Popular Front for the Liberation of Palestine member Ilich Ramírez Sánchez—the infamous "Carlos the Jackal"—committed attacks on a Paris café and on Paris-Orly Airport. In June 1975, French authorities attempted to arrest Ramírez. He shot and killed two French intelligence agents and made his escape. For the next two decades, French authorities sought to apprehend him and try him for these shootings.[36]

Meanwhile, FRG socio-revolutionary actors committed a series of dramatic attacks abroad; in turn West German officials shifted their multilateral initiatives to target homegrown violent actors more than Palestinians. In February 1975, members of the 2 June Movement kidnapped mayoral candidate Peter Lorenz in West Berlin. Schmidt's cabinet exchanged Lorenz for several extremist Red Army Faction (RAF) and 2 June Movement members incarcerated in West Berlin. The kidnappers and released prisoners boarded a flight to South Yemen and vanished. On April 24, 1975, six RAF members occupied the FRG embassy in Stockholm, Sweden, killing two FRG diplomats. Swedish police stormed the embassy after the attackers accidentally set off their own explosives. Under Swedish law, authorities could not extradite the attackers to the FRG for crimes within Sweden, but they did expel them for immigrations violations and turned them over to FRG authorities, who convicted them for two counts of murder.[37] Together, these incidents marked a turning point, as Schmidt privately decided not to publicly concede to West German extremist actors' demands in the future.[38] The Schmidt cabinet prioritized the creation of extradition agreements that would allow FRG authorities to regain custody of West German citizens.

European allies also diversified their understanding of international terrorism in this period. In the United States, a mid-level working group called the Cabinet Committee to Combat Terrorism coordinated the U.S. government's antiterrorism initiatives. In September 1975, the working group's chairman, State Department diplomat Robert Fearey, publicly identified the RAF and the Japanese Red Army as international terrorism organizations alongside Palestinian extremists.[39] Japanese Red Army members had committed both the 1972 Lod Airport massacre and a 1974 French embassy takeover in The Hague. Fearey's interview showcased that U.S. officials were also increasingly diversifying their understanding of international terrorism to add non-Palestinian actors.

Following the incidents in the spring of 1975, Vogel and Lecanuet introduced the idea of a new extradition convention in the Council of Europe. On May 22, 1975, Vogel mentioned extradition regulations for international terrorists at a meeting of the Council of Europe's justice ministers in Obernai, France. Knowing that delegates in the UNGA, ICAO, Council of Europe, and elsewhere had held charged discussions over the sensitive issue of regulating politically motivated violence, Vogel and Lecanuet did not formally table the issue. Instead, they raised it in casual conversation with other European justice ministers, convincing the other ministers to dedicate resources toward a new antiterrorist extradition agreement. This approach allowed the justice ministers to broach this politically contentious issue informally and privately.

The main controversy, as in earlier U.S. initiatives, came from Vogel's insistence that international terrorism was solely a crime. By speaking informally and secretly to his colleagues, Vogel launched another attempt to remove the largest loophole in previous extradition agreements, the political offense exception. This standard inclusion in extradition treaties protects politically motivated actors from extradition. States can invoke the exception to refuse extradition in cases where their respective authorities accept that an offender was politically motivated, or if they assume that an offender would face politically motivated charges if extradited. This exception is a crucial mechanism for political dissidents, insurgents, and similar actors. If a state decides not to extradite someone on the basis of the political offense exception, it acknowledges (and to a certain degree validates) their political motivations and the actor's right to pursue them.

The U.S. State Department had attempted to remove the political offense exception from agreements concerning hijacking, attacks on civil aviation, and attacks on diplomats since 1968 in order to be able to accuse Cuba and other leftist regimes of harboring criminals. However, neither U.S. allies nor recently independent states were willing to support the idea because they feared that it would cut into states' sovereign handling of their own legal systems. Arab, African, and nonaligned states accused the United States of pursuing imperial geopolitical goals and seeking to discredit the political agency of national liberation movements. Meanwhile, both the UK and Lecanuet's justice ministry voiced general worries about damaging an anticommunist tool and undermining political dissidents' civil rights, especially under authoritarian regimes. The United States and other Western countries used the political offense exception to refuse extradition requests from Soviet Bloc states and Cuba.[40] The political offense exception was thus an important Cold War mechanism for the United States, the UK and their allies to shame and critique leftist regimes. Because the political offense exception was a standardized and politically useful aspect of extradition treaties, Vogel faced an uphill struggle. Like the U.S. State Department's failed efforts, his initiative to curtail the political offense exception would infringe on other states' sovereign legal systems as well as on international law protections for political dissidents.

Yet with Lecanuet's support, Vogel's conversations at least opened new negotiations. The justice ministers green-lighted a Council of Europe antiterrorism initiative though in as vague terms as possible. The ministers decided that their expert bureaucrats should collaborate. The goal was to define a "politically motivated act" (as covered under the political offense exception) so that acts of international terrorism did not qualify.

This formulation did not provide any hints toward a substantive solution. Nevertheless, the ministers agreed that an extradition agreement covering international terrorism should be ready to sign by their next meeting in June 1976.[41] Until then, their subordinate officials would have to figure out how to address the political offense exception in a manner that eighteen European states with differing legal traditions, values, and practices could agree on.[42]

THE COUNCIL OF EUROPE NEGOTIATIONS AND GERMAN-FRENCH DIVISIONS

Overall, the Council of Europe justice ministers agreed to fill a tall order. Lower-ranking bureaucrats now had to draft a convention that criminalized international terrorism by redrawing the political offense exception so narrowly that acts of international terrorism (in all its forms) would not meet the requirements for the exception. All involved knew that committees in the UN, ICAO, and OAS had failed at this task.

The ball now passed to specialized mid-level justice ministry and judicial officials to figure out what was going to happen and how. After their informal discussions at Obernai, the justice ministers gave control of the issue to the Council of Europe's Committee on Crime Problems, where expert specialists could negotiate details. The committee included justice ministry officials from all Council of Europe member states. Also present were law enforcement officials, foreign and interior ministry bureaucrats, and academics.[43] Delegates met at the Council of Europe headquarters in Strasbourg, France. This committee instituted the subordinate ad hoc committee to examine certain new forms of concerted acts of violence and to work out details of a new convention in October 1975. Golsong handled meeting invitations and logistics. Pötz or Corves usually represented the FRG with assistants. Pötz chaired the October meeting, though he afterward passed control to Belgian delegate Suzanne Oschinsky. Delegates from the UK, Charles Prior (head of crime policy planning in the Home Office) and Michael Wood (legal adviser in the Foreign and Commonwealth Office), were both also heavily involved in other multilateral efforts against international terrorism, especially the FRG interior ministry's domestic security initiative. They had experience with multilateral antiterrorism collaboration.[44]

At the heart of negotiations was the issue of who to extradite for what offense. The eighteen Council of Europe members held a wide variety of legalistic traditions and had enacted differing domestic laws against national and transnational nonstate violence. German and French justice officials knew that they would have to bridge these varying regulations. What offenses should the new extradition convention cover? The convention needed to be broad enough to encompass acts of international terrorism in general yet precise enough to actually be of use in concrete extradition proceedings.

FRG officials championed a convention based on the "extradite or prosecute" formula, which the other delegations quickly agreed upon because it was relatively simple to implement domestically.[45] This formulation did not require any changes to a state's domestic criminal law; it merely specified that states should in fact pass domestic criminal laws against the offenses specified by the convention and apply those laws uniformly. Together with universal jurisdiction, "extradite or prosecute" could be a useful deterrent for international terrorism, since attackers could now expect to be placed on trial for their crimes even if they fled abroad to other European states. Additionally, nonstate offenders had to rely on state officials if they wanted an exception from extradition due to political motivation. This approach gave state officials definitional authority and undercut attackers' attempts to label themselves as insurgents, revolutionaries, combatants, or prisoners of war. In particular, RAF members framed their actions as occurring within a war against the FRG, and thus demanded protections under the laws of war.[46] The "extradite or prosecute" approach undermined such claims.

The ad hoc committee now had to solve two closely related challenges: It had to define what exactly constituted an act of "terrorism," and it had to delineate how far the political offense exception could be scaled back so that it would not apply to such acts of terrorism. The greatest controversy in the working group was over the question of whether to touch the exception at all. The 1957 European Extradition Convention generally stated that perpetrators with political motivations could not be extradited. The location or severity of the crime did not matter—state officials' sovereign interpretation (political or not) did. In contrast, West German delegates wanted to abolish the political offense exception in the new convention completely and make all international terrorism attacks extraditable as ordinary crimes. Many other delegations were hesitant to cut too deeply into the exception. They stressed its overall use, arguing that it provided a legal safety net for all political dissidents and protected them from being returned to a state that might violate their civil liberties.[47]

The committee delegates discussed ways to define terrorism and narrow the political offense exception at their first meeting in December 1975. Under the leadership of Oschinsky, a doctor of law and managing director in the Belgian justice ministry, the delegates brainstormed what to do. The most radical option was to eliminate the political offense exception altogether. The delegates' second option was to create broad categories of crimes that should never fall under the label of politically motivated offenses, including acts that threatened many lives, acts that threatened innocent lives, or acts that displayed unusual cruelty in their execution.[48] This was the only option that attempted to define terrorism (through a list of these categories). Another choice was to focus on the cross-border aspects of international terrorism and require extradition for extremists if their attack occurred in a state unconnected to their political motivation. A final option was to just retain the exception.

The earlier conventions against specific acts of terroristic violence had retained the political offense exception but combined it with a list of never-exempt crimes. This combination created a significant loophole. It gave states the right to invoke the political offense exception even if an attack fell on the list of covered crimes. The resulting conventions were weak and their lists of never-exempt crimes unenforceable. But these conventions only gained enough ratification to enter into force precisely because they were so weak. The ICAO, OAS, and Diplomats Conventions did not require states to amend their legal traditions or to extradite politically motivated offenders. It was their loopholes and ambiguities that made these conventions widely acceptable in the international community.

Two weeks later, the hostage takeover at the OPEC headquarters in Vienna highlighted to citizens and officials worldwide that committers of "international terrorism" were not just Palestinian but hailed from an expanding network within and beyond the Global South. As discussed in chapter 3, Palestinian extremist leader Wadie Haddad planned the attack and Venezuelan "Carlos the Jackal" led it. One of the attackers was Gabriele Kröcher-Tiedemann, a West German who had been released earlier that year as part of the Lorenz exchange. For the committee members, the attack affirmed how crucial the issue of extradition would be to stop not just Palestinians but also their own citizens from traveling between states and seeking a safe haven abroad.

Acting with haste, the committee chose the solution to the question of the political offense exception that members believed would be easiest to implement. They replicated the setup used in earlier conventions. In its second meeting, which took place February 2–6, 1976, the group agreed to retain the political offense exception. Yet the committee also listed offenses that, in the future, would not qualify for the exception. This list formally laid out what types of attacks the Council of Europe would consider to be international terrorism.

The delegates included in the list both clear and vague offenses. On the one hand, the first article of their convention draft listed specific attacks that would generally be considered crimes, not politically motivated acts: all acts covered under the ICAO's Hague and Montreal Conventions and the UN Diplomats Convention, and all other attacks on diplomats, hostage-takings, and bombings. The delegates explicitly defined these acts as international terrorism. Listing specific types of crimes had functioned well before. The previously mentioned ICAO and UNGA conventions all contained such lists. States that did not want to infringe on the agency of national liberation actors or political dissidents could still accept these lists because of their clearly defined, unambiguous scope. The convention draft's first article and its listing of covered offenses did not cause any controversy.

In contrast, article two of the convention draft contained an additional vague definition of terrorism, extending it to include all "serious offenses against the life, physical integrity, or liberty of a person."[49] Like in the South African and similar repressive antiterrorist laws, and like in the United States' failed UNGA convention, this definition delineated the term so broadly that it could have almost any meaning. This approach left significant leeway for individual states to choose whether an act was a "serious offense" worthy of the international terrorism label. It permitted European states to brand almost any attack as a terrorist "serious offense." In contrast, however, the vague definition also allowed states to deny that a (less brutal) violent act was a "serious offense."

Such a vague definition held the potential to cause significant controversies. As the 1972 UNGA terrorism debate had shown, Arab, African, and nonaligned officials were invested in the success of anticolonial, national liberation, and self-determination movements. These UNGA delegates had rejected a vague definition of terrorism because it gave states broad powers to declare an attack a terrorist and thus exclusively criminal offense. Arab and African delegates in particular feared that the United States, Israel, South Africa, and others could use such vagueness at leisure to criminalize insurgents or political dissidents as terrorists in pursuit of imperialist and authoritarian aims.[50] They pointed to instances like South Africa's 1967 terrorism bill or Uruguay's suppression of the Tupamaros as already existing examples of such suppression. Yet the Council of Europe working group showed little concern for such prosecution. The Arab, African, and other nonaligned countries were not represented in the Council of Europe. Additionally, the FRG, Belgian, and later UK delegates most in favor of the convention emphasized the strong rule of law and democratic institutions among the Council of Europe member states. They argued that those states did not need to fear that their fellow member states might engage in political repression.[51]

The committee's delegates agreed that their two-pronged definition of terrorism was the fastest, best solution feasible under the current circumstances. Their precise list specified some offenses that the political offense exception would never apply to. Additionally, the vague definition placed all the power to determine who was a terrorist or what was a terroristic act in the hands of state officials. It thus strengthened their authority to define and prosecute terrorism.[52] When deciding whether to label an attack as a "serious offense," state officials could ignore any input from nonstate actors such as civil rights activists or terrorists themselves. Unmentioned was the advantage that these definitions of terrorism focused on the actual offense and not on surrounding context. Officials would not need to consider offenders' national origins, race, or political affiliations—factors that amplified attackers' political grievances and their connection to national liberation ideology.

Most committee delegates were relieved to have settled on a convention draft. The FRG Council of Europe delegation knew that their draft included loopholes and still contained the political offense exception. Yet they were pleased that the quickly negotiated convention draft seemed to fit most of their needs and allowed them to seek extradition for a wide range of violent acts.[53] Meanwhile, British officials in the Home and Foreign and Commonwealth Offices expressed hope that the convention would enable the extradition of IRA members who had fled to Ireland after committing attacks in the UK.[54] So far, Ireland had declared all such actors politically motivated and nonextraditable.[55] In fact, the Irish government had strong reservations about the convention draft and was attempting to downplay the importance of extradition in it, emphasizing that states should primarily try offenders at home.[56]

West German officials hoped that the resulting convention could serve as a model for future antiterrorist agreements. By early 1976, the FRG interior and justice ministries seemed well on their way to successfully implementing their respective sought-after collaboration against international terrorism. The EC states' interior ministers, including FRG's Werner Maihofer, had agreed to a conference on domestic security in the summer of 1976. The result of the conference was the TREVI network. Meanwhile, Hans-Dietrich Genscher, now foreign minister, saw an opportunity to introduce an "extradite or prosecute" convention against hostage-taking in the UNGA.[57] The Foreign Office began discussing such a narrow convention against hostage-taking with other foreign ministries in January 1976. Arab, African, and nonaligned states had been hostile to U.S. efforts to draft an antiterrorism convention in 1972, but they had compromised in 1973 and adopted a more limited protection-of-diplomats convention. The head of the Foreign Office's Political Division, Günther van Well, hoped that another limited convention against the specific crime of hostage-taking would be as acceptable. Van Well was a career diplomat and had previously served in the FRG's UN mission. He also pointed out that some Arab states might be in the process of shifting their opinion on terrorism.[58] Though he did not say so specifically, the fact that the OPEC attackers directly targeted Saudi Arabia and other (Arab) oil-producing states, for the first time, played a role in his considerations and Foreign Office planning.

Knowing that previous ICAO, OAS, and UN negotiations had been difficult, in January 1976 FRG Foreign Office and interior and justice ministry officials decided to keep their respective antiterrorism initiatives separate.[59] In splitting their efforts, FRG officials emphasized that if one of these initiatives failed, the others might succeed. This approach differed from the British and French methods. The UK Home Office and Foreign and Commonwealth Office viewed all multilateral initiatives against terrorism in the UNGA, ICAO, EC, and Council of Europe as far more interconnected than their West German counterparts.[60] They heavily preferred working on the most effective initiatives and opposed a diffusion of efforts into many separate international institutions. Meanwhile, French officials were not interested in general agreements against international terrorism at all. But they were willing to discuss related issues such as secret intelligence-sharing or European judicial integration. Vogel, Maihofer, and Genscher counted on the fact that one successful FRG initiative could become a model to support the others. In January 1976, the justice ministry's extradition convention in the Council of Europe was the first FRG initiative approaching completion. The Foreign Office and interior ministry wanted the adoption of this convention to serve as a successful case study, bolstering the FRG policy positions for their respective public UNGA lobbying efforts and secret TREVI cooperation.[61]

As the working group completed its convention draft, however, the collaboration between French and German delegates broke down. Neither side was willing to give up the interests that had driven them into the negotiations. After a series of fine-tuning edits, the convention draft went to a higher Council of Europe body, the ministers' deputies, for approval in June 1976; they attempted to have the draft signed on June 25, 1976. Ireland abstained, which did not impede the convention adoption, but it also meant that it would not be bound to the convention. The French delegation actually rejected the convention, however, and refused to sign. This rejection halted all adoption proceedings. The other delegates were flabbergasted—they had not been expecting this move.[62]

French officials justified their refusal by emphasizing that the convention draft did not address French national interests. When prompted, French interior minister Michel Poniatowski told Maihofer that the convention was too imprecise for the French government to accept or ratify.[63] French objections centered on the vague definition of terrorism and the "serious offenses" article. The convention did not clarify what a "serious offense" was. On the one hand, this article provided European states with broad authority to label any violent act, even if committed for political purposes, as a criminal or terrorist attack. French leftists would oppose this powerful tool to define terrorism. In addition, the French foreign ministry worried that an endorsement of this blanket authority to criminalize any violent extremist might harm French diplomatic relations with Arab states that supported Palestinian national liberation efforts.

On the other hand, however, from a French perspective the convention draft was also too weak on crime and terrorism. States could still use the political offense exception or simply deny that an attack was a "serious offense." Therefore, French Gaullist leaders could not claim they had negotiated a tough convention that undoubtedly increased domestic security in Europe.[64] Golsong speculated that French officials would not be able to present the convention as a prestigious European integration project.[65] West German justice officials were anxious to pass the convention because it generally covered their interests; French officials did not see their goals realized and pulled the figurative emergency brake.

Worse still from the FRG perspective, the French government leveraged Bonn's desperation to pass the existing convention draft to achieve French geopolitical interests. These interests were to advance European integration under French guidance. In his discussion with Maihofer, Poniatowski requested that the antiterrorism negotiations move from the Council of Europe to the smaller EPC, a set of informal ad hoc working groups in which the nine EC states coordinated foreign policy. Poniatowski argued that the EC members would cooperate more efficiently and create a more politically relevant agreement.[66] With fewer involved states and an informal setting, France would also hold more influence in new negotiations. French officials wanted a convention that would bind together a small group of states (maximizing French influence) with significant judicial integration measures—ideally ones that included more than just extradition.

Oddly enough, the Entebbe hijacking played into French demands to shift antiterrorism negotiations to the EC. Two days after the French rejection of the Council of Europe's convention draft, on June 27, 1976, two Palestinians and two FRG leftist extremists hijacked an Air France aircraft to Entebbe, Uganda. Israeli Special Forces rescued the hostages in a clandestine raid on July 4, 1976. The UN and most international organizations condemned the hijacking. The European Council was the EPC's most senior foreign policy ad hoc group and was comprised of placeholders for the EC heads of state. The European Council reacted with a resolution on July 13, 1976. It requested that the EC states develop an "extradite or prosecute" agreement against hostage-taking.[67] French officials leveraged this resolution to argue that all discussions about extradition, crime, and international terrorism should move from the Council of Europe into the EPC's working groups. While the perpetrators of the Entebbe hijacking sought anticolonial and anti-Israeli aims, French judicial authorities broached the attack in a completely different European context.

Neither the FRG nor France was willing to compromise on its national interests. Their political wrangling called into question the reach and utility of the proposed Council of Europe convention. French aims to create a prestigious convention among the nine EC members clashed with the FRG's goal to cut off safe havens for FRG extremists, regulate the extradition of international terrorists quickly, and get as many of the eighteen Council of Europe members as possible on board. The Schmidt cabinet had more extradition-related headaches at the time. In July 1976, Greek authorities arrested Rolf Pohle, one of the prisoners released in the Lorenz exchange. The Greek government initially considered deporting (and thus freeing) him. Schmidt and Genscher intervened at top levels to have Pohle extradited to the FRG. After much wrangling, the Greek Supreme Court finally agreed.[68] Meanwhile, Helmut Schmidt's cabinet placed significant pressure on the French government to sign the Council of Europe convention. Schmidt ordered all three ministries involved in any projects against international terrorism—the Foreign Office and Ministries of Justice and the Interior—to undercut French objections to the convention draft. The ministries emphasized that the convention was a completed draft that could be signed immediately.[69]

In subsequent weeks, the FRG Foreign Office sent van Well and its Paris ambassador, Axel Herbst, to pressure French officials in Paris, the Council of Europe, and the EPC. The two stressed that the Council of Europe convention had an immediate effect because it would reduce safe havens for border-crossing international terrorists throughout Northern, Western, and Southern Europe, even if it did include loopholes.[70] Van Well also tried to shape the European Council's July 13 proclamation to his benefit, arguing that France should sign the Council of Europe convention now because French interests would be met in the future through a new EC convention.[71] Though these arguments met little receptivity in the French foreign and justice ministries, FRG officials continued their lobbying for several months.

In September 1976, van Well persuaded the French to sign the convention by promising another loophole—the option of issuing a reservation.[72] A reservation allows a state to become party to an international agreement even if said agreement has clauses that are unacceptable to that state. The reservation is a unilateral declaration; it declares that all content of the agreement applies to a state—except for the clause about which the state has issued the reservation.[73] This option weakened the convention overall by permitting states to opt out of specific articles. But it enabled the French justice ministry to gather support for the convention at home. With the option of filing a reservation, the French justice ministry could placate the Ministry of Foreign Affairs and French leftists. Somewhat ironically, this compromise created further loopholes, which was one of the concerns that French interior minister Poniatowski had expressed in the first place.

The West German justice ministry worried about reservations' potential to weaken the convention, since any country could declare that it was not bound to segments of the convention. However, FRG officials decided that a French signature would be preferable to a continued veto and that a compromised convention was better than none at all.[74] The UK Foreign and Commonwealth Office officials also discussed the issue with Golsong and the FRG Foreign Office. They pushed for a quick signing to be able to apply the convention against IRA members abroad, especially in Ireland.[75] In the last months of 1976 Golsong quickly moved the convention through the various bureaucratic stages of adoption. The EC states also began negotiations about a convention against hostage-taking. These negotiations happened solely among the nine EC members, which French officials wanted more than the Council of Europe negotiations. In November 1976, a newly instituted EPC working group of senior expert officials met to discuss the European Council's Entebbe resolution.

Meanwhile, the Irish government voiced late-stage opposition to the convention draft. On June 25, 1976, the Irish delegation had abstained from signing the convention draft, announcing that their government did not want to adhere to this convention because it perceived the convention as encouraging extradition over prosecution at home. The Irish constitution forbid such a priority; accepting the convention would thus infringe on a crucial part of Irish sovereignty. As a former colony of the UK, Ireland's main interest was to protect former colonial subjects from the colonizing state, particularly in the context of political turmoil in Northern Ireland. The Irish government refused to extradite Irish citizens who had committed violent attacks in the UK. And Justice Minister Patrick Cooney's subordinates insisted that the Council of Europe convention draft needed to be reformulated so that states first had to consider the political offense exception and offenders' political grievances. Such consideration needed to come before all other steps to prosecute or extradite.[76] This position grew directly out of the Northern Irish conflict.

In fact, British officials pursued every step they thought possible to push Ireland into extraditing Irish citizens who attacked British targets. This pressure occurred despite new reciprocal prosecution regulations between the UK and Ireland that allowed both to try offenses committed in the other state. These regulations entered into law for the UK in the summer of 1975 and Ireland in June 1976. Clandestine incursions by UK Special Forces into Ireland additionally inflamed Irish national sentiments. For example, during the Flagstaff Hill incident in May 1976, Irish officials arrested eight Special Air Services members in civilian garb on Irish soil near the border to Northern Ireland.

Overall, Irish claims about the convention draft were well-founded. The UK government's main goal for the European Convention was to pressure Ireland into extraditing Irish citizens, particularly IRA and similar leftist actors, back to the UK. The FRG justice ministry was in fact also lobbying the other Council of Europe states to prioritize extradition over other options, especially in cases involving West German offenders.[77] Irish efforts to change the convention draft increased after September 1976, when French opposition decreased. Yet Pötz and Wood downplayed the Irish objections, and the other Council of Europe delegations followed suit.[78] They prioritized the idea that within the Council of Europe territory, states followed the rule of law and had little considerations for postcolonial context. Ireland again abstained from signing the subsequent convention. Since Ireland was a small European state and did not actually reject the convention, however, the others did not consider this position a material problem.

Ultimately, all Council of Europe states except for Ireland signed the European Convention on the Suppression of Terrorism (European Convention) on January 27, 1977.[79] It was the first European antiterrorism agreement in the post–World War II period and the first postwar agreement to regulate terrorism itself. The European Convention went significantly beyond the conventions of the early 1970s to focus on terrorism and not on more specific types of attacks such as hijackings. This convention enabled states to delineate who was a terrorist and extradite them as criminals. It increased state authority and took definitional power away from activists and nonstate actors. The convention closed safe havens because it required states to have the capacity to prosecute attackers domestically— even if the attack happened abroad. The last-minute reservation compromise between the FRG and France weakened the convention by allowing states to cherry-pick which sections to adhere to. Overall, however, this convention strengthened European states' normative treatment of violent acts meant to generate terror as criminal. It politically delegitimized violent extremists.

Most participants in the working group were relieved. FRG officials hoped that the convention would ease extradition requests, especially for West German extremists hiding in neighboring countries. In addition, it symbolized a unified European stance against international terrorism and highlighted European (and FRG) adherence to the rule of law. Several smaller states, such as the Netherlands, had engaged in the negotiations principally to foster a unified European position, and also saw their goal achieved.[80] Officials in the UK also saw the European Convention as an important step for multilateral antiterrorism practices. Yet the relief was short-lived.

The mood at the signing soured when former French justice minister Jean Taittinger tabled the French reservation to the European Convention; France stated that it would not ratify or adhere to the European Convention until the EC passed another (French-desired) convention.[81] The other delegates were astonished; they believed they had convinced the French to commit to the European Convention. The European Convention required only a minority of three ratifications to enter into effect and was not dependent on French ratification. Both the practical and the symbolic downsides of France's refusal were not lost on any delegation present, however. This formal reservation allowed France to avoid criticism from its Arab trading partners and domestic leftists. It also deeply undercut the convention's symbolic and practical usefulness, if a powerful European country such as France was unwilling to adhere to it.

SEEKING A DOUBLE-TRACK EPC COMPROMISE

For the next three years, Vogel and the FRG justice ministry attempted to persuade their French counterparts to commit to the terms of the European Convention, while new French justice minister Alain Peyrefitte pushed the nine EC states to adopt their own new convention. Peyrefitte unflinchingly pursued a broader criminal justice convention. French officials wanted the EC states to adopt identical processes when collaborating with one another in crime-related matters. Such processes included (but were not limited to) extradition and mutual assistance in criminal matters. Overall, Peyrefitte aimed to create a common "European legal space" where all EC states utilized the same mechanisms and structures when they had bilateral or multilateral legal interactions concerning criminal law. Such a multilateral legal space would require individual states to adapt their national legislation, law and security structures, and legal traditions to meet supernational requirements. Thus, Peyrefitte was proposing a massive project that would take a long time to negotiate, implement, and ratify. Approving it would provide further evidence of French leadership in the process of Europeanization. The French-envisioned convention was an anticrime agreement, not an antiterrorist one.

The other EC states did not embrace this idea of a common European legal space because it required substantive cuts into their sovereignty. The French proposal would extend multilateral governance into legal traditions, security hierarchies, and criminal legislation. This governance cut into states' regulation of violence on their territories. It would abridge national sovereignty much more significantly than a narrow "extradite or prosecute" convention against terrorism (with readily recognizable loopholes). Though Peyrefitte presented this endeavor as a key step toward European integration, the other justice ministries did not consider such a step to be in their national interest. They were far more interested in getting France to adhere to the European Convention, which gave their officials authority over delineating and regulating terrorism without abridging national sovereignty.

As demanded by France, negotiations in the EPC concerning an anticrime convention had begun in November 1976. The EPC was an informal and closely knit set of working groups among only the EC states, namely the FRG, France, the UK, the Benelux states, Denmark, Italy, and Ireland. Generally speaking, EPC meetings were organized and hosted by the country that held the rotating six-month EC presidency. The EPC was an informal process to integrate EC states' foreign policy while the Council of Europe was an established international organization specializing only in rule of law and human rights questions; EPC membership was much smaller, but its agreements had the potential to affect the EC states more profoundly. Over the next four years, the EPC antiterrorism negotiations served two purposes. One was to follow upon and get France to adhere to the European Convention; the other was to negotiate a French-envisioned new convention.

The European Council's Entebbe Resolution acted as the foundation for negotiations. The resolution called only for the nine EC members to prepare an "extradite or prosecute" convention against hostage-takers. The new EPC expert working group on this issue took up deliberations in November 1976—after the French government agreed to sign the European Convention, but before its actual signature date. The EPC group included many of the same officials who had drafted the European Convention in the Council of Europe. Oschinsky was on the Belgian delegation in 1976. The FRG delegation was headed throughout by Corves or Pötz, often accompanied by members of the FRG Foreign Office's European integration and legal divisions. Meanwhile, Charles Prior and Michael Wood again took point in the UK delegation. These experts were invested in the success and ratification of the European Convention that they themselves had drafted.

The first major question that the EPC group faced was what, precisely, it was doing there. The group's initial meeting in The Hague on November 17, 1976, highlighted the discrepancies between the aims of the French delegation and those of the other EC states. Several days before the meeting, the French delegation circulated a draft of a new convention to fulfill the European Council's demands. It covered all serious crimes (not just hostage-taking) and focused on integrating the EC states' processes concerning mutual assistance in criminal matters. Its section on extradition completely abolished the political offense exception.[82] This French draft was larger in scale and stricter concerning politically motivated offenders than the Council of Europe convention draft. From the outset, the French aims for the EPC negotiations differed from the others. Emerging as defenders of the soon-to-be European Convention, Corves, Prior, and Oschinsky questioned whether a separate EC convention was practical or even necessary. Overall, the delegates discussed whether a separate EPC convention was needed, whether it had to solely address hostage-takings, and whether it should be limited in membership to EC states.[83] They reached no solution and turned to their foreign ministers to ask what they should be doing. At an EPC meeting in January 1977, the foreign ministers decided that the working group could work on a French-desired broad-coverage convention limited to the EC states.[84]

FRG and UK interests converged quickly and focused on getting France to ratify the European Convention. The FRG Foreign Office had started preparations to negotiate a convention against hostage-taking in the UNGA in early 1976.[85] The justice ministry did not want to duplicate or impede the Foreign Office's work. Though the FRG justice ministry considered the idea of an integrated European legal space an interesting theoretical future possibility, officials worried that such a convention would take many years to negotiate and ratify.[86] It could also impinge on the jurisdiction of the European Convention and undermine its use. Corves and Pötz focused on the ratification of the European Convention that they had already managed to pass.

The UK delegation became the FRG's staunchest ally in the EPC negotiations. Like the FRG, UK officials wanted to secure the ratification of the European Convention; they were mainly interested in consolidating antiterrorism initiatives that the European states had achieved. Both delegations wanted the same practical results: to increase their extradition options for citizens and foreigners engaged in international terrorism without acknowledging these actors' political motivations. They worked to ensure that the European Convention entered into effect. During early 1977, a slew of exchanges through the EC's official telegram network, Coreu, revealed deep anxieties in both the FRG justice ministry and the UK Home Office. Both agencies worried that Peyrefitte was trying to replace the European Convention with an unfeasible, too broad convention.[87] A British telegram pointed out that the French convention draft abolished the political offense exception—an endeavor that had failed several times in past years. The FRG and British position was to avoid any complication that prevented the ratification of the European Convention.

Meanwhile, Anglo-Irish frictions over extradition remained. As the only EC member with a recent colonized history, the Irish EPC delegation worried about a potential repeal of the political offense exception. Irish officials accused France, the FRG, and especially the UK of seeking to gain custody of extremists in direct violation of Irish sovereign control over its legal system.[88] They refused to sign an EPC agreement, just like they had abstained from signing the European Convention. And unlike the Council of Europe, the EPC's smaller membership and requirement that decisions be unanimous amplified Irish demands.

By the time the experts met again on March 14, 1977, divergent fronts were clear between delegates who wanted quick and practical extradition mechanisms for nonstate extremists and ones who had different priorities in regard to anticolonial and politically motivated actors. Delegates representing the UK, the FRG, Belgium, and the Netherlands, all of whom had faced severe violent acts from nonstate attackers at home, demanded that any new convention build upon and improve the European Convention. As an aside, British and FRG officials were also sharing their negotiating and policy-making experiences with U.S. counterparts such as Robert Kupperman, chief scientist at the Arms Control and Disarmament Agency. They collaborated with North American, European, and Israeli academics as well, creating a network of contacts who discussed legal and tactical responses to terrorism more than political context.[89] In contrast to the British and other states' position, though, the Irish delegation requested that the European Convention and any new convention unequivocally prioritize the political offense exception and respect the political rights of attackers.

French officials sought a convention that was broadly about European integration on crime-related legal processes and barely touched upon the issue of terrorism. A crime-based convention might receive institutional and popular support within France, but a terrorism convention would not. French officials had almost no domestic support for the European Convention, which codified violent nonstate actors within Europe principally as criminals even if they claimed to be anticolonial actors or political dissidents. The powerful French leftist scene rejected this approach. The French Ministry of Foreign Affairs was still adamantly resisting any endorsement of the European Convention, worried that this step would undermine France's relations to Arab states.[90] By early 1977, the FRG Council of Europe delegation speculated that the French government also sought to placate leaders in the Palestinian national liberation movement in order to make France less of a target for international terrorism. Unlike their counterparts in Italy, the UK, or the FRG, French legislators had passed no specific domestic antiterrorism laws. The French police did not put effort into arresting Palestinian Fedayeen on French territory.

The French arrest of Abu Daoud in January 1977 fit into this pattern. The d'Estaing administration quickly instituted deportation proceedings and let Abu Daoud travel to Algeria, where he was out of reach of European judicial systems. To frustrated West German and enraged Israeli diplomats, French officials explained that the West German extradition request had procedural faults and did not include the alias under which Abu Daoud had entered France. His identity was thus in question and an extradition out of the question. Exemplifying their respective national policies, to French authorities the arrested man was only a potentially dangerous actor whose civil rights were of primary concern, while to the FRG he was an extraditable criminal with a history of substantive brutal violence.

The French focus in the EPC negotiations was completely on the integration of judicial regulations and mechanisms. Compared to the FRG's extradition aims, French goals were thus less controversial in the Global South—but more controversial within the EC. The French convention draft stipulated that all states would use the same processes for extradition and mutual assistance requests, with the possibility of further integration of actual criminal laws down the road.[91] This suggestion was radical in its scope. From March 1977 onward, Christian Le Gunehec led the French delegation in the EPC working group. He was director of Criminal Matters and Pardons at the French justice ministry and would go on to serve as a top-tier judge in France's Court of Cassation and Law Court of the Republic. Le Gunehec criticized the European Convention for allowing each country to maintain its own legal tradition and decide on what constituted a terrorist "serious offense." He claimed that this ambiguity would lead to a range of contradictory practices and interpretations. As a solution, the French draft contained general regulations for any sort of multilateral interaction or processes concerning all "serious crimes," not just terrorist acts. It also required each EC member to abandon national practices concerning the political offense exception. French delegates knew their draft would require substantial time to negotiate, and that states might need to revise existing law or even their constitutions to comply. They emphasized that its long-term utility was greater than the European Convention, though, and would offset the short-term delay.[92] This stance diverged strongly from the aims of the other EC delegates in the working group.

To address both West German/British and French interests, the EPC working group took a pragmatic approach and decided that it would create two new multilateral agreements—one for each side. These agreements would keep all parties invested in the negotiations. The first agreement catered to most delegates' interest in preserving and fortifying the European Convention. The delegates conceptualized it as an addendum to the European Convention. The addendum required EC states to adhere to the statutes and practices set up within the European Convention, even if the state in question had not signed or ratified the convention. It would bind France to the requirements of the European Convention without requiring French ratification of that convention. In the meantime, the group would also discuss a second, separate EC convention based on the French draft. This step met French demands and kept Peyrefitte and Le Gunehec invested in the working group. This second convention would standardize European extradition and mutual assistance procedures.[93] It would create a common European legal space.

Meanwhile, the West German RAF continued to operate across borders and collaborate with Palestinian extremists. These attacks heightened FRG demands for fast and easily acceptable extradition mechanisms. From April to October 1977, the RAF hit the FRG with a series of assassinations, kidnappings, and a Palestinian hijacking of a Lufthansa flight in a period known as the "German Autumn."

The West German offenders often plotted and hid in the Netherlands, France, and other states bordering the FRG. The violence of their actions motivated the Schmidt cabinet to request that neighboring governments arrest these FRG citizens and extradite them back to the FRG. By the fall of 1977, even French authorities collaborated. In July 1977, one of the lawyers representing the incarcerated RAF leadership, Klaus Croissant, fled to France to avoid a West German arrest warrant that claimed that he was criminally conspiring with his clients. Croissant settled in Paris and filed a petition for political asylum, claiming that FRG authorities wanted to punish him for his defense of RAF clients. He enjoyed significant public support. Over two hundred French luminaries signed a petition in favor of his asylum claim.[94] Yet in a spectacular media-frenzied case, French officials denied Croissant's claims and extradited him back to the FRG in November 1977.[95] In December 1977 Swiss authorities arrested Gabriele Kröcher-Tiedemann, the 2 June Movement member who had been released in the Lorenz exchange and who had participated in the OPEC takeover. Swiss authorities prosecuted Kröcher-Tiedemann themselves for shooting and wounding two customs officials during her arrest. She also had ransom money from a prominent recent kidnapping in Austria on her. After serving the main part of her Swiss sentence, authorities extradited Kröcher-Tiedemann to the FRG in 1986.

Since the FRG, the UK, and smaller EC states were committed to strengthening the European Convention, work progressed quickly on the addendum that was to bind France to it. In early October 1977, the EPC working group agreed that the addendum would apply to the entire European Convention. By December, the working group had outmaneuvered Le Gunehec and decided that the addendum would require all EC states to adhere to the European Convention, even if a state had not ratified the European Convention or if that state had ratified the convention with reservations.[96] Unlike the Council of Europe, in the EPC decisions and votes had to be unanimous. If passed, the addendum would force France to adhere to the premises of the European Convention. The Irish delegation was unhappy about the phrasing, but finally prioritized European integration and being "good Europeans" as long as the negotiations did not include a requirement to extradite.[97] All in all, the addendum would allow the FRG to emphasize that the Western European states shared a common understanding of international terrorism as criminal; the addendum would end the negative symbolic repercussions of France's current refusal to adhere to the European Convention. The working group finished its addendum draft in April 1978.[98]

The French delegation in the meantime threatened to withdraw from the negotiations if its own proposed convention was not addressed. If the French delegation left, their absence would render the addendum to the European Convention moot. The other EC states thus had to emphasize their willingness to work with French officials in order to keep them engaged in the working group and actually pass the addendum. Throughout early 1978, the heads of state and justice ministers of the other eight EC states assured Giscard d'Estaing and Peyrefitte that they would support French political aims in the EPC—if France would only agree to the addendum. In February 1978, Le Gunehec resubmitted the French convention draft. It proposed that the EC states standardize their legal interaction on extradition, mutual assistance in criminal matters, the transfer of criminal prosecution, recognition and enforcement of foreign criminal judgments, and the transfer of convicts.[99] The convention draft completely erased the political offense exception. This step made the French draft unacceptable for Ireland and raised concerns in the UK Foreign and Commonwealth Office about whether this draft would be passable at all.[100] Yet the other delegates agreed to continue negotiations in order to move the adoption of the addendum forward and tie France to the European Convention.[101]

FIGURE 4.1. The body of Aldo Moro, former Italian prime minister, found in Rome, May 9, 1978. The leftist Italian Red Brigades kidnapped Moro in March 1978 and finally murdered him in an attack that shook the general public as well as Italian and European politicians. Keystone Press / Alamy Stock Photo.

In mid-March 1978, the Italian Red Brigades kidnapped former Italian president Aldo Moro. The kidnappers demanded the release of their incarcerated members. Italian media covered the kidnapping around the clock; Italian society hotly debated how to respond. In May, Moro's body was found stuffed into the trunk of a car.[102] Though this incident had no immediately visible transnational ties, it did highlight that high-level state officials in Europe were prime targets of nonstate extremists. The EC justice ministers reaffirmed their support for multilateral initiatives against terrorism.[103]

Peyrefitte continued to link progress on the addendum to progress on the French-proposed EC convention. He informed Vogel that the French justice ministry needed negotiation successes on the European legal space convention draft and for the other EC states to demonstrate continuous support. Otherwise, Peyrefitte could not overcome significant opposition to the addendum from the French Ministry of Foreign Affairs.[104] In the summer of 1978, another series of French petitions to the FRG justice ministry stated that Peyrefitte was losing interest in the addendum. French justice and foreign ministry officials sharply critiqued other EPC delegations for alienating the French president and themselves; these delegations did not treat the French convention draft as a prestigious European integration project.[105] Only such a prestige project had a shot at passing the French legislature—an antiterrorism agreement did not.

The FRG justice ministry became more conciliatory to the French position after the European Convention entered into force on August 4, 1978. It had the three necessary ratifications from the FRG, Austria, and Sweden. Vogel then wrote to Peyrefitte. In an assuaging tone, Vogel offered to support the French convention draft and its European legal space concept at an upcoming meeting of the EC justice ministers.[106] Pötz adopted a more conciliatory tone, as well, and promised to treat the French convention draft with the appropriate gravitas.[107] Meanwhile, the UK Home Office and the FRG justice ministry continued lobbying the other Council of Europe members to ratify the European Convention.

By the fall of 1978, the EPC working group had reached a stalemate in which the French and FRG/British sides paid lip service to the other's goals to protect their own respective draft agreements. This stalemate slowed any overall progress to a crawl. In October 1978, the working group discussed the contours of the French-sought European legal space convention, despite the fact that most delegates had no significant interest in it. The delegates postponed major decisions about the content of the draft. The convention was to standardize judicial collaboration among the EC states. Yet the details were unclear. What sorts of crimes should the EC states collaborate on? Should they limit their judicial process collaboration to murder and manslaughter, for example, or include slighter infractions as well? The French had included extradition in their convention drafts, which threw up questions debated in negotiations over the European Convention. Should the new European legal space convention also include the "extradite or prosecute" requirement? What about the political offense exception? The delegates could not answer these questions.[108] In the meantime, the finished addendum to the European Convention went before the EC justice ministers. The ministers accepted the addendum on October 10, 1978, leaving only formal translations and the signing ceremony to be completed.

However, little further progress occurred, and the stalemate held. The delegates conducted multilateral negotiations but prioritized national goals and sovereignty. Details on the French-desired European legal space convention remained spotty. Working group meetings in January and March 1979 passed without any agreement about the sorts of offenses or mechanisms that this convention should cover. A French proposal to extend the convention even further, to encompass civil law as well as criminal law, met with instant rejection. Prior announced that the UK would not be able to ratify even the current draft of the European legal space convention without an extensive reform of British extradition law.[109] In April, the working group sought high-level guidance and asked the EC justice ministers to decide what offenses and mechanisms should be included.[110] The ministers did not reach agreement on any of the issues either, though, and neither did subsequent working group meetings in June and September 1979. The other EC justice ministries were not willing to hand off control over their legal processes in the way that the French convention draft envisioned.

Meanwhile, the French justice ministry, which held the EPC presidency from January to June 1979 and thus controlled meeting agendas, delayed the final work on the addendum to keep the other delegations focused on the European legal space convention. The presidency-holding state hosted meetings and had discretion over their agenda. Le Gunehec demanded that the translations of the addendum into the seven official EC languages match perfectly. The translation process was lengthy and took up the entire French EPC presidency.[111] Overall, the EPC stalemate on both agreements highlighted that delegates wanted multilateral solutions and European integration but were not willing to submit to multilateral governance if it infringed too far on their sovereign control of their legal systems.

After two years with few results, tempers began to fray. The seven delegations pushing the addendum (all but France and Ireland) became more aggressive about passing it. Ironically, it was under Irish supervision, during a September 1979 working group meeting, that translations of the addendum were complete. Crucially, the Irish delegation again did not raise formal objections, accepting that the addendum and the European Convention's "extradite or prosecute" formulation would not require Ireland to extradite anyone. This position allowed the working group to move forward with the addendum adoption. However, the French delegation announced scheduling difficulties with an October 1979 adoption date.

During a high-level EPC dinner, the director of political affairs in the Belgian foreign ministry, Alfred Cahen, sharply accused his French counterpart of delay tactics. He pointed out that the European legal space concept was unpopular in the EPC working group and in the ruling Belgian Socialist party, and that Belgium as well as other EC states had fulfilled their part of the compromise by working on both agreements. He threatened that his government would not support the "European legal space" convention if France did not sign the addendum.[112]

In late 1979, Corves and other working group delegates placed substantial pressure on their French counterparts, finally convincing them that the European legal space convention would fail if they stalled further on the addendum.[113] On December 4, 1979, all nine EC member states signed the addendum to the European Convention and send it to the individual states to be ratified.[114] Just days later, the UNGA adopted the Foreign Office's envisioned convention against hostage-taking.[115] The FRG initiatives appeared to be moving forward. However, the FRG Foreign Office notified the justice ministry that significant domestic opposition to the European Convention still existed in France, and that the French authorities were unlikely to ratify the European Convention or its EC addendum if they could no longer use these agreements as leverage for the European legal space draft.[116]

Yet the delegates also lost patience with this European legal space convention. After years of inconclusive discussions, most delegates realized that the EC states were unlikely to sacrifice sovereign control over legal processes to multilateral governance. In a late February 1980 working group meeting in Rome, delegates from all states except for France informally conducted intense discussions about the future of the negotiations in hallway settings and over coffee breaks. They questioned whether a European legal space convention was even possible, and agreed that the negotiations (no matter the outcome) should be quickly finished, ideally by the end of Italy's EPC presidency in June.[117] In addition, they decided that because of the difficulty of negotiating multilaterally on antiterrorism and legal matters, no new antiterrorism initiatives should be attempted until all had ratified the European Convention and its addendum.

In its twentieth meeting in May 1980, the EPC working group agreed on hasty and legally sloppy compromises and declared the European legal space convention draft complete. For example, the working group declared that the new convention would not contain the political offense exception.

However, states could issue reservations, and they could for example issue a reservation about the clause that abolished the political offense exception.[118] There was no right to introduce a general reservation about more than a single convention clause, however. In addition, no mechanism existed for a state to leave the agreement once it had signed on. No obvious mechanism allowed states to modify the convention either. This hasty compromise proved to be a mistake.

For the first time during the EPC negotiations, the smaller EC states overtly challenged the idea of standardizing judicial processes, claiming that this integrative step came at too high of a cost for their own national sovereignty. Previously, Dutch, Belgian, and Danish delegates had supported the negotiations in hopes of improving European integration. After the hasty European legal space convention draft was complete, the smaller EC states labeled it as unacceptable. All were wary because the draft abolished the political offense exception yet contained no mechanisms for a country wishing to leave, amend the treaty, or voice a general reservation about more than one article.[119] The draft required all EC states to adapt their legal systems without giving them further options to revise the parameters for change in the future. In circular telegrams to the other delegations, these smaller EC states claimed that the draft locked them into a politically and judicially problematic agreement.[120] Dutch minister of justice Job de Ruiter led the opposition. He speculated that France was attempting to reinforce its EC leadership, utilizing the informal EPC working group process to undermine the smaller EC members' sovereign control of their legal systems.[121]

Dutch resistance destroyed the compromise that France would accept the addendum to the European Convention if only the other delegations cooperated on the European legal space agreement. In early June 1980, the Dutch cabinet declared that it would not sign the European legal space convention.[122] EPC agreements were unanimous, and the Dutch rejection set off last minute scrambling to save the convention as well as the addendum (mainly the addendum, which would not be ratified by France otherwise). These last-minute steps failed, and the European legal space convention draft was never opened for signature. On June 19, 1980, the French undersecretary of justice, Jean-Paul Mourot, announced that France would not ratify the addendum to the European Convention.[123] After four years of work, the EPC negotiations achieved no presentable results.

By this time, the judicial experts who had worked in the Council of Europe and the EPC on international terrorism were exhausted. Even the West Germans were done. The cost-benefit ratio of the negotiations was too asymmetric. The sheer effort and number of meetings that had gone into the European Convention and the EPC negotiations were not proportional to the utility the convention offered. By 1980, the EC justice ministries agreed with the U.S. State Department's 1973 decision that "extradite or prosecute" conventions were a lot of work for little political payoff. The European Convention had a symbolic effect against international terrorism by demonstrating that European states were willing to collaborate against such attackers. Yet antiterrorism was too complex a field and infringed on too much national sovereignty in legal matters to advance multilateral governance and European integration on a large scale—at least in the 1970s. Two decades later, the European Union gradually created a common legal space in its "area of freedom, security, and justice." It also introduced the 2004 European Arrest Warrant system, which operated without the political offense exception.[124] Yet these developments would take decades more to implement and were not specifically tied to antiterrorism initiatives.

During the mid to late 1970s, negotiations about terrorism and extradition became part of the process of European integration. Wide-reaching efforts to shape these antiterrorism agreements into a new facet of European integration failed, however, despite the general increase of European unification throughout the 1970s. Loopholes and sovereignty considerations meant that, ironically, the European Convention solidified terrorism as a criminal problem within European relations and yet offered insufficient means to address or resolve that problem. Once again, the patterns established in the ICAO, the OAS, and UNGA repeated themselves. Antiterrorism conventions passed when addressing specific offenses—ideally in a precisely defined list. But they were politically burdensome, cost substantial effort to implement, and did not generate immediate payoffs. For these reasons, they did not lend themselves to larger political initiatives such as French Gaullist policy. In addition, states contested antiterrorism extradition specifications and judicial integration because they infringed on national interests and eroded sovereignty in ways that officials were not prepared to accept. Multilateral negotiations about terrorism and political violence were too politically divisive to create straightforward outcomes.

The European Convention institutionalized terrorism as a security threat in European politics, however, and solidified what kinds of violent attacks would fall under the label *terrorism* in foreign relations on the continent. It created a normative change even if it did not provide substantial antiterrorism mechanisms. The European Convention's list of covered offenses helped codify a number of violent acts as terrorism and managed for the first time to regulate the term itself as a criminal offense in international law. The European Convention thus defined the act as a crime in international law, a feat which the U.S. State Department had not been able to achieve within the UNGA. It also gave state officials the power to identify "serious offenses" as terrorist crimes—and took definitional power away from nonstate actors such as political activists or the terrorists themselves. The negotiations around the European Convention significantly normalized the idea that nonstate violent actors with transnational connections were criminals, not insurgents, combatants, revolutionaries, protostate officials, or politically motivated dissidents. The European Convention thus strengthened the Western trend, which had been developing since 1968, to handle international terrorism as a crime. In subsequent years, networks of conservatives in the United States, Europe, and Israel would seize on this interpretation of terrorists as criminals and deploy it to advance their own political ends.

Chapter Five

FROM INTERNATIONAL LAW TO MILITARIZED COUNTERTERRORISM

Yonatan Netanyahu became a hero after his death. On June 27, 1976, two Palestinians and two West Germans hijacked Air France Flight 139 from Tel Aviv to Paris via Athens. The Palestinians belonged to Wadie Haddad's Popular Front for the Liberation of Palestine—External Operations (PFLP-EO), an extremist Palestinian national liberation splinter group dedicated to attacking Israeli targets outside of Israel. The West Germans were members of the ideologically affiliated group Revolutionary Cells. In Entebbe, Uganda, at least four others waited to join the arriving hijackers. The Ugandan dictator Idi Amin ordered his army to surround Entebbe Airport, but Amin for all intents and purposes supported the hijackers and their plans. Holding 254 hostages, the hijackers demanded the release of fifty-three incarcerated Palestinians and associated European and Japanese extremists. On June 29, the attackers separated Israeli from non-Israeli hostages in a procedure that reminded some onlookers of the Holocaust. Gradually, the attackers released most non-Israelis but continued to detain 106 hostages. On the evening of July 3, 1976, the Israeli Special Forces unit Sayeret Matkal landed with four transport aircraft at the airport, stormed the buildings, and freed 102 hostages. Three hostages died, as did several dozen Ugandan soldiers. Commander Netanyahu was the only Israeli Special Forces casualty. From a tactical perspective, the Entebbe raid was a failure for the hijackers and a resounding success for the Israelis. In turn, the raid facilitated two interrelated counterterrorism developments. Global North officials' prior conceptualization of international terrorists as criminals—actors whose politics were irrelevant—solidified within international relations and law. However, especially in the United States the ideological justification and mechanisms of counterterrorism gradually militarized to serve new (and highly political) purposes.

In the late 1970s and early 1980s, U.S. officials slowly adopted military means against international terrorism because earlier international law initiatives had created strong normative conceptions of terrorism in the Global North but did not provide effective mechanisms to prevent and punish attackers. The Entebbe hijacking boosted European initiatives to criminalize international terrorism with multilateral agreements. West German foreign minister Hans-Dietrich Genscher used the attack to advocate for a convention against hostage-taking in the United Nations. The Group of Seven (G7) states later passed a resolution against hijacking. The Entebbe attack thus allowed especially West German officials to solidify their multilateral, crime-focused approach to international terrorism. The result was a normative Global North understanding of international terrorism as a crime. Yet on the other hand, Yonatan Netanyahu's brother and future Israeli prime minister Benjamin Netanyahu used the attack to valorize his deceased sibling and advance Israeli conceptions of militarized counterterrorism. His advocacy resonated especially with the burgeoning conservative movement (as exemplified by Ronald Reagan) in the United States. These conservatives appreciated military approaches for their visible effectiveness and political utility. Using Israeli cues, conservatives emphasized that terrorism was an existential, communist-directed threat to Western societies and tied its prevention into their own militant anticommunist platforms. Though Global North governments still adhered to the legal agreements that described terrorism as a criminal activity, the Reagan administration slowly but surely prioritized military countermeasures against this ostensibly existential threat.

By the late 1970s, U.S. and European officials habitually cooperated to regulate specific acts of terrorism as criminal offenses and to undermine other states' support for extremist attackers. Though these multilateral initiatives were driven by diverse political interests, officials presented them as apolitical technical endeavors to protect and secure their civilian populations. Global North officials consolidated a corresponding international law

FIGURE 5.1. Benjamin Netanyahu speaks to students as he stands in front of a banner depicting his late brother Yonatan Netanyahu, September 1, 2019.
Benjamin Netanyahu valorized his brother, the only Israeli operative killed during the 1976 Entebbe operation, and used his memory to lobby for militant antiterrorism measures in Israel and around the world.
UPI / Alamy Stock Photo.

framework and used the conventions and strategies they had accumulated throughout the 1970s to circumvent opposition from recently independent states, political activists, and terrorists themselves. In international organizations, they no longer attempted to regulate the undefined term of terrorism. Instead, they returned to regulating only specific, easily delineable acts of violence as criminal and illegitimate. In the United Nations General Assembly (UNGA), the Federal Republic of Germany (FRG) convinced other states to adopt a convention against hostage-taking. However, Global North officials were aware that these agreements were complex and time-consuming to negotiate. As such, they also began collaborating among themselves on controversial issues, especially on how to enforce antiterrorism conventions. The G7 states adopted the 1978 "Statement on Air-Hijacking," which threatened sanctions against states that harbored hijackers. The G7 also invited other states to copy their example. These initiatives had few practical antiterrorism results. But Global North states codified the act of terrorism within international law in the way that they perceived it (as individual and criminal). Having achieved this aim, these states scaled back their international law initiatives on this difficult and time-consuming issue by the early 1980s.

As earlier officials began withdrawing from legal antiterrorism initiatives, hawkish conservatives appropriated the crime-focused discourse on terrorism for their own anticommunist political aims. In 1979, Netanyahu and Israeli leaders convinced conservative politicians, officials, and activists from the United States and Europe to view terrorism as a Cold War problem. Through a transnational network of policymakers, politicians, and political pundits, conservatives claimed that the Soviet Union supported terrorists as illegal proxy combatants. American, Global North, and right-wing actors had held similar views in the 1960s. Different now was that several multilateral agreements codified terrorist acts as predominantly criminal no matter the political context. Soviet and other states' support of terrorists thus violated international norms more than in the past. To counter these transgressions, U.S. conservatives and their European counterparts advocated for the implementation of the military options against terrorists that the Israelis had favored all along. Based on unsound and distorted facts, this perception did not accurately reflect the realities of international terrorism.[1] As U.S. conservatives took power through the Reagan administration in 1981, nevertheless, they disseminated this idea of a Soviet-controlled "terror network," adapting the ostensibly apolitical criminal view of terrorism and inserting their own political ideology and aims in order to recodify counterterrorism as a militaristic endeavor.

These U.S. and Global North strategies solidified the global contestation around the label of terrorism and the right to use political violence.

In 1970s international organizations, participants sought to convince one another that their own position on international terrorism was accurate and should be adopted within international law. This effort failed as Global North and South states developed distinct positions. Global North state officials continued to conceptualize terrorist actors and attacks as predominantly criminal. Meanwhile, recently independent states still viewed terrorism as an aspect of decolonization and national independence. By the 1980s, officials, experts, and interested parties found it increasingly easier to pursue their own antiterrorism initiatives without seeking common global positions. For example, the Reagan administration pursued Cold War priorities as it labeled left-wing actors in Latin America as terrorists and, contrastingly, supported right-wing Nicaraguan contras and Afghani *mujahideen*. In addition, high-level Reagan administration members now became increasingly interested in military solutions. The international controversy about whether terrorism was a criminal or anticolonial issue remained even as the United States gradually transitioned to military counterterrorism measures. By the 1980s, international discussions concerning the definition of terrorism diversified into unresolvable avenues.

NORMALIZING GLOBAL NORTH CONCEPTUALIZATIONS OF TERRORISM IN INTERNATIONAL LAW

By the late 1970s, Global North states firmly established their normative conception of international terrorism—as an individual criminal act—through further multilateral collaboration. Their efforts downplayed and even ignored any anticolonial political context. Officials cemented their antiterrorism practices in two ways. They created new extradition conventions against specific violent acts. They also collaborated informally to find enforcement mechanisms for the existing conventions. In the early 1980s, Western officials soon believed that they had exhausted the opportunities to solidify their normative understanding of terrorism as a criminal offense in international law and among the global community of states.

By 1976, three ratified multilateral conventions regulated extradition for attacks on civil aviation and attacks on diplomats.[2] Two more would soon be ratified.[3] These conventions framed the violence that they covered in a specific way: as an individual, politically illegitimate, and intrinsically criminal act. Attacks such as hijackings, the kidnapping or assassination of diplomats, and bombings were already illegal according to most states' criminal laws. The conventions specified that states were to actually employ these domestic criminal laws, especially in cases of violent attacks with international dimensions. The conventions implied that terroristic offenders were neither political dissidents nor national liberation insurgents. Signatory states pledged to apply criminal law against terroristic offenders as opposed to the laws of war. The conventions all had loopholes, including the political offense exception. However, the conventions vested the authority to label and prosecute attackers in the hands of state officials. They denied agency and sovereignty to protostate or nonstate actors. Western states thus branded international terrorism acts as ordinary criminal violations of a state's sovereign control over violence.

Within Europe, FRG officials remained the most vehement driving force for antiterrorism collaboration that spanned national boundaries. FRG elites had promoted extensive domestic security reforms in the late 1960s and early 1970s. In addition, the FRG leadership was badly shaken emotionally by the 1972 Munich attack. FRG officials saw antiterrorism initiatives as a means to improve their local and regional domestic security in tandem with European unification. As West German citizens committed more acts of terror outside the FRG in the mid to late 1970s, the cabinet of Chancellor Helmut Schmidt also wanted to develop mechanisms to deny FRG terrorists safe haven abroad and extradite them back to the FRG. British officials supported this endeavor because they were very interested in extraditing Northern Irish attackers from Ireland to the UK during the Troubles. In the FRG, Hans-Dietrich Genscher was the main high-level proponent of international antiterrorism initiatives. After becoming foreign minister in 1974, he retained his interest in multilateral antiterrorism projects.[4]

Genscher soon asked the FRG's Foreign Office to develop further multilateral antiterrorism collaboration. Following the Organization of Petroleum Exporting Countries (OPEC) attack, Genscher began planning to create a new convention against the increasingly common act of taking hostages. The OPEC attackers had targeted Saudi and other Arab officials, showcasing that insufficiently radical Arab bureaucrats were now a target of international terrorism as well and might be convinced to collaborate with their Global North counterparts. The Foreign Office's plan was to create another narrow convention against a specific violent act, hostage-taking. This approach held more promise of success that did targeting the ambiguous category of terrorism. Genscher's main goals were to deny safe haven abroad to FRG terrorists and also to increase the FRG's international prestige. As a recent UN member, the FRG could display global leadership by shepherding a major multilateral convention against individual violent actors to completion.[5]

FRG UN ambassador Rüdiger von Wechmar announced the initiative after the 1976 Entebbe hijacking,[6] which led to a wave of calls for new international regulations against the taking of hostages in peacetime (hostage-taking in war already fell under international humanitarian law). In the Council of Europe and European Community, the Entebbe attack precipitated a new wave of negotiations concerning the almost completed European Convention, terrorism, and mutual assistance in criminal matters.[7] For their burgeoning UN initiative, the Foreign Office's United Nations division recommended the format of an "extradite or prosecute" convention, just like the Montreal, Hague, Diplomats, and European Conventions.[8] Such conventions had proven widely acceptable to most states due to their loopholes and lack of enforcement mechanisms. Yet they branded the specific act they covered as an extraditable criminal offense.

Von Wechmar spent the fall of 1976 advocating for the FRG initiative in the UN. He could count on the support of most other European states, as the Council of Europe was in the final process of adopting the European Convention and the EC members had just set up the TREVI network. Problematic was the UNGA's large membership of recently decolonized countries, who prioritized protections for national liberation actors and had shaped UNGA terrorism-related discussions since 1972. Genscher and von Wechmar faced the same problems that had plagued then-U.S. secretary of state William Rogers and UN ambassador George H. W. Bush in their 1972 UNGA initiative against international terrorism. Like Rogers and Bush, the FRG Foreign Office sought extradition and criminal law regulations.

Many Arab, African, and other delegates from recently independent states used the UNGA Ad Hoc Committee on International Terrorism to claim that national liberation movements and the term *terrorism* both needed be addressed as anticolonial self-determination issues. In the fall of 1976, they attempted to transfer the hostage-taking convention initiative into the terrorism committee to link the issues and prevent any potential abrogation of national liberation movements' rights. Van Wechmar assuaged them by promising that any actions by legitimate self-determination movements, acting as protostate actors, would already fall under the laws of war and were not covered by the FRG initiative.[9] On December 15, 1976, the UNGA agreed to have its Sixth Committee, responsible for legal issues, draft a convention against hostage-taking.[10] An ad hoc committee for this purpose met for several weeks in August 1977. The FRG provided an "extradite or prosecute" convention draft to discuss.[11] The committee made little headway, but the delegates agreed to ask the UNGA to renew their mandate and continue negotiating a potential convention. The UNGA approved this continuation in December 1977.[12] The FRG delegation still had a lot of convincing to do.

West German officials specifically wanted to avoid any references to warfare, national liberation, and military antiterrorism approaches.[13] Ongoing negotiations on the laws of war complicated the situation. In the mid-1970s, UN members negotiated addendums to the Geneva Conventions, the laws of war, and international humanitarian law. The major controversy of these negotiations was whether national liberation actors should have access to special rights accorded to sovereign states' soldiers, including combatant and prisoner of war status. Most Global North states said no. Most recently independent states said yes. The final result was a compromise. The 1977 Protocol I and II to the Geneva Conventions included special rights for nonstate self-determination actors as long as they themselves could uphold all statist obligations under the Geneva Conventions. Thus, national liberation groups had to be able to, for example, treat captured opponents as prisoners of war and offer the International Red Cross access to them. Such qualifications were impossible to meet. The protocols also contained ambiguous formulations for how to determine whether an actor met those criteria. The text's vagueness ensured that Global North states could rather easily refuse to acknowledge that national liberation movements upheld Geneva Convention obligations. The United States, the UK, and other Global North states were not interested in renegotiating, clarifying these qualifications, or potentially allowing nonstate actors to gain clearer access to specific statist rights.[14] The FRG's initiative had the potential to open that can of worms.

Issues of nonstate political violence were contentious not just between Global North and South states, but also among the Global North states themselves and their close allies. Israeli and French diplomats created the same headaches for von Wechmar that they had caused Bush in 1972. The Israeli foreign minister Yigal Allon undermined the FRG position by supporting military counterterrorism efforts. He suggested that a hostage-taking convention could be applicable in situations such as the Entebbe raid.[15] Most Arab and Eastern European states, as well as the Soviet Union, considered the Israeli operation at Entebbe an armed foreign intervention. These positions were sharply in contrast with FRG (and earlier U.S.) efforts to address terrorism as a crime, not a military issue. In a similar vein, French diplomats argued that a new convention would undermine existing international humanitarian law by superseding rules against hostage-taking in the Geneva Conventions. A new convention could thus generate situations in which hostage-taking by national liberation movements could fall into problematic legal grey areas.[16] Building on its policies not to antagonize French-Arab relations, the French Ministry of Foreign Affairs preferred not to negotiate a new convention at all. The 1972 UN initiative by the United States to draft a convention against terrorism had faced similar Israeli and French opposition. West German and U.S. allies contested among themselves how to handle border-crossing extremists.

The FRG initiative had one major advantage in that it addressed a specific and already heavily regulated problem: hostage-taking. The 1972 UNGA negotiations for a terrorism convention failed because participants could not agree on how to define terrorism or who would be covered under the convention's provisions. However, conventions against more specific attacks such as hijacking were easier because these attacks carried less definitional ambiguity. Also, some specific attacks were subject to existing UN regulation. The UN General Assembly had adopted the 1973 Diplomats Convention in part because diplomats were already protected persons under international law. Its supporters argued that the Diplomats Convention merely reinforced earlier requirements.[17] Similarly, as emphasized by French UN delegates, hostage-taking was already prohibited under the 1949 Geneva Conventions.[18] The Additional Protocols to the Geneva Conventions reaffirmed this ban when they were completed in 1977. West German diplomats emphasized that they were only prohibiting hostage-taking in nonwarfare and civilian settings. They were not addressing national liberation or warfare situations.[19] Overall, the focus on a specific violent act with prior international law regulations allowed the FRG to sidestep some of the controversy over definition and scope that had choked the 1972 U.S. initiative against the broader and more contentious issue of terrorism.

The FRG UN delegation developed strategies to address the difficulties caused by the Arab, African, Israeli, and French delegations. Genscher personally endorsed and at times participated in the negotiations. Richard Nixon, Henry Kissinger, and William Rogers had avoided such political risk to themselves in the early 1970s. Genscher's status in the international community improved after the 1977 Mogadishu operation. Unlike the Israelis at Entebbe, Schmidt and Genscher secured permission from Somali president Siad Barre before sending a tactical unit to free the hijacked Lufthansa plane. Even African states acknowledged that the FRG leadership had respected Somali sovereignty.[20] Genscher's personal influence increased commensurately.

Another FRG strategy was to discuss the proposed convention in semi-private venues where FRG officials could speak to Arab, African, and non-aligned delegates away from the public eye. The goal was to avoid posturing while generating willingness to negotiate without the pressure of having to adhere to public stances. The FRG Foreign Office supported the 1976 revival and yearly renewal of the UN Ad Hoc Committee on International Terrorism. Genscher and von Wechmar wanted this committee to serve as a venue for recently independent states to discuss terrorism and national liberation movements separately from the hostage-taking negotiations. They outmaneuvered all attempts to link the terrorism and hostage-taking committees.[21]

In the meantime, from 1978 onward the West Germans channeled the hostage-taking committee away from New York City. In February 1978, the committee met in small and off-the-record working groups at the UN office in Geneva. This format gave all involved parties the opportunity to make concessions without losing public face. The Israelis removed a potential point of contention by agreeing not to participate. Meanwhile, the Camp David Accords signaled that Arab states would no longer stand united against Israel or support Palestinians' agency in pursuit of self-determination.[22] The FRG's negotiator was Carl-August Fleischhauer, head of the legal department of the Foreign Office. Fleischhauer was an experienced bureaucrat with a doctorate in international law; he had been working on West German antiterrorism collaboration since 1972. He wound up collaborating, surprisingly, especially with the Algerian delegate. The two relied on their Nigerian colleague to mediate between them. The committee members took conciliatory steps toward a convention that criminalized hostage-taking as long as such a convention had strict limitations and did not imply a blanket condemnation of violent national liberation actors.[23] After the formal negotiations ended, the West Germans continued their lobbying among all delegations in New York City. The FRG Foreign Office thus slowly undermined massive potential resistance to its convention draft. The UNGA renewed the hostage-taking convention committee again for 1979.[24]

In the third committee meeting in early 1979, the small working groups achieved a breakthrough. They agreed on a convention draft that applied the principle of "extradite or prosecute" to hostage-taking. Once again, the draft required signatory states to pass and apply domestic criminal laws against hostage-taking. The political offense exemption gave states the option to acknowledge the criminals' political motivation. Yet the basic principle that the perpetrators should be handled as ordinary criminals remained. The convention's generous jurisdiction clauses allowed any state whose territory, citizens, or interests were affected to claim jurisdiction and prosecute an offender. The French delegation accepted the draft due to an article that placed wartime or martial situations under the sole jurisdiction of the Geneva Conventions.[25]

That same article placated Arab and African delegates who supported national liberation movements. The Geneva Conventions's recently adopted Protocols I and II contained provisions for national liberation actors, though who qualified was vague. Arab and African delegates hoped that national liberation actors' behavior would fall under the Geneva Conventions, international humanitarian law, and the laws of war, not this convention that focused on criminal law and civilian situations.[26] Recognition as participants in the Geneva Conventions could provide national liberation movements legitimacy as protostate actors and give them a potential seat at the table in international relations. Meanwhile, most Western delegations knew that being recognized as a Geneva Conventions participant would be very difficult for nonstate groups due to the ambiguity of the actual text and the requirement that groups uphold all aspects of the Geneva Conventions.[27] Thus, the hostage-taking convention draft served Western states' interest in regulating and politically delegitimizing hostage-taking by nonstate actors. Yet it in principle (if not in practice) retained loopholes for recognized national liberation actors to be handled under the Geneva Conventions.

The final discussions and adoption of the convention proceeded quickly in the tumult surrounding the Iran hostage crisis. On November 4, 1979, Iranian students stormed the U.S. embassy in Tehran and took sixty-three U.S. embassy staff hostage. The Carter administration responded with a plethora of diplomatic initiatives and threats, including in the UN. The UN Security Council met from December 1 to 4, 1979, and passed Resolution 457 calling for the release of the hostages. By the end of December, the United States demanded economic sanctions against Iran in the Security Council. Its Resolution 461 of December 31, 1979, introduced such sanctions.[28] In this politically charged climate, the UNGA Sixth Committee discussed and approved the FRG's long-sought convention draft from November 27 to December 7, 1979. The UN General Assembly adopted the International Convention Against the Taking of Hostages (Hostages Convention) on December 17, 1979.[29] Facing long odds, the FRG Foreign Office had successfully negotiated another multilateral convention against a specific violent act. The Hostages Convention entered into force with twenty-two ratifications in 1983.

In addition, 1979 also saw the adoption of a similar convention to protect nuclear materials. In 1974, the U.S. State Department had begun discussions about the security of nuclear materials with other nuclear states.[30] A year later, the first conference to review the progress of the 1968 Nuclear Non-Proliferation Treaty took place. The conference attendees endorsed the creation of a convention to safeguard nuclear materials. The International Atomic Energy Agency (IAEA) supervised negotiations from 1977 to 1979, and in 1980 its members adopted the Convention on the Physical Protection of Nuclear Material (Nuclear Material Convention).[31] It required its signatories to institute domestic laws against the theft or careless handling of nuclear materials in border-crossing transport. The convention also contained "extradite or prosecute" requirements for offenders.[32] It entered into force in 1987. The Nuclear Material Convention was part of the expanding global nonproliferation regime yet also served as an antiterrorism convention.

Alongside negotiations for new agreements, the FRG also collaborated with the United States, the UK, and other close allies to enforce the existing international law conventions. The main goal of FRG, U.S., and other Western officials was to pressure other states to respond to cross-border violent acts in a certain way—by treating them as criminal but not political offenses. Such a treatment served Global North states' various domestic and geopolitical interests. The United States could demand that Latin American and Arab states discount the political claims of extremists. The FRG could request the extradition of its own terrorist citizens home. The UK sought more extradition options from Ireland during the Troubles.

The conventions against terroristic violence were not enforceable, however. They did not include mechanisms that would allow Western states to pressure other states into adhering to them. Within international law, signing and ratifying a convention is voluntary. Not all states were eligible to sign all conventions—the European Convention restricted signings to Council of Europe states, for example. And all conventions contained a loophole in the form of the political offense exemption.

But these issues had not stopped the U.S. State Department from trying to create enforcement mechanisms in the early 1970s. President Richard Nixon's goal had been to punish states that did not adhere to the U.S. interpretation of the spirit of the various conventions, regardless of their voluntary nature or legal loopholes. State Department officials attempted to introduce punitive clauses into the Hague, Montreal, and Diplomats Conventions. Specifically, the State Department wanted to include the option of placing economic sanctions on states that harbored people who had committed attacks covered by the conventions. In 1973, the State Department attempted to create a sanction-focused convention in the International Civil Aviation Organization (ICAO) but failed. Most other states rejected the U.S. efforts as unfeasible, unwise, and simply not achievable. International law is based on voluntary state participation, and only very few actions such as genocide are forbidden with enforcement mechanisms.

During most of the 1970s, the United States and its European allies thus relied on unilateral and bilateral measures to enforce their interpretation that international terrorists were predominantly criminals and not political actors. The Nixon administration introduced legislation, the 1974 Anti-Hijacking Act, which gave the U.S. president the right to unilaterally sanction any state harboring hijackers.[33] No president used that law in the 1970s, however. On the European side, the FRG interior ministry hoped that the TREVI network would improve the enforcement of national, bilateral, and multilateral domestic security collaboration. Officials particularly wanted their neighboring states to collaborate in police training and border patrols, but European states used TREVI mainly as an informal information-sharing network. The FRG, the UK, France, Italy, Belgium, and others did negotiate a range of bilateral extradition and domestic security agreements among themselves that covered terroristic actors and violence. Yet until 1978, no multilateral mechanisms existed to enforce antiterrorism agreements in the international sphere.

In mid-1978, Japanese officials generated a new means to enforce the ICAO conventions against attacks on civil aviation. In 1977, the Japanese government faced diplomatic pressure from its allies, including the FRG and the United States, to strengthen its antihijacking policies. On September 28, 1977, members of the communist militant Japanese Red Army, a group with well-documented connections to extremist Palestinians, hijacked Japan Airlines Flight 472. The Japanese government traded six imprisoned Japanese Red Army members and paid a ransom of six million dollars for the safe return of the 151 hostages.[34] This prisoner release was in line with other Western states' concessions in the early 1970s. But by the middle of the decade, the United States, the FRG, and others were changing their policies. After the 1973 murder of three diplomats in Khartoum, Sudan, Nixon publicly announced that he would not make concessions for extremist attackers.[35] This policy gradually took hold in the U.S. federal government. Likewise, FRG chancellor Schmidt and his cabinet decided during the 1975 Stockholm embassy takeover that the FRG would not give in to demands, though this stance did not become public knowledge until 1977.[36] Meanwhile, most Western states were training tactical units to deploy in hijacking situations such as Entebbe. Particularly after the FRG rescue of a hijacked plane in Mogadishu, Somalia, in October 1977, other industrialized states vigorously and publicly criticized Japan for acceding to the terrorists' demands. The Japanese government in turn sought easy, politically expedient means to demonstrate its commitment against hijackings worldwide.[37]

Meanwhile, President Jimmy Carter's incoming administration reassessed all U.S. antiterrorism measures and became more open to new multilateral initiatives. It abolished the interagency working group of the Cabinet Committee to Combat Terrorism (CCCT), which had previously coordinated antiterrorism policy planning for the U.S. federal government.

It created the similar National Security Council/Special Coordinating Committee Working Group on Terrorism, which included representatives from a vast array of federal agencies.[38] The new working group reported to national security adviser Zbigniew Brzezinski's military assistant, General William Odom. Brzezinski and Odom focused on effective antiterrorism measures, including the use of the military.[39] For example, they supported the creation of the U.S. Special Forces unit Delta Force. Odom personally met with West German border police in December 1977 to learn more about their antiterrorism tactical unit.[40] Overall, the new working group discussed practical and effective means to address terrorism, including the possibility of sponsoring new multilateral initiatives.[41]

In July 1978 Global North officials met in Bonn at the G7, an economic forum and unlikely place to discuss terrorism or political violence. In the wake of the 1973 oil crisis, the seven most influential Global North states held a series of summit meetings, which they named the G7, to coordinate economic policies.[42] Their main goal was to alleviate pressures of the economic shocks of the 1970s through shared measures and collaboration. During the G7 summit from July 16 to 17, 1978, Japanese prime minister Takeo Fukuda proposed at lunch that the G7 heads of state publish a joint statement against hijacking. Chancellor Schmidt quickly embraced the idea, as did Canadian prime minister Pierre Trudeau and U.S. president Carter.[43] The established French position was ambivalent at best toward multilateral antiterrorism initiatives. Yet French president Valéry Giscard d'Estaing agreed to the statement, possibly swayed by the fact that it was first and foremost "an expression of political will," and by Carter's insistence that the G7 leaders should use only their existing domestic powers to enforce it.[44] The G7 heads of state decided to announce that they would collaborate to sanction states that did not prosecute and convict hijackers. They also agreed to use their influence to convince other states to do likewise. On July 17, they released the Bonn Declaration, which affirmed their joint determination to sanction states that harbored hijackers.[45] It allowed Japan to participate in a largely symbolic statement against terrorism.

Since 1969, the U.S. State Department had sought but failed to introduce multilateral sanctions related to attacks on civil aviation within the international community. The G7 Bonn Declaration changed that. The G7 countries promised to sanction any state that refused to either prosecute or extradite hijackers as ordinary criminals. Specifically, the G7 heads of

FIGURE 5.2. The G7 heads of state at lunch during the Bonn Summit, July 16, 1978. Chancellor Helmut Schmidt and the others agreed to adopt a joint statement against hijacking during the summit. Bundesarchiv (German Federal Archives), Photo B 145 Bild-00010587 / Engelbert Reineke.

state declared that they would cut off their states' civil aviation service to and from the offending country. Airlines registered in a G7 country would no longer be permitted to land in that country, and the offender's national airlines would not receive landing rights in any G7 state. The G7 states' airports and airlines handled about 70 percent of the civil aviation industry outside of the Soviet Bloc. These states wielded the economic power to make their sanctions a credible threat to others.[46] The G7 heads of state also intended the Bonn Declaration to serve as a recruiting tool. They hoped that their statement would generate a snowball effect—motivating other states to publicly commit to similar sanctions.[47]

The declaration's goal was to signal to the world that the major economic powers were taking a cohesive and firm stance against aviation-related violence. Even though it had not originated as a West German idea, the FRG Foreign Office adopted the declaration as another multilateral project. Fleischhauer invited counterpart G7 bureaucrats for a follow-up meeting on implementation strategies in August 1978. The officials decided to send a worldwide invitation for other states to adopt the same sanctions.[48] In addition, the G7 states continued to emphasize their commitment to the Bonn Declaration at subsequent summit meetings in Tokyo (1979), Venice (1980), and Ottawa (1981). Relatedly, the G7 UN ambassadors lobbied through the fall of 1979 to ensure that the FRG's Hostages Convention was adopted without snares in December.[49] The G7 states thus collaborated collectively to create the impression that they would not tolerate aviation attacks.

Nevertheless, this initiative created little response. Few states committed to the Bonn Declaration.[50] Furthermore, the G7 only actually applied sanctions related to the Bonn Declaration in one case in which Cold War considerations predominated. In March 1981, hijackers took over Pakistani International Airlines Flight 326. They killed a Pakistani diplomat and secured the release of fifty Pakistani prisoners. Subsequently, the G7 states accused the Soviet-backed regime in Afghanistan of granting the hijackers asylum. The G7 states terminated landing rights for Ariana Airlines, Afghanistan's national air carrier, until 1986.[51] The Bonn Declaration meanwhile faded into obscurity. During the late 1970s the G7 states committed themselves to a common narrative about terrorists being extraditable criminals and attempted to enforce it but with weak results.

These complex multilateral initiatives were also exhausting for the involved officials, and Global North policymakers scaled back their efforts. By 1980, Schmidt, Genscher, and the FRG leadership no longer considered transnationally active terrorists an existential threat. The "German Autumn" wave of attacks had ended. Though West German extremists such as the Red Army Faction (RAF) continued their attacks, FRG officials, pundits, and public became more confident that such violence could not undermine their democratic institutions. Furthermore, the Hostages Convention was complete, and the FRG justice ministry realized that negotiations since 1976 to extend European judicial collaboration against terrorism were unlikely to come to fruition.[52] The FRG Foreign Office and interior and justice ministries did not begin new initiatives, instead securing what they had achieved in the 1970s. Along similar lines, the UK Home and Foreign and Commonwealth Offices had advocated for a consolidation of existing agreements since 1977.[53] The new British government under Prime Minister Margaret Thatcher continued to adopt harsh antiterrorism legislation at home. Abroad, it focused mainly on the implementation of existing international law agreements against terrorists.[54]

French officials still preferred to avoid public international action against terrorism throughout the 1970s and early 1980s.[55] Meanwhile, Brzezinski and Odom focused more on the state-centered Iranian hostage crisis than on legal options against nonstate actors. Global North officials thus felt that they had achieved the possible and had little drive to create new international law agreements.

At this moment, however, they had not resolved their core underlying disagreements with states such as Algeria, Cuba, and increasingly, Libya. The debate around appropriate international responses to terrorism remained. These states argued that transnational extremist violence was a side effect of imperialist oppression, and that only resolving colonial and postcolonial issues would end this type of violence. In a 1979 working paper for the UNGA terrorism committee, Algeria, India, Nigeria, Syria, and several other recently independent states also emphasized that "the struggle of liberation movements comes within the purview of the Geneva Conventions of 1949 and the Additional Protocols thereto of 1977 and cannot be identified with terrorist acts."[56] Global North states' framing of extremist violence as an ordinary (extraditable) crime in international law sharply contradicted this view. Thus, by the early 1980s Global North states solidified their conceptualization of terrorism in a way that kept the debate around the term unresolved.

NEOCONSERVATIVES, ANTICOMMUNISM, AND INTERNATIONAL TERRORISM AT THE JERUSALEM CONFERENCE

By 1979, U.S., FRG, and other Western officials had established a series of multilateral conventions in international law that addressed violent extremists as illegitimate and criminal offenders. Together with Israeli counterterrorism experts, the conservative movement in the United States and Europe adapted these norms to promote Cold War anticommunist policies, especially in the United States. Conservatives emphasized that communist states supported or condoned attackers and stressed the alleged connections between leftist terrorists and their ostensible state supporters. Subsequent U.S. counterterrorism efforts relied on the core criminal conceptualization of terrorism formed during the 1970s yet militarized to serve the Reagan administration's Cold War prerogatives.

In the 1970s, conservatives became a formidable grassroots political movement within the United States. Figures such as Ronald Reagan and Phyllis Schlafly successfully united economic and social conservatives to form the Moral Majority. The economic recession after the 1973 oil crisis and deindustrialization increasingly motivated white working-class American citizens to support this movement.[57] Arguing that individuals had the right to shape their own economic and social communities, conservative leaders and grassroots members supported fewer government regulations, a free capitalist market, anticommunism, and religious and breadwinner-family oriented values even as they opposed détente, the civil rights movement, and large government programs. By the late 1970s, conservatives had emerged as a powerful political group in U.S. local, state, and national politics.[58]

Conservatives in the United States strongly argued for a foreign policy dedicated principally to anticommunism.[59] Echoing earlier bipartisan statements, these conservatives held a zero-sum view of international relations. They preferred simple, bipolar foreign policy structures over complex multilateral systems. Conservatives warned of a decline in U.S. hard power due to détente. In the United States, the Committee on the Present Danger (CPD) was the most aggressive conservative foreign-policy interest group. Its wide-ranging conservative membership included prominent officials such as former Director of Central Intelligence William Colby, foreign policy experts such as Paul Nitze, journalists such as *Commentary's* editor-in-chief Norman Podhoretz, and academics such as Harvard University's Richard Pipes, a historian of Russia. CPD members argued that the United States needed to pursue all means to counter the rising influence of the Soviet Union, even if that meant taking morally dubious actions such as supporting right-wing dictators.[60] They called for a strong American military buildup as soon as possible to offset ostensible Soviet geopolitical and nuclear weaponry gains that created a "window of vulnerability" and placed not only allies but the continental United States at risk.[61] Later, the CPD disseminated anti-Soviet writing like the "Team B" report, which accused the Central Intelligence Agency (CIA) of recklessly underestimating the Soviet Union's military buildup and its expansionist intentions.[62]

Conservatives also increasingly communicated in transnational networks across state boundaries. Many conservative politicians in the United States, Western Europe, Southeast Asia, and Latin America shared a deep fear of communism and collaborated on anticommunist foreign policy platforms that called for military responses to counter the rising Soviet influence throughout the Global South.[63] Less well known and outside of formal politics or diplomacy, radical right-wing and conservative activists increasingly funded, supported, and engaged in violent guerilla tactics against leftist states such as Cuba or Nicaragua.[64] Right-wing Latin American and U.S. politicians almost never applied to right-wing violent actors the terrorism label they used to criminalize and depoliticize leftist extremists. By the late 1970s, conservatives thus cooperated across borders in myriad ways to advance anticommunist foreign policy agendas.

Part of this overall development, though not limited to conservatives, was an improvement in U.S.-Israeli relations and civil society contacts. After the 1967 Six-Day War, the U.S. government steadily increased its military aid to Israel. In 1975, President Ford promised not to recognize the Palestine Liberation Organization (PLO) until it recognized the right of the state of Israel to exist. Meanwhile, Israeli and U.S. activist groups worked hard to foster a positive view of Israel in the United States and influence both public and government opinion, often appealing to U.S. evangelical sensitivities.[65] Many Arab states had working relationships with the Soviet Union. Claiming Cold War considerations, Israeli leaders and American advocates, including evangelical Christians, Zionist Jews, and an emerging neoconservative coalition that crossed party lines, agreed that it would be in both countries' best interests to foster an American foreign policy friendly toward Israel as a U.S. regional ally in the Middle East.

Due to an Israeli initiative, neoconservative activists, politicians, and opinion leaders began to consider the fields of terrorism and counterterrorism in the late 1970s. Since the 1960s Israeli officials had attempted to influence the U.S. federal government to support its military-focused counterterrorism program against Palestinian Fedayeen. Unlike the U.S. and Western European states, the Israeli government viewed Palestinian Fedayeen as hostile combatants supported by surrounding Arab states. Israeli antiterrorism measures included counterinsurgency tactics against the Fedayeen themselves, such as the use of Special Forces teams and the exercise of military control of majority-Palestinian areas, as well as armed campaigns against Fedayeen bases and support structures in neighboring Arab states. In contrast, during the 1970s American, West German, and other European officials sought to codify terrorism as a criminal, not military, threat. They wanted to avoid conceptual links between terrorism and warfare because they feared that such links would validate Palestinians' political grievances. Israeli military activity subverted U.S. and FRG efforts to regulate international terrorism through crime-focused conventions in the UN and ICAO.

In July 1979, a new Israeli think tank named the Jonathan Institute held a large conference in Jerusalem that shaped how Western neoconservatives conceptualized the term *terrorism*. Benjamin Netanyahu, a young Israeli conservative and future prime minister, ran both. He was an Israeli Special Forces veteran, had recently completed graduate school in the United States, and was starting to make a name for himself as an antiterrorist specialist. The Jonathan Institute was named in honor of his brother (Yonatan in Hebrew), who was in command at Entebbe and was the lone Israeli fatality during the operation. The institute was a mouthpiece for the Israeli government. Its administrative committee was full of high-ranking current and former Israeli officials, including President Ephraim Katzir, Prime Minister Menachem Begin, Foreign Minister Moshe Dayan, Defense Minister Ezer Weizman, and former Prime Ministers Golda Meir and Yitzhak Rabin.[66]

The Jonathan Institute's main purpose was to support and disseminate the Israeli government's military-oriented position regarding terrorism. Netanyahu openly stated that he planned for the conference to be an intervention to change the discourse on terrorism in Israel's favor.[67] Records on the preparation of the Jerusalem Conference are currently unavailable, but Netanyahu published the papers and discussion transcripts. These publications offer valuable insights into the conceptualization of terrorism that Netanyahu and the Jerusalem Conference's organizers wanted to disseminate.[68] The conference spread the concept that Palestinian Fedayeen were a military Cold War threat. This anticommunist interpretation noted that Palestinian extremists were illegal proxy combatants in the service of the Soviet Union.[69] Such a concept appealed to (U.S.) neoconservatives.

High-level Israeli officials and luminaries contributed to the conference, which ran from July 2 to 5, 1979, and emphasized this framing of terrorism. Presenters included Menachem Begin, former Defense Minister Shimon Peres, Aharon Yariv (former Israeli chief of intelligence), and Shlomo Gazit (head of Israel's military intelligence).[70] Senior Israeli diplomats chaired most panels; in one case the chair was Meir Shamgar, a justice of the Supreme Court of Israel.[71] Israeli president Yitzak Navon was also in attendance.[72]

The Jerusalem Conference catered first and foremost to neoconservative anticommunist activists—not to antiterrorism experts. Some of the most ardent anticommunist pundits of the day were present. An example was Brian Crozier, director of the Institute for the Study of Conflict, a London-based neoconservative think tank. Another was Crozier's associate Robert Moss, a British-based journalist and editor of *Foreign Report*, the private intelligence bulletin of *The Economist*. Both published strongly anticommunist works during the 1970s, likely received CIA funding for their writing, and also participated in antiterrorism conferences.[73] The non-Israeli terrorism experts present at the conference also held notably conservative viewpoints, such as Hans-Josef Horchem, head of the FRG intelligence service Office for the Protection of the Constitution in Hamburg, West Germany.[74] Noticeably absent from the conference program were contributions from a number of antiterrorism experts who had gained prominence in the 1970s but did not share Netanyahu's ideas, such as RAND Corporation's Brian Jenkins.[75]

The Israeli organizers of the conference also invited a vast range of neoconservatives from North America and Western Europe to disseminate their intervention into the global discourse on terrorism. Invitations went out to over four hundred journalists.[76] Conference presenters included prominent conservative politicians, policy-makers, journalists, pundits, and academics. Among the speakers were former heads of state, former cabinet members, and active members of parliament from the Western European states and Canada.[77] However, American anticommunists comprised the largest delegation at the conference. Notable foreign policy hawk Senator Henry M. "Scoop" Jackson (Dem, WA) presented, as did George H. W. Bush. Bush had overseen the 1972 UNGA terrorism discussions as Richard Nixon's ambassador to the United Nations and afterward, as Gerald Ford's CIA director, approved the Team B exercise. At least ten CPD members presented papers, including Congressman Jack Kemp (Rep, NY) and conservative intellectuals such as Norman Podhoretz and Richard Pipes (who chaired Team B).[78] Other committee members in attendance included Richard Allen, who would be appointed Reagan's first national security adviser, and Henry Jackson aide Richard Perle.[79] Many of these actors would gain positions in the Reagan administration. Other prominent attendees were conservative journalist George Will and Soviet dissident Vladimir Bukovsky.

The neoconservative anticommunist majority at the conference shaped its discussions. Participants argued that Western states needed to treat terrorists as Soviet proxy combatants. The conference's main aim was to portray counterterrorism as a component of military anticommunism efforts. This view was similar to 1950s and 1960s conceptions of terrorism as leftist insurgent threats. However, the crime-focused norms developed during the 1970s now amplified certain Cold War elements.

Most conference panelists began by alleging that terrorists despised the freedom inherent in democratic societies. This claim was easier to make than it might have been a decade earlier because U.S. and European officials had developed the habit of downplaying, ignoring, and delegitimizing leftist extremists' motivations and political context. This erasure was particularly glaring in Palestinian and Latin American cases where the offenders articulated clear anticolonial and national liberation goals. Now, conservatives introduced their own interpretations of terrorists' political aims. The conference speakers conflated Global North industrialized states with "the West," a set of countries with intrinsically democratic values and freedoms (not specifically defined). They then accused terrorists of fundamentally rejecting and striving to undermine such democratic values.[80] Center for Strategic and International Studies (CSIS) executive director Ray S. Cline, who had worked as a CIA officer since the 1940s and as a State Department analyst in the 1960s and early 1970s, argued, "Terrorism is intended by those who finance it, arm it and ideologically inspire it, to weaken and ultimately dissolve the fabric of civilized behavior in open, pluralistic societies."[81] The conference attendants massively simplified terrorists' aims to fit their own ideological convictions. Officials in the United States and other countries had considered attackers' leftist and communist rationales in the past, especially during the 1950s and 1960s. However, Cline and other conference attendees now portrayed terrorists as a more large-scale, irrational, Manichean, and civilizational threat than earlier scholars and policymakers had done.

The attendees' core argument was that the Soviet Union heavily supported international terrorists as proxy combatants against the West. Having accused terrorists of hating Western "freedoms," panelists discussed how such views aligned with Soviet ones. A series of presenters, especially

Americans, postulated that the Soviet Union and its satellite states were actively training, fostering, and supporting terrorists. During the 1950s and 1960s, most writing about terrorism had focused on leftist and Soviet-backed insurgents as well, but had taken into account terrorists' rational political goals and context.[82] Now, Jerusalem Conference presenters dismissed terrorists' autonomy and instead strongly focused on the ostensible benefits that the Soviets were drawing from their sponsorship of terrorism. Senator Henry M. Jackson stated that the Soviet Union fostered terrorism as "a form of 'warfare by remote control' waged against free nations or against non-democratic but moderate states which dare to sympathize with freedom."[83] Brian Crozier claimed that Soviet leaders supported terrorists because "terrorism contributes to the enfeeblement and destabilization of non-Communist regimes."[84] Ray S. Cline postulated that terrorism was a form of low-intensity warfare, waged against the "open societies" of the world.[85] George Bush called terrorism "surrogate warfare" to be prevented "by the free nations of the world."[86] These ideas all fit neoconservative warnings that the Soviet Union was building its capacities to be an existential military threat in the late 1970s.

The Soviet Union did offer material aid to Palestinian national liberation actors and leftist extremists, as did Eastern European states. Recent historical research has highlighted military aid and hardware, training, and safe havens that particularly East Germany provided to the PLO, the RAF, and other nonstate actors. Such assistance was small in scale, however. Contemporary CIA reports and later research also highlighted that the Soviets, East Germans, and others were never able to direct the movements of such independent actors in the manner that the Jerusalem Conference participants worried about.[87] As well, conference speakers insufficiently sourced their assertions.

To support their claims, many speakers presented unverified facts and speculated freely. Crozier and Cline, for example, listed Soviet state organizations that might coordinate actions and sites where Soviet terrorist training camps might be located.[88] They offered no supporting evidence. Other speakers presented questionable proof. Robert Moss identified specific Soviet training institutions, such as "the military academy at Simferopol," as well as the terrorists being educated there—"mixed groups (usually numbering about 60 trainees at a time) including Fatah, Saiqa, the PFLP and the PLF [Palestine Liberation Front]."[89] Moss also made spectacular claims, including that Soviet-trained PLO members were acting "as the nucleus of a new secret police, a revolutionary SAVAK [Iranian secret police]" in Iran.[90] Thus, the Soviets were ostensibly undermining U.S. regional influence through extremist agents.

But even a short source analysis of these ostensibly factual claims reveals massive problems. To support his statements, Moss referred to "a series of important intelligence defectors, including the Czech General Sejna."[91] Jan Šejna defected to the United States in early 1968, so any of his statements were at least eleven years out of date.[92] Since the PFLP and other extremist Palestinians did not begin hijacking large civil airplanes until July 1968, after Sejna's defection, his knowledge of Soviet or Czech policies on international terrorism was questionable. It is also possible the CIA used Sejna to plant anticommunist propaganda, which Moss then fell for. Journalist Bob Woodward claimed in a 1987 book that CIA analysts gave doctored statements from Sejna on the subject of terrorism to a right-wing Italian newspaper in 1979 to discredit the leftist Red Brigades terror organization.[93] Overall, Moss's evidence was problematic.

Most conference attendees accepted these speakers' statements without question, however. For example, Richard Pipes stated that "concrete examples of Soviet support of terrorist organizations have been given by others," utilizing presentations such as Moss, Crozier, and Cline's to justify his own analysis of contemporary Soviet policy.[94] Anyone who did not share the apocryphal views of the Soviets and international terrorism faced heavy criticism in the question and answer sessions. Ironically, conservatives derided these suggestions as "confused in his theory" or as "hopes or fears or delusions."[95] The consensus among the conference participants was that the Soviet Union utilized terrorist groups to destabilize Western liberal democracies. Therefore, terrorism was a vital and previously underrated aspect of the Cold War. If the Israeli organizers of the conference planned to justify their counterterrorism efforts as military anticommunism practices, then they succeeded.[96]

Emphasizing the immediate existential threat of terrorism and its ostensible Soviet and communist backers, the conference attendees heavily criticized Western states' existing domestic and multilateral antiterrorism efforts as ineffective. Discussants claimed that domestic security and international law initiatives in the United States, UK, FRG, and elsewhere were not enough to stop a global network of terrorists backed by the Soviet

Union. Presenters lamented that legislative restrictions placed on U.S. intelligence agencies in the 1970s prevented successful information gathering.[97] The prominent physicist Edward Teller, who had contributed to the hounding of Robert Oppenheimer in the 1950s, sent a talk to the conference to be read; Teller warned that Western industrialized states were currently unable to prevent terrorists from acquiring weapons-grade nuclear material and posing an existential threat to civilization itself.[98] A panel on "Terrorism and the Media" came to the conclusion that the uncensored Western media aided terrorism by displaying "a dangerous lack of understanding of terrorism and its aims," by sensationalizing terrorist acts in progress, and by creating overly nuanced descriptions when reporting on terrorism.[99]

The last and most crucial topic at the conference was therefore how Western states needed to handle international terrorism as a military Cold War threat. Speakers emphasized that the Soviet Union's involvement changed the parameters of what was permissible. Accordingly, conference participants contended, Western states should respond to Soviet-backed proxy actors with militarized countermeasures.[100] The former executive chairman of Israel's El Al airline, Mordecai Ben-Ari, called for a "policy of active defense" that included "active intelligence; active pre-emptive measures . . . [and] active opposition and offensive action."[101] Speakers advocated that Western intelligence agencies should have more capacities and less supervision.[102] They recommended that the media be required to censor itself, like in wartime, in order to deprive terrorists of publicity and audiences.[103] Drawing from his own experience, Bush argued that the UN was unable and unwilling to act, and that multilateral conventions and criminal law were not enough.[104] Conference speakers thus discussed terrorism as a Soviet Cold War tactic and advocated for militarized countermeasures in response.

Led by Israeli officials and U.S. Cold War hardliners, participants in the Jerusalem Conference developed a powerful new narrative about international terrorism. To them, the Soviet Union supported (even if it did not fully control) all terrorist groups worldwide. Soviet backing linked these groups in a collective effort to destabilize liberal democratic societies. The conference's closing statement postulated, "Whatever the ideological or nationalist aspirations of individual terrorist groups, they have a common interest, which they share with the Soviet Union, in destroying the fabric of democratic, lawful societies all over the world."[105] This conception ignored

Palestinian Fedayeen's postcolonial and national liberation context. Instead, it hyperemphasized the leftist, Maoist, and Marxist ideals held by the PFLP and similar violent groups in Latin America, Europe, and elsewhere.

The conference participants thus adopted Israeli-introduced conceptions of terrorism and counterterrorism for their own anticommunist political aims. They postulated that international terrorism was an illegitimate measure utilized by the Soviet Union to gain a distinct advantage in the Cold War. Therefore, Western states needed to employ aggressive military measures to combat terrorism. This conceptualization focused exclusively on leftist terrorist actors and neatly overlooked instances of right-wing violence and terror. To disseminate awareness of this existential threat and potential solutions, panelists stressed the need for an "aware public" that was willing to support unequivocal policies against both terrorists and the Soviet Union.[106] In its closing statement, the conference members called for "an energetic and continuing effort to alert public opinion to the dangers of terrorism to civil liberties and to the rights of individuals in a free society and the need for effective measures to combat it."[107] After the Jerusalem Conference, its organizers and participants intervened in prevailing discussions about terrorism in the United States and Europe to disseminate their new narrative.

THE "TERROR NETWORK" THEORY

Viewing leftist terrorism as an existential and civilizational threat, neoconservatives sought to disseminate their conceptualization of terrorism and counterterrorism as quickly as possible. They began a media offensive that initially made little headway and remained a fringe view. After the U.S. presidential election of 1980, the incoming Reagan administration included many CPD members and quite a few Jerusalem Conference attendees. Reagan and his high-level appointees adopted the neoconservative, Cold War conception of terrorism. They disseminated this view, though they initially struggled to introduce related policies.

Jerusalem Conference attendees quickly followed Netanyahu's call to spread its warnings. During the conference, British historian and presenter Paul Johnson published an article in the London *Evening Standard* warning readers that the Provisional Irish Republican Army was part of a vast network of terrorist groups.[108] Days later, Congressman Jack Kemp inserted the conference's summary statement as well as his conference presentation into the U.S. Congressional Record.[109] Kemp's act provided publicity and an on-the-record source for the Jerusalem Conference's findings.[110] Since conference participants had very little other evidence for their claims, Kemp's insertion was a crucial reference for later writers. In the following months, conservative conference attendees such as Moss, Crozier, and Horchem published articles in U.S. and European newspapers and journals to accuse the Soviet Union of abetting Palestinian and other terrorist organizations.[111] So did renowned conservative commentator George Will.[112] The American filmmaker Herbert Krosney produced a documentary, "The Russian Connection," in September 1979 that explicitly stated that the Soviet Union manipulated Palestinian terrorists for the Soviets' own purposes.[113] Meanwhile, Netanyahu published several conference papers and then a full transcript of the conference proceedings.[114]

The participants at the Jerusalem Conference struggled to break into the mainstream media in the United States or Europe, though. Two factors worked against them. First, the Iranian hostage crisis diverted public attention. Ayatollah Sayyid Ruhollah Khomeini's emerging theocratic state took control of the hostage U.S. embassy staff from the initial hostage-takers. The new Iranian regime was antagonistic toward the Soviet Union and in 1982 suppressed the Iranian communist party. The Iranian hostage crisis did not fit into a conceptual framework in which Soviet agents controlled nonstate actors' terrorism or hostage-taking. Second, conference participants lacked publicly available evidence to prove their allegations. Even if they had access to intelligence sources on Soviet, East German, and similar states' support for violent actors, much of this intelligence was classified and not citable.[115] Instead, they either referred to problematic intelligence sources, such as Moss, or cross-cited one another.[116] For example, Krosney included statements from Crozier, Cline, and Moss in his documentary. Reactions were not positive. For example, the *New York Times* television critic John O'Connor mocked "The Russian Connection" for being "more preoccupied with plucking emotions than with dispassionate analysis."[117] And overall, such publications did not garner significant public attention in the United States or Western Europe.

During the 1980 presidential election season, however, conservatives' views on terrorism fit neatly into the alarmist anticommunist rhetoric of the Reagan campaign. The CPD and other foreign policy conservatives emphasized again and again that the Soviet Union's power and influence were advancing around the world. Their primary accusation against President Carter was that the United States was militarily and otherwise unprepared to counter the Soviet Union's advance. Carter himself fed into this narrative with his shocked reaction to the Soviet invasion of Afghanistan in December 1979.

A good example of such conservative views during the 1980 election season is Paul Nitze's "Strategy in the Decade of the 1980s." Chairman of Policy Studies at the CPD, Nitze wrote about Soviet geopolitical ambition in the fall 1980 issue of *Foreign Affairs*.[118] His article drew connections between Soviet expansion and international terrorism and highlighted why the Jerusalem Conference's conceptualization was so appealing to American foreign policy hawks. Nitze claimed that the Soviet Union's goal was to maximize its military capabilities and global outreach to gradually eclipse U.S. power.[119] He portrayed the support of international terrorism as one in a series of measures undertaken by the Soviet Union to gain an advantage over the United States and its allies. Nitze stated that the Soviet Union "focuses on the training, organization, and support of terrorist activities designed to break down the confidence of groups not under their control. The evidence . . . supports the view that the Soviet Union has been, and is, a principal supporter of terrorism, both with material aid and in its politics and propaganda."[120] He provided no evidence except for one citation to a January 1980 Robert Moss article.[121] In this article, Moss repeated his Jerusalem Conference claims, especially an assertion that Soviet-trained PLO members were acting as a secret police for the revolutionary Iranian state.[122] Moss's claims had no traceable evidentiary basis at the time. However, Nitze cited Moss's article without qualification and linked the downfall of U.S. global influence to the Soviet Union and (among other things) international terrorism.

Conservatives' mutual cross-referencing continued. In November 1980, Moss wrote an even more alarmist article about the Soviet Union's support of terrorism. He now tried to integrate the Iranian hostage crisis into conservatives' framing of terrorism. The new Iranian state was not interested in developing friendly relations with the Soviet Union. Yet Moss claimed that behind the scenes, the PLO supported Iran and Khomeini. The Soviets supported the PLO and indirectly benefited from its ostensible actions in Iran. Moss thus linked the United States' primary Cold War opponent and the ongoing Iranian hostage crisis.[123] As evidence, he referenced several Eastern Bloc defectors, including Jan Šejna. Moss also pointed to a Jerusalem Conference statement from the former head of Israeli military intelligence, Shlomo Gazit, who asserted that terrorists were training in more than forty different military schools in the Soviet Union.[124] Both Nitze and Moss thus relied on statements from the Jerusalem Conference and articles about the conference to make their case. They used the Jerusalem Conference's idea that Soviets sponsored terrorists to argue in favor of a more militant American foreign policy, a turn away from détente, and increased American defense expenditures.

In 1981, neoconservatives' conceptualization of terrorism shifted from the fringe to the mainstream of U.S. politics with the election and inauguration of Ronald Reagan. Regan brought many CPD members and Jerusalem Conference attendees into his administration. Richard Allen became Reagan's national security adviser, while Richard Pipes was installed as director of Soviet Affairs in the National Security Council. Later additions to the Reagan administration included Henry Jackson acolyte Richard Perle, union leader Lane Kirkland, nuclear scientist Edward Teller, and journalist Midge Decter, the wife of Norman Podhoretz.[125] Brian Crozier, now writing a regular column for the National Review, advised Reagan on foreign policy during the 1980 presidential campaign.[126] After Reagan's election, Crozier maintained contact with the national security advisers Allen, William Clark, and Robert McFarlane.[127] The new administration members did not specifically reference the Jerusalem Conference. But they brought their neoconservative conceptions of terrorism with them into the White House.

The Reagan administration embraced the idea that terrorism was a Soviet-sponsored threat to Western societies. In January 1981, Alexander Haig, Reagan's new secretary of state, declared that terrorism would replace human rights as a central concern for the administration. Haig had not been at the conference. But he was especially concerned about terrorism because he had survived an assassination attempt by the West German RAF two years earlier. Conference presenter Michael Ledeen also served as Haig's adviser. Haig stated in his first official press conference in January 1981 that the Soviet Union trained, funded, and equipped terrorists. He announced that the United States would prioritize policies against terrorism in the future that permitted " 'swift and effective retribution' " against

Soviet-backed terrorists.[128] The implication was that the United States would pursue military counterterrorism policies over multilateral collaboration. After all, multilateral efforts (especially in the UN) required compromise with the Soviets, states with revolutionary foreign policy agendas such as Algeria or Libya, and other supporters of leftist nonstate movements.[129] The National Security Council's director of Soviet Affairs, Richard Pipes, and the Moscow deputy chief of mission, Jack Matlock, joined Haig's position in administration-internal correspondence, asserting that the Soviets broadly sponsored leftist terrorists who were misleadingly labeled "national liberation actors."[130] However, Haig and other top administration officials faced immediate pushback to their assertions.

Haig's statements surprised officials with antiterrorism experience in the CIA, the State and Defense Departments, and other U.S. agencies. These officials were well aware of Soviet support for revolutionary states and leftist movements in the late 1970s. But they saw little concrete evidence of the Soviet Union's control over terrorists around the world to the extent that Haig claimed. For example, a CIA research paper titled "International Terrorism in 1979" mentioned the Soviet Union only as a victim.[131]

Analysts at Langley and Foggy Bottom also pushed back against the idea that terrorism was a form of Soviet warfare.[132] CIA Director William Casey was critical of his agency's intelligence-gathering capacities.[133] Immediately after taking office, Casey ordered a new study about the Soviet Union's involvement in international terrorism, hoping to prove the Soviet Union's complicity with all sorts of international terrorist organizations.[134] However, CIA and other intelligence analysts working on this Special National Intelligence Estimate (SNIE) upheld their own analyses even when these did not sufficiently condemn the Soviet Union for Casey's taste; Ronald Spiers, director of the State Department's Bureau of Intelligence and Research, warned against any analysis for the SNIE based solely on "policy preferences."[135] Likewise, RAND Corporation's noted terrorism expert, Brian Jenkins, who had provided the U.S. federal government with terrorism-related papers throughout the 1970s, wrote a paper in March 1981 on the issue. Jenkins acknowledged Soviet support of terrorism but warned explicitly about "leap[ing] from evidence of Soviet involvement to a conspiracy theory of terrorism."[136] Jenkins advocated a nuanced antiterrorism approach that relied on multilateral conventions and sanctions against all state supporters of terrorism.

Despite this bureaucratic ambivalence, Reagan and his top officials made further statements along the lines of the neoconservative understanding of terrorism in the spring of 1981. That February, the *Washington Post* ran an article on Pipes's assessment of the Soviet Union. The article reaffirmed his claims (from the Jerusalem Conference, but unattributed) that the Soviet Union "encourages and employs terrorism because terrorism is a handy and cheap weapon in their arsenal to destroy Western societies."[137] Ronald Reagan also emphasized that leftist terrorist groups worked in tandem with socialist and dangerous states. In an interview with Walter Cronkite about his policy toward El Salvador, Reagan stated on March 3 that the Soviet Union, other communist states, and a range of left-leaning actors such as Cuba, Libya, and the PLO sponsored terrorism there.[138] Three days later, Reagan replied to a question about El Salvador at a press conference that the United States government was "trying to stop this destabilizing force of terrorism and guerilla warfare and revolution from being exported in here, backed by the Soviet Union and Cuba and those others that we've named."[139] Reagan thus conflated leftist political aims and revolutionary political goals with terrorism—a criminal and illegitimate act. This interpretation matched U.S. conceptions in the 1950s and 1960s of terrorism as leftist insurgent activity. New was the focus on the Soviet Union as the central hub in a web of interconnected actors, as well as the disregard for potential indigenous political context.

Of note, Reagan remained silent about similar U.S. support for antileftist actors, for example in Nicaragua or Afghanistan. In public, Reagan praised nonstate actors such as the Nicaraguan Contras and Afghani *mujahideen* (those who engage in divine war) as "freedom fighters" and revolutionaries.[140] These statements aligned with the anticommunist values set forward by CPD member Jeanne Kirkpatrick in her seminal 1979 article "Dictatorship and Double Standards." But when speaking about leftist violent groups, Reagan's wording changed. He labeled their activity as terrorism, an existential and deplorable threat.

Alongside their own public statements, Reagan's high-level officials also worked with other Jerusalem Conference participants who wished to propagate the concept of a Soviet-backed terror network. The most prominent was journalist Claire Sterling. An American living in Italy, Sterling had covered Italian and international terrorism since the early 1970s. She had coauthored an article on Soviet influence on Italian communists with

Michael Ledeen and was present at the Jerusalem Conference.[141] When the Reagan administration came into office, Sterling was in the final stages of writing a book on the interconnections between the Soviet Union and terrorists groups. Sterling and the new administration provided each other with substantial publicity. Sterling's 1981 book *The Terror Network* supported administration pronouncements and widely publicized the concept of a Soviet-backed "terror network." Sterling wrote that terror was "about destabilizing the West, by extending the classic Von Clausewitz definition of war as the continuation of politics by other means."[142] She claimed that the Soviet Union supplied terrorists with support[143] and spoke of "guerilla training camps for tens of thousands of terrorists," "colossal supplies of weapons," as well as sanctuaries, intelligence information, and diplomatic cover for terrorists.[144] Though she conducted interviews with a range of European, Israeli, and U.S. terrorism experts and officials, she could not cite them in her book. She principally relied on newspaper articles and secondary literature to make her claims. And like Robert Moss, she used the questionable statements by General Šejna as a source.[145]

Members of the Reagan administration loved Sterling's work. Casey claimed that Sterling's book provided more information than all of the analysts working under him at the CIA combined. Haig and Casey handed out copies of *The Terror Network* within the federal government.[146] Meanwhile, Sterling's publishers advertised her book with Haig and other administration members' public statements.[147] Sterling received considerable media and administration attention.

The Reagan administration thus played a vital role in conservative and also Israeli propaganda efforts concerning international terrorism. For the first time, wide U.S. audiences heard about the theory of a Soviet-backed terror network. The administration's statements placed terrorism firmly within a Cold War framing while ignoring or downplaying any decolonization context. Reagan, Haig, and others ensured that reporters scrambling to cover the new American government also wrote about their conception of international terrorism.

Yet resistance to the terror network theory continued in Langley and Foggy Bottom. Especially in the CIA, professional antiterrorism analysts questioned their superiors' claims.[148] In particular, the 1981 SNIE study that Casey had commissioned, "Soviet Support for International Terrorism and Revolutionary Violence," hesitated to connect the Soviet Union and terrorist organizations. It did state that "Soviets are deeply involved in the support of revolutionary violence worldwide" and that "there is conclusive evidence that the USSR directly or indirectly supports a large number of national insurgencies and some separatist-irredentist groups."[149] Nevertheless, the study emphasized that the Soviet Union differentiated between terrorist organizations and supported them based on their alignment with Soviet ideals. Secular national liberation movements received support, ethnic or religious separatists rarely, and "strictly terrorists" none.[150] The study denied that the Soviet Union controlled or fostered terrorist organizations to the degree that the Jerusalem Conference claimed. Casey disagreed. But the only way he could include his own ideas in the SNIE study was to place them as "alternative opinions" in the footnotes.[151]

The study also discounted Sterling's *The Terror Network* as "uneven and the reliability of its sources varies widely. Significant portions are correct; others are incorrect or written without attending to important detail."[152] Moreover, Bob Woodward claims that CIA analysts realized in the course of preparing the study that the ostensible Šejna statements at the core of both Robert Moss and Claire Sterling's claims were CIA plants. The Jerusalem Conference had picked up CIA propaganda efforts and presented them as facts to both the public and (ironically) the CIA itself. This revelation was an embarrassment for Casey.[153]

In the academic community, the Soviet terror network theory was also heavily controversial. Most academics and experts who had begun writing about terrorism during the 1970s rejected the Jerusalem Conference's narrative. All pointed out that this conceptualization catered to strong ideological biases.[154] These discrepancies generated a cycle of public contention in the United States about the definition of and appropriate responses to terrorism.

Nevertheless, the Reagan administration continued to view terrorism through a Cold War "terror network" framework as the administration's first term progressed. The administration did not engage in further multilateral efforts that might require collaborating with the Soviet Union. The only multilateral exception was the G7 states' civil aviation sanctions against Afghanistan, which aligned neatly with the administration's Cold War policies. And gradually, U.S. academic experts and political pundits focused more and more on the (Cold War) morality of terroristic acts. They increasingly condemned terrorists' wickedness. Those who did not participate in this moral condemnation found themselves sidelined from U.S. antiterrorism debates and perhaps even labeled a terrorist sympathizer.[155]

Nevertheless, the Reagan administration waited, like earlier U.S. administrations, to institute substantial antiterrorism policies until a major attack forced a reaction. By the early 1980s, new religiously oriented violent actors operated in the Middle East. The Iranian Revolution propelled to power religious authorities who restructured politics, law, society, and culture in Iran based on Shia Islamic teachings.[156] The new Islamic Republic of Iran inspired other religious groups and organizations in the region to increase their political activity. Some became violent. In 1982, Israel invaded southern Lebanon to uproot the PLO leadership situated there. During the resultant Israeli occupation and subsequent Lebanese civil war, various factions waged low-intensity warfare to control the region. Shia militias consolidated into the group Hezbollah. Soon, Hezbollah committed violent acts within and outside of Lebanon. In 1983, its operatives bombed the U.S. barracks in Beirut, causing 307 deaths.

The Reagan administration's response to the Lebanon attack was more nuanced than the administration's earlier statements on a terror network might have suggested. The administration gradually increased its commitment to the military counterterrorism measures it had openly advocated. On April 3, 1984, Reagan adopted National Security Decision Directive 138, "Combatting Terrorism." This directive called for a long-term program to develop active (and not reactive) measures against terrorism, especially through military and intelligence capacities.[157] Yet Reagan hesitated to actually implement such measures and face the potential fallout. He considered an air strike after the 1983 bombing but chose to withdraw U.S. forces from Lebanon instead of risking further casualties.[158]

The Reagan administration turned to covert action, public condemnation, and unilateral legal steps to shape its immediate responses to attacks and to reinforce its Cold War framing. While publicly condemning terrorism and its state supporters, the United States also clandestinely supported violent actors. In subsequent years, Hezbollah took several U.S. officials and citizens in Beirut hostage, including senior CIA agent William Buckley. Reagan and his advisers avoided military reprisals to keep these hostages safe (Buckley was nevertheless killed).[159] In addition, National Security Council officials laid the groundwork for what would become the Iran-Contra scandal. They sold weapons to the Iranian government, generating cash to support Latin American right-wing insurgents and curry goodwill with Iranian leaders who (the administration hoped) could influence Hezbollah to release its U.S. hostages. Reagan was aware that these actions violated stated U.S. policy and Congressional legislation. Somewhat ironically given their claims of Soviet support for terrorism, the administration also covertly supported Afghani rebels. Religiously motivated groups, *mujahideen*, became the key resisters of Soviet occupying forces in Afghanistan after 1980. They branded themselves as holy combatants in the service of Islam. The United States, Saudi Arabia, the Gulf states, Egypt, and other U.S. allies in the region offered them substantial material support.[160]

Meanwhile, Reagan continued to publicly lambast the Soviet Union, Libya, and other states for their support of terrorism. Just days after the Lebanon bombing, Reagan justified the 1983 invasion of Grenada with the claim that the island was "being readied as a major military bastion to export terror and undermine democracy. . . . Not only has Moscow assisted and encouraged the violence in [Lebanon and Grenada], but it provides direct support through a network of surrogates and terrorists."[161] And his administration kept fostering the idea of a Soviet terror network in subsequent years. From June 24 to 26, 1984, Benjamin Netanyahu and the Jonathan Institute hosted the Second Conference on International Terrorism, a follow-up to the Jerusalem Conference, in Washington, DC, at the invitation of the Reagan administration. Many attendees from the 1979 conference were again present, including Yitzhak Rabin, Congressman Kemp, Vladimir Bukovsky, and conservative writers George Will, Norman Podhoretz, and Midge Decter. However, the conference speakers also included a plethora of high-ranking Reagan administration members, such as the secretary of state George Shultz, counselor to the president Edwin Meese III, U.S. UN ambassador Jeane Kirkpatrick (author of "Dictatorships and Double Standards"), and FBI director William Webster.[162] These top officials brought the prestige of their offices.[163] The conference centered on an ostensible "larger struggle, one between the forces of civilization and the forces of barbarism."[164] The administration also sponsored further studies and academic symposia.[165] For example, the Department of Defense commissioned a study on state-sponsored terrorism from Ray Cline and his coworkers at CSIS.[166]

The Reagan administration also took unilateral and bilateral legal steps hailing from 1970s antiterrorism initiatives to demonstrate U.S. resolve in the face of terrorist challenges. In 1985, the United States signed a supplement

FIGURE 5.3. President Reagan holds a National Security Council meeting on the TWA hijacking in the White House Situation Room, June 16, 1985.
Reagan and his advisers increasingly considered military responses against international terrorism. Courtesy of the Ronald Reagan Library.

to its existing extradition treaty with the United Kingdom. Since the 1970s, U.S. courts had employed the political offense exemption to refuse the extradition of several violent Northern Irish extremists back to the United Kingdom—to the consternation of the British government. The new treaty stated that most violent acts were extraditable offenses, enabling U.S. courts to extradite extremists more easily.[167]

Meanwhile, in June 1985 two Hezbollah agents hijacked Trans World Airlines Flight 847 and killed a U.S. service member on board. Reagan and his advisers considered a Special Forces rescue operation but finally rejected it as too risky.[168] Instead, Reagan applied the 1974 Anti-Hijacking Act. This act, meant to translate the Hague Convention into U.S. law, allowed the president to unilaterally sanction states that supported hijackers.[169] Reagan ordered U.S. airlines not to fly to Beirut and embargoed all Lebanese airlines from flying into the United States.[170]

Gradually, Reagan and his top officials increased their use of military and covert action. In response to the TWA 847 hijacking, Robert McFarlane, the national security adviser, advocated military reprisals against Libya. He argued that Hezbollah, Iran, and Libya were collaborating against the United States as part of the terror network. Reagan was cautious, but McFarlane convinced him to clandestinely support insurgents in Libya against its ruling dictator, Muammar Gaddafi.[171] Reagan and McFarlane did not acknowledge the irony that in Libya (as in Afghanistan, El Salvador, and Nicaragua), they were engaging in the same type of support for guerilla and insurgent actors for which they condemned Soviet leaders.

After years of public advocating and contrasting policy restraint, the Reagan administration employed direct military responses during the *Achille Lauro* crisis in October 1985. Four PLF members hijacked the cruise ship *Achille Lauro* and killed a U.S. citizen. Concealing this death to prevent a further escalation of violence, Egyptian authorities let the attackers and PLF leader Abu Abbas leave by air. This attack was one too many for Reagan. When he learned of the American's death, he decided to demonstrate that the United States was not only capable of a military response but also willing to employ it. Fighters intercepted the attackers' plane and forced it to land in Italy, where it was surrounded by U.S. Joint Special Operations Command forces, including Delta Force. Though the Italian police then seized the hijackers and tried them in Italy, the Reagan administration was pleased that the United States had credibly followed up on its threat to employ its military.[172] The hijacking prompted the International Maritime Organization to negotiate a new convention against the seizure of ships. The 1988 Convention for the Suppression of Unlawful Acts Against the Safety of Maritime Navigation and its supplemental protocol on deep-sea platforms mirrored the Hague and similar conventions.[173] It branded attacks on ships as extraditable offenses and required that states "extradite or prosecute" attackers. Yet by this point, the Reagan administration was much more invested in military counterterrorism.

Reagan committed to a direct military response against a state sponsor of terrorism in 1986. In April, a U.S. soldier was killed in a bombing at La Belle discothèque in West Berlin. The Reagan administration had enough intelligence to connect the perpetrators to Gaddafi and ordered a series of air strikes, code-named Operation El Dorado Canyon, on Libya.[174] The president initially encountered resistance from British prime minister Margaret Thatcher, who refused to let U.S. airplanes stationed in the UK conduct the raid because it was an act of retaliation and thus against international law. In a personal telephone conversation, Reagan assured Thatcher that the United States would hit only targets related to international terrorism. Thatcher encouraged Reagan to portray the raid as an act of self-defense.[175] In subsequent years, the Iran-Contra scandal shook the Reagan administration. It carried out no further military engagements against terrorists and their sponsors. However, in 1985 and 1986, the Reagan administration made good on its earlier promises to militarily engage terrorists and their alleged state sponsors. It signaled that the U.S. federal government would be capable in the future of responding to terrorist incidents with military counterterrorism.

International law conventions were now low on the U.S. list of priorities. In 1988, the ICAO added a protocol to the 1971 Montreal Convention to increase its scope, making not only attacks on aviation facilities but also specifically on airports extraditable offenses.[176] The United States signed it. Yet the U.S. federal government soon ignored the convention's central premise "to extradite or prosecute" in its efforts to enforce criminal punishment for attackers. That December, a bomb destroyed Pan Am Flight 103 over Lockerbie, Scotland, killing 270 people. By 1991, Scottish officials and the FBI determined that two Libyan officials planted the bomb. One, Abdelbaset al-Megrahi, was an intelligence officer and head of security for Libyan Arab Airlines. The Bush administration discussed whether to react with military means, as in 1986, but ultimately decided to handle the attack as a criminal case.[177] Gaddafi refused to extradite the two offenders, claiming that he would prosecute them domestically. Libya had signed the Montreal Convention, and Gaddafi's claims were in line with its requirements. The Bush administration thought it unlikely that Gaddafi would prosecute the attackers, though. Officials in the United States demanded a trial outside Libya, valuing the enforcement of punishment over adherence to the actual convention. The involved states agreed in 1999 to institute a court of Scottish law in the neutral Netherlands. This court found al-Megrahi guilty of murder and sentenced him to life in prison. Even when pursuing criminal law responses, the U.S. government thus preferred enforcing punishment more than getting all states to adhere to the same convention.

The Reagan administration's overall perception of terrorism was heavily filtered through Cold War biases. These views aligned with 1950s and 1960s perceptions of terrorism. New in the 1980s was the Reagan administration's single-minded focus on the Soviet Union as the source of terrorism worldwide. Reagan's top officials believed in a leftist terror network that aimed to undermine American and other democratic societies with the backing of the Soviet Union (and other state sponsors such as Iran and Libya). Reagan and his officials saw terrorism as one facet in the Cold War zero-sum game—if terrorism weakened the United States, the Soviets gained from it. Since they believed that terrorists were illegitimate Soviet proxies, Reagan and his cabinet considered military countermeasures appropriate when Nixon, for example, had not. Due to the ostensible existential threat and urgency of the situation, Reagan and his advisers were less interested in the barely-enforceable multilateral solutions of the 1970s. By supporting the terror network theory and gradually employing military counterterrorism measures, the Reagan administration adapted U.S. counterterrorism efforts to the political developments of the 1980s.

FROM THE 1980S TO THE GLOBAL WAR ON TERROR

By the early 1980s, U.S., FRG, and other Global North states moved away from their 1970s strategy to pursue new international law initiatives against terrorism. On the one hand, many officials believed that they had done what was possible along these lines. They had achieved the conventions against attacks on air travel, diplomats, and civilians that the international community was willing to support. On the other hand, the creation of multilateral conventions was difficult. Negotiating them was complex, time-consuming, and required significant compromise, and the conventions had normative, but few practical results. As Global North states' priorities concerning terrorism changed, each had less interest in making such investments.

In the 1980s, the Global North states took on discrete international antiterrorism efforts that best suited their foreign policy requirements. In particular, the Reagan administration increasingly favored military counterterrorism approaches more than international law collaboration. Meanwhile, the UK and France had more nuanced responses. The British government under Margaret Thatcher continued its militarized domestic counterterrorism at home. Abroad, Thatcher advocated for the enforcement of international law against terrorists and their state supporters, though British intelligence agencies collaborated with American counterparts on terrorism issues. France experienced a wave of leftist, nationalist, and Islamist terrorist attacks from 1982 onward. Like the United Kingdom, French authorities introduced harsher domestic antiterrorism legislation and law enforcement and militarized practices. In the international arena, French officials gradually ratified the antiterrorism conventions of the 1970s.[178] The United States, the UK, and France thus to varying degrees blended military, intelligence, law enforcement, and international law practices against cross-border terrorism.

Meanwhile, FRG leaders stopped championing international antiterrorism collaboration. The FRG had been a crucial driver of multilateral antiterrorism collaboration, especially in international law, during the 1970s. But Schmidt and Genscher, along with mid-level bureaucrats, had emphasized more so than the U.S. federal government that these initiatives served FRG domestic security purposes. And by the early 1980s, FRG domestic, bilateral, and multilateral efforts to address terrorist violence provided promising results. The wave of attacks known as the 1977 "German Autumn" ended with numerous arrests and no political gains for the responsible extremists. Subsequently, attacks in the FRG declined, as did the number of attacks committed by FRG terrorists abroad. Though the FRG's most notorious terrorist organization, the RAF, continued attacks and assassinations throughout the 1980s, both the government and public viewed terrorism as far less of an immediate and urgent threat.[179] While the Reagan administration increased its focus on terrorism as a military Cold War issue, the FRG government desecuritized terrorism and political elites' nonpartisan support of harsh antiterrorism initiatives yielded to more normative political debates and wrangling.[180] Because of these changing priorities, the FRG no longer took center stage on complex, long-term multilateral collaboration against terrorism.

In the 1970s, Global North states collaborated on multilateral conventions and a criminal understanding of terrorism that barely, if ever, accounted for attackers' postcolonial background. By the early 1980s, they adopted new antiterrorism policies that did not prioritize time-consuming cooperation on extradition and international law mechanisms.

At this time, Global North officials had still not bridged the conceptual gap between themselves and states and actors who primarily saw terrorism within the context of decolonization. The basic contestation of the 1970s about the definition and scope of terrorism remained. International law declined in relevance as a shared way to address terrorism—both conceptually and practically. By the late 1980s, religiously-oriented Islamist terrorist groups drew more upon religion as well as secular political concepts to justify their actions.[181] The United States, its close European allies, and recently independent states such as Libya and Algeria pursued increasingly distinct terrorism-related policies beyond a common international law framework. The U.S. government in particular viewed terrorism as a civilizational threat and took military countersteps. Incomprehension of violent actors' motives and moral outrage at their attacks increased over time and would reach a fever peak after the attacks on September 11, 2001. The resulting U.S. Global War on Terror in turn included a definitional and legal lack of clarity and postcolonial context. These aspects developed through Global North states' antiterrorism initiatives in the course of the 1970s.

CONCLUSION

Ilich Ramírez Sánchez, also known as Carlos the Jackal, was in Sudan in the summer of 1994 to undergo a minor surgical procedure. French authorities caught wind of his location, as did the U.S. Central Intelligence Agency. Both began negotiating with the Sudanese government. On August 14, 1994, Ramírez's state-appointed Sudanese bodyguards drugged him and handed him over to French security agents, who spirited him away to France in an extraordinary rendition. In the following days, headlines and news broadcasts around the world announced the capture of the elusive and infamous terrorist. He had evaded Global North authorities for two decades. But as U.S. and European officials expanded their Special Forces and antiterrorism tactical units as well as their military and intelligence capacities against transnational terrorism, these approaches achieved what law enforcement and extradition requirements had not. Ramírez was tried in France for several 1970s murders and in 1997 was sentenced to life in prison without parole. French authorities' acquisition of Ramírez did not adhere to international law. But it had the desired effect.

Our current understanding of terrorism is specific to our time and place. It developed in the past and is historically contingent. In the 1970s, violent extremists increasingly targeted the Global North with cross-border attacks. They oftentimes framed their actions as anticolonial in purpose. In collaborative responses, the United States and its European allies prioritized international law, extradition, and law enforcement solutions. These steps ignored attackers' anticolonial and national liberation claims by highlighting the brutality of their violent acts and the ways in which these acts violated domestic criminal laws. Overall, many Global North officials were almost compulsively unwilling to discuss the political context of violent actors who traveled from the Global South to commit violent acts in Global North territory. This depoliticizing view extended to Global North citizens who collaborated with Global South actors. Through their cooperation, Global North officials established an understanding of international terrorists as individual, illegitimate, and criminal actors. This conception contrasted earlier views of terrorists as (communist-affiliated) political agents that were prevalent in the 1950s and 1960s.

European and U.S. antiterrorism collaboration in the 1970s created normative changes but delivered fewer practical results than contemporaries expected. Altogether, eight multilateral conventions were ratified or adopted by the end of the decade. These extradition conventions required all signatory states to address people who committed certain cross-border violent attacks as criminals, and to arrest, prosecute, and extradite them. This approach sidelined the political and military context of the era, however: that of decolonization, national liberation, and counterinsurgency. To make the conventions palatable for recently independent states who prioritized such political context, the conventions contained loopholes, especially in the form of the political offense exception. They were also unenforceable. The conventions did not have significant immediate effects, though they set precedents and facilitated the adoption of terrorist offenses into bilateral extradition agreements around the world.

With these agreements and practices, officials established a normative U.S. and European approach against international terrorism. Officials developed a conception of terrorism as an individual, nonstate, and criminal offense. In contrast, they emphasized that Global North states' authority to prosecute and prevent such attacks was legitimate and legal. The global community did not wholeheartedly adopt this conception. It remained a Global North normative understanding. But this approach became the foundation for modern U.S. and European counterterrorism practices.

In the meantime, Global North officials fostered related forms of antiterrorism security collaboration. These included domestic security cooperation such as the TREVI network and the development of aviation security measures. Overall, officials introduced several conventions and policies with the premise that terrorists were individual and criminal actors. But the most attractive novel change was the founding of tactical antiterrorism units around the world. Based on military Special Forces teams, these units quickly resolved terrorist crises, often in ways that made policymakers look competent in the face of international terrorism threats. Going into the 1980s, U.S. officials in particular adopted more militarized outlooks and then policies against cross-border extremists. Military and special operations approaches provided faster and more media-attractive solutions that policymakers could directly control. Ramírez's arrest fit into this pattern.

Most historical studies on counterterrorism remain focused within national boundaries. Future histories of counterterrorism should enrich national frameworks with an international perspective. Because terroristic actors traveled frequently across borders, Global North states collaborated with one another to create responses against them. Global North officials, when creating national and international policies against terrorism, also had to consider diplomatic implications—how their actions affected multilateral projects with allies, and how their own antiterrorism policies might alienate recently independent (oil-rich) states as well as anticolonial and other political activists. Considering such international and transnational factors will allow historians to more significantly address larger processes, including imperialism and decolonization, multilateralism, globalization, and long-running U.S. military commitments.

Since the 1970s, cross-border counterterrorism has been juxtaposed between crime-focused law enforcement and international law approaches on the one hand and militarized practices that offer faster, more direct, and more controllable results for policymakers on the other. This book covered a specific historical moment of the 1970s when state officials emphasized multilateral legal initiatives as key antiterrorism steps. Later events and initiatives, from the 1980s onward, occurred in a different international and historical context in which large-scale multilateral endeavors were not so prioritized and happened alongside new militarized antiterrorism efforts. The Reagan administration inserted distinct Cold War ideological frameworks and militarized responses into its counterterrorism policies. During the late 1980s and 1990s, new extremist Islamic groups such as al Qaeda emerged out of earlier radical organizations.[1] Such groups honed terroristic attacks with high casualty rates, especially suicide bombings.[2] At the same time, U.S. military and intelligence services engaged more and more in the question of how to address terrorism. And since the attacks of September 11, 2001, the Global War on Terror has been ongoing. The United States and its allies have entered a constant state of long-running warfare against an irregular target.

Officials in the United States frame the Global War on Terror as a military engagement. Yet crime-focused approaches also continue. Global North leaders often categorize terrorists as "illegal combatants" or "unlawful combatants" who act outside of the normal processes and laws of war.[3] And since the 1970s, contemporaries have continued to craft antiterrorism conventions, including the 1997 UN International Convention for the Suppression of Terrorist Bombings, the 1999 UN International Convention for the Suppression of the Financing of Terrorism, and the 2005 UN International Convention on the Suppression of Acts of Nuclear Terrorism. Many regional organizations adopted their own antiterrorism conventions in the late 1990s and early 2000s. These agreements generally rely on the "extradite or prosecute" formula, showcasing that the 1970s conventions set the scope for what is possible against terrorism within international law. After 9/11, UN Security Council Resolution 1373 required all states to criminalize terrorism, though it did not say how. International law initiatives against terrorism have become more difficult to negotiate, with "a decentralized rush by states to criminalize terrorism . . . and . . . to invent a customary crime of terrorism."[4] Current UN negotiations to create a comprehensive convention against terrorism (and finally define terrorism) have stalled since 2000. All in all, the 1970s conventions established weak compromises, but these compromises set the precedent for international law and criminal approaches to terrorism even today. The Global War on Terror and modern counterterrorism thus have complex roots not only in military policies but also in the history of law enforcement, international law, and extradition regulations.

By questioning this history, researchers can interrogate assumptions inherent in the Global War on Terror and our modern counterterrorism efforts. One is the use of the war metaphor to describe counterterrorism efforts. With their collaborative 1970s agreements and practices, Global North officials established a normative U.S. and European approach against international terrorism. Officials conceptualized international terrorism as an individual, nonstate, and criminal offense. If such terrorism is primarily a criminal threat, what should the role, mission, and capacity of the military be going forward against irregular criminal actors? These questions address problematic human rights developments like detention at Guantanamo Bay and the concept of "illegal" or "unlawful" combatants. A sovereignty and state-building angle is important to consider as well. If terrorists and anyone associated with terrorism are illegitimate and criminal actors, then they cannot engage in state-building. In contrast, only governments whose authority is legitimate and legal can. Deploying such labels is thus a powerful tool to delegitimize and exclude actors from political governance. This approach downplays revolutionary, postcolonial, leftist, and similar views, views that threaten the global status quo and the predominance of Global North countries in today's international system. If Global North states held such assumptions in the early 2000s, then researchers will need to analyze the implications of these assumptions for the conduct of the wars in Afghanistan and Iraq, especially for U.S. and European state-building efforts therein.

In today's world, many people and most governments consider terrorism to be a crime; they do not consider it an act of war or a rational act of political dissidence. This crime-focused understanding covers domestic violent actors as well as attackers who cross national boundaries, such as hijackers. And yet U.S. officials in particular emphasize the central role of the military in counterterrorism. To a lesser extent, many European states do so as well. And most attackers hold specific political goals and frame these goals in militarized terms. Terrorism is, paradoxically, a crime punished through military means. Questioning its international history is crucial to clarify and analyze the complexities, problems, and potential solutions involved.

NOTES

INTRODUCTION

1. See John Newsinger, *British Counterinsurgency: From Palestine to Northern Ireland* (Basingstoke, UK: Palgrave MacMillan, 2016); Douglas Porch, *Counterinsurgency: Exposing the Myths of the New Way of War* (Cambridge: Cambridge University Press, 2013); David French, *The British Way in Counter-Insurgency, 1945–1967* (New York: Oxford University Press, 2012); and Robert Holland, ed., *Emergencies and Disorder in the European Empires After 1945* (London: Routledge, 2012). Case studies include Fabian Klose, *Human Rights in the Shadow of Colonial Violence: The Wars of Independence in Kenya and Algeria*, trans. Dona Geyer (Philadelphia: University of Pennsylvania Press, 2013) and Martin Evans, *Algeria: France's Undeclared War* (New York: Oxford University Press, 2012).

2. See Teishan Latner, *Cuban Revolution in America: Havana and the Making of a United States Left, 1968–1992* (Chapel Hill: University of North Carolina Press, 2018); Jeffrey James Byrne, *Mecca of Revolution: Algeria, Decolonization, and the Third World Order* (Oxford: Oxford University Press, 2016); and Matthew Connelly, *A Diplomatic Revolution: Algeria's Fight for Independence and the Origins of the Post-Cold War Era* (Oxford: Oxford University Press, 2003). A slightly later example is Piero Gleijeses, *Visions of Freedom: Havana, Washington, Pretoria, and the Struggle for Southern Africa, 1976–1991* (Chapel Hill: University of North Carolina Press, 2013).

3. See Paul Thomas Chamberlin, *The Global Offensive: The United States, the Palestine Liberation Organization, and the Making of the Post-Cold War Order* (New York: Oxford University Press, 2012); and Lien-Hang Nguyen, *Hanoi's War: An International History of the War for Peace in Vietnam* (Chapel Hill: University of North Carolina Press, 2012).

4. Greg Grandin and Gilbert Joseph, eds., *A Century of Revolution: Insurgent and Counterinsurgent Violence During Latin America's Long Cold War* (Durham, NC: Duke University Press, 2010).

5. Stephen G. Rabe, *The Killing Zone: The United States Wages Cold War in Latin America* (New York: Oxford University Press, 2012); and Michael McClintock, *Instruments of Statecraft: U.S. Guerilla Warfare, Counter-Insurgency, and Counter-Terrorism, 1940–1990* (New York: Pantheon, 1992).

6. Kyle Burke, *Revolutionaries for the Right: Anticommunist Internationalism and Paramilitary Warfare in the Cold War* (Chapel Hill: University of North Carolina Press, 2018).

7. The domestic antiterrorism initiatives in European states have been most closely researched. Comparative studies include Johannes Hürter, ed., *Terrorismusbekämpfung in Westeuropa: Demokratie und Sicherheit in den 1970er und 1980er Jahren* (Oldenbourg, Germany: De Gruyter, 2015); Jussi Hanhimäki and Bernhard Blumenau, eds., *An International History of Terrorism: Western and Non-Western Experiences* (London: Routledge, 2013); Matthias Dahlke, *Demokratischer Staat und Transnationaler Terrorismus: Drei Wege zur Unnachgiebigkeit in Westeuropa 1972–1975* (Munich: Oldenbourg, 2011); and David A. Charters, ed., *The Deadly Sin of Terrorism: Its Effect on Democracy and Civil Liberty in Six Countries* (Westport, CT: Greenwood, 1994).

8. Studies of multilateral antiterrorism efforts include Bernhard Blumenau, "The Group of 7 and International Terrorism: The Snowball Effect That Never Materialized," *Journal of Contemporary History* 51, no. 2 (April 2016): 316–34; Bernhard Blumenau, "The Other Battleground of the Cold War: The UN and the Struggle Against International Terrorism in the 1970s," *Journal of Cold War Studies* 16, no. 1 (Winter 2014): 61–84; and Bernhard Blumenau, *The United Nations and Terrorism: Germany, Multilateralism, and Antiterrorism Efforts in the 1970s* (Basingstoke, UK: Palgrave MacMillan, 2014).

9. *Global Terrorism Database*, National Consortium for the Study of Terrorism and Responses to Terrorism, 2009–2020, accessed March 18, 2020, https://www.start.umd.edu/gtd/access/.

10. Historical studies on U.S. counterterrorism are rare and include Philip Travis, *Reagan's War on Terrorism in Nicaragua: The Outlaw State* (Lanham, MD: Lexington, 2017); Mattia Toaldo, *The Origins of the US War on Terror: Lebanon, Libya and American Intervention in the Middle East* (New York: Routledge, 2012); Timothy J. Naftali, *Blind Spot: The Secret History of American Counterterrorism* (New York: Basic Books, 2005); and David C. Wills, *The First War on Terrorism: Counter-Terrorism Policy During the Reagan Administration* (Lanham, MD: Rowman and Littlefield, 2003).

11. Large overview works include Daniel J. Sargent, *A Superpower Transformed: The Remaking of American Foreign Relations in the 1970s* (New York: Oxford University Press, 2015); Tim Borstelmann, *The 1970s: A New Global History from Civil Rights to Economic Inequality* (Princeton, NJ: Princeton University Press, 2012); and Niall Ferguson, Charles S. Maier, Erez Manela, and Daniel J. Sargent, eds., *The Shock of the Global: The 1970s in Perspective* (Cambridge, MA: Belknap Press of Harvard University Press, 2011).

12. On the spread of air travel, see Jenifer Van Vleck, *Empire of the Air: Aviation and the American Ascendancy* (Cambridge, MA: Harvard University Press, 2013); and Jeffrey Engel, *Cold War at 30,000 Feet: The Anglo-American Fight for Aviation Supremacy*

(Cambridge, MA: Harvard University Press, 2007). Strong hijacking case studies include Eric Scott, "The Hijacking of Aeroflot 244: States and Statelessness in the Late Cold War," *Past and Present* 243 (May 2019): 213–45; and Teishan A. Latner, "Take Me to Havana! Airline Hijacking, U.S.-Cuban Relations, and Political Protest in Late Sixties' America," *Diplomatic History* 39, no. 1 (January 2015): 16–44.

13. "Regime theory" hails from Stephen Krasner, ed., *International Regimes* (Ithaca, NY: Cornell University Press, 1983). See also John Gerald Ruggie, ed., *Multilateralism Matters: The Theory and Praxis of an Institutional Form* (New York: Columbia University Press, 1993); and Robert Keohane, "Multilateralism: An Agenda for Research," *International Journal* 45, no. 4 (Autumn 1990): 731–64).

14. For human rights see Steven L. B. Jensen, *The Making of International Human Rights: The 1960s, Decolonization, and the Reconstruction of Global Values* (Cambridge: Cambridge University Press, 2016); Sarah Snyder, *Human Rights Activism and the End of the Cold War: A Transnational History of the Helsinki Network* (Cambridge: Cambridge University Press, 2011); Roland Burke, *Decolonization and the Evolution of International Human Rights* (Philadelphia: University of Pennsylvania Press, 2010); and Samuel Moyn, *The Last Utopia: Human Rights in History* (Cambridge, MA: Belknap Press of Harvard University Press, 2010).

Studies on economic, racism, and self-determination issues include Samuel Moyn, *Not Enough: Human Rights in an Unequal World* (Cambridge, MA: Belknap Press of Harvard University Press, 2018); Christopher R. W. Dietrich, *Oil Revolution: Anticolonial Elites, Sovereign Rights, and the Economic Culture of Decolonization* (Cambridge: Cambridge University Press, 2017); Blumenau, "The Other Battleground of the Cold War, 61–84; Brenda Gayle Plummer, *In Search of Power: African Americans in the Era of Decolonization, 1956–1974* (Cambridge: Cambridge University Press, 2013); Chamberlin, *The Global Offensive;* and Ryan Irwin, *Gordian Knot: Apartheid and the Unmaking of the Liberal World Order* (Oxford: Oxford University Press, 2012).

15. Studies on the formation of state sovereignty include Charles S. Maier, *Once Within Borders: Territories of Power, Wealth, and Belonging Since 1500* (Cambridge, MA: Harvard University Press, 2016); Daniel Philpott, *Revolutions in Sovereignty: How Ideas Shaped Modern International Relations* (Princeton, NJ: Princeton University Press. 2001); and Janice E. Thompson, *Mercenaries, Pirates, and Sovereigns: State-Building and Extraterritorial Violence in Early Modern Europe* (Princeton, NJ: Princeton University Press, 1994).

Theoretical studies on sovereignty within international relations are Dieter Grimm, *Sovereignty: The Origin and Future of a Political and Legal Concept,* trans. Belinda Cooper (New York: Columbia University Press, 2015); Robert Jackson, *Sovereignty: The Evolution of An Idea* (Cambridge, MA: Polity, 2007); and Benedict Anderson, *Imagined Communities: Reflection on the Origins and Spread of Nationalism,* rev. ed. (London: Verso, 2006).

16. See Barry Buzan, Ole Waever, and Jaap de Wilde, *Security: A New Framework for Analysis* (London: Lynne Rinner, 1998); Thierry Balzacq, "The Three Faces of Securitization: Political Agency, Audience, and Context," *European Journal of International Relations* 11, no. 2 (June 2005): 171–201; and Markus Lammert, "Ein neues Analysemodell für die historische Terrorismusforschung? Securitization-Prozesse in Frankreich und Deutschland in den 1970er und 1980er Jahren," in *Terrorismusbekämpfung*

in Westeuropa: Demokratie und Sicherheit in den 1970er und 1980er Jahren, ed. Johannes Hürter (Oldenbourg, Germany: De Gruyter, 2015), 201–15.

17. The concept of "epistemic communities" stems from Peter Haas, "Introduction: Epistemic Communities and International Policy Coordination," *International Organization* 46, no. 1 (Winter 1992): 1–35. See also Mai'a K. Davis Cross, "Rethinking Epistemic Communities Twenty Years Later," *Review of International Studies* 39, no. 1 (January 2013): 137–60. "Transgovernmental networks" was coined by Robert O. Keohane and Joseph S. Nye, "Transgovernmental Relations and International Organizations," *World Politics* 27, no. 1 (October 1974): 39–62. Studies on it include Anne-Marie Slaughter, *A New World Order* (Princeton, NJ: Princeton University Press, 2004); and Kal Raustiala, "The Architecture of International Cooperation: Transgovernmental Networks and the Future of International Law," *Virginia Journal of International Law* 43 (Fall 2002): 1–92.

18. See Giovanni Mantilla, "The Political Origins of the Geneva Conventions of 1949 and the Additional Protocols of 1977," in *Do the Geneva Conventions Matter?*, ed. Matthew Evangelista and Nina Tannenwald (New York: Oxford University Press, 2017), 35–68.

19. The key publication on terrorism and international law is Ben Saul, *Defining Terrorism in International Law* (New York: Oxford University Press, 2006). See also Vincent DeFabo, "Terrorist or Revolutionary: The Development of the Political Offender Exception and Its Effects on Defining Terrorism in International Law," *American University National Security Law Brief* 2, no. 2 (Fall 2012): 69–104. Studies of *aut dedere aut judicare* include Kriangsak Kittichaisaree, *The Obligation to Extradite or Prosecute* (New York: Oxford University Press, 2018); and M. Cherif Bassiouni and Edward Wise, *Aut Dedere Aut Judicare: The Duty to Extradite or Prosecute in International Law* (Dordrecht, The Netherlands: Martinus Nijhoff, 1995).

20. For antiterrorism initiatives within European integration, see Eva Oberloskamp, *Codename TREVI: Terrorismusbekämpfung und die Anfänge einer europäischen Innenpolitik in den 1970er Jahren* (Oldenbourg, Germany: De Gruyter, 2017); Bernhard Blumenau, "Taming the Beast: West Germany, the Political Offence Exception and the Council of Europe Convention on the Suppression of Terrorism," *Terrorism and Political Violence* 27, no. 2 (March 2015): 310–30; and Bernhard Blumenau, "The European Communities' Pyrrhic Victory: European Integration, Terrorism, and the Dublin Agreement of 1979," *Studies in Conflict & Terrorism* 37, no. 5 (February 2014): 405–21. For the process of European integration, see Wilfried Loth, *Building Europe: A History of European Unification* (Berlin: De Gruyter Oldenbourg, 2015); Daniel Mockli, *European Foreign Policy During the Cold War: Heath, Brandt, Pompidou and the Dream of Political Unity* (London: I. B. Tauris, 2008); and Alan Milward, *The European Rescue of the Nation State* (London: Routledge, 2000).

21. See Oberloskamp, *Codename TREVI*; and Aviva Guttmann, "Combatting Terror in Europe: Euro-Israeli Counterterrorism Intelligence Cooperation in the Club de Berne (1971–1972)," *Intelligence and National Security* 33, no. 2 (Summer 2017): 158–75, doi: 10.1080/02684527.2017.1324591.

22. National Foreign Assessment Center, "Patterns of International Terrorism: 1980," research paper, June 1981, Central Intelligence Agency Freedom of Information Act Electronic Reading Room (CREST), General CIA Records, CIA-RDP90-01137R000100050001-3, iii; and National Foreign Assessment Center, Research

Paper "International Terrorism in 1979," April 1980, CREST, General CIA Records, CIA-RDP86B00985R000200260002-1, 1.

23. See Ami Pedahzur, *The Israeli Secret Services and the Struggle Against Terrorism* (New York: Columbia University Press, 2009); and J. Paul de B. Taillon, *The Evolution of Special Forces in Counter-Terrorism: The British and American Experiences* (Westport, CT: Praeger, 2000).

24. For the United Kingdom, a significant historiography exists on the Troubles and the IRA. Recent works include Tommy McKearney, *The Provisional IRA: From Insurrection to Parliament* (New York: Palgrave MacMillan, 2011); Andrew Sanders, *Inside the IRA: Dissident Republicans and the War for Legitimacy* (Edinburgh: Edinburgh University Press, 2011); and Cilian McGrattan, *Northern Ireland: The Politics of Entrenchment* (New York: Palgrave MacMillan, 2010). See also Johannes Hürter, "Regieren gegen Terrorismus: Die Beispiele Westminster, Bonn und Rom in den 1970er Jahren," in *Terrorismusbekämpfung in Westeuropa*, ed. Johannes Hürter (Oldenbourg, Germany: De Gruyter, 2015), 63–80; and Bruce B. Warner, "Great Britain and the Response to International Terrorism," in *The Deadly Sin of Terrorism: Its Effect on Democracy and Civil Liberties in Six Countries*, ed. David Charters (Westport, CT: Greenwood, 1996), 13–42.

For France, see Markus Lammert, *Der Neue Terrorismus: Terrorismusbekämpfung in Frankreich in den 1980er Jahren* (Oldenbourg, Germany: De Gruyter, 2017); and Markus Lammert, "The Absent Terrorism: Leftist Political Violence and the French State, 1968–1974," in *An International History of Terrorism: Western and Non-Western Experiences*, ed. Jussi Hanhimäki and Bernhard Blumenau (New York: Routledge, 2013), 86–99.

For Italy see Tobias Hof, *Staat und Terrorismus in Italien 1969–1982* (Oldenbourg, Germany: De Gruyter, 2011).

For West Germany see Sabine Bergstermann, *Stammheim: Eine Moderne Haftanstalt als Ort der Auseinandersetzung zwischen Staat und RAF* (Oldenbourg, Germany: De Gruyter, 2016); Karrin Hanshew, *Terror and Democracy in West Germany* (New York: Cambridge University Press, 2012); Stephan Scheiper, *Innere Sicherheit: Politische Anti-Terror-Konzepte in der Bundesrepublik Deutschland während der 1970er Jahre* (Paderborn, Germany: Verlag Ferdinand Schönign, 2010); and Wolfgang Kraushaar, ed., *Die RAF und der linke Terrorismus*, 2 vols. (Hamburg: Hamburger Editionen, 2006).

25. See Oberloskamp, *Codename TREVI*; Hürter, ed., *Terrorismusbekämpfung in Westeuropa*; Blumenau, *The United Nations and Terrorism*; Hanhimäki and Blumenau, *An International History of Terrorism*; and Dahlke, *Demokratischer Staat und Transnationaler Terrorismus*.

26. See Richard Bach Jensen, *The Battle Against Anarchist Terrorism: An International History, 1878–1934* (Cambridge: Cambridge University Press, 2014); and Mathieu Deflem, *Policing World Society: Historical Foundations of International Police Cooperation* (New York: Oxford University Press, 2002).

27. U.S.-centric works focusing on the early twentieth century are Mary S. Barton, "The Global War on Anarchism: The United States and International Anarchist Terrorism, 1898–1904," *Diplomatic History* 39, no. 2 (April 2015): 303–30; and Beverly Gage, *The Day Wall Street Exploded: A Story of America in Its First Age of Terror* (New York: Oxford University Press, 2009).

28. Histories of recent U.S. counterterrorism practices are Mattia Toaldo, *The Origins of the US War on Terror*; Naftali, *Blind Spot*; and Wills, *The First War on Terrorism*.
29. Early publications include Paul Wilkinson, *Political Terrorism* (New York: Halsted, 1974); Brian Jenkins, *International Terrorism: A New Kind of Warfare*, P-5261 (Santa Monica, CA: RAND Corporation, 1974); and Walter Laqueur, *Terrorism* (Boston: Little, Brown, 1977).
30. Landscape terrorism overviews are Bruce Hoffman, *Inside Terrorism*, 3rd ed. (New York: Columbia University Press, 2017); David C. Rapoport, ed., *Terrorism: Critical Concepts in Political Science*, 4 vols. (London: Routledge, 2006); Louise Richardson, *What Terrorists Want: Understanding the Enemy, Containing the Threat* (New York: Random House, 2006); and Walter Laqueur, *The New Terrorism: Fanaticism and the Arms of Mass Destruction* (New York: Oxford University Press, 2000).
    Studies on the root causes of terrorism include Marc Sageman, *Misunderstanding Terrorism* (Philadelphia: University of Pennsylvania Press, 2016); and Tore Bjørgo, ed., *Root Causes of Terrorism: Myths, Reality, and Ways Forward* (London: Routledge, 2005).
31. See for example Andrew Silke, ed., *The Routledge Handbook of Terrorism and Counterterrorism* (London: Routledge, 2018); Martha Crenshaw and Gary LaFree, *Countering Terrorism* (Washington, DC: Brookings Institution, 2017); Dorle Hellmuth, *Counterterrorism and the State: A Comparative Analysis of European and American Responses to 9/11* (Philadelphia: University of Pennsylvania Press, 2016); Ronald Crelinsten, *Counterterrorism* (Cambridge: Polity, 2009); and Charters, *The Deadly Sin of Terrorism*. For a critical view of the field see John Mueller and Mark G. Stewart, *Chasing Ghosts: The Policing of Terrorism* (New York: Oxford University Press, 2016).
32. See Raphael Bossong, *The Evolution of EU Counter-Terrorism: European Security Policy After 9/11* (London: Routledge, 2012); Peter Romaniuk, *Multilateral Counter-Terrorism: The Global Politics of Cooperation and Contestation* (London: Routledge, 2010); and Martha Crenshaw, *Terrorism and International Cooperation* (New York: Routledge, 1989).
33. See Richard Jackson, ed., *The Routledge Handbook of Critical Terrorism Studies* (New York: Routledge, 2016). The field's main journal, *Critical Studies in Terrorism*, has existed since 2007.
34. See Ondrej Ditrych, *Tracing the Discourses of Terrorism: Identity, Genealogy, and State* (Basingstoke, UK: Palgrave MacMillan, 2014); Lisa Stampnitzky, *Disciplining Terror: How Experts Invented "Terrorism"* (Cambridge: Cambridge University Press, 2013); and Mikkel Thorup, *An Intellectual History of Terror: War, Violence, and the State* (London: Routledge, 2012).
35. Joseph J. Easson and Alex P. Schmid, "Appendix 2.1: 250-plus Academic, Governmental, and Intergovernmental Definitions of Terrorism," in *The Routledge Handbook of Terrorism Studies*, ed. Alex P. Schmid (New York: Routledge, 2011), 99–157.
36. For a discussion of the differences and the frequent practical overlap between these categories, see Hoffman, *Inside Terrorism*, 36–38; and Crenshaw and LaFree, *Countering Terrorism*, 17–18.
37. Gérard Chaliand and Arnaud Blin, "Zealots and Assassins," in *The History of Terrorism: From Antiquity to Al Qaeda*, ed. Gérard Chaliand and Arnaud Blin (Berkeley: University of California Press, 2007), 55–78. See also Mark Andrew Brighton, *The Sicarii in Josephus' Judean War: Rhetorical Analysis and Historical Observations*

(Atlanta: Society of Biblical Literature, 2009); and Meriem Pagès, *From Martyr to Murderer: Representations of the Assassins in Twelfth- and Thirteenth-Century Europe* (Syracuse, NY: Syracuse University Press, 2014).

38. See Verena Erlenbusch, "Terrorism and Revolutionary Violence: The Emergence of Terrorism in the French Revolution," *Critical Studies on Terrorism* 8, no. 2 (June 2015): 193–210; and Thorup, *An Intellectual History of Terror*.

39. See Lynn Patyk, *Written in Blood: Revolutionary Terrorism and Russian Literary Culture, 1861–1881* (Madison: University of Wisconsin Press, 2017); Claudia Verhoeven, *The Odd Man Karakozov: Imperial Russia, Modernity, and the Birth of Terrorism* (Ithaca, NY: Cornell University Press, 2009); and Anna Geifman, *Thou Shalt Kill: Revolutionary Terrorism in Russia, 1894–1917* (Princeton, NJ: Princeton University Press, 1993).

40. See Barton, "The Global War on Anarchism," 303–30; and Richard Bach Jensen, "The United States, International Policing and the War Against Anarchist Terrorism, 1900–1914," in *Terrorism: Critical Concepts in Political Science*, vol. 1: *The First or Anarchist Wave*, ed. David C. Rapoport (London: Routledge, 2006), 369–400.

41. See Jensen, *The Battle Against Anarchist Terrorism*; Mathieu Deflem, *Policing World Society*; and His-Huey Liang, *The Rise of the Modern Police and the European State System from Metternich to the Second World War* (New York: Cambridge University Press, 1992).

42. See Ray Wilson and Ian Adams, *Special Branch: A History: 1883–2006* (London: Biteback, 2015).

43. See Felicitas Fischer von Weikersthal, "From Terrorists to Statesmen: Terrorism and Polish Independence," *Studies in Conflict & Terrorism* 43, no. 1 (2020): 5–23.

44. A strong case study is Mary S. Barton, "The British Empire and International Terrorism: India's Separate Path at the League of Nations, 1934–1937," *Journal of British Studies* 56, no. 2 (April 2017): 351–73.

45. See Mary S. Barton and David Wright, "The United States and International Terrorism," *Oxford Research Encyclopedia of American History*, ed. Mark Lawrence, June 25, 2019, accessed October 3, 2019, https://oxfordre.com/americanhistory/view/10.1093/acrefore/9780199329175.001.0001/acrefore-9780199329175-e-743.

46. League of Nations, "Convention for the Prevention and Punishment of Terrorism," World Digital Library, accessed November 25, 2019, https://www.wdl.org/en/item/11579/.

47. See Ditrych, *Tracing the Discourses of Terrorism*, 39–54; and Ben Saul, "The Legal Response of the League of Nations to Terrorism," *Journal of International Criminal Justice* 4 (2006): 78–102, doi:10.1093/jicj/mqiO96.

48. "Convention (IV) relative to the Protection of Civilian Persons in Time of War. Geneva, 12 August 1949," International Committee of the Red Cross, accessed March 19, 2020, https://ihl-databases.icrc.org/applic/ihl/ihl.nsf/c525816bde96b7fd41256739003e636a/72728b6de56c7a68c12563cd0051bc40, article 33.

49. Overview works include Newsinger, *British Counterinsurgency*; Porch, *Counterinsurgency*; Klose, *Human Rights in the Shadow of Colonial Violence*; and French, *The British Way in Counter-Insurgency*.

50. The classic counterinsurgency treatise along these lines is David Galula, *Pacification in Algeria: 1956–1958*, new introduction by Bruce Hoffman (Santa Monica, CA: RAND Corporation, 2006).

51. See, for example, Hannah Arendt, "Ideology and Terror: A Novel Form of Government," *Review of Politics* 15, no. 3 (July 1953): 303–27.
52. See note 2.
53. See especially Nguyen, *Hanoi's War: An International History of the War for Peace in Vietnam.*
54. See Chamberlin, *The Global Offensive.*
55. An excellent study of the Tupamaros' transnational connections is Lindsey Churchill, *Becoming the Tupamaros: Solidarity and Transnational Revolutionaries in Uruguay and the United States* (Nashville, TN: Vanderbilt University Press, 2014).
56. Gérard Chaliand and Arnaud Blin, "Terrorism in Time of War: From World War II to the Wars of National Liberation," in Chaliand and Blin, *The History of Terrorism*, 221–54.
57. See Naftali, *Blind Spot*, 26; and Lisa Stampnitzky, *Disciplining Terror*, 51–54.
58. See Churchill, *Becoming the Tupamaros*; and Jamil Ddamulira Mujuzi, "South Africa," in *Comparative Counter-Terrorism Law*, ed. Kent Roach (Cambridge: Cambridge University Press, 2015), https://doi.org/10.1017/CBO9781107298002.019.

1. FROM ANTICOLONIAL TO CRIMINAL ACTS: HIJACKINGS, ATTACKS ON DIPLOMATS, AND EXTRADITION CONVENTIONS, 1968-1971

1. See for example Bruce Hoffman, *Inside Terrorism*, 3rd ed. (New York: Columbia University Press, 2017); and Peter Romaniuk, *Multilateral Counter-Terrorism: The Global Politics of Cooperation and Contestation* (London: Routledge, 2010).
2. See Annette Vowinckel, *Flugzeugentführungen: Eine Kulturgeschichte* (Göttingen, Germany: Wallstein, 2011), 22.
3. See David MacKenzie, *ICAO: A History of the International Civil Aviation Organization* (Toronto: University of Toronto Press, 2010), 250.
4. Even small aircrafts with little fuel capacity could make this trip. See Teishan A. Latner, "Take Me to Havana! Airline Hijacking, U.S.-Cuban Relations, and Political Protest in Late Sixties' America," *Diplomatic History* 39, no. 1 (January 2015): 16–44.
5. Federal Aviation Administration (FAA) administrator John Shaffer to Congressman Richard Shoup, letter, June 30, 1972, with attached chart "Worldwide Reported Hijacking Attempts," National Archives and Records Administration (NARA), Record Group 237: Records of the Federal Aviation Administration (RG 237), Administrative History (A1), Office of the Administrator (14), Box 399, 1972, 8040A Hijacking (4 of 6).
6. See Latner, "Take Me to Havana!" 27.
7. "What to Do When the Hijacker Comes," *Time* 92, no. 23, December 6, 1968.
8. Air Line Pilots Association (ALPA) president Charles H. Ruby to Senator Philip A. Hart, letter, August 22, 1968, Wayne State University, Walter P. Reuther Library, Archive of Urban and Labor Affairs (AULA), ALPA Collection (ALPA), ALPA President's Department Records Part II (Pres-II), 10–2 Hijacking Correspondence 1968–1969.
9. See Department of Transportation, FAA, Office of Compliance and Security, "Report of Program Accomplishment Compliance and Security: FY 1968," December 19,

1968, NARA, RG 237, A1 14, Box 281, 1600 Security-1968; John Shaffer to all regional directors, memorandum "Potential for Civil Disobedience Directed Against Air Transportation Facilities: Director of Investigations and Security's Briefing and Discussions, 25 June 1970," with attachment "IS-1 Briefing, Regional Directors, 25 June 1970, Security of Air Transportation Facilities: Basic Recommendations," July 1, 1970, NARA, RG 237, A1 14, Box 314, 1600 Security–1970.

10. Henry Kissinger, the national security adviser, to President Richard Nixon, memorandum, "Aircraft Hijacking," Washington, DC, February 7, 1969, *Foreign Relations of the United States (FRUS)*, 1969–1976, Volume E-1: Documents on Global Issues, 1969–1972, Document 122, accessed February 5, 2020, https://history.state.gov/historicaldocuments/frus1969-76ve01/d122; and Embassy Bern to Department of State, Telegram 356, February 4, 1969, Richard Nixon Presidential Library (NPL), National Security Council (NSC) Files Collection, Country Files—Europe, Box 707, Switzerland Vol. I 1969 & 1970 [1 of 2].

11. Fidel Castro, "Text of Castro Havana University Speech: 03/14/1968," *Latin American Network Information Center, Castro Speech Database*, accessed January 8, 2020, http://lanic.utexas.edu/project/castro/db/1968/19680314.html.

12. Office of the Under Secretary for Global Affairs, "Frank E. Loy, Under Secretary of State for Global Affairs: Biography," November 2, 1998, *U.S. Department of State Archive: Information Released Online Prior to January 20, 2001*, accessed January 25, 2019, https://1997-2001.state.gov/about_state/biography/loy.html.

13. See Latner, "Take Me to Havana!" 27.

14. See Paul Thomas Chamberlin, *The Global Offensive: The United States, the Palestine Liberation Organization, and the Making of the Post-Cold War Order* (New York: Oxford University Press, 2012), 71.

15. Kissinger to Nixon, memorandum, February 7, 1969, *FRUS*, 1969–1976, Volume E-1, Document 122; Department of State to Embassy Mexico City, Telegram 260705, October 24, 1968, *FRUS*, 1964–1968, Volume XXXIV: Energy Diplomacy and Global Issues, Document 297, accessed October 4, 2019, https://history.state.gov/historicaldocuments/frus1964-68v34/d306.

16. Thomas Williams (Bureau of Economic Affairs), memorandum of conversation, "Hijacking of Commercial Aircraft," April 25, 1968, *FRUS*, 1964–1968, Volume XXXIV, Document 297, accessed October 4, 2019, https://history.state.gov/historicaldocuments/frus1964-68v34/d297.

17. Frank Loy, memorandum of telephone conversation, July 17, 1968, *FRUS*, 1964–1968, Volume XXXIV, Document 299, accessed October 4, 2019, https://history.state.gov/historicaldocuments/frus1964-68v34/d299.

18. Terry Richard Kane, "Prosecuting International Terrorists in United States Courts: Gaining the Jurisdictional Threshold," *Yale Journal of International Law* 12 (1987): 294–341.

19. Harry Feehan, Bureau of Economic Affairs, memorandum of conversation, "Conference with IATA Officials on Airplane Hijacking," August 1, 1968, *FRUS*, 1964–1968, Volume XXXIV, Document 301, accessed October 4, 2019, https://history.state.gov/historicaldocuments/frus1964-68v34/d301.

20. See MacKenzie, *ICAO*, 51–56.

21. See Jeffrey Engel, *Cold War at 30,000 Feet: The Anglo-American Fight for Aviation Supremacy* (Cambridge, MA: Harvard University Press, 2007).

22. Donald J. Agger, "Report of the United States Delegation to the Sixteenth Session of the Assembly of International Civil Aviation Organization, Buenos Aires, Argentina, September 3–26, 1968," October 29, 1968, NARA, Record Group 59: Records of the Department of State (RG 59), Central Foreign Policy Files (CFPF) 1967–1969, AV3 ICAO 10/1/68, 23.

23. International Civil Aviation Organization (ICAO), "Convention on Offences and Certain Other Acts Committed on Board Aircraft, signed at Tokyo on September 14, 1963" *United Nations*, accessed November 25, 2019, https://treaties.un.org/doc/db /Terrorism/Conv1-english.pdf.

24. International Civil Aviation Organization, "Convention on Offences and Certain Other Acts Committed on Board Aircraft," Article 3, Paragraph 1; and Article 4.

25. See Luc Reydams, *Universal Jurisdiction: International and Municipal Legal Perspectives* (Oxford: Oxford University Press, 2003).

26. ICAO, "Tokyo Convention," Article 11, Paragraph 2.

27. Mackenzie, *ICAO*, 253–54.

28. Feehan, "Conference with IATA Officials on Airplane Hijacking."

29. U.S. Consulate Montreal to Department of State, Telegram 745, October 19, 1968, *FRUS*, 1964–1968, Volume XXXIV, Document 305, accessed October 7, 2019, https:// history.state.gov/historicaldocuments/frus1964-68v34/d305.

30. Covey Oliver to Dean Rusk, memorandum, "Hijacking of Aircraft to Cuba," December 6, 1968, *FRUS*, 1964–1968, Volume XXXIV, Document 309, accessed October 7, 2019, https://history.state.gov/historicaldocuments/frus1964-68v34/d309.

31. See Timothy J. Naftali, *Blind Spot: The Secret History of American Counterterrorism* (New York: Basic, 2005), 39.

32. MacKenzie, *ICAO*, 255–58.

33. See Chamberlin, *The Global Offensive*, 73–74.

34. See Chamberlin, *The Global Offensive*, 70–73.

35. Department of State to Embassies Beirut and Tel Aviv, Telegram CA-740, February 4, 1969, NARA, RG 59, CFPF 1967–1969, AV3 ICAO 2/1/69.

36. Department of State to Consulate Montreal, Telegram 8296, January 16, 1969, *FRUS*, 1969–1976, Volume E-1, Document 3, accessed September 21, 2017, https://history.state .gov/historicaldocuments/frus1969-76ve01/d3.

37. Airgram A-1110, September 26, 1968, NARA, RG 59, CFPF 1967–1969, AV3 ICAO 9/1/68.

38. Kissinger to Nixon, memorandum, February 7, 1969, *FRUS*, 1969–1976, Volume E-1, Document 122.

39. Knute Malmborg, "Report of the United States Delegation to the Subcommittee on Unlawful Seizure of Aircraft, International Civil Aviation Organization, Montreal, Canada, February 10 through 21, 1969," June 16, 1969, NARA, RG 59, CFPF 1967–1969, AV3 ICAO 6/1/69, 4.

40. Legal Committee, International Civil Aviation Organization, "Report of the Subcommittee on Unlawful Seizure of Aircraft, 10–21 February 1969," February 21, 1969, NARA, RG 59, CFPF 1967–1969, AV3 ICAO 6/1/69, 5.

41. Malmborg, "Report of the United States Delegation to the Subcommittee on Unlawful Seizure of Aircraft," 13.

42. Kriangsak Kittichaisaree, *The Obligation to Extradite or Prosecute* (New York: Oxford University Press, 2018).

43. Giovanni Mantilla, "The Political Origins of the Geneva Conventions of 1949 and the Additional Protocols of 1977," in *Do the Geneva Conventions Matter?*, ed. Matthew Evangelista and Nina Tannenwald (New York: Oxford University Press, 2017), 35–68.

44. Malmborg, "Report of the United States Delegation to the Subcommittee on Unlawful Seizure of Aircraft," 13.

45. The State Department's NEA and Henry Kissinger's NSC staff were not involved in the ICAO negotiations.

46. Robert Boyle, the U.S. ICAO representative, to John Meadows, director of the Office of Aviation, Department of State, letter, May 14, 1969, NARA, RG 59, CFPF 1967–1969, AV3 ICAO 5/1/69; and Charles King to ALPA President Charles Ruby, memorandum, "Report on the Second Session of the ICAO Legal Subcommittee on Unlawful Seizure of Aircraft, Montreal, Canada, September 23–October 3, 1969," October 9, 1969, AULA, ALPA, Pres-II, 10–2 Hijacking Correspondence 1968–1969.

47. See, for example, John S. Meadows to Jerome A. Huisentruitt, assistant general counsel, Air Transportation Association of America, letter, August 21, 1970, NARA, RG 59, CFPF 1970–1973, AV 3 ICAO, 7/1/70.

48. Embassy Rome to Department of State, Telegram 5480, August 29, 1969, NARA, RG 59, CFPF 1967–1969, AV 12 US, 8/1/69; Telegram 13069 from Embassy Paris to Department of State, Telegram 13069, August 29, 1969, NARA, RG 59, CFPF 1967–1969, AV 12 US, 8/1/69; Department of State to Embassy Tel Aviv, Action Telegram 146780, August 29, 1969, NARA, RG 59, CFPF 1967–1969, AV 12 US, 8/1/69.

49. Joseph Sisco, assistant secretary of state for Near Eastern and South Asian Affairs to William Rogers, information memorandum, "TWA Hijacking: Status Report," September 5, 1969, *FRUS*, 1969–1976, Volume E-1, Document 18, accessed February 11, 2020, https://history.state.gov/historicaldocuments/frus1969-76ve01/d18.

50. Embassy Rome to Department of State, Telegram 5496, August 30, 1969, NARA, RG 59, CFPF 1967–1969, AV 12 US, 8/1/69; Department of State to Embassy Rome, Telegram 147491, August 30, 1969, *FRUS*, 1969–1976, Volume E-1, Document 8, accessed November 21, 2017, https://history.state.gov/historicaldocuments/frus1969-76ve01/d8.

51. Memorandum of conversation between Charles Tillingham, TWA chairman of the board, Tom Huntington, TWA vice president, and Frank Loy, Subject: TWA Hijacking, September 3, 1969, *FRUS*, 1969–1976, Volume E-1, Document 16, accessed February 2, 2018, https://history.state.gov/historicaldocuments/frus1969-76ve01/d16.

52. Department of State to Embassy Tel Aviv, Telegram 147454, August 30, 1969, NARA, RG 59, CFPF 1967–1969, AV 12 US, 8/1/69.

53. The executive secretary of the Department of State, Theodore Eliot, to Henry Kissinger, memorandum, "Follow-up Report on the TWA Incident," September 10, 1969, *FRUS*, 1969–1976, Volume E-1, Document 19, accessed January 14, 2019, https://history.state.gov/historicaldocuments/frus1969-76ve01/d19.

54. Viron P. Vaky (NSC Staff) to Henry Kissinger, memorandum, "Cuba's New Anti-Hijacking Law—A Significant Development," September 23, 1969, *FRUS*, 1969–1976, Volume E-1, Document 123, accessed September 26, 2017, https://history.state.gov/historicaldocuments/frus1969-76ve01/d123.

55. John Volpe to William Rogers, letter, October 21, 1969, *FRUS*, 1969–1976, Volume E-1, Document 124, accessed September 26, 2017, https://history.state.gov/historicaldocuments/frus1969-76ve01/d124.

56. Report by Knute Malmborg, "Report of the United States Delegation to the Sub-committee on Unlawful Seizure of Aircraft, International Civil Aviation Organization, Montreal, Canada, September 23 through October 3, 1969," December 4, 1969, NARA, RG 59, CFPF 1967–1969, AV3 ICAO 10/1/69, 8.

57. Department of State to Embassy Tel Aviv, Telegram 159327, September 19, 1969, FRUS, 1969–1976, Volume E-1, Document 21, accessed February 11, 2020, https://history .state.gov/historicaldocuments/frus1969-76veo1/d21.

58. Frank Loy to Knut Hammarskjöld, letter, November 25, 1969, NARA, RG59, CFPF 1967–1969, AV 12 US, 11/1/69; and Philip Trezise (Bureau of Economic Affairs) to the under secretary for political affairs, U. Alexis Johnson, briefing memorandum, "Reception for Hijacking Meeting," December 15, 1969, NARA, RG59, CFPF 1967–1969, AV 12 US, 11/1/69.

59. See Mackenzie, ICAO, 260.

60. John Volpe to William Rogers, letter, October 21, 1969, FRUS, 1969–1976, Volume E-1, Document 124, accessed September 26, 2017, https://history.state.gov/histori -caldocuments/frus1969-76veo1/d124; William Rogers to President Richard Nixon, memorandum, "Cuban Hijacking Decree," October 31, 1969, FRUS, 1969–1976, Volume E-1, Document 125, accessed September 26, 2017, https://history.state.gov /historicaldocuments/frus1969-76veo1/d125; and National Security Adviser Henry Kissinger to President Richard Nixon, memorandum, "Note to Cuban Government on Hijacking," November 12, 1969, FRUS, 1969–1976, Volume E-1, Document 126, accessed February 11, 2020, https://history.state.gov/historicaldocuments /frus1969-76veo1/d126.

61. Department of State to Embassy Bern, Telegram 199293, November 28, 1969, FRUS, 1969–1976, Volume E-1, Document 128, accessed September 26, 2017, https://history .state.gov/historicaldocuments/frus1969-76veo1/d128.

62. Henry Kissinger to President Richard Nixon, memorandum, "Note to Cuban Government on Hijacking," May 28, 1970, FRUS, 1969–1976, Volume E-1, Document 130, accessed September 26, 2017, https://history.state.gov/historicaldocuments/frus1969 -76veo1/d130.

63. Kissinger to Nixon, memorandum, "Note to Cuban Government on Hijacking," May 28, 1970, FRUS, 1969–1976, Volume E-1, Document 130.

64. Department of State, Office for Combatting Terrorism, report, "Terrorist Skyjackings: A Statistical Overview of Terrorist Skyjackings from January 1968 Through June 1982," July 1982, 2, Central Intelligence Agency (CIA) Freedom of Information Act Electronic Reading Room (CREST), Argentina Declassification Project—The "Dirty War" (1976–83), 05164489.

65. Embassy Seoul to Department of State, Telegram A-256 with Enclosure "The KAL Incident," May 27, 1970, NARA, RG59, CFPF 1970–73, AV3 ICAO 5/19/70.

66. Michael Newton, "Belon, Christian Reni: kidnapper," The Encyclopedia of Kidnappings (New York: Checkmark, 2002), 23.

67. The group had faced serious setbacks five months earlier, when many members had been arrested in a remote training camp. See Patricia G. Steinhoff, "Kidnapped Japanese in North Korea: The New Left Connection," Journal of Japanese Studies 30, no. 1 (Winter 2004): 123–142,127.

68. See "Arabs Reviewing Airliner Attack," New York Times, February 25, 1970, 1, 10; and "Swiss Suspect Link in 2 Air Explosions," New York Times, February 28, 1970, 33.

69. Embassy Paris to Department of State, Airgram A-1277, October 17, 1970, NARA, RG 59, CFPF 1970–73, AV3 ECAC, 6/1/70.

70. Department of State to all diplomatic posts except Africa, action telegram 017617, February 5, 1970, NARA, RG59, CFPF 1970–73, AV3 ICAO 2/1/70.

71. Codification Division Publications, "Diplomatic Conferences," *Codification Division, Office of Legal Affairs, United Nations*, accessed February 8, 2019, http://legal.un .org/diplomaticconferences/.

72. United Nations, "Vienna Convention on Diplomatic Relations, Done at Vienna on 18 April 1961," *United Nations*, accessed November 25, 2019, http://legal.un.org/ilc/texts /instruments/english/conventions/9_1_1961.pdf, Article 29.

73. Large-scale overviews include Stephen Rabe, *The Killing Zone: The United States Wages Cold War in Latin America*, 2nd ed. (New York: Oxford University Press, 2015); Hal Brands, *Latin America's Cold War* (Cambridge, MA: Harvard University Press, 2012); Greg Grandin, *The Last Colonial Massacre: Latin America in the Cold War*, 2nd ed (Chicago: University of Chicago Press, 2011). See also Greg Grandin and Gilbert Joseph, eds., *A Century of Revolution: Insurgent and Counterinsurgent Violence During Latin America's Long Cold War* (Durham, NC: Duke University Press, 2010).

74. An excellent study of an individual group is Lindsey Churchill, *Becoming the Tupamaros: Solidarity and Transnational Revolutionaries in Uruguay and the United States* (Nashville, TN: Vanderbilt University Press, 2014).

75. See Brands, *Latin America's Cold War*, 60–61, 71–78, and Grandin, *The Last Colonial Massacre*.

76. See for example the statements on terrorism by the U.S. representative to the Organization of American States, Ellsworth Bunker, to President Lyndon B. Johnson, memorandum, "Present Situation in the Dominican Republic," October 28, 1966, *FRUS, 1964–1968*, Volume XXXII, Dominican Republic; Cuba; Haiti; Guyana, Document 185, accessed February 14, 2020, https://history.state.gov/historicaldocuments /frus1964-68v32/d185; and Embassy Santo Domingo to State Department, Telegram 1461, January 9, 1968, *FRUS*, Volume XXXII, Document 208, accessed February 14, 2020, https://history.state.gov/historicaldocuments/frus1964-68v32/d208.

77. Michael McClintock, *Instruments of Statecraft: U.S. Guerilla Warfare, Counterinsurgency, and Counterterrorism, 1940–1990* (New York: Pantheon, 1992), 185–188.

78. William Macomber, deputy under secretary of state for Administration, to Senator William Fulbright, letter, October 31, 1967, NARA, RG59, CFPF 1967–1969, POL 23–8 LA, 1/1/1967.

79. Naftali, *Blind Spot*, 27.

80. Department of State to all diplomatic and consular posts, action telegram 151166, September 6, 1968, NARA, RG59, CFPF 1967–1969, POL 23–9.

81. Arlan L. Kinney (Office of Security, Department of State), report, "Kidnapping— Donald J. Crowley, Lt. Colonel, USAF Attache," April 1, 1970, NPL, White House Special Files, Staff Member and Office Files (SMOF), John Dean Collection, Subject File: Demonstrations and Domestic Intelligence, Box 99, Threats Against Ambassadors; "Dominicans Seize U.S. Air Attache," *New York Times*, March 25, 1970, accessed February 18, 2019, https://www.nytimes.com/1970/03/25/archives/dominicans-seize -us-air-attache-guerrillas-ask-release-of-21-held.html.

82. William Macomber to U. Alexis Johnson, action memorandum, "U.S. Policy Toward Politically Motivated Kidnapping of U.S. Officials Abroad," April 2, 1970, *FRUS*,

1969–1976, Volume E-1, Document 38, accessed February 18, 2019, https://history .state.gov/historicaldocuments/frus1969-76veo1/d38.

83. Robert Hurwitch, deputy assistant secretary of state for Inter-American Affairs, and Marvin Gentile, deputy assistant secretary of state for Security, to William Macomber, memorandum, "Kidnapping of U.S. Officials Abroad," April 2, 1970, *FRUS*, 1969–76, Volume E-1, Document 37, accessed February 18, 2019, https://history .state.gov/historicaldocuments/frus1969-76veo1/d37.

84. Macomber to Johnson, action memorandum, "Political Program Designed to Inhibit Kidnapping," April 3, 1970, *FRUS*, 1969–76, Volume E-1, Document 39, accessed September 21, 2017, https://history.state.gov/historicaldocuments/frus1969-76veo1 /d39.

85. For a detailed analysis of the U.S. position on Cuba and the Soviet Union in Latin America, see Ray S. Cline (Bureau of Intelligence and Research) to William Rogers, intelligence brief, "Cuba: Castro's April 22 Speech a Sign of Increasing Hemispheric Flexibility," April 29, 1970, NARA, RG 59, CFPF 1970–1973, POL 23–9 LA, 1/1/70. Cline was a former Central Intelligence Agency officer.

86. Macomber to Johnson, action memorandum, "Political Program Designed to Inhibit Kidnapping," *FRUS*, 1969–76, Volume E-1, Document 39.

87. Memorandum for the record, "Kidnapping of U.S. Officials/Dependents," April 15, 1970, *FRUS*, 1969–76, Volume E-1, Document 40, accessed February 18, 2019, https:// history.state.gov/historicaldocuments/frus1969-76veo1/d40.

88. A recent study of this development is Federico Finchelstein, *The Ideological Origins of the Dirty War: Fascism, Populism, and Dictatorship in Twentieth Century Argentina* (Oxford, U.K., New York: Oxford University Press, 2014). For U.S. foreign policy on the dirty war, see William Michael Schmidli, *The Fate of Freedom Elsewhere: Human Rights and U.S. Cold War Policy Toward Argentina* (Ithaca, NY: Cornell University Press, 2013).

89. Department of State to Embassy Buenos Aires, Telegram 053134, April 10, 1970, NARA, RG59, CFPF 1970–1973, POL 23–8 LA 1/1/70.

90. Department of State to Embassy Buenos Aires, Telegram 0545589, April 14, 1970, NARA, RG59, CFPF 1970–1973, POL 23–8 LA 1/1/70.

91. Department of State to all Latin American posts, Telegram 059835, April 22, 1970, NARA, RG59, CFPF 1970–1973, POL 23–8 LA 1/1/70; and Department of State to All Latin American Posts, Priority Telegram 096478, June 18, 1970, NARA, RG59, CFPF 1970–1973, POL 23–8 LA 6/1/70.

92. Mission United Nations to Department of State, Telegram 731, April 21, 1970, NARA, RG59, CFPF 1970–1973, POL 17, 1-1-70.

93. Department of State to Mission United Nations, Telegram 061555, April 24, 1970, NARA, RG59, CFPF 1970–1973, POL 17, 1-1-70.

94. Macomber to Johnson, action memorandum, "Political Program Designed to Inhibit Kidnapping," *FRUS*, 1969–76, Volume E-1, Document 39.

95. Department of State, "Issues Paper: OAS Policy and Action on Terrorism and Kidnapping (Agenda Item 13)," Enclosure to Executive Secretary of the Department of State Theodore Eliot to National Security Adviser Henry Kissinger, memorandum, "OAS General Assembly Agenda Item on Terrorism and Kidnapping," June 24, 1970, *FRUS*, 1969–76, Volume E-1, Document 41, accessed September 21, 2017, https://history .state.gov/historicaldocuments/frus1969-76veo1/d41.

96. Macomber to Johnson, Action Memorandum "Political Program Designed to Inhibit Kidnapping," *FRUS*, 1969–76, Volume E-1, Document 39.

97. Mark Feldman to Charles Meyer, memorandum, "IAJC Draft Convention on Terrorism," November 27, 1970, NARA, RG59, CFPF 1970–1973, POL 23–8 LA 6/1/70.

98. MacKenzie, *ICAO*, 262–63, 341.

99. The UK minister of state for Foreign and Commonwealth Affairs, Joseph Godber, to Reginald Maudlin, M.P., letter, August 25, 1971, The National Archives of the United Kingdom (TNA), FCO 14/886.

100. Chamberlin, *The Global Offensive*, 114–24.

101. An excellent recent overview of the PFLP and Dawson's Field Crisis is Alex Hobson, "Creating a World Stage: Revolution Airport and the Illusion of Power," *The International History Review* (November 2019), https://doi.org/10.1080/07075332.2019.1683050.

102. Washington Special Action Group, meeting report, "Contingencies for Hijacking Crisis," September 9, 1970, NPL, NSC Files Institutional Files, Meeting Files, H-077, WSAG and SRG Meeting Middle East and Hijacking 9/9/70.

103. Chamberlin, *The Global Offensive*, 121.

104. Kissinger to Nixon, memorandum, "Hijacking Status," September 9, 1970, *FRUS*, 1969–76, Volume E-1, Document 54; Deputy National Security Adviser Alexander Haig to President Richard Nixon, memorandum, "Middle East Hijacking Status Report," September 7, 1970, *FRUS*, 1969–76, Volume E-1, Document 47, accessed November 21, https://history.state.gov/historicaldocuments/frus1969-76ve01/d47.

105. For example, see Hans-Jürgen Wischnewski's description of his contact with PFLP and PLO representatives on behalf of the FRG government in Hans-Jürgen Wischnewski, *Mit Leidenschaft und Augenmass: In Mogadischu und Anderswo, Politische Memoiren* (Munich: C. Bertelsmann, 1989), 127–32.

106. P. J. S. Moon to J. A. N. Graham, letter, September 30,1970, TNA, PREM 15/203.

107. "Memorandum for the President," September 10, 1970, *FRUS*, 1969–1976, Volume E-1, Document 56, accessed June 2, 2016, https://history.state.gov/historicaldocuments/frus1969-76ve01/d56; and Department of State to All Diplomatic Posts, Circular Telegram 149917, September 12, 1970, NARA, RG 59, CFPF 1970–1973, AV 12 US, 9/12/70.

108. Israel instituted armed air marshals on its El Al flights after the first PFLP hijacking in August 1968. See Mitch Ginsburg, "How to Thwart a Gunman at 29,000 Feet, by the Only Pilot Who Ever Did," *Times of Israel*, March 24, 2014, accessed February 18, 2019, https://www.timesofisrael.com/how-to-defeat-airplane-terrorists-from-the-only-pilot-who-ever-foiled-a-skyjacking/.

109. The director of the Office of Management and Budget, George P. Shultz, to President Richard Nixon, memorandum, "Anti-hijacking Program," May 14, 1971, NPL, White House Central Files (WHCF): Subject Files (SF), Judicial-Legal Matters (JL) 3–2 Hijacking, EX JL3-2 Hijacking Apr.–Sept. 1971; Chairman United States Civil Commission Robert P. Hampton to President Richard Nixon, memorandum, November 30, 1970, NPL, WHCF: SF, JL 3–2, EX JL3-2 Hijacking Nov. 1970–Mar. 1971.

110. MacKenzie, *ICAO*, 264.

111. Arnold Nachmanoff (NSC Staff) to Henry Kissinger, memorandum, "Clearance of Cable Containing Note to the Cuban Government on Hijacking Negotiations," December 22, 1970, *FRUS*, 1969–1976, Volume E-1, Document 133, accessed

September 26, 2017, https://history.state.gov/historicaldocuments/frus1969-76veo1 /d133. Latner, "Take Me to Havana!" 38–40 discusses Roa's insistence on reciprocity in the context of U.S. colonialism.

112. Embassy Paris to Department of State, Telegram 12815, September 22, 1970, NARA, RG59, CFPF 1970–1973, AV3 ICAO 9/1/70; and Embassy Paris to Department of State, Telegram 12669, September 19, 1970, NARA, RG59, CFPF 1970–1973, AV3 ICAO 9/1/70.

113. Franklin Willis to John Rheinlander et al., memorandum, "Legal Subcommittee on Sanctions: Canadian-United States Consultations on April 1–2," March 30, 1971, NARA, RG59, CFPF 1970–1973, AV3 ICAO 3/10/71.

114. Embassy London to Department of State, Telegram 8466, October 14, 1970, NARA, RG59, CFPF 1970–1973, AV3 ICAO 10/9/70.

115. International Civil Aviation Organization, "Convention for the Suppression of Unlawful Seizure of Aircraft, Signed at The Hague on 16 December 1970," United Nations Treaty Series, No. 12325 (1973): 106–11, accessed November 25, 2019, https://treaties.un.org/doc/db/Terrorism/Conv2-english.pdf, Article 7.

116. Franciszek Przetacznik, Protection of Officials of Foreign States According to International Law (Boston: Martinus Nijhoff, 1983), 62n116.

117. Macomber to Johnson, action memorandum, "U.S. Policy Toward Politically Motivated Kidnapping of U.S. Officials Abroad," FRUS, 1969–1976, Volume E-1, Document 38.

118. Meyer to Rogers, action memorandum, "Request for Authority to Negotiate and Conclude an Inter-American Convention on Kidnapping and Terrorism," Including Position Paper "Inter-American Cooperation in Suppressing Terrorism and Kidnapping," January 23, 1971, NARA, RG59, CFPF 1970–1973, POL 23–8 LA 1/1/71, position paper 1.

119. The six delegations were from Brazil, Argentina, Paraguay, Guatemala, Ecuador, and Haiti.

120. Organization of American States, "Convention to Prevent and Punish the Acts of Terrorism Taking the Form of Crimes Against Persons and Related Extortion That Are of International Significance, Signed at the Third Special Session of the General Assembly, in Washington, D.C., February 2, 1971," Organization of American States, accessed November 25, 2019 http://www.oas.org/juridico/english/treaties/a-49.html. It entered into force immediately for each ratifying state. The United States ratified it in 1976.

121. Department of State to all Latin American posts, Telegram 008163, January 16, 1971, NARA, RG59, CFPF 1970–1973, POL 23–8 LA 1/1/71.

122. Organization of American States, "Convention to Prevent and Punish the Acts of Terrorism," article 1.

123. Organization of American States, "Convention to Prevent and Punish the Acts of Terrorism," article 6.

124. An analysis of the label terrorism in the 1930s can be found in Ondrej Ditrych, Tracing the Discourses of Terrorism: Identity, Genealogy and the State (Basingstoke, UK: Palgrave MacMillan, 2014), 39–54.

125. See Lisa Stampnitzky, Disciplining Terror: How Experts Invented "Terrorism" (Cambridge: Cambridge University Press, 2013), for a detailed discussion of the dissemination of the term terrorism in the 1970s.

126. Department of State to Embassy Bonn et al., Telegram 187138, November 14, 1970, NARA, RG59, CFPF 1970–1973, POL 17, 6-1-70; Department of State to Mission NATO, Telegram 164674, October 6, 1970, NARA, RG59, CFPF 1970–1973, POL 17, 6-1-70.

127. On Italian domestic terrorism, see Tobias Hof, *Staat und Terrorismus in Italien 1969–1982* (Oldenbourg, Germany: De Gruyter, 2011).

128. Embassy Rome to Department of State, Telegram 4386, August 12, 1970, NARA, RG59, CFPF 1970–1973, POL 17, 6-1-70.

129. Rome to State, Telegram 4386, August 12, 1970, NARA, RG59, CFPF 1970–1973, POL 17, 6-1-70; Embassy Rome to Department of State, Embassy Bonn, et al., Telegram 4589, August 21, 1970, NARA, RG59, CFPF 1970–1973, POL 17, 6-1-70; Embassy Rome to Department of State, Telegram 4942, September 9, 1970, NARA, RG59, CFPF 1970–1973, POL 17, 6-1-70.

130. Embassy Bonn to Department of State, Telegram 10010, September 1, 1970, NARA, RG59, CFPF 1970–1973, OAS 3, 7-1-70; Embassy Bonn to Department of State, Telegram 10462, September 11, 1970, NARA, RG59, CFPF 1970–1973, OAS 3, 7-1-70.

131. Embassy Rome to Department of State, Telegram 6736, November 20, 1970, NARA, RG59, CFPF 1970–1973, POL 17, 6-1-70; Embassy Paris to Department of State, Telegram 3281, March 3, 1971, NARA, RG59, CFPF 1970–1973, POL 17, 1-1-71.

132. See chapter 2, International Terrorism at the United Nations General Assembly.

133. Franklin Willis to John Stewart, Pat Boyle, et al., memorandum, "Summary of Results at ICAO Legal Committee and Next Steps," May 14, 1971, NARA, RG59, CFPF 1970–1973, AV3 ICAO 5/1/71.

134. Thomas Ainsworth to Murray Jackson, memorandum, "Proposed United States Delegation to the Legal Subcommittee on Sanctions, International Civil Aviation Organization (ICAO), Montreal, April 14–27, 1971," April 12, 1971, NARA, RG59, CFPF 1970–1973, AV3 ICAO 4/1/71.

135. See chapter 2, From Multilateralism to Unilateralism.

136. International Civil Aviation Organization, "Convention for the Suppression of Unlawful Acts Against the Safety of Civil Aviation (with Final Act of the International Conference on Air Law Held Under the Auspices of the International Civil Aviation Organization at Montreal in September 1971). Concluded at Montreal on 23 September 1971," *United Nations Treaty Series* 974, No. I-14118 (1975): 177–248, accessed February 13, 2020, https://treaties.un.org/doc/Publication/UNTS/Volume%20974/volume-974-I-14118-English.pdf.

137. Memorandum of conversation between William Rogers and Swiss ambassador Schnyder, "Hijacking," November 16, 1972, *FRUS*, 1969–1976, Volume E-1, Document 135, accessed September 26, 2017, https://history.state.gov/historicaldocuments/frus1969-76ve01/d135.

138. Kissinger to Nixon, memorandum, "Secretary Rogers to See Swiss Ambassador to Cuba on Monday to Hand Him U.S. Draft Proposal on Hijacking," December 3, 1972, *FRUS*, 1969–1976, Volume E-1, Document 138, accessed January 22, 2019, https://history.state.gov/historicaldocuments/frus1969-76ve01/d138.

139. Serban Vallimarescu (NSC staff) to Brent Scowcroft, deputy national security adviser, memorandum, "Hijacking Agreement with Cuba," February 13, 1973, *FRUS*, 1969–1976, Volume E-1, Document 142, accessed September 26, 2017, https://history.state.gov/historicaldocuments/frus1969-76ve01/d142.

2. WHAT IS INTERNATIONAL TERRORISM? THE 1972 DEBATES ON EXTREMIST VIOLENCE AND NATIONAL LIBERATION AT THE UNITED NATIONS

1. The rich recent historiography on these states' agency includes Steven L. B. Jensen, *The Making of International Human Rights: The 1960s, Decolonization, and the Reconstruction of Global Values* (Cambridge: Cambridge University Press, 2016); Jeffrey James Byrne, *Mecca of Revolution: Algeria, Decolonization, and the Third World Order* (Oxford: Oxford University Press, 2016); Piero Gleijeses, *Visions of Freedom: Havana, Washington, Pretoria, and the Struggle for Southern Africa, 1976–1991* (Chapel Hill: University of North Carolina Press, 2013); Lien-Hang T. Nguyen, *Hanoi's War: An International History of the War for Peace in Vietnam* (Chapel Hill: University of North Carolina Press, 2012); and Matthew Connelly, *A Diplomatic Revolution: Algeria's Fight for Independence and the Origins of the Post-Cold War Era* (Oxford: Oxford University Press, 2003).

2. Studies of Nixon's Middle East peace process in the 1970s barely mention the issue of international terrorism. See Richard Moss, *Nixon's Back Channel to Moscow: Confidential Diplomacy and Détente* (Lexington: University Press of Kentucky, 2017); Craig Daigle, *The Limits of Detente: The United States, the Soviet Union, and the Arab-Israeli Conflict, 1969–1973* (New Haven, CT: Yale University Press, 2012); and Geoffrey Wawro, *Quicksand: America's Pursuit of Power in the Middle East* (New York: Penguin, 2010).

3. These measures are covered in chapter 3, s.v. The TREVI Network: Multilateral Collaboration against International Terrorism and Crime, and chapter 4, s.v. The Council of Europe Negotiations and German-French Divisions.

4. These conventions were the International Civil Aviation Organization (ICAO) 1970 "Convention for the Suppression of Unlawful Seizure of Aircraft" (Hague Convention), the Organization of American States (OAS) 1971 "Convention to Prevent and Punish the Acts of Terrorism Taking the Form of Crimes Against Persons and Related Extortion That Are of International Significance" (OAS Convention), and the ICAO 1971 "Convention for the Suppression of Unlawful Acts against the Safety of Civil Aviation" (Montreal Convention).

5. The executive secretary of the State Department, Theodore Eliot, to Henry Kissinger, "Memorandum: Status Report on Hijacked TWA Aircraft," October 21, 1969, *Foreign Relations of the United States (FRUS), 1969–1976*, Volume E-1: Documents on Global Issues, 1969–1972, Document 31, accessed August 30, 2018, https://history.state.gov/historicaldocuments/frus1969-76ve01/d31.

6. A good study of the ICAO is David MacKenzie, *ICAO: A History of the International Civil Aviation Organization* (Toronto: University of Toronto, 2010).

7. The assistant legal adviser for European Affairs, Charles Brower, "Memorandum for the Under Secretary: Talking Points for Ambassador Bush's Meeting with the Attorney General, May 11," May 10, 1971, National Archives and Records Administration (NARA), Record Group 59: Records of the Department of State (RG 59), Central Foreign Policy Files (CFPF) 1970–1973, POL 17, 1-1-71.

8. Martin Arnold, "Bomb Explodes in Midtown Soviet Trade Office," *New York Times*, April 23, 1971, 41.

9. Department of State to U.S. Embassy Moscow, Telegram 45380, March 18, 1971, NARA, RG59, CFPF 1970–1973, POL 13–10 US, 1-2-71; Embassy Moscow to Department of State, Telegram 2073, April 3, 1971, NARA, RG59, CFPF 1970–1973, POL 13–10 US, 1-2-71.

10. The assistant secretary of state for Administration, Joseph Donelan, to the Office of Management and Budget International Programs division chief, James Frey, memorandum, February 12, 1973, *FRUS, 1969–1976*, Volume E-3: Documents on Global Issues, 1973–1976, Document 205, accessed June 25, 2018, https://history.state.gov/historicaldocuments/frus1969-76ve03/d205.

11. John V. Lindsay to the assistant secretary of the Treasury, Eugene Rossides, letter, February 8, 1971, Richard Nixon Presidential Library (NPL), White House Special Files (WHSF), Staff Member and Office Files (SMOF), John Dean Collection, Subject Files, Box 77, UN Re: Security of Missions, Draft Resolutions.

12. The deputy under secretary of state for Management, William B. Macomber Jr. to the counsel to the president, John W. Dean III, memorandum "Protection of Missions to the United Nations," December 8, 1971, NPL, WHSF, SMOF, John Dean Collection, Subject Files, Box 65, Protection of UN Missions 3 of 3.

13. See Byrne, *Mecca of Revolution*; Paul Thomas Chamberlin, *The Global Offensive: The United States, the Palestine Liberation Organization, and the Making of the Post-Cold War Order* (New York: Oxford University Press, 2012); and Connelly, *A Diplomatic Revolution.*

14. See, for example, Mission United Nations to Department of State, Airgram A-2933, December 5, 1969, NARA, RG59, CFPF 1967–1969, AV 12, 11/1/69; and Federal Republic of Germany Observer Post United Nations to Foreign Office, Telegram 1477, November 12, 1970, Political Archive of the Foreign Office, Federal Republic of Germany (B), Auslandsvertretungen Neues Amt, Vol. 18459.

15. Eliot to Kissinger, memorandum, "International Law Commission's Work on Draft Articles Concerning Crimes Against Persons Entitled to Special Protection Under International Law," March 31, 1972, NARA, RG59, CFPF 1970–1973, POL 5–2 ILC, 11-12-71.

16. Mission United Nations to Department of State, Telegram 4092, November 8, 1971, NARA, RG59, CFPF 1970–1973, POL 5–2 ILC, 8-9-71.

17. Mission United Nations to Department of State, Airgram A-1551, October 19, 1971, NARA, RG59, CFPF 1970–1973, POL 17, 8-17-71.

18. Embassy Rome to Department of State, Embassy Bonn, et al., Telegram 4589, August 21, 1970, NARA, RG59, CFPF 1970–1973, POL 17, 6-1-70; Embassy Rome to Department of State, Telegram 4942, September 9, 1970, NARA, RG59, CFPF 1970–1973, POL 17, 6-1-70; Embassy Brussels to Department of State, Telegram 632, February 24, 1971, NARA, RG59, CFPF 1970–1973, POL 17, 1-1-71; Assistant Legal Advisor for Intra-American Affairs Mark Feldman to John W. Ford (U.S. OAS Delegation), "Memorandum: Protection of Diplomats—Council of Europe," March 11, 1971, NARA, RG59, CFPF 1970–1973, POL 17, 1-1-71; Embassy London to Department of State, Telegram 2711, March 26, 1971, NARA, RG59, CFPF 1970–1973, POL 17, 1-1-71; Mark Feldman, "Memorandum for the Files: Protection of Diplomats—Council of Europe," April 5, 1971, NARA, RG59, CFPF 1970–1973, POL 17, 1-1-71.

19. Embassy Rome to Department of State, Telegram 6736, November 20, 1970, NARA, RG59, CFPF 1970–1973, POL 17, 6-1-70; Embassy Paris to Department of State, Telegram 3281, March 3, 1971, NARA, RG59, CFPF 1970–1973, POL 17, 1-1-71.

20. Embassy Rome to Department of State, Telegram 6233, October 1, 1971, NARA, RG59, CFPF 1970–1973, POL 17, 8-17-71.
21. Mission United Nations to Department of State, Telegram 3756, October 22, 1971, NARA, RG59, CFPF 1970–1973, POL 5-2 ILC, 8-9-71; Embassy London to Department of State, Telegram 9862, October 27,1971, NARA, RG59, CFPF 1970–1973, POL 23-8, 1970–1971; Department of State to Embassy London, Telegram 194206, October 22, 1971, NARA, RG59, CFPF 1970–1973, POL 23-8, 1970–1971; Embassy London to Department of State, Telegram 9862, October 27, 1971, NARA, RG59, CFPF 1970–1973, POL 5-2 ILC, 8-9-71.
22. Department of State to Mission United Nations, Telegram 186160, October 9, 1971, NARA, RG59, CFPF 1970–1973, POL 5-2 ILC, 8-9-71; Embassy Paris to Department of State, Telegram 18020, October 26, 1971, NARA, RG59, CFPF 1970–1973, POL 5–2 ILC, 8-9-71.
23. United Nations to State, Telegram 4092, November 8, 1971, NARA, RG59, CFPF 1970–1973, POL 5-2 ILC, 8-9-71; Mission United Nations to Embassy Rome, Telegram 4045, November 4, 1971, NARA, RG59, CFPF 1970–1973, POL 5-2 ILC, 8-9-71.
24. Mission United Nations to Department of State, Telegram 4310, November 18, 1971, NARA, RG59, CFPF 1970–1973, POL 17, 8-17-71.
25. See Chamberlin, *The Global Offensive*, 121–74.
26. See Nguyen, *Hanoi's War*.
27. See Nancy L. Clark and William H. Worger, *South Africa: The Rise and Fall of Apartheid*, 2nd ed. (New York: Routledge, 2011); and Henri Boshoff, Anneli Botha, and Martin Schönteich, *Fear in the City: Urban Terrorism in South Africa* (Pretoria: Institute for Security Studies, 2001).
28. See Lindsey Churchill, *Becoming the Tupamaros: Solidarity and Transnational Revolutionaries in Uruguay and the United States* (Nashville, TN: Vanderbilt University Pres, 2014).
29. Markus Lammert, "The Absent Terrorism: Leftist Political Violence and the French State, 1968–1974," in *An International History of Terrorism: Western and Non-Western Experiences*, ed. Jussi Hanhimäki and Bernhard Blumenau (New York: Routledge, 2013), 86–99.
30. Karrin Hanshew, *Terror and Democracy in West Germany* (Cambridge: Cambridge University Press, 2012).
31. Bryan Burrough, *Days of Rage: America's Radical Underground, the FBI, and the Forgotten Age of Revolutionary Violence* (New York: Penguin, 2015).
32. Hanshew, *Terror and Democracy in West Germany*.
33. "Irish Republican Army (IRA) statement concerning a prisoner in Mountjoy Prison, Dublin, (6 September 1971)," *Conflict Archive on the Internet*, Ulster University, accessed February 20, 2020, https://cain.ulster.ac.uk/othelem/organ/ira/ira060971.htm.
34. For a detailed analysis of later RAF claims in this regard, see Leith Passmore, "International Law as an Extralegal Defense Strategy in West Germany's Stammheim Terror Trial," *Law, Culture and the Humanities* 9, no. 2 (June 2011): 375–94.
35. The West Germans were quickly asked to return home, due to their drinking and the women's European bathing attire. See Tobias Wunschik, "Baader-Meinhof international?," *Aus Politik und Zeitgeschichte* 40–41 (2007): 23–29.
36. Translated from German by the author. Rote Armee Fraktion, "Anschlag auf das Hauptquartier der US-Army in Frankfurt/Main," May 14, 1972, in *Rote Armee*

2. WHAT IS INTERNATIONAL TERRORISM?

Fraktion: Texte und Materialien zur Geschichte der RAF (Berlin: ID Verlag, 1997), 145. See also Rote Armee Fraktion, "Die Rote Armee Aufbauen: Erklärung zur Befreiung Andreas Baaders vom 5. Juni 1970," June 5, 1970, in *Rote Armee Fraktion: Texte und Materialien*, 24–26.

37. See Patricia G. Steinhoff, "Portrait of a Terrorist: An Interview with Kozo Okamoto," *Asian Survey* 16, no. 9 (September 1976): 830–45.

38. Good media examples include "Lebanese, Israelis Take Precautions at Airports," *Washington Post*, June 2, 1972, A16; and "L'Avertissement de Jérusalem sommant les dirigeants de Beyrouth de neutraliser les terroristes accroit l'inquiétude des Libanais," *Le Monde*, June 3, 1972.

39. Mission United Nations to Department of State, Telegram 2029, June 1, 1972, NARA, RG59, CFPF 1970–1973, AV14 ISR, 6-1-72.

40. United Nations to State, Telegram 2029, June 1, 1972, NARA, RG59, CFPF 1970–1973, AV14 ISR, 6-1-72.

41. Embassy Beirut to Department of State, Telegram 6066, June 5, 1972, NARA, RG59, CFPF 1970–1973, POL 23-8, 1-1-72; Embassy Moscow to Department of State, Telegram 5405, June 7, 1972, NARA, RG59, CFPF 1970–1973, POL 23-8, 1-1-72.

42. See Chamberlin, *The Global Offensive*, 153–54.

43. Eva Oberloskamp, "Das Olympia-Attentat 1972: Politische Lernprozesse im Umgang mit dem transnationalen Terrorismus," *Vierteljahrshefte für Zeitgeschichte* 60, no. 3 (July 2012): 321–52, doi: 10.1524/vfzg.2012.0018.

44. See for example Manuel Lucbert, "La police avait l'ordre d'empêcher le départ des terroristes," *Le Monde*, September 7, 1972, http://www.lemonde.fr/archives/article/1972/09/07/la-police-avait-l-ordre-d-empecher-le-depart-des-terroristes_2389991_1819218.html?xtmc=munich&xtcr=59; and Rudolf Augstein, "Terror und kein Ende," *Der Spiegel*, September 11, 1972, 20.

45. See Eva Oberloskamp, "Das Olympia-Attentat 1972," 333–34.

46. Central Intelligence Agency (CIA) Directorate of Intelligence, "Weekly Review," September 15, 1972, 3, CIA Freedom of Information Act Electronic Reading Room (CREST), FOIA Collection, 0000656074.

47. CIA Directorate of Intelligence, "Weekly Review," September 15, 1972, 3, CREST, FOIA Collection, 0000656074.

48. Tripoli LNA, "Tunisian Delegation Arrives," September 12, 1972, translated by Foreign Broadcast Information Service, *Foreign Broadcast Information Service*, daily report, White Book, FBIS-FRB-72-179, A1; Tunis Domestic Service, "Fatah Praises Tunisians," September 12, 1972, translated by Foreign Broadcast Information Service, *Foreign Broadcast Information Service*, daily report, White Book, FBIS-FRB-72-179, A1; See also Chamberlin, *The Global Offensive*,164, 166.

49. Embassy Tripoli to Department of State, Telegram 9178, September 10, 1972, NARA, RG59, CFPF 1970–1973, POL 23-8 9-6-72.

50. "Murder in Munich," *New York Times*, September 6, 1972, 44.

51. See for example James Yuenger, "The Tentacles of Terror," *Chicago Tribune*, September 10, 1972, A1.

52. Walter Laqueur, "The Terrorist Attacks: An Exercise in Futility: Arab Terror: More to Come," *Washington Post*, September 10, 1972, B1, B5.

53. See Chamberlin, *The Global Offensive*, 162–66.

54. Oberloskamp "Das Olympia-Attentat 1972," 330–31.

55. See chapter 3, s.v. The Proliferation of Antiterrorism Tactical Units During the 1970s.

56. See Timothy J. Naftali, *Blind Spot: The Secret History of American Counterterrorism* (New York: Basic Books, 2005), 39, 55–60.

57. Richard Kearney to Henry Kissinger, memorandum, "Action to Combat Terrorism," September 23, 1972, Gerald Ford Presidential Library (FPL), White House Central Files (WHCF), Special Files 355: Cabinet Committee to Combat Terrorism; Henry Kissinger and John Ehrlichman, the White House's domestic affairs adviser to President Richard Nixon, memorandum, "Action to Combat Terrorism," undated, FPL, WHCF, Special Files 355: Cabinet Committee to Combat Terrorism.

58. President Richard Nixon to heads of departments and agencies, memorandum, "Action to Combat Terrorism," September 25, 1972, *FRUS, 1969–1976*, Volume E-1, Document 109, accessed June 25, 2018, https://history.state.gov/historicaldocuments/frus1969-76ve01/d109.

59. Department of State to Embassy UK and other posts, Circular Telegram 164986, September 9, 1972, *FRUS, 1969–1976*, Volume E-1, Document 99, accessed June 25, 2018, https://history.state.gov/historicaldocuments/frus1969-76ve01/d99.

60. Recent studies of this support include Jensen, *The Making of International Human Rights*; Bernhard Blumenau, "The Other Battleground of the Cold War: The UN and the Struggle Against International Terrorism in the 1970s," *Journal of Cold War Studies* 16, no. 1 (Winter 2014): 61–84; and Brenda Gayle Plummer, *In Search of Power: African Americans in the Era of Decolonization, 1956–1974* (Cambridge: Cambridge University Press, 2013).

61. Department of State to Embassy UK and other posts, Circular Telegram 164986, September 9, 1972, *FRUS, 1969–1976*, Volume E-1, Document 99.

62. See Embassy Moscow to Department of State, Telegram 9300, September 14, 1972, NARA, RG59, CFPF 1970–1973, POL 23-8, 9-13-72; Samuel M. Hoskinson and Fernando Rondon of the National Security Council staff to Henry Kissinger, memorandum, "International terrorism at the UN," September 6, 1972, *FRUS, 1969–1976*, Volume E-1, Document 96, accessed September 7, 2018, https://history.state.gov/historicaldocuments/frus1969-76ve01/d96.

63. Department of State to all diplomatic posts, Circular Telegram 167609, September 13, 1972, NARA, RG59, CFPF 1970–1973, POL 23-8, 9-13-72.

64. Mission United Nations to Department of State, Telegram 3289, September 15, 1972, NARA, RG59, CFPF 1970–1973, POL 23-8, 9-13-72.

65. Mission United Nations to Department of State, Telegram 3256, September 14, 1972, NARA, RG59, CFPF 1970–1973, POL 23-8, 9-13-72.

66. Mission United Nations to Department of State, Telegram 3356, September 20, 1972, NARA, RG59, CFPF 1970–1973, POL 23-8, 9-16-72; Mission United Nations to Department of State, Telegram 3340, September 19, 1972, NARA, RG59, CFPF 1970–1973, POL 23-8, 9-16-72.

67. Mission United Nations to Department of State, Telegram 3412, September 22, 1972, NARA, RG59, CFPF 1970–1973, POL 23-8, 9-21-72; Mission United Nations to Department of State, Telegram 3452, September 25, 1972, NARA, RG59, CFPF 1970–1973, POL 23-8, 9-22-72.

68. Mission United Nations to Department of State, Telegram 3486, September 26, 1972, NARA, RG59, CFPF 1970–1973, POL 23-8, 9-25-72; and Mission United Nations

to Department of State, Telegram 3527, September 28, 1972, NARA, RG59, CFPF 1970–1973, POL 23-8, 9-27-72.

69. "UNGA Draft," September 23, 1972, NPL, National Security Council Files, Subject Files, Box 310, Cabinet Committee on Terrorism, 17.

70. Department of State to all diplomatic posts, Circular Telegram 175954, September 26, 1972, NARA, RG59, CFPF 1970–1973, POL 17, 7-10-72.

71. United Nations General Assembly Sixth Committee, Agenda Item 92, "United States of America: Working Paper," September 25, 1972, NARA, RG59, CFPF 1970–1973, POL 23-8, 9-25-72.

72. Republic of South Africa, "Terrorism Act 1967, Act No. 83 of 1967," in *Statutes of the Union of South Africa* (Pretoria: Government Printer, 1967), 1236–46, article 2.

73. Eliot to Kissinger, memorandum, "International Law Commission's Work on Draft Articles Concerning Crimes Against Persons Entitled to Special Protection Under International Law," March 31, 1972, NARA, RG59, CFPF 1970–1973, POL 5-2 ILC, 11-12-71.

74. William Rogers to President Richard Nixon, memorandum, "Actions to Combat International Terrorism," November 7, 1972, *FRUS*, 1969–1976, Volume E-1, Document 115, accessed December 12, 2018, https://history.state.gov/historicaldocuments/frus1969-76veo1/d115.

75. Mission United Nations to Department of State, Telegram 3745, October 7, 1972, NARA, RG59, CFPF 1970–1973, POL 5-2 ILC, 11-12-71; Mission United Nations to Department of State, Telegram 3777, October 9, 1972, NARA, RG59, CFPF 1970–1973, POL 5-2 ILC, 11-12-71.

76. Mission United Nations to Department of State, Telegram 3881, October 13, 1972, NARA, RG59, CFPF 1970–1973, POL 23-8, 10-6-72; Mission United Nations to Department of State, Telegram 3777, October 9, 1972, NARA, RG59, CFPF 1970–1973, POL 5-2 ILC, 11-12-71.

77. Mission United Nations to Department of State, Telegram 3663, October 4, 1972, NARA, RG59, CFPF 1970–1973, POL 5-2 ILC, 11-12-71.

78. Mission United Nations to Department of State, Telegram 3745, October 7, 1972, NARA, RG59, CFPF 1970–1973, POL 5-2 ILC, 11-12-71.

79. Mission United Nations to Department of State, Telegram 3906, October 20, 1972, NARA, RG59, CFPF 1970–1973, POL 5-2 IA, 10-06-72.

80. Fernando Rondon and Richard Kennedy of the National Security Council staff to Henry Kissinger, memorandum, "Terrorism: United Nations Action," October 25, 1972, *FRUS*, 1969–1976, Volume E-1, Document 113, accessed December 12, 2018, https://history.state.gov/historicaldocuments/frus1969-76veo1/d113.

81. Anonymous, "Arrest of Arab Terrorist Courier," in Central Intelligence Agency, "Weekly Situation Report on International Terrorism," November 1, 1972, CREST, General CIA Records, CIA-RDP79-01209A000100010001-7, 6–7.

82. Embassy Beirut to Department of State, Telegram 12044, November 6, 1972, NARA, RG59, CFPF 1970–1973, POL 23-8, 11-2-72; Department of State to Embassy Tel Aviv, Embassy Amman, et al., Telegram 197114, October 30, 1972, NARA, RG59, CFPF 1970–1973, POL 23-8, 10-13-72.

83. "Flugzeugentführung: Terroristen Befreit," *Die Zeit* 44, November 3, 1972, accessed February 19, 2020, https://www.zeit.de/1972/44/terroristen-befreit.

84. Department of State to Mission United Nations, Telegram 201467, November 4, 1972, NARA, RG59, CFPF 1970–1973, POL 23-8, 11-2-72; Department of State to Embassy

Buenos Aires et al., Circular Telegram 201469, November 4, 1972, NARA, RG59, CFPF 1970–1973, POL 23-8, 11-2-72; and Department of State to Mission United Nations, Telegram 198884, November 1, 1972, NARA, RG59, CFPF 1970–1973, POL 23-8, 11-2-72.

85. Mission United Nations to Department of State, Telegram 4511, November 10, 1972, NARA, RG59, CFPF 1970–1973, POL 23-8, 11-2-72

86. Mission United Nations to Department of State, Telegram 4510, November 10, 1972, NARA, RG59, CFPF 1970–1973, POL 23-8, 11-2-72.

87. Mission United Nations to Department of State, Telegram 4510, November 10, 1972, NARA, RG59, CFPF 1970–1973, POL 23-8, 11-2-72.

88. FAA administrator John H. Shaffer to all regional directors (Except EU and Centers), memorandum, January 4, 1973, NARA, Records of the Federal Aviation Administration (RG237), Office of the Administrator: Subject and Correspondence Files, 1959–82 (A1 14), 8040-A Hijacking 1973, January–June.

89. John H. Shaffer to Eastern Air Lines President S. L. Higginbottom, president of Eastern Air Lines, letter, January 3, 1973, NARA, RG237, A1 14, 8040-A Hijacking 1973, January–June.

90. Alexander Butterfield, FAA administrator, to all regional directors (Except AEU and Centers), memorandum, October 8, 1973, NARA, RG237, A1 14, 8040-A Hijacking 1973, July–December

91. Mission United Nations to Department of State, Telegram 4645, November 14, 1972, NARA, RG59, CFPF 1970–1973, POL 23-8, 11-2-72; Mission United Nations to Department of State, Telegram 4697, November 16, 1972, NARA, RG59, CFPF 1970–1973, POL 23-8, 11-2-72.

92. Mission United Nations to Department of State, Telegram 4758, November 17, 1972, NARA, RG59, CFPF 1970–1973, POL 23-8, 11-2-72; Mission United Nations to Department of State, Telegram 4545, November 10, 1972, NARA, RG59, CFPF 1970–1973, POL 23-8, 11-2-72; Embassy Tel Aviv to Department of State, Telegram 7441, November 13, 1972, NARA, RG59, CFPF 1970–1973, POL 23-8, 11-2-72.

93. Mission United Nations to Department of State, Telegram 4759, November 17, 1972, NARA, RG59, CFPF 1970–1973, POL 23-8, 11-2-72.

94. Mission United Nations to Department of State, Telegram 4817, November 18, 1972, NARA, RG59, CFPF 1970–1973, POL 23-8, 11-2-72; and Kathleen Teltsch, "Israel Warns the UN that Governments Will Act on Terrorism," New York Times, November 17, 1972.

95. Mission United Nations to Department of State, Telegram 4697, November 16, 1972, NARA, RG59, CFPF 1970–1973, POL 23-8, 11-2-72. See also Embassy Paris to Department of State, Telegram 21734, November 13, 1972, NARA, RG59, CFPF 1970–1973, POL 23-8, 11-2-72.

96. The sponsors of the Italian draft were Australia, Belgium, Canada, Costa Rica, Italy, Japan, New Zealand, the UK, and Iran.

97. Mission United Nations to Department of State, Telegram 4855, November 21, 1972, NARA, RG59, CFPF 1970–1973, POL 23-8, 11-2-72.

98. Department of State to Mission United Nations, Telegram 222138, December 7, 1972, NARA, RG59, CFPF 1970–1973, POL 23-8, 12-1-72; Mission United Nations to Department of State, Telegram 5461, December 9, 1972, NARA, RG59, CFPF 1970–1973, POL 23-8, 12-1-72; and Department of State to Embassy Buenos Aires,

Embassy Gaberones, et al., Telegram 223323, December 9, 1972, NARA, RG59, CFPF 1970–1973, POL 23-8, 12-1-72.

99. Department of State to Embassy The Hague, Mission United Nations, Telegram 214763, November 27, 1972, NARA, RG59, CFPF 1970–1973, POL 23-8, 11-2-72. 7

100. The sponsors of the nonaligned draft were Afghanistan, Algeria, Guyana, India, Kenya, Yugoslavia, and Zambia.

101. Mission United Nations to Department of State, Telegram 5086, November 28, 1972, NARA, RG59, CFPF 1970–1973, POL 23-8, 11-2-72.

102. "U.N. General Assembly Resolution on Measures to Prevent International Terrorism," *International Legal Matters* 12, no. 1 (January 1973): 218–20.

103. Mission United Nations to Department of State, Telegram 5582, December 15, 1972, NARA, RG59, CFPF 1970–1973, POL 23-8, 12-1-72.

104. US Mission NATO to Department of State, Telegram 5424, December 16, 1972, NARA, RG59, CFPF 1970–1973, POL 23-8, 12-1-72.

105. Department of State to Embassy Rome, Embassy London, Embassy Paris, and Mission United Nations, Telegram 227601, December 16, 1972, NARA, RG59, CFPF 1970–1973, POL 23-8, 12-1-72.

106. J. Dodds (UK Foreign and Commonwealth Office, Maritime and Transport Division) to Mr. Whitehead and Mr. Woodland, memorandum "ICAO Legal Committee Meeting in Montreal, January 19, 1973, TNA, FCO 76/619.

107. The coordinator for Combating Terrorism, Lewis Hoffacker, and Carlyle Maw, the deputy legal adviser, to Henry Kissinger, action memorandum, "Terrorism: Soviet Proposal for Bilateral," December 29, 1973, *FRUS*, 1969–1976, Volume E-3, Document 213, accessed October 4, 2019, https://history.state.gov/historicaldocuments/frus1969-76ve03/d213.

108. Terence Smith, "Israelis Down a Libyan Airliner in the Sinai, Killing at Least 74; Say It Ignored Warnings to Land," *New York Times*, February 22, 1973, 1.

109. Department of State to Embassy Tokyo, Telegram 171985, August 29, 1973, NARA, RG59, CFPF 1973–1979, Electronic Telegrams 1973 (/Electronic Telegrams), 1973STATE171985, accessed April 25, 2015.

110. Consulate Montreal to Department of State, Telegram 0479, March 9, 1973, NARA, RG59, CFPF 1973–1979/Electronic Telegrams, 1973MONTRE00479, accessed April 25, 2015.

111. J. Mellon, "UK Statement in Plenary Session of ICAO Assembly," attachment to J. Mellon to J. P. Ritter, letter, September 28, 1973, The National Archives of the United Kingdom (TNA), FCO 76/629.

112. Rogers to Nixon, memorandum, "Protection for Foreign Diplomats Here, and Ours Abroad," March 29, 1973, NARA, RG59, CFPF 1970–1973, POL 17, 1-3-73; William Rogers to Richard Nixon, Memorandum "Combating Terrorism," June 17, 1973, *FRUS*, 1969–1976, Volume E-3, Document 210, accessed June 25, 2018, https://history.state.gov/historicaldocuments/frus1969-76ve03/d210.

113. Ronald Ziegler, memorandum, "Department of State Luncheon with Secretary William P. Rogers and State Department Officials, Tuesday, March 6, 1973 at 12:50 p.m.," March 6, 1973, *FRUS*, 1969–1976, Volume E-3, Document 207, accessed June 25, 2018, https://history.state.gov/historicaldocuments/frus1969-76ve03/d207. In 1974, Sudan found the attackers guilty, but handed their custody to the PLO. The United States and European states were outraged, and Nixon took actions that he

had avoided in 1973. He halted economic assistance and recalled the U.S. ambassador to Sudan.

114. Department of State to Mission United Nations and Embassy Brussels, Telegram 070919, March 28, 1973, NARA, RG59, CFPF 1970–1973, POL 23-8, 4-2-73.

115. Mission United Nations to Department of State, Airgram A-1135, August 24, 1973, NARA, RG59, CFPF 1970–1973, POL 23-8, 5-1-73.

116. Juan de Onis, "Lebanon Accuses Israel of Piracy in Jet Intercept," *The New York Times*, August 12, 1973, 1.

117. Embassy Rome to Department of State, Telegram 9280, September 7, 1973, NARA, RG59, CFPF 1973–1979/Electronic Telegrams, 1973ROME09280, accessed April 25, 2015; Department of State to Embassy Rome, Telegram 172929, August 30, 1973, NARA, RG59, CFPF 1973-79/Electronic Telegrams, 1973STATE172929, accessed April 25, 2015.

118. UK Embassy Rome to Foreign and Commonwealth Office and UK Mission New York, Telegram 645, September 22, 1973, TNA, FCO 76/629.

119. Hoffacker to Kissinger, briefing memorandum, "Major Problems in Combating Terrorism," October 4, 1973, *FRUS*, 1969–1976, Volume E-3, Document 211, accessed June 25, 2018, https://history.state.gov/historicaldocuments/frus1969-76ve03/d211; Department of State to all diplomatic and consular posts, airgram A-8515, October 11, 1973, NARA, RG59, CFPF 1970–1973, POL 23-8, 5-1-73.

120. The director of the Office of Management and Budget, James Lynn, to President Gerald Ford, memorandum, "Enrolled Bill H.R. 12—Executive Protective Service Sponsor—Rep. Jones (D) Alabama and 2 others," November 26, 1975, *FRUS*, 1969–1976, Volume E-3: Documents on Global Issues, 1973–1976, Document 224, accessed September 23, 2019, https://history.state.gov/historicaldocuments/frus1969-76ve03/d224.

121. The deputy director of Central Intelligence General, Vernon Walters, to Henry Kissinger, backchannel message, November 4, 1973, *FRUS*, 1969–1976, Volume XXV, Document 318, accessed May 15, 2019, https://history.state.gov/historicaldocuments/frus1969-76v25/d318.

122. Department of State to Consulate Montreal, Telegram 226496, November 16, 1973, NARA, RG59, CFPF 1973–1979/Electronic Telegrams, 1973STATE226496, accessed April 25, 2015; Department of State to Consulate Montreal, Telegram 233628, November 28, 1973, NARA, RG59, CFPF 1973–1979/Electronic Telegrams, 1973STATE233628, accessed April 25, 2015; and Mackenzie, *ICAO*, 262.

123. Department of State to Embassy Kuwait, Telegram 228111, September 22, 1977, NARA, RG59, CFPF 1973–1979/Electronic Telegrams, 1977STATE228111, accessed March 20, 2015.

124. See International Civil Aviation Organization, "The Convention on International Civil Aviation: Annexes 1 to 18," *International Civil Aviation Organization*, accessed November 25, 2019, http://www.icao.int/safety/airnavigation/nationalitymarks/annexes _booklet_en.pdf, Annex 17; and Mackenzie, *ICAO*, 262.

125. U. S. House of Representatives, "Public Law 93–366," August 5, 1974, Office of the Law Revision Counsel, U.S. Code, accessed November 25, 2019, http://uscode .house.gov/statutes/pl/93/366.pdf, 413–414.

126. "Public Law 93–366," August 5, 1974, 418.

127. State Department, Bureau of International Security and Nonproliferation, "Convention on the Physical Protection of Nuclear Material," *U.S. Department of State Archive*, accessed September 13, 2019, https://2009-2017.state.gov/t/isn/5079.htm.

128. See chapter 5, s.v. Normalizing Global North Conceptualizations of Terrorism in International Law.

129. See, for example, Robert Kupperman, "Nuclear Terrorism: Armchair Pastime or Genuine Threat?," *Jerusalem Journal of International Relations* 3, no. 4 (Summer 1978): 19–26.

130. A strong example from Mark Feldman can be found in Embassy Mexico City to Department of State, Telegram 4674, June 28, 1973, NARA, RG59, CFPF 1970–1973, POL 5–2 ILC, 10-20-72.

131. Hoffacker and Maw to Kissinger, action memorandum, "Terrorism: Soviet Proposal for Bilateral," December 29, 1973, *FRUS*, Volume E-3, Document 213, accessed October 4, 2019, https://history.state.gov/historicaldocuments/frus1969-76ve03/d213.

132. United Nations, "Convention on the Prevention and Punishment of Crimes Against Internationally Protected Persons, Including Diplomatic Agents: General Assembly Resolution 3166 (XXVIII) of 14 December 1973," December 14, 1973, *International Law Commission*, accessed November 25, 2019, http://legal.un.org/ilc/texts/instruments/english/conventions/9_4_1973.pdf.

133. Hoffacker to Kissinger, briefing memorandum, "Terrorism: The Busy Month of December," December 27, 1973, *FRUS*, 1969–1976, Volume E-3: Documents on Global Issues, 1973–1976, Document 212, accessed December 12, 2018, https://history.state.gov/historicaldocuments/frus1969-76ve03/d212; First Councilor K. Hoffmann (FRG Foreign Office Legal Department), memorandum, "Konvention zur Verhinderung und Bestrafung von Verbrechen gegen international geschützte Personen einschliesslich diplomatischer Vertreter (Diplomatenschutzkonvention): Verlauf und Ergebnis der Verhandlungen im 6. Ausschuss der VN waehrend der XXVIII. Vollversammlung," December 28, 1973, Political Archive of the Foreign Office, Federal Republic of Germany (B)83, Vol. 1225.

134. United Nations, "Convention on the Prevention and Punishment of Crimes Against Internationally Protected Persons, Including Diplomatic Agents."

135. Department of State to all diplomatic and consular posts, Circular Telegram 256207, October 15, 1976, *FRUS*, 1969–1976, Volume E-3: Documents on Global Issues, 1973–1976, Document 228, accessed September 23, 2019, https://history.state.gov/historicaldocuments/frus1969-76ve03/d228.

136. See chapter 3, s.v. Setting the Scene: The FRG's Response to the 1972 Munich Olympic Games Attack.

137. See chapter 5, s.v. Normalizing Global North Conceptualizations of Terrorism in International Law.

3. TACTICAL ANTITERRORISM COLLABORATION IN EUROPE AND THE GLOBAL NORTH

1. A detailed analysis of the kidnapping is Matthias Dahlke, " 'Nur eingeschränkte Krisenbereitschaft': Die staatliche Reaktion auf die Entführung des CDU-Politikers Peter Lorenz 1975," *Vierteljahrshefte für Zeitgeschichte* 55, no. 4 (October 2007): 641–78.

2. Richard Bach Jensen, *The Battle Against Anarchist Terrorism: An International History, 1878–1934* (Cambridge: Cambridge University Press, 2014).

3. Christopher Daase, "Die Historisierung der Sicherheit. Anmerkungen zur historischen Sicherheitsforschung aus politikwissenschaftlicher Sicht," *Geschichte und Gesellschaft* 38, no. 3 (July 2012): 387–405, 388.

4. Little research exists on TREVI. The definitive work is Eva Oberloskamp, *Codename TREVI: Terrorismusbekämpfung und die Anfänge einer europäischen Innenpolitik in den 1970er Jahren* (Oldenbourg, Germany: De Gruyter, 2017).

5. David A. Charters, ed., *The Deadly Sin of Terrorism: Its Effect on Democracy and Civil Liberty in Six Countries* (Westport, CT: Greenwood, 1994) provides an overview of domestic efforts and institutions in Israel, the United States, Italy, the FRG, France, and the UK.

6. For French counterinsurgency in Algeria, see Douglas Porch, *Counterinsurgency: Exposing the Myths of the New Way of War* (New York: Cambridge University Press, 2013); Martin Evans, *Algeria: France's Undeclared War* (New York: Oxford University Press, 2012); and Martin S. Alexander and J. F. V. Keiger, eds., *France and the Algierian War, 1954–62: Strategy, Operations, and Diplomacy* (London: Frank Cass, 2002). For French domestic developments, see Markus Lammert, *Der Neue Terrorismus: Terrorismusbekämpfung in Frankreich in den 1980er Jahren* (Oldenbourg, Germany: De Gruyter, 2017), 27–33, 36–39, 41–43.

7. Markus Lammert, "The Absent Terrorism: Leftist Political Violence and the French State, 1968–1974," in *An International History of Terrorism: Western and Non-Western Experiences*, ed. Jussi Hanhimäki and Bernhard Blumenau (New York: Routledge, 2013), 86–99.

8. Lammert, *Der Neue Terrorismus*, 33–38, 43–47.

9. Histories of the RAF include Stefan Aust, *The Baader-Meinhof Complex*, Rev. ed. (London: Bodley Head, 2008); Wolfgang Kraushaar, ed. *Die RAF und der linke Terrorismus*, 2 vols. (Hamburg: Hamburger Editionen, 2006); and Jeremy Varon, *Bringing the War Home: The Weather Underground, the Red Army Faction, and Revolutionary Violence in the Sixties and Seventies* (Berkeley: University of California Press, 2004).

10. "Wer Waren die Mitglieder der RAF?," *Die Welt*, accessed March 12, 2019, https://www.welt.de/politik/deutschland/gallery726024/Wer-waren-die-Mitglieder-der-RAF.html.

11. Ulrike Meinhof, "Das Konzept Stadtguerilla," in *Rote Armee Fraktion: Texte und Materialien zur Geschichte der RAF* (Berlin: ID Verlag, 1997), 27–48, 32–33.

12. Achim Saupe, " 'Innere Sicherheit' und 'law and order': Die politische Semantik von Ordnung, Sicherheit und Freiheit in der bundesdeutschen Innenpolitik," in Hürter, *Terrorismusbekämpfung in Westeuropa*, 171–200.

13. Oberloskamp, *Codename TREVI*, 198–99.

14. See Karrin Hanshew, *Terror and Democracy in West Germany* (New York: Cambridge, 2012), and Boris Spernol, *Notstand der Demokratie. Der Protest gegen die Notstandsgesetze und die Frage der NS-Vergangenheit* (Essen, Germany: Klartext, 2008).

15. See Hanshew, chapters 3 and 5, *Terror and Democracy in West Germany*.

16. See Johannes Hürter, "Regieren gegen Terrorismus: Die Beispiele Westminster, Bonn und Rom in den 1970er Jahren," in *Terrorismusbekämpfung in Westeuropa*, ed. Johannes Hürter (Oldenbourg, Germany: De Gruyter, 2015), 63–80.

17. On the years of lead, see Tobias Hof, *Staat und Terrorismus in Italien 1969–1987* (Munich: Oldenbourg, 2011); and Johannes Hürter and Gian Enrico Rusconi, eds., *Die bleiernen Jahre: Staat und Terrorismus in der Bundesrepublik Deutschland und Italien, 1969–1982* (Munich: R. Oldenbourg, 2010).

18. Hof, *Staat und Terrorismus in Italien, 70–83*.
19. Hof, *Staat und Terrorismus in Italien*, 108, 111.
20. "Arab Guerillas Kill 31 in Rome During Attack on U.S. Airliner, Take Hostages to Athens, Fly on," *New York Times*, December 18, 1973, 1.
21. *Global Terrorism Database*, National Consortium for the Study of Terrorism and Responses to Terrorism, 2009–2020, accessed March 18, 2020, https://www.start .umd.edu/gtd/access/. A significant historiography exists on the Troubles and the IRA. Recent works include Tommy McKearney, *The Provisional IRA: From Insurrection to Parliament* (New York: Palgrave MacMillan, 2011); Andrew Sanders, *Inside the IRA: Dissident Republicans and the War for Legitimacy* (Edinburgh: Edinburgh University Press, 2011); and Cilian McGrattan, *Northern Ireland: The Politics of Entrenchment* (New York: Palgrave MacMillan, 2010).
22. Hürter, "Regieren gegen Terrorismus," 66–68; and Bruce B. Warner, "Great Britain and the Response to International Terrorism," in *The Deadly Sin of Terrorism: Its Effect on Democracy and Civil Liberties in Six Countries*, ed. David Charters (Westport, CT: Greenwood, 1996), 13–42.
23. Wilfried Loth, *Building Europe: A History of European Unification* (Berlin: De Gruyter Oldenbourg, 2015), and Alan S. Milward, *The European Rescue of the Nation-State*, 2nd ed. (London: Routledge, 2000).
24. Timothy Andrews Sayle, *Enduring Alliance: A History of NATO and the Postwar Global Order* (Ithaca, NY: Cornell University Press, 2019).
25. Stefanie Schmahl and Marten Breuer, eds., *The Council of Europe: Its Law and Policies* (New York: Oxford University Press, 2017); and Aline Royer, *Der Europarat* (Strasbourg: Council of Europe Publishing, 2010).
26. Lorenzo Ferrari, "How the European Community Entered the United Nations, 1969–1976, and What It Meant for European Political Integration," *Diplomacy & Statecraft* 29 no. 2 (April 2018): 237–54, doi: 10.1080/09592296.2018.1452430.
27. See European Political Co-operation (EPC) Press and Information Office "Introduction to EPC (European Political Cooperation)," Federal Republic of Germany, 5th ed., 1988, accessed March 10, 2020, http://aei.pitt.edu/1895/1/EPC_intro.pdf. See also Giuliana Laschi, ed., *The European Community and the World: A Historical Perspective* (Bern, Switzerland: Peter Lang, 2014).
28. Charles Maier, *Once Within Borders: Territories of Wealth, Power, and Belonging since 1500* (Cambridge, MA: Belknap Press of Harvard University Press, 2016).
29. See Mary S. Barton, "The Global War on Anarchism: The United States and International Anarchist Terrorism, 1898–1904," *Diplomatic History* 39, no. 2 (April 2015): 303–30; Jensen, *The Battle Against Anarchist Terrorism*; Peter Andreas and Ethan Nadelmann, *Policing the Globe: Criminalization and Crime Control in International Relations* (New York: Oxford University Press, 2008), 59–87; and Mathieu Deflem, *Policing World Society: Historical Foundations of International Police Cooperation* (New York: Oxford University Press, 2004), 45–77.
30. See Aviva Guttmann, "Combatting Terror in Europe: Euro-Israeli Counterterrorism Intelligence Cooperation in the Club de Berne (1971–1972)," *Intelligence and National Security* 33, no. 2 (Summer 2017): 158–75, doi: 10.1080/02684527.2017.1324591.
31. Pompidou Group, "History," Council of Europe, accessed April 18, 2019, https:// www.coe.int/en/web/pompidou/about/history.
32. Hans-Dietrich Genscher, *Vom Traum zum Terror—München 72*, documentary, directed by Marc Brasse and Florian Huber, CITY: Spiegel TV, 2012.

33. Matthias Dahlke, *Der Anschlag auf Olympia '72: Die Politischen Reaktionen auf den Internationalen Terrorismus in Deutschland* (Munich: Martin Meidenbauer, 2008), 93–98.
34. Eva Oberloskamp, "Das Olympia-Attentat 1972: Politische Lernprozesse im Umgang mit dem transnationalen Terrorismus," *Vierteljahrshefte für Zeitgeschichte* 60, no. 3 (July 2012): 321–52, doi: 10.1524/vfzg.2012.0018, 330–331; Dahlke, *Der Anschlag auf Olympia '72*, 42, 46–53.
35. Offices 200, 502, 230 (FRG Foreign Ministry), Current Position Paper "Gemeinsame Europäische Massnahmen gegen Terrorismus (Empfehlungen Nr. 674 und 684 der Beratenden Versammlung)," December 11, 1972, Political Archive of the Foreign Office (hereafter: PA AA) Federal Republic of Germany (hereafter: B83 Vol. 980).
36. Councilor Dr. Fleischhauer to Berndt von Staden, director of the Political Office of the Foreign Officememorandum, "Bekämpfung des Terrorismus: Hausbesprechung vom 15. Sept. 1972," September 19, 1972, Political Archive of the Foreign Office (hereafter: PA AA), Federal Republic of Germany (hereafter: B83 Vol. 980).
37. Offices 200, 502, 230, current position paper, "Gemeinsame Europäische Massnahmen gegen Terrorismus," December 11, 1972, PA AA, B83 Vol. 980.
38. Undersecretary Paul-Günter Pötz (B II 5) to the federal minister of justice, Hans-Jochen Vogel, memorandum, "Vorbereitung des EG-Justizministerrats vom 26.11.1974," November 25, 1974, Federal Archives Germany (BArch), Federal Republic of Germany (B) Records of the Ministry of Justice (141)-65262, pages 46–48.
39. US Mission NATO to Department of State, Telegram 5424, December 16, 1972, National Archives and Records Administration, Record Group 59: Records of the Department of State, Central Foreign Policy Files (CFPF) 1970–1973, POL 23-8, 12-1-72.
40. See Jensen, *The Battle Against Anarchist Terrorism*; and Deflem, *Policing World Society*.
41. Oberloskamp, *Codename TREVI*, 220–23.
42. Councilor Dr. Born (Office for Constitutional and Administrative Law (510), Foreign Office) to FRG interior minister Hans-Dietrich Genscher, memorandum, "Vorbereitung einer europäischen Konferenz über innere Sicherheit: Ihr Schreiben vom 25. April 1973," May 15, 1973, PA AA, B83 Vol. 825; undersecretary Merk (Public Security, Division 2, FRG Interior Ministry) to Hans-Dietrich Genscher, memorandum, "Vorbereitung einer Europäischen Konferenz über Innere Sicherheit," August 10, 1973, PA AA, B83 Vol. 825.
43. Merk to Genscher, memorandum, "Vorbereitung einer Europäischen Konferenz über Innere Sicherheit," August 10, 1973, PA AA, B83 Vol. 825; Consultative Assembly of the Council of Europe, "Recommendation 703 (1973) on International Terrorism," 16 May 1973, PA AA, B83 Vol. 981.
44. Gerhard von Löwenich (Public Security, FRG Interior Ministry) to Hans-Dietrich Genscher, memorandum, "Vorbereitung einer Europäischen Konferenz für Innere Sicherheit: Vorlage des Referates ÖS 2 vom 10. August 1973, Vortrag bei Ihnen am 17. August 1973," September 4, 1973, PA AA, B82 Vol. 1032.
45. Von Löwenich to Genscher, memorandum, "Vorbereitung einer Europäischen Konferenz für Innere Sicherheit," September 4, 1973, PA AA, B82 Vol. 1032; Public Security Office 2, "Ergebnisvermerk über eine Besprechung mit Ressorts, BfV, BKA, und Referaten im BMI am 15. August 1974," August 23, 1974, PA AA, B82 Vol. 1032.

46. Hans-Dietrich Genscher to French interior minister Raymond Marcellin, letter, October 23, 1973, PA AA, B82 Vol. 1032.
47. FRG Embassy Paris to Foreign Office, Telegram 162, January 15, 1974, PA AA, B83 Vol. 980; FRG Embassy Paris to Foreign Office, Telegram 405, February 5, 1974, PA AA, B83 Vol. 980.
48. Oberloskamp, *Codename TREVI*, 215–16.
49. First secretary Dr. Birmelin to FRG Embassy Paris, Telegram 2740, January 29, 1974, PA AA, B82 Vol. 1032.
50. Oberloskamp lays out these fears well in *Codename TREVI*, 214–15.
51. Offices 200, 502, 230, current position paper, "Gemeinsame Europäische Massnahmen gegen Terrorismus," December 11, 1972, PA AA, B83 Vol. 980. See also Oberloskamp, *Codename TREVI*, 58, 141; and Lammert, *Der Neue Terrorismus*, 33–38, 43–47.
52. Bernhard Blumenau, "Taming the Beast: West Germany, the Political Offence Exception and the Council of Europe Convention on the Suppression of Terrorism," *Terrorism and Political Violence* 27, no. 2 (March 2015): 310–30.
53. Born to Genscher, memorandum, "Vorbereitung einer europäischen Konferenz über innere Sicherheit," May 15, 1973, PA AA, B83 Vol. 825; FRG Embassy Paris to Foreign Office, Telegram 405, February 5, 1974, PA AA, B83 Vol. 980.
54. FRG Embassy Paris to Foreign Office, Telegram 405, February 5, 1974, PA AA, B83 Vol. 980; FRG interior minister Werner Maihofer to Foreign Office, memorandum, "Europäische Konferenz über Innere Sicherheit: Bildung einer deutsch-französischen Arbeitsgruppe für Allgemeine Fragen der Inneren Sicherheit," August 2, 1974, PA AA, ZA Vol. 109198.
55. FRG Embassy Paris to Foreign Office, Telegram 2798, September 4, 1974, PA AA, ZA Vol. 109198.
56. FRG Embassy Paris to Foreign Office, Telegram 2742, August 23, 1975, B Records of the Chancellery (136)-25202, pp. 10–13.
57. See chapter 4 for the justice ministries' creation of European extradition agreements based on earlier conventions against specific acts of political violence.
58. Oberloskamp, *Codename TREVI*, 61.
59. "Terrorists Land, Relinquish Money," *New York Times*, September 19, 1974, 1.
60. "Two Rockets Fired at Israeli Jet in Paris," *New York Times*, January 14, 1975, 1; Flora Lewis, "Arabs Free 10 at Orly, Surrender in Iraq," *New York Times*, January 21, 1975, 1.
61. Translated from French by the author. Jean-Paul Sartre, "La mort lente d'Andreas Baader," *Libération*, December 7, 1974.
62. Dahlke, "Nur eingeschränkte Krisenbereitschaft."
63. Translated from German by the author. Andreas Baader, "Auszug aus dem Wortprotokoll vom 4. Mai 1976," in Gisela Diewald-Kerkmann, "Die Rote Armee Fraktion im Original-Ton: Die Tonbandmitschnitte vom Stuttgarter Stammheim-Prozess," *Studies in Contemporary History*, 5 no. 2 (2008), 299–312, http://www.zeithistorische-forschungen.de/16126041-Diewald-Kerkmann-2-2008.
64. Dahlke, "Nur eingeschränkte Krisenbereitschaft," 672; Michael März, *Die Machtprobe 1975: Wie RAF und Bewegung 2. Juni den Staat erpressten* (Leipzig, Germany: Forum Verlag Leipzig, 2007).
65. Memorandum, attachment 3, Maihofer to the head of the chancellery, Manfred Schüler, letter, August 28, 1975, BArch, B136-25202, pp. 20–27.
66. Oberloskamp, *Codename TREVI*, 61, 63–67.

67. Memorandum, attachment 3, Maihofer to Schüler, letter, August 28, 1975, BArch, B136-25202, pp. 20–27.

68. Robert Armstrong (Home Office) to Michael Butler (Foreign and Commonwealth Office), letter, July 31, 1975, The National Archives of the United Kingdom (TNA), FCO 30/2614.

69. Tobias Hof, "Anti-Terrorismus-Gesetze und Sicherheitskräfte in der Bundesrepublik Deutschland, Großbritannien und Italien in den 1970er und 1980er Jahren," in Hürter, *Terrorismusbekämpfung in Westeuropa*, 7–34, 19; and Peter R. Neumann, "The Myth of Ulsterization in British Security Policy in Northern Ireland," *Studies in Conflict and Terrorism* 26, no. 5 (May 2003): 365–377.

70. Maihofer to French interior minister Michel Poniatowski, letter, September 18, 1975, BArch, B, Records of the Interior Ministry (106)-78829; undersecretary Streicher (Public Security, Division 1, Interior Ministry) to Maihofer, memorandum, "Europäische Konferenz für Innere Sicherheit: Einladung des Herrn Ministers zu einem Besuch in London," September 1975, BArch, B106-78829, folder 1; British Embassy Bonn to state secretary Siegfried Fröhlich (FRG interior ministry), diplomatic note with attachment memorandum, "European Political Cooperation: Proposal for a Meeting of Ministers of the Interior of the Nine," October 22, 1975, BArch, B106-78829, folder 1.

71. Maihofer to FRG Mission Brussels, memorandum, "Vorbereitung einer Europäischen Konferenz für Innere Sicherheit," December 30, 1975, PA AA, B83 Vol. 980; Dr. Feit (Office for France, Andorra, Monaco, Belgium, Netherlands, Luxembourg (202), Foreign Office), memorandum of conversation "Deutsch-französische Direktorenkonsultationen am 12.1.76 in Paris, Terrorismusbekämpfung," January 23, 1976, PA AA, B83 Vol. 980.

72. Clyde H. Farnworth, "Terrorists Raid OPEC Oil Parley in Vienna, Kill 3," *New York Times*, December 22, 1975, 59.

73. Brian Jenkins, *Embassies Under Siege: A Review of 48 Embassy Takeovers, 1971–1980* (Santa Monica, CA: RAND Corporation, 1981), 31.

74. Alice Siegert, "Europe's Reign of Terror: No One Is Immune," *Chicago Tribune*, February 8, 1976, A1.

75. See Paul Thomas Chamberlin, *The Global Offensive: The United States, the Palestine Liberation Organization, and the Making of the Post-Cold War Order* (New York: Oxford University Press, 2012), 224–25, 235–38, 246–53.

76. Early publications include Brian M. Jenkins, *International Terrorism: A New Kind of Warfare* (Santa Monica, CA: RAND Corporation, 1974), accessed March 21, 2019, https://www.rand.org/content/dam/rand/pubs/papers/2008/P5261.pdf; Paul Wilkinson, *Political Terrorism* (New York: Halsted, 1974); Yonah Alexander, ed. *International Terrorism: National, Regional, and Global Perspectives* (New York: Prager, 1976); and Walter Laqueur, *Terrorism* (Boston: Little, Brown, 1977).

77. Lisa Stampnitzky, *Disciplining Terror: How Experts Invented 'Terrorism' "* (Cambridge: Cambridge University Press, 2013), 60–61.

78. See chapter 2, s.v. From Multilateralism to Unilateralism.

79. Robert Kupperman, *Facing Tomorrow's Terrorism Incidents Today* (Washington, DC: Law Enforcement Assistance Administration, 1977), i, Hoover Institution Archives (Hoover), Robert H. Kupperman Papers (Kupperman), Box 4, folder 5.

80. Arms Control and Disarmament Agency (ACDA), chief scientist Robert Kupperman to Jakov Katwan, Institute for International Scientific Exchange, letter, June 22, 1978, Hoover, Kupperman, Box 5, folder 7.

81. CCCT chairman Robert Fearey to Fred Ikle, memorandum, "Commendation of Dr. Robert H. Kupperman," August 18, 1976, Hoover, Kupperman, Box 6, folder 5. This folder also holds correspondence related to the trip.

82. Hans-Josef Horchem, *West Germany's Red Army Anarchists* (London: Institute for the Study of Conflict, 1974); Hans-Josef Horchem, *Right-Wing Extremism in Western Germany* (London: Institute for the Study of Conflict, 1975).

83. Jakov Katwan, Institute for International Scientific Exchange, to ACDA chief scientist Robert Kupperman, letter, September 29. 1978, Hoover, Kupperman, Box 5, folder 7.

84. FRG Consulate Bilbao to Foreign Office, memorandum, "Besuch des Präsidenten des Landesamts für Verfassungsschutz Hamburg, Dr. Horchem, in Spanien," July 24, 1978, BArch, B136-15685, folder 3; FRG Embassy Madrid to Foreign Office, Telegram 458, July 26, 1978, BArch, B136-15685, folder 3.

85. See chapter 4, s.v. The Council of Europe Negotiations and German-French Divisions, and chapter 5, s.v. Normalizing Global North Conceptualizations of Terrorism in International Law.

86. Streicher to Maihofer, memorandum, "Vorbereitung einer Europäischen Konferenz für Innere Sicherheit: Pakt gegen den Terrorismus," January 30, 1976, BArch, B106-78829, folder 2.

87. Foreign and Commonwealth Office, memorandum, "Terrorism: European Council Declaration," August 6, 1976, TNA, FCO 76/1221.

88. Rome Coreu to Bonn Coreu, EC-Internal Coreu Telegram 3019, December 31, 1975, BArch, B106-78829, folder 1.

89. Streicher to Maihofer, memorandum, "Vorbereitung einer Europäischen Konferenz für Innere Sicherheit: Vorbereitende Gespräche mit der dänischen und luxemburgischen Seite," February 17, 1976, BArch, B106-78829, folder 2; Mr. Henatsch (Office for European Integration et al. (200), Foreign Office), note for the record, "Vorbereitung der Konferenz der Innenminister der Neun über Fragen der Inneren Sicherheit: Beamtentreffen der Neun in Luxemburg am 20.02.76," February 24, 1976, PA AA, B83 Vol. 980.

90. Mr. Henatsch, note for the record, "Vorbereitung der Konferenz der Innenminister der Neun über Fragen der Inneren Sicherheit."

91. Mr. H. P. Bochmann (Public Security, Division 9, FRG Interior Ministry), memorandum for the record, "Vorbereitung einer Europäischen Konferenz für Innere Sicherheit: Vorbereitung der Sitzung der Hohen Beamten am 29.04.1976," April 27, 1976, BArch, B106-106774, folder 1.

92. Coreu Luxembourg to all other Coreu states, EC Internal Coreu Telegram 629, February 25, 1976, BArch, B106-78829, folder 3.

93. Translated from German by the author. Draft press communiqué, undated, attachment to Chief Executive Officer Bracht (Public Security, Division 1, FRG Interior Ministry) to State Secretary F, memorandum, "Europäische Konferenz für Innere Sicherheit am 19. Juni 1976 in Luxemburg: Ergebnisse," July 2, 1976, BArch, B106-106774, folder 1.

94. TREVI Office Netherlands to all other TREVI offices, Telegram 31624, October 4, 1976, BArch, B106-106774, folder 2.

95. Oberloskamp, *Codename TREVI*, 3-4.

96. Public Security Division, Office 1, FRG Interior Ministry, to Office 8 et al., memorandum, "Europäische Zusammenarbeit 'Innere Sicherheit': Einstufung des unter dem Codewort 'TREVI' laufenden Schriftverkehrs," January 13, 1977, BArch, B106-106774, folder 3.

97. Oberloskamp, *Codename TREVI*, 243-54.

98. FRG interior officials were displeased that not enough officials with the capacity to think broadly across issues were present. Merk, memorandum for the record "Europäische Zusammenarbeit 'Innere Sicherheit': Erfahrungen in der ersten Sitzungsrunde der fünf Arbeitsgruppen—Überlegungen für weiteres Vorgehen," October 26, 1976, BArch, B106-106774, folder 3.

99. Division P, FRG interior ministry, to FRG interior minister Gerhard Baum, memorandum, "Europäische Zusammenarbeit bei der Terrorismusbekämpfung (TREVI): Randverfügungen Herrn Ministers auf der Ergebnisniederschrift über die Sitzung des Ausschusses der Hohen Beamten am 4./5. Dezember in Luxemburg," December 18, 1980, BArch, B106-106812, folder 1.

100. See, for example, "Liste des Participants," attachment, Merk to Maihofer, memorandum, "Europäische Zusammenarbeit Innere Sicherheit: Sitzung der 'hohen Beamten' am 26. September 1976 in den Haag," September 28, 1976, BArch, B106-106774, folder 2; and "Liste des Participants," attachment, Bochmann to Maihofer, memorandum, "Europäische Zusammenarbeit Innere Sicherheit: 1. Sitzung der EG-Arbeitsgruppe 'Terrorismus,' " October 20, 1976, BArch, B106-106774, folder 3.

101. Federal Office for the Protection of the Constitution to Maihofer, memorandum, "Zusammensetzung der deutschen Delegation bei den Sitzungen der TREVI-Arbeitsgruppe I," February 21, 1978, BArch, B106-106775, folder 2.

102. Oberloskamp, *Codename TREVI*, 135-40.

103. Public Security, Division 9, FRG Interior Ministry to Maihofer, memorandum, "Entführung Aldo Moro," March 17, 1978, BArch, B106-107064, folder 1.

104. Bochmann to president of the Bundeskriminalamt, Horst Herold, et al., memorandum, "Europäische Zusammenarbeit Innere Sicherheit: EG-Arbeitsgruppe 'Terrorismus,'" November 15, 1976, BArch, B106-106774, folder 3.

105. Anonymous undated memorandum, "Protokoll über die Sitzung der "Hohen Beamten" der EWG-Mitgliedsstaaten, die am 30. Mai 1980 gehalten worden ist," attachment to Italian interior ministry to FRG interior ministry, letter, July 24, 1980, BArch, B106-106811, folder 1.

106. Oberloskamp, *Codename TREVI*, 142-50.

107. Oberloskamp, *Codename TREVI*, 63-68, 120-21.

108. Hürter, "Regieren gegen Terrorismus"; Hof, "Anti-Terrorismus-Gesetze und Sicherheitskräfte in der Bundesrepublik Deutschland, Großbritannien und Italien in den 1970er und 1980er Jahren"; and Gisela Diewald-Kerkmann, "Justiz gegen Terrorismus: 'Terroristenprozesse' in der Bundesrepublik, Italien, und Grossbritannien," in Hürter, *Terrorismusbekämpfung in Westeuropa*, 35-62.

109. Oberloskamp, *Codename TREVI*, 121-22.

110. Head of Home Defence and Emergency Services Division, M. J. Moriarity, memorandum for the record, "Meeting with M. Bigay, 14 January 1977," January 17, 1977,

TNA, HO 306/138; A. E. Corben, memorandum for the record "Anglo-German Talks," June 21, 1978, TNA, HO 306/136.

111. *Global Terrorism Database*, National Consortium for the Study of Terrorism and Responses to Terrorism, 2009–2020, accessed March 18, 2020, https://www.start.umd.edu/gtd/access/.

112. See Raphael Bossong, *The Evolution of EU Counter-Terrorism: European Security Policy After 9/11* (New York: Routledge, 2013).

113. See for example briefing note "TOP 3f: Terrorismus und Medien," undated, attachment to Mr. Schenk (PI2/IS2) to Office IS6 (both FRG interior ministry), memorandum, "TREVI-Zusammenarbeit: Sitzung des Ausschusses Hoher Beamter am 27. März 1979 in Paris," March 14, 1979, BArch, B106-106809, folder 2.

114. See James D. Ladd, *SAS Operations* (London: Robert Hale, 1986); and Robin Neillands, *In the Combat Zone: Special Forces Since 1975* (New York: New York University Press, 1998).

115. Porch, *Counterinsurgency*, 156; David French, *The British Way in Counterinsurgency, 1945–1967* (New York: Oxford University Press, 2011), 94–137.

116. See David Tucker and Christopher J. Lamb, *United States Special Operations Forces* (New York: Columbia University Press, 2007); and Ami Pedahzur, *The Israeli Secret Services and the Struggle Against Terrorism* (New York: Columbia University Press, 2009).

117. Kay Schiller and Christopher Young, *The 1972 Munich Olympic Games and the Making of Modern Germany* (Berkeley: University of California Press, 2010), 197–201.

118. For a contrasting example of how U.S. police forces adopted counterinsurgency practices, see Stuart Schrader, *Badges Without Borders: How Global Counterinsurgency Transformed American Policing* (Oakland: University of California Press, 2019).

119. Ortex Telegram 99, November 4, 1972, PA AA, B82 Vol. 1031.

120. Ulrich Wegener to Hans-Dietrich Genscher, experience report, "Sonderlehrgang bei den israelischen Verteidigungsstreitkräften (MAHAL) vom 30.10.–12.11.1972," November 28, 1972, BArch, B106-115427, folder 1.

121. This unit became the Escadron spécial d'intervention in 1974. See Police Fédérale, "CGSU: Unités spéciales de la police fédérale," *Police Haute Senne*, accessed March 15, 2019, http://www.policelocale.be/5328/actualites/95-cgsu-unites-speciales-de-la-police-federale.

122. "Unit Interventie Mariniers," Dutch Defense Press, accessed March 15, 2019, https://www.dutchdefencepress.com/unit-interventie-mariniers/.

123. Hof, "Anti-Terrorismus-Gesetze und Sicherheitskräfte," 17.

124. Groupe d'Intervention de la Gendarmerie Nationale, "Historique," *Gendarmerie Nationale*, accessed March 1, 2018, https://www.gendarmerie.interieur.gouv.fr/gign/Historique/Historique.

125. See Bruce Hoffman, *Inside Terrorism*, 3rd ed. (New York: Columbia University Press, 2017), 132.

126. Anthony Cragg to Hayden Phillips, letter, March 24, 1975, TNA, DEFE 24/720.

127. Wegener to Maihofer, memorandum, "2. Internationale Konferenz über Methoden und Einsatzmittel terroristischer Organisationen vom 12.-23.5.1975 in Deepcut/Grossbritannien: Bericht Kommandeur GSG 9," June 19, 1975, BArch, B106-371631, folder 2.

128. Oberloskamp, *Codename TREVI*, 122.
129. A recent summary of the crisis is Saul David, *Operation Thunderbolt: Flight 139 and the Raid on Entebbe Airport, the Most Audacious Hostage Rescue Mission in History* (New York: Little, Brown, 2015). See also Markus Eikel, "Keine Atempause: Das Krisenmanagement der Bundesregierung und die Flugzeugentführung von Entebbe 1976," *Vierteljahrshefte für Zeitgeschichte* 61, no. 2 (April 2013): 239–61.
130. "Amin Says Uganda Retains the Right to Reply to Raid," *New York Times*, July 6, 1976, 1.
131. Jeffrey Herf, *Undeclared Wars with Israel: East Germany and the West German Far Left 1967–1989* (New York: Cambridge University Press, 2016), 323.
132. See, for example, "Israelis Lose Commando, 3 Hostages, Kill All Hijackers," *Washington Post*, July 5, 1976, A1; and Dietrich Strothmann, "Im Teufelskreis des Terrors," *Die Zeit*, July 9, 1976, accessed March 1, 2018, http://www.zeit.de/1976/29/im-teufelskreis-des-terrors.
133. Edwin Eytan, "Freed Hostages Tell Their Stories," *Jewish Telegraph Agency: Daily News Bulletin*, June 2, 1976, 1–2.
134. See Markus Eikel, "Keine Atempause"; and Matthias Dahlke, "Nur eingeschränkte Krisenbereitschaft."
135. Tim Geiger, "Westliche Anti-Terrorismus-Diplomatie im Nahen Osten," in Hürter, *Terrorismusbekämpfung in Westeuropa*, 259–88.
136. Mr. Strecker (Border Patrol II, Interior Ministry) to Foreign Office, memorandum, "Deutsch-Britische Zusammenarbeit auf dem Polizeisektor: Besuch der GSG9 durch 2 Beamte des Special Air Service in der Zeit vom 9.-12. November 1976," October 21, 1976, BArch, B106-371631, folder 2; Mr. Krassmann (Border Patrol II) to Border Patrol Command West, letter, February 25, 1977, BArch, B106-371631, folder 2; and Dr. Reuter (Border Patrol II, Interior Ministry) to Border Patrol Command West, Border Patrol Administration West, memorandum, "Anordnung einer Dienstreise," April 29, 1977, BArch, B106-371631, folder 2.
137. P. A. Rotheram, PR brief, "SAS Assistance to the Dutch," May 25, 1977, TNA, FCO 76/1750; Foreign and Commonwealth Office to Embassy The Hague, Telegram 89, May 25, 1977, TNA, FCO 76/1752.
138. Department of State to U.S. Embassies London, Paris, Bonn, Tel Aviv, Consulate Munich, Telegram 28099, December 6, 1976, Hoover, Kupperman, Box 5, folder 5.
139. Pieter Bakker Schut, *Stammheim: Der Prozess gegen die Rote Armee Fraktion* (Kiel, Germany: Neuer Malik, 1986), 37.
140. See note 23 for historical studies on the RAF and the "German Autumn."
141. FRG Consulate Jeddah to Foreign Office, Telegram 550, October 17, 1977, BArch, B106-106684, folder 1.
142. Foreign Office to FRG Embassy Mogadishu, Telegram 7648, November 3, 1977, PA AA, B150 Vol. 379; memorandum of conversation between FRG state minister Hans-Jürgen Wischnewski and Somali ambassador to the FRG Bokah, November 11, 1977, November 14, 1977, PA AA, B150 Vol. 379.
143. Ulrich Wegener to Klaus-Herbert Becker (Bundeskriminalamt), memorandum, "Teilbericht Einsatz 'Landshut' der GSG 9 am 18.10.1977: Darstellung des Sachverhalts des Kampfes in der Maschine," February 14, 1978, BArch, B106-106684, folder 2.
144. Translated from German by the author. "Deutsche können stark und menschlich sein," *Der Spiegel*, October 24, 1977, 4–9; another example is Henry Tanner, "German

Troops Free Hostages on Hijacked Plane in Somalia; Four Terrorist Killed in Raid," *New York Times*, October 18, 1977, 77.

145. FRG Embassy Belgrade to Foreign Office, Telegram 675, October 18, 1977, PA AA, B83 Vol. 1004; FRG Mission Geneva to Foreign Office, Telegram 1625, October 19, 1977, PA AA, B83 Vol. 1004.

146. See, for example, Werner Maihofer to Hans Bausch, director of the ARD network, and the director of the ZDF network, letter, October 18, 1977, BArch, B106-106684, folder 1.

147. Anonymous memorandum for the record, "Deutsch-Britishes Expertengespräch zum Erfahrungsaustausch über das 'crisis management' im Falle Schleyer/Mogadischu," November 2, 1977, BArch, B136-16493; Office 213, FRG Chancellery, memorandum, "Informationsgespräch mit Vertretern der niederländischen Botschaft über Entführung der Lufthansa-Maschine 'Landshut,' " November 23, 1977, BArch, B136-16493.

148. George A. Carver (U.S. Embassy Bonn) to the Border Patrol inspector General Kurt Schneider, letter, November 18, 1977, BArch, B106-371685, folder 1; Adam F. Henritzy (U.S. Army Europe Liaison Officer Bonn) to Schneider, letter, December 6, 1977, BArch, B106-371685, folder 1; and Anonymous, Program "The GSG 9, Its Mission, Organization and Training: Description of Operation 'Landshut,' " December 8, 1977, BArch, B106-371685, folder 1.

149. Office 300 (Argentina, Uruguay, Paraguay, Brazil, and Caribbean), FRG Foreign Office, memorandum for the record, January 11, 1978, PA AA, ZA Vol. 111188.

150. Mr. Meyer-Landrut (Office 300 [Argentina, Uruguay, Paraguay, Brazil, and Caribbean], FRG Foreign Office) to Hans-Dietrich Genscher, memorandum, "Internationaler Terrorismus: Unterstützung von ausländischen Sicherheitskräften zur Terrorismusbekämpfung durch deutsche Experten," with attachment, June 8, 1978, PA AA, ZA Vol. 111188.

151. Martin Morland, head of the Maritime, Aviation, and Environment Department, to Miss Brown and Sir A. Duff, memorandum, "Terrorism, Military Intervention Overseas: Exercise 'Joybell' 19/20 October," October 11, 1978, TNA, FCO 30/3775.

152. See, for examples, Schneider to Border Patrol Command West, Border Patrol Administration West, memorandum, "Anordnung einer Auslandsdienstreise," June 15, 1978, BArch, B106-371631, folder 2; Wegener to interior ministry, memorandum, "Erfahrungsaustausch mit ausländischen Sicherheitsbehörden: Schweiz, GB, USA," August 16, 1978, BArch, B106-371685, folder 1; Zimmermann to Wegener, memorandum, "Zusammenarbeit mit Grossbritannien bei der Terrorismusbekämpfung," January 15, 1979, BArch, B106-371631, folder 2; Mr. Strecker (Division P III 1, Interior Ministry) to Border Patrol Command West, Border Patrol Administration West, memorandum, "Besuch bei britischen Spezialeinheiten in Hereford/Gross -britannien: Weisung Direktor i. BGS Wegener vom 1. Febr. 1980," February 1, 1980, BArch, B106-371631, folder 2.

153. Division P III 1, FRG Interior Ministry, to GSG 9, memorandum, "Übungsvorhaben der GSG 9 in Lydd/Grossbritannien vom 1–12.4.79," March 27, 1979, BArch, B106-371631, Folder 2.

154. Army School of Ammunition, Temple Herdewyke, Warwickshire, "Joining Instructions (Part 2)," August 1980, BArch, B106-371631, folder 2.

155. Officer Dee (GSG 9) to FRG interior ministry, memorandum, "Ausbildungshilfe für Scotland Yard," August 5, 1980, BArch, B106-371631, folder 2.

156. Mr. Grützner (Division SV P III 1, Interior Ministry) to State Secretary F, memorandum, "Zusammenarbeit bei der Bekämpfung des internationalen Terrorismus: Zusammenarbeit mit Grossbritannien," April 30, 1980, BArch, B106-371631,
folder 1; and GSG 9 to FRG interior ministry, Telegram 856, May 6, 1981, BArch,
B106-371631.

157. U.S. Army War College Commandant Robert C. Yerks to Admiral Kurt Seizinger,
letter, October 28, 1977, BArch, B106-371685, folder 1; and FBI Director William H.
Webster to Maihofer, letter, April 12, 1978, BArch, B106-371685, Folder 1.

158. Schneider to Border Patrol Command West, Border Patrol Administration West,
memorandum, "Anordnung von Auslandsdienstreisen," June 13, 1978, BArch, B106-
371685, folder 1; and Mr. Baumann (Division P III 1, FRG Interior Ministry) to
Border Patrol Command West, Border Patrol Administration West, memorandum,
"Teilnahme an einer Ausbildungsveranstaltung in Fort Bragg, USA: Anordnung
einer Auslandsdienstreise für Kommandeur GSG 9, LtdPD i. BGS Wegener," October 29, 1979, BArch, B106-371685, folder 1.

159. Wegener to FRG interior ministry, memorandum, "Erfahrungsaustausch mit aus-
ländischen Sicherheitsbehörden," August 16, 1978, BArch, B106-371685, folder 1;
GSG 9 to Police Director Strecker (FRG Interior Ministry), memorandum, "Aus-
bildung und Unterstützung ausländischer Sicherheitsorgane," October 13, 1978,
BArch, B106-371685, folder 1; Krassmann (Division P III 1, FRG Interior Ministry)
to the state secretary Dr. Hiele (FRG Ministry of Defense), letter, October 16, 1978,
BArch, B106-371685, folder 1; and Krassmann to Border Patrol Command West,
Border Patrol Administration West, memorandum, "Teilnahme an einem Spezial-
symposium in Fort Bragg, USA: Technischer Erfahrungsaustausch," November 1,
1979, BArch, B106-371685, folder 1.

160. U.S. defense attaché Jack G. Callaway (Embassy Bonn) to Kurt Schneider, letter,
December 27, 1978, BArch, B106-371685, folder 1; and Mr. Schrecker (Division P III
1, FRG Interior Ministry), memorandum for the record, "Dienstreise LPD Wegener
in die USA," January 22, 1979, BArch, B106-371685, folder 1.

161. Letter from Krassmann to Callaway, letter, November 26, 1979, BArch, B106-371685,
folder 1.

162. Director for Special Operations, Federal Border Patrol, to Rear Admiral Samuel H.
Packer (Director, Operations Directorate, U.S. European Command), letter, Janu-
ary 20, 1981, BArch, B106-371685, folder 1; Commander, Support Operations Task
Force, Europe, to U.S. Defense Attaché Office, Embassy Bonn, Telegram, April 7,
1981, BArch, B106-371685, folder 2; and memorandum, Mr. Siegele (Division P I 2,
FRG interior ministry) to FRG interior minister Friedrich Zimmermann, "Ameri-
kanisch-Deutsche Terrorismusübung 'Ellipse Bravo '82,' " November 25, 1982,
BArch, B106-371685, folder 2.

163. Zimmermann (Division P III 1, FRG Interior Ministry) to State Secretary F (FRG
interior ministry), memorandum, "Internationaler Lehrgang für Angehörige von
Spezialeinheiten zur Terrorismusbekämpfung an der FBI-Akademie in Quantico,
USA," December 15, 1978, BArch, B106-371685, folder 1; and Officer Grützner (Division SV P III 1, FRG interior ministry) to the head of Division P, FRG interior
ministry, memorandum, "Hostage Training Course beim FBI, Quantico, vom 11.
Bis 23. January 1981," December 8, 1980, BArch, B106-371685, folder 1.

164. Police superintendent Walter R. Lee (Port Authority of New York and New Jersey) to Vice Consul Manfred R. Haedelt (vice consul, FRG consulate New York), letter, March 21, 1978, BArch, B106-371631, folder 2; Krassmann (Border Patrol II, FRG Interior Ministry) to Foreign Office, telex, May 1978, BArch, B106-371631, folder 2; Wegener to FRG interior ministry, Telegram 5956, September 29, 1978, BArch, B106-371685, folder 1; Border Patrol Command West to FRG interior ministry, Telegram 5142, April 28, 1980, BArch, B106-371685, folder 1; and Associate Professor Wolfred K. White (College of Law Enforcement, Eastern Kentucky University) to FRG interior minister Gerhart Baum, letter, March 19, 1980, BArch, B106-371685, folder 1.

165. H. P. Bochmann (Public Security, Division 9, FRG Interior Ministry) to German Parliament Member Hermann Biechele, Letter, January 14, 1978, BArch, B106-106930, folder 1.

166. It still carries this name. Jim Weiss and Mickey Davis, "Cobra: Austria's Special Police Commandos," *Law and Order*, July 2009, 48–52.

167. Hof, "Anti-Terrorismus-Gesetze und Sicherheitskräfte," 17–18.

168. Meyer-Landrut to Genscher, memorandum, "Internationaler Terrorismus," with attachment, June 8, 1978, PA AA, ZA Vol. 111188.

169. Office 300 (Argentina, Uruguay, Paraguay, Brazil, and Caribbean), FRG Foreign Office, to FRG Embassy Jeddah, memorandum, "Terrorismusbekämpfung: Zusammenarbeit mit Saudi Arabien," with attachment Aide-Memoire of October 25, 1978, October 26, 1978, BArch, B106-115427, folder 3.

170. Division P I 1, FRG Foreign Office, memorandum of conversation, "Deutsch-Spanische Zusammenarbeit auf dem Gebiet der Inneren Sicherheit: Besuch des Spanischen Innenministers beim Bundesminister des Innern am 3./4. Juli 1978," July 7, 1978, BArch, B136-15685, folder 2.

171. FRG Embassy Lisbon to FRG Foreign Office, memorandum, "Bekämpfung des Internationalen Terrorismus in Portugal: Aufbau einer Anti-Terror-Spezialgruppe," 28, 1979, PA AA, B83 Vol. 1385.

172. Anonymous, report, "Bericht über den Besuch des Bundesministers des Innern in Moskau und Leningrad vom 23. bis 27. Mai 1979," undated, BArch, B106-106940, folder 1.

173. Dr. Bochmann (Division P I 2, FRG Interior Ministry) to Dr. Wieck (FRG Embassy Moscow), memorandum, "Zusammenarbeit mit der Sowjetunion bei der Terrorismusbekämpfung: Erledigung noch offenstehender Wünsche der sowjetischen Seite aus den Gesprächen anlässlich des Besuchs von Bundesminister Baum in Moskau Ende Mai 1979," July 6, 1970, BArch, B106-106940, folder 2.

174. Zimmermann (Division P III 1) to Division P I 2, FRG Foreign Office, memorandum, "Deutsch-rumänische Zusammenarbeit: Besuch einer rumänischen Delegation im BMI am 4.5.1979," June 29, 1979, BArch, B106-106930, folder 2.

175. Meyer-Landrut to Genscher, memorandum, "Internationaler Terrorismus: Unterstützung von ausländischen Sicherheitskräften," with attachment, June 8, 1978, PA AA, ZA Vol. 111188.

176. Anthony Goodenough (Foreign and Commonwealth Office), draft memorandum, "Counter-Terrorism: Aid to Other Countries," undated, TNA, FCO 76/1763; Graham Angel (Section F4 Home Office), draft memorandum, "Counter-Terrorism

Arrangements: Requests from Other Countries for Advice, Equipment or Training," with annexes, December 21, 1977, TNA, FCO 76/1763.

177. Home Office, "Note of a Meeting Held 13 June 1978: Saudi Arabia: Police Training Co-Operation," June 21, 1978, TNA, FCO 8/3138; 22 Special Air Service (SAS) Regiment, "Final Report: Op Chicane," June 30, 1978, TNA, FCO 8/3100; 22 SAS Regiment, "Final Report: Operation Secondary," January 22, 1979, TNA, FCO 93/1975; 22 SAS Regiment, "Final Report: Op Consolidate," January 21, 1980, TNA, FCO 8/3500.

178. D. B. Omand (Ministry of Defense) to Mr. Alexander, memorandum, "Prime Minister's Visit to the SAS," December 22, 1980, TNA, FCO 8/3838.

179. B. Watkins (Defense Department) to Mr. Gillmore, memorandum, "U.K. Military Assistance: OD Paper," August 24, 1979, with attachment report "United Kingdom Military Training Assistance Note by Officials," TNA FCO 46/2123.

180. Office II 2, FRG Federal Authority for Audit Matters, to Division P II 2, FRG Interior Ministry, Memorandum, July 28, 1981, BArch, B106-371685, folder 2.

181. Division P III 1, FRG interior ministry, to Office 300 (Argentina, Uruguay, Paraguay, Brazil, and Caribbean), FRG Foreign Office, memorandum, "Internationaler Wettkampf für Spezialeinheiten bei der GSG 9," March 5, 1985, PA AA, ZA Vol. 135331.

182. The plane landed in Italy, and after a standoff with the U.S. Special Forces Italian authorities arrested the hijackers. See Mattia Toaldo, *The Origins of the US War on Terror: Lebanon, Libya, and American intervention in the Middle East* (New York: Routledge, 2013), 117–19; and David C. Wills, *The First War on Terrorism: Counter-Terrorism Policy During the Reagan Administration* (Lanham, MD: Rowman and Littlefield, 2003), 155–59.

4. SOVEREIGNTY-BASED LIMITS TO ANTITERRORISM IN EUROPEAN INTEGRATION, 1974-1980

1. FRG Mission Council of Europe to Foreign Office, memorandum, "Unterzeichnung der Konvention zur Bekämpfung des Terrorismus," February 3, 1977, Political Archive of the Foreign Office (hereafter: PA AA) Federal Republic of Germany (hereafter: B)83 Vol. 982. See also Thomas E. Carbonneau, "The Provisional Arrest and Subsequent Release of Abu Daoud by French Authorities," *Virginia Journal of International Law* 17, no. 3 (Spring 1977): 495–513.

2. European Integration Department, Foreign and Commonwealth Office, memorandum, "Council of Ministers (Foreign Affairs) Brussels, 18 January 1977: International Terrorism," undated, The National Archives of the United Kingdom (TNA), Home Office (HO) 306/137.

3. Council of Europe, "European Convention on the Suppression of Terrorism," *Council of Europe*, accessed November 25, 2019, https://rm.coe.int/16800771b2.

4. These conventions regulated only specific types of attacks. Their formal titles are the International Civil Aviation Organization (ICAO) 1963 Convention on Offences and Certain Other Acts Committed on Board Aircraft (Tokyo Convention), the ICAO 1970 Convention for the Suppression of Unlawful Seizure of Aircraft (Hague Convention), the ICAO 1971 Convention for the Suppression of

Unlawful Acts Against the Safety of Civil Aviation (Montreal Convention), and the United Nations 1973 Convention on the Prevention and Punishment of Crimes Against Internationally Protected Persons, Including Diplomatic Agents (Diplomats Convention). European officials rarely considered the similar Organization of American States (OAS) 1971 Convention to Prevent and Punish the Acts of Terrorism Taking the Form of Crimes Against Persons and Related Extortion That Are of International Significance (OAS Convention) because it was an exclusively regional convention from the Americas.

5. Undersecretary Paul-Günter Pötz (B II 5) to FRG justice minister Hans-Jochen Vogel, memorandum, "Vorbereitung des EG-Justizministerrats vom 26.11.1974," November 25, 1974, Federal Archives Germany (BArch), Federal Republic of Germany (B) Records of the Ministry of Justice (141)-65262, pp. 46–48.

6. See United Nations, "Convention on the High Seas," *United Nations*, accessed March 10, 2020, https://www.gc.noaa.gov/documents/8_1_1958_high_seas.pdf, articles 14–21.

7. Councilor Dr. Fleischhauer to Berndt von Staden, director of the Political Office of the Foreign Office, memorandum, "Bekämpfung des Terrorismus: Hausbesprechung vom 15. Sept. 1972," September 19, 1972, PA AA, B83 Vol. 980; Legal Department V4 (Foreign Office) to Legal Department V1 (Foreign Office), memorandum, "Bekämpfung des Terrorismus: Dortige Zuschrift—nachrichtlich—vom 19.9.1972," September 26, 1972, PA AA, B82 Vol. 1031.

8. For a good overview, see Alan S. Milward, *The European Rescue of the Nation-State*, 2nd ed. (London: Routledge, 2000).

9. During the period of this chapter, the EC included France, the FRG, Italy, the United Kingdom, Ireland, Denmark, the Netherlands, Belgium, and Luxemburg.

10. See European Political Cooperation (EPC) Press and Information Office, "Introduction to EPC (European Political Cooperation)," 5th ed., 1988, accessed March 10, 2020, http://aei.pitt.edu/1895/1/EPC_intro.pdf.

11. See Sarah Snyder, *Human Rights Activism and the End of the Cold War: A Transnational History of the Helsinki Network* (Cambridge: Cambridge University Press, 2011).

12. See Stefanie Schmahl and Marten Breuer, eds., *The Council of Europe: Its Law and Policies* (New York: Oxford University Press, 2017); and Aline Royer, *Der Europarat* (Strasbourg: Council of Europe Publishing, 2010).

13. See chapter 1, s.v. Adopting the Conventions.

14. See chapter 3, s.v. Setting the Scene: The FRG's Response to the 1972 Munich Olympic Games Attack.

15. Legal counsellor H. G. Darwin to Mr. Smith (Security Department, Foreign and Commonwealth Office), memorandum, "UN Item on Terrorism," September 29, 1972, TNA, HO 306/134.

16. Pötz to Vogel, memorandum, "Vorbereitung des EG-Justizministerrats vom 26.11.1974," November 25, 1974, BArch, B141-65262, pp. 46–48.

17. A. P. B. Smart (Security Department, Foreign and Commonwealth Office) to Mr. Marsden (European Integration Department) et al., memorandum, "EEC Consultations on Terrorism," June 1973, with attachment draft memorandum, "Belgian Proposal for a Convention of the Nine Community Countries on Extradition of Terrorists," undated, TNA, Foreign and Commonwealth Office (FCO) 41/1085.

18. Undersecretary Merk (Public Security Office, Division 2, FRG Interior Ministry) to FRG interior minister Hans-Dietrich Genscher, memorandum, "Vorbereitung einer

Europäischen Konferenz über Innere Sicherheit," August 10, 1973, PA AA, B83 Vol. 825.

19. Council of Europe, "European Convention on Extradition," *Council of Europe*, accessed November 25, 2019, https://rm.coe.int/CoERMPublicCommonSearchServices/Displ ayDCTMContent?documentId=0900001680064587.

20. Fleischhauer to von Staden, memorandum, "Bekämpfung des Terrorismus: Hausbe-sprechung vom 15. Sept. 1972," September 19, 1972, PA AA, B83 Vol. 980.

21. Council of Europe, "Recommendation 684 (1972): International Terrorism," *Council of Europe*, accessed November 25, 2019, http://assembly.coe.int/nw/xml/XRef/Xref -XML2HTML-en.asp?fileid=14718&lang=en.

22. P. A. Grier (UK delegation to the Council of Europe) to David MacLennan (Western Organizations Department, Foreign and Commonwealth Office), memorandum, "Inter-national Terrorism—Recommendation 684," January 29, 1973, TNA, FCO 41/1085.

23. Consultative Assembly of the Council of Europe, "Recommendation 703 (1973) on International Terrorism," May 16, 1973, PA AA, B83 Vol. 981.

24. Grier to MacLennan, memorandum, "International Terrorism and Some Wider Matters," December 21, 1973, TNA FCO 41/1085.

25. Council of Europe Minister's Committee, "Resolution 74(3) on International Terror-ism," unofficial German translation, undated, BArch, B141-65262, pp. 235–36.

26. John Robey (UK delegation to the Council of Europe) to George Lee (Western Orga-nizations Department, Foreign and Commonwealth Office), memorandum, "Inter-national Terrorism," October 3, 1973, with attachment Minutes of the Ministers' Deputies, pages 13–15, undated, TNA, FCO 41/1085.

27. Pötz to Vogel, memorandum, "Treffen der Justizminister des Europarates am 22. Mai 1975 in Obernai b. Strassburg: Fragen der internationalen Zusammenarbeit bei der Bekämpfung des Terrorismus," May 16, 1975, BArch, B141-65262, pp. 226–34.

28. See chapter 3, s.v. The TREVI Network: Multilateral Collaboration Against Interna-tional Terrorism and Crime.

29. FRG justice minister Gerhard Jahn to Hans-Dietrich Genscher, memorandum, "Vorbereitung einer Europäischen Konferenz über Innere Sicherheit: Ihr Schreiben vom 15. August 1973," December 21, 1973, PA AA, B83 Vol. 980. For a discussion of the two ministries' competencies, see Eva Oberloskamp, *Codename TREVI: Ter-rorismusbekämpfung und die Anfänge einer europäischen Innenpolitik in den 1970er Jahren* (Oldenbourg, Germany: De Gruyter, 2017), 54–56.

30. Pötz to Vogel, memorandum, "Treffen der Justizminister des Europarates am 22. Mai 1975 in Obernai," May 16, 1975, BArch, B141-65262, pp. 226–34.

31. Pötz to Vogel, memorandum, "Treffen der Justizminister des Europarates am 22. Mai 1975 in Obernai."

32. These discussions were the first step to founding TREVI. See chapter 3, s.v. The TREVI Network: Multilateral Collaboration Against International Terrorism and Crime.

33. Pötz to Vogel, memorandum, "Treffen der Justizminister des Europarates am 22. Mai 1975 in Obernai."

34. See Bernhard Blumenau, "Taming the Beast: West Germany, the Political Offence Exception and the Council of Europe Convention on the Suppression of Terrorism," *Terrorism and Political Violence* 27, no. 2 (March 2015): 310–30.

35. For Gaullism in French foreign policy, see Francis Choisel, *Comprendre le Gaullisme: A Propos de Quelques Contresens sur la Pensée et l'Action du Général de Gaulle* (Paris:

Harmattan, 2016); and Frédéric Bozo, *French Foreign Policy Since 1945: An Introduction* (New York: Berghahn, 2016).

36. French authorities persuaded Sudanese authorities to hand over Ramírez in a middle-of-the-night covert operation in 1994.

37. See Terry Richard Kane, "Prosecuting International Terrorists in United States Courts: Gaining the Jurisdictional Threshold," *Yale Journal of International Law* 12 (1987): 294–341.

38. For an analysis of the Lorenz kidnapping, see Matthias Dahlke, " 'Nur eingeschränkte Krisenbereitschaft': Die staatliche Reaktion auf die Entführung des CDU-Politikers Peter Lorenz 1975," *Vierteljahrshefte für Zeitgeschichte* 55, no. 4 (October 2007): 641–78. On the political repercussions of releasing FRG terrorists during the Lorenz kidnapping, see Markus Eikel, "Keine Atempause: Das Krisenmanagement der Bundesregierung und die Flugzeugentführung von Entebbe 1976," *Vierteljahrshefte für Zeitgeschichte* 61, no. 2 (April 2013): 239–61.

39. "Terrorism: 'Growing and Increasingly Dangerous': Interview with Robert A. Fearey, Special Assistant to the Secretary of State and Co-ordinator for Combating Terrorism," *U.S. News and World Report*, September 29, 1975, 77–79.

40. For example, the FRG did not extradite hijackers from Eastern Europe. A large set of case files describes Eastern European hijackers who landed in West Berlin and whom the FRG refused to extradite. See PA AA, B83 Vol. 1475.

41. Pötz to Vogel, memorandum, "Internationale Massnahmen zur Bekämpfung des Terrorismus, hier: Dem BMJ nachrichtlich zugegangenes Schreiben des Chefs des Bundeskanzleramtes an den BMI," June 13, 1975, BArch, B141-65263, pp. 7–14.

42. In 1975, the eighteen Council of Europe member states included the nine EC states (the FRG, France, Italy, the Netherlands, Belgium, Luxembourg, Denmark, the UK, and Ireland) as well as Norway, Sweden, Austria, Switzerland, Greece, Turkey, Malta, Cyprus, and Iceland. Between 1976 and 1978, Portugal, Spain, and Liechtenstein also joined, increasing membership to twenty-one. In 2018, the Council of Europe included forty-seven member states encompassing most of the European continent.

43. Pötz memorandum, "Europarat—XXIV. Vollsitzung des Europäischen Ausschusses für Strafrechtsfragen vom 26. bis 30. Mai 1975 in Strassburg, hier: TOP I 11—Konferenz über die Kriminalpolitik (März 1975) und Arbeitsprogramm für die künftige Tätigkeit des CEPC," June 1975, PA AA, B83 Vol. 981.

44. Legal adviser M. C. Wood to Mr. Furness (Security Department, Foreign and Commonwealth Office), memorandum, "Council of Europe: Ad Hoc Meeting on Certain New Forms of Concerted Acts of Violence: Meeting of 6–8 October 1975," October 14, 1975, TNA, FCO 41/1607.

45. Council of Europe, European Committee on Crime Problems, "Committee to Examine the Problems Raised by Certain New Forms of Concerted Acts of Violence: Preliminary Draft Convention: Prepared by the Drafting Group at Its Meeting in Brussels on 4 and 5 December 1975," December 8, 1975, PA AA, B83 Vol. 981.

46. Leith Passmore, "International Law as an Extralegal Defense Strategy in West Germany's Stammheim Terror Trial," *Law, Culture, and the Humanities* 9, no. 2 (June 2013): 375–94.

47. European Committee on Crime Problems, "Committee: Preliminary Draft Convention," December 8, 1975, PA AA, B83 Vol. 981.

48. European Committee on Crime Problems, "Committee: Preliminary Draft Convention."
49. Council of Europe, European Committee on Crime Problems, "Committee to Examine the Problems Raised by Certain New Forms of Concerted Acts of Violence: Preliminary Draft European Convention on the Suppression of Terrorism: Adopted by the Committee at its Meeting in Strasbourg from 2 to 6 February 1976," February 10, 1976, PA AA, B83 Vol. 981.
50. See chapter 2, s.v. International Terrorism at the United Nations General Assembly.
51. FRG Council of Europe delegation, "Stellungnahme der Delegation der Bundesrepublik Deutschland zu den Dokumenten DPC/CEPC/AV (76) 2. Rév. und DPC/CEPC/AV (76) 3," undated, p. 10, PA AA, B83 Vol. 981; Charles Prior (C3, Home Office) to Mr. Lyon and secretary of state for Home Affairs, memorandum, "Extradition: Proposals for Legislation," November 7, 1975, TNA, HO 306/129; Private secretary J. C. Maund to private secretary W. J. A. Innes, memorandum, "Terrorism and Extradition Developments in the Council of Europe," December 2, 1975, TNA, HO 306/129.
52. European Committee on Crime Problems, "Committee: Preliminary Draft European Convention on the Suppression of Terrorism," February 10, 1976, PA AA, B83 Vol. 981, p. 2.
53. FRG Council of Europe delegation, "Stellungnahme der Delegation der Bundesrepublik Deutschland zu den Dokumenten DPC/CEPC/AV (76) 2. Rév. und DPC/CEPC/AV (76) 3," undated, PA AA, B83 Vol. 981.
54. D. H. J. Hilary to Mr. Cairncross et al., memorandum, "Terrorism and Extradition Developments in the Council of Europe," November 27, 1975, TNA, HO 306/129; Foreign and Commonwealth Office, memorandum, "Terrorism: European Council Declaration," August 6, 1976, TNA, FCO 76/1221.
55. Geoff Gilbert, "The Irish Interpretation of the Political Offense Exception," *International and Comparative Law Quarterly* 41 (January 1992): 66–84.
56. Legal adviser Michael Wood to C. M. Bentley (Western European Department), memorandum, "Council of Europe: Meeting of Ministers' Deputies, June 8, 1976, TNA, FCO 87/580.
57. See chapter 5, s.v. Normalizing Global North Conceptualizations of Terrorism in International Law.
58. Günther van Well to Ernst Friedrich Jung, NATO's assistant secretary general for Political Affairs, memorandum, "Internationale Zusammenarbeit bei der Bekämpfung von Terroristen: Vorbereitung einer Initiative im Rahmen der VN," January 12, 1976, PA AA, B83 Vol. 983.
59. Undersecretary Streicher (ÖS1, FRG Interior Ministry) to FRG interior minister Werner Maihofer, memorandum, "Vorbereitung einer europäischen Konferenz für Innere Sicherheit: 'Pakt gegen den Terrorismus,' " January 30, 1976, BArch, B Records of the Ministry of the Interior (106)-78829.
60. Wood to Mr. Furness, memorandum, "Proposed Council of Europe Convention against Terrorist Offences," December 9, 1975, TNA, FCO 41/1607.
61. First councilor Otto von der Gablenz (Political Division 2, Foreign Office) to Hans-Dietrich Genscher, memorandum, "Haltung der Bundesregierung zur Anti-Terrorismus-Konvention des Europarats (EuR)," July 9, 1976, PA AA, B83 Vol. 982.
62. George Lee (UK delegation to the Council of Europe) to Adolf McCarthy (Western European Department), "European Convention on Terrorism," June 25, 1976, TNA, FCO 87/580.

63. Von der Gablenz to Division 011, Foreign Office, memorandum, "Sachstand: Anti-Terrorismus-Konvention des Europarats," July 22, 1976, PA AA, B83 Vol. 982; and Blumenau, "Taming the Beast," 316.
64. See Blumenau, "Taming the Beast," 317.
65. P. M. Foster (UK delegation to the Council of Europe) to A. D. S. Goodall (Western European Department), memorandum, "Terrorism," July 28, 1976, TNA, FCO 87/580.
66. Von der Gablenz to Genscher, memorandum, "Haltung der Bundesregierung zur Anti-Terrorismus-Konvention des Europarats (EuR)," July 9, 1976, PA AA, B83 Vol. 982.
67. Von der Gablenz to Division 011, Foreign Office, memorandum, "Sachstand: Zusammenarbeit der Neun Innen-oder Justizminister im Bereich der Inneren Sicherheit," July 22, 1976, PA AA, B83 Vol. 982.
68. FRG Embassy Athens to Foreign Office, Telegram 569, July 29, 1976, in Ilse Dorothee Pautsch, Matthias Peter, Michael Ploetz, and Tim Geiger, eds., *Akten zur Auswärtigen Politik der Bundesrepublik Deutschland (1976)* (Munich: R. Oldenbourg, 2007), Document 250, pp. 1157–60.
69. Von der Gablenz to Division 011, memorandum, "Zusammenarbeit der Neun Innen-oder Justizminister im Bereich der Inneren Sicherheit," July 22, 1976, PA AA, B83 Vol. 982.
70. Von der Gablenz to Division 011, memorandum, "Sachstand: Anti-Terrorismus-Konvention des Europarats," July 22, 1976, PA AA, B83 Vol. 982.
71. Von der Gablenz to FRG Embassy Paris, Telegram 2726, July 14, 1976, BArch, B141-77289, pp. 6–8.
72. Director of the Legal Division (Foreign Office) to Division 511 (Foreign Office), "Anti-Terrorismus-Konvention des Europarats," September 23, 1976, PA AA, B83 Vol. 982.
73. United Nations, "Vienna Convention on the Law of Treaties (with Annex)," May 23, 1969, *United Nations*, accessed November 25, 2019, https://treaties.un.org/doc/publication /unts/volume%20l155/volume-1155-i-18232-english.pdf, article 2d; and article 19.
74. Von der Gablenz to Division 011, "Anti-Terrorismus-Konvention des Europarats," July 22, 1976, PA AA, B83 Vol. 982; FRG Embassy Paris to Foreign Office, Telegram 2511, September 7, 1976, PA AA, B83 Vol. 982.
75. R. F. Cornish (British Embassy Bonn) to Ivor Roberts (European Integration Department), memorandum, "Terrorism," September 22, 1976, TNA, FCO 87/580; Michael Wood to Mr. Morris (Western European Department), memorandum, "Draft European Convention on the Suppression of Terrorism," October 4, 1976, TNA, FCO 87/580.
76. Adolf McCarthy to Mr. Sutherland, memorandum, "Draft European Convention on the Suppression of Terrorism," October 13, 1976, TNA, FCO 87/580.
77. See Blumenau, "Taming the Beast," 313–14.
78. Von der Gablenz to Genscher, memorandum, "Europäische Konvention zur Bekämpfung des Terrorismus," October 13, 1976, PA AA, B83 Vol. 982.
79. Council of Europe, "European Convention on the Suppression of Terrorism."
80. Philippa Drew to Charles Prior and D. H. J. Hilary, memorandum, "Visit to The Hague," May 30, 1977, TNA, HO 306/140.
81. FRG Mission Council of Europe to Foreign Office, memorandum, "Unterzeichnung der Konvention zur Bekämpfung des Terrorismus," February 3, 1977, PA AA, B83 Vol. 982.

82. Senior government official Walter (B II 5, Justice Ministry) to Hans-Jochen Vogel, memorandum, "Initiative des Europäischen Rats vom 13. Juli 1976 für eine Konvention gegen Geiselnahmen, hier: Vorbereitung der Sitzung eines Expertenkommittees am 17. November 1976 in Den Haag," November 16, 1976, BArch, B141-77290, pp. 1–4.

83. Von der Galblenz to Division 02, Foreign Office, memorandum, "Sachstand: Ausführung der Erklärung des Europäischen Rats vom 13.07.1976 zum Internationalen Terrorismus," January 6, 1977, BArch, B141-77291, pp. 1–3.

84. Helen Watson (Maritime and General Department) to Philippa Drew (Home Office), memorandum, "Follow-Up of the European Council Declaration on Terrorism," with attachment "Draft Presidency Report," April 29, 1977, TNA, FCO 76/1742.

85. Councilor Jung (International Organizations Division 230, Foreign Office) to FRG Mission United Nations, Telegram "Massnahmen gegen den Terrorismus: Initiative zum Abschluss einer Konvention gegen Geiselnahme," January 14, 1976, PA AA, B83, Vol. 983.

86. Von der Galblenz to Division 02, "Ausführung der Erklärung des Europäischen Rats vom 13.07.1976," January 6, 1977, BArch, B141-77291, pp. 1–3.

87. Coreu London to Coreu Bonn, Coreu Telegram 823, March 2, 1977, PA AA, B83 Vol. 982.

88. Von der Galblenz to Division 02, "Ausführung der Erklärung des Europäischen Rats vom 13.07.1976," January 6, 1977, BArch, B141-77291, pp. 1–3.

89. See, for example, Robert Kupperman's records on the International Centre for Comparative Criminology, Université de Montréal, seminar, "Research Strategies for the Study of International Political Terrorism," held in Italy in May–June 1977, in Hoover Institution Archives (Hoover), Robert H. Kupperman Papers (Kupperman), Box 4, folder 4. Corves and Golsong attended as well. See also Corves's records on the 1978 State Department "International Conference on Legal Aspects of International Terrorism" in BArch, B141-65268.

90. Vogel, memorandum, "Europäische Zusammenarbeit bei der Bekämpfung des Terrorismus," June 24, 1978, PA AA, B83 Vol. 1234.

91. Coreu Paris to Coreu Copenhagen, Coreu Telegram 1099, April 11, 1978, BArch, B141-77295, pp. 37–40.

92. Pötz to Vogel, memorandum, "Initiative des Europäischen Rats vom 13.07.1976 für eine Konvention gegen den Terrorismus, hier: 2. Sitzung der Expertengruppe am 14. März 1977 in London," May 20, 1977, BArch, B141-77291, pp. 60–63.

93. Pötz to Vogel, memorandum, "Initiative des Europäischen Rats vom 13.07.1976 für eine Konvention gegen den Terrorismus, hier," 21–24.

94. "Hörnchen in Folie," Der Spiegel, October 17, 1977, 201.

95. A detailed, though partisan, narrative of events can be found in Pieter Bakker Schut, Stammheim: Der Prozess gegen die Rote Armee Fraktion (Kiel, Germany: Neuer Malik, 1986), 223ff.

96. Pötz to Vogel, memorandum, "Initiative des Europäischen Rats vom 13.07.1976 für eine Konvention gegen Geiselnahmen, hier: Behandlung der Angelegenheit auf der nächsten Sitzung des Europäischen Rats am 5. und 6. 12. 1977; Stand der Angelegenheit," November 29, 1977, BArch, B141-77292, pp. 76–80; and Pötz to Vogel, memorandum, "Initiative des Europäischen Rats vom 13.07.1976 für eine Konvention gegen Geiselnahmen, hier: Bericht über die 5. Sitzung der Arbeitsgruppe leitender Beamter," December 13 1977, BArch, B141-77293, pp. 31–36.

97. UK Embassy Dublin to Foreign and Commonwealth Office, Telegram 513, November 29, 1977, TNA, FCO 76/1743.

98. Senior government official Behrens (II B 5, FRG Justice Ministry) to Vogel, memorandum, "Arbeiten im Rahmen der Mitgliedsstaaten der EG zur Bekämpfung des Terrorismus, hier: Bericht der deutschen Präsidentschaft über die 8. Sitzung der aufgrund der Initative des Europäischen Rats vom 13.7.1976 eingesetzten Arbeitsgruppe leitender Beamter in der Zeit vom 24.-26.7.1978 in Bonn," August 2, 1978, BArch, B141-77298, pp. 4–16.

99. Pötz to Vogel, memorandum, "Initiative des Europäischen Rats vom 13.07.1976 für eine Konvention gegen Geiselnahmen, hier: Bericht über die 6. Sitzung der Arbeitsgruppe leitender Beamter in Kopenhagen (1./2.2.1978)," February 3, 1978, BArch, B141-77294, pp. 89–94.

100. Maritime, Aviation, and Environmental Department, confidential brief, "French Foreign Minister's Talks with the Secretary of State, 2 December 1977," November 30, 1977, TNA, FCO 76/1743.

101. Behrens to Vogel, memorandum, "Bericht der deutschen Präsidentschaft über die 8. Sitzung der Arbeitsgruppe leitender Beamter," August 2, 1978, BArch, B141-77298, pp. 4–16.

102. For a detailed description of the kidnapping and reactions, see Tobias Hof, *Staat und Terrorismus in Italien 1969–1982* (Munich: Oldenbourg, 2011), 208–23.

103. Walter to Vogel, "Arbeiten im Rahmen der Neun zur Bekämpfung des Terrorismus," June 2, 1978, PA AA, B83 Vol. 1234.

104. Pötz to Vogel, memorandum, "Initiative des Europäischen Rats vom 13.07.1976 für eine Konvention gegen Geiselnahme, hier: Deutsch-französische Expertengespräche in der Zeit vom 29.-31. März in Paris," April 11, 1978, BArch, B141-77295, pp. 67–74; Pötz to Vogel, memorandum, "Arbeiten im Rahmen der Neun zur Bekämpfung des Terrorismus, hier: Bericht über die 9. Sitzung der Arbeitsgruppe leitender Beamter vom 18.-20.4.1978 in Kopenhagen," April 25, 1978, BArch, B141-77296, pp. 10–21; and Vogel, memorandum, "Europäische Zusammenarbeit bei der Bekämpfung des Terrorismus," June 24, 1978, PA AA, B83 Vol. 1234.

105. Alain Peyrefitte to Hans-Jochen Vogel, letter, August 1, 1978, BArch, B141-77298, pp. 33–34; Division 202, Foreign Office, memorandum for the record, "Weitere Behandlung des französischen Projekts einer 'espace judiciare', hier: Demarche des französischen Gesandten M. Henry bei Herrn Dg 20 am 3.8.1978," August 9, 1978, BArch, B141-77298, pp. 39–40.

106. Vogel to Peyrefitte, letter, August 29, 1978, BArch, B141-77298, pp. 63–65.

107. Under-Division-Head IV B to Vogel, memorandum, "3. EG-Justizministertagung, hier: Schreiben des französischen Justizministers vom 1. August 1978," August 10, 1978, BArch, B141-77298, pp. 41–45.

108. Erich Corves (II B 5, FRG Justice Ministry) to Division 200, Foreign Office, memorandum, "Arbeiten im Rahmen der Mitgliedsstaaten der Europäischen Gemeinschaften zur Bekämpfung des Terrorismus und zur Schaffung eines einheitlichen europäischen Rechtraums, hier: Bericht der deutschen Präsidentschaft über die 9. Sitzung der aufgrund der Initative des Europäischen Rats vom 13.7.1976 eingesetzten Arbeitsgruppe leitender Beamter in der Zeit vom 7. bis 10. November 1978 in Bonn," November 17, 1978, BArch, B141-77299. A further meeting in the following month defined a "serious offense" as a crime with at least one year's sentence.

109. Division 200, memorandum, "Espace Judiciare," March 29, 1979, BArch, B141-77303, pp. 82–85; Division 200, "EPZ—Zusammenarbeit der neun EG-Staaten zur Bekämpfung des Terrorismus und zur Schaffung eines europäischen Rechtsraumes," January 28, 1980, PA AA, B83 Vol. 1238.

110. Walter to Vogel, memorandum, "Zweite EG-Justizministerkonferenz im Rahmen der Europäischen Politischen Zusammenarbeit (EPZ) am 23.4.1979 in Paris, hier: Vorbereitung der Sitzung," April 12, 1979, BArch, B141-77304, pp. 78–82.

111. Division 200, memorandum, "Espace Judiciare," March 29, 1979, BArch, B141-77303, pp. 82–85.

112. Division 200, memorandum, "Espace Judiciare, hier: Europäisches Terrorismusabkommen," October 16, 1979, BArch, B141-77309, pp. 68–69.

113. Walter to Vogel, memorandum, "Arbeiten im Rahmen der Mitgliedsstaaten der EG zur Bekämpfung des Terrorismus und zur Schaffung eines einheitlichen europäischen Rechtraums, hier: Bericht über die 16. Sitzung der aufgrund der Initative des Europäischen Rats vom 13.7.1976 eingesetzten Arbeitsgruppe leitender Beamter in der Zeit vom 5.-7.11.1979 in Dublin," November 12, 1979, BArch, B141-77310, pp. 1–9.

114. Walter to Vogel, memorandum, "Espace Judiciare: Justizministertreffen vom 4.12.1979 in Dublin," December 5, 1979, BArch, 141-77312, pp. 57–61.

115. See chapter 5, s.v. Normalizing Global North Conceptualizations of Terrorism in International Law.

116. Division 200, memorandum, "EPZ—Zusammenarbeit der neun EG-Staaten zur Bekämpfung des Terrorismus und zur Schaffung eines europäischen Rechtsraumes," January 28, 1980, PA AA, B83 Vol. 1238.

117. Walter to Vogel, memorandum, "Arbeiten im Rahmen der Mitgliedsstaaten der EG zur Bekämpfung des Terrorismus und zur Schaffung eines einheitlichen europäischen Rechtraums, hier: Bericht über die 18. Sitzung der aufgrund der Initative des Europäischen Rats vom 13.7.1976 eingesetzten Arbeitsgruppe leitender Beamter in der Zeit vom 26. bis 29. Februar 1980 in Rom," March 4, 1980, BArch, B141-77315, pp. 54–66.

118. Walter to Vogel, memorandum, "Arbeiten im Rahmen der Mitgliedsstaaten der EG zur Bekämpfung des Terrorismus und zur Schaffung eines einheitlichen europäischen Rechtraums, hier: Bericht über die 20. Sitzung der aufgrund der Initiative des Europäischen Rats vom 13.7.1976 eingesetzten Arbeitsgruppe leitender Beamter in der Zeit vom 6. bis 12. Mai 1980 in Rom," May 16, 1980, BArch, B141-77319, pp. 53–60.

119. FRG Embassy The Hague to Foreign Office Bonn, Telegram 255, June 16, 1980, BArch, B141-77321, p. 30.

120. Coreu Rome to Foreign Office, Coreu Telegram 2214, June 13, 1980, BArch, B141-77320, p. 47; and Coreu Rome to Foreign Office, Coreu Telegram 2237, June 16, 1980, BArch, B141-77320, p. 48.

121. Immo Stabreit (Division 200), memorandum, "Espace Judiciare," Undated (after September 4, 1980), BArch, B141-77321, pp. 142–43.

122. The Hague to Foreign Office, Telegram 255, June 16, 1980, BArch, B141-77321, p. 30.

123. Vogel, memorandum, "Espace judiciare civile, hier: Ergebnisse der EG-Justizministerkonferenz in Rom am 19. Juni 1980," June 20, 1980, PA AA, B83 Vol. 1240; and FRG Embassy Rome to Foreign Office, Telegram 650, June 23, 1980, PA AA, B83 Vol. 1240.

124. European Commission, "European Arrest Warrant," *European Commission: Policies, Information, and Services*, accessed June 4, 2019, https://ec.europa.eu/info/law /cross-border-cases/judicial-cooperation/types-judicial-cooperation/european-arrest -warrant_en.

5. FROM INTERNATIONAL LAW TO MILITARIZED COUNTERTERRORISM

1. See Lisa Stampnitzky, *Disciplining Terror: How Experts Invented "Terrorism"* (Cambridge: Cambridge University Press, 2013), 119–20; and Adrian Hänni, "Global Terror Networks: Die Diskursive Konstruktion der Terroristischen Bedrohung in den USA, 1886–1986" (dissertation, Institute of Social and Economic History, University of Zurich, 2013), 63–64.
2. In effect were the International Civil Aviation Organization (ICAO) 1970 Convention for the Suppression of Unlawful Seizure of Aircraft (Hague Convention), the Organization of American States (OAS) 1971 Convention to Prevent and Punish the Acts of Terrorism Taking the Form of Crimes Against Persons and Related Extortion That Are of International Significance (OAS Convention), and the ICAO 1971 Convention for the Suppression of Unlawful Acts Against the Safety of Civil Aviation (Montreal Convention). The ICAO conventions were based on the 1963 Convention on Offences and Certain Other Acts Committed on Board Aircraft (Tokyo Convention).
3. These were the United Nations 1973 Convention on the Prevention and Punishment of Crimes Against Internationally Protected Persons, Including Diplomatic Agents (Diplomats Convention) and the Council of Europe's 1977 European Convention on the Suppression of Terrorism (European Convention).
4. Bernhard Blumenau, *The United Nations and Terrorism: Germany, Multilateralism, and Anti-Terrorism Efforts in the 1970s* (Basingstoke, UK: Palgrave MacMillan, 2014), 118–19.
5. Blumenau, *The United Nations and Terrorism*, 3–5.
6. FRG Mission United Nations to Foreign Office, Telegram 1585, August 3, 1976, Political Archive of the Foreign Office (hereafter: PA AA) Federal Republic of Germany (hereafter: B)83 Vol. 984.
7. See chapter 4, s.v. The Council of Europe Negotiations and German-French Divisions.
8. First Councilor Dr. Gorenflos (Office 230: United Nations, Foreign Office) to FRG foreign minister Hans-Dietrich Genscher, memorandum, "Vorbereitung unserer VN-Initiative zur Bekämpfung der Geiselnahme," August 13, 1976, PA AA, B83 Vol. 984. See also Blumenau, *The United Nations and Terrorism*, 142.
9. Blumenau, *The United Nations and Terrorism*, 146–47, 170–71.
10. FRG Mission United Nations to Foreign Office, Telegram 3597, December 12, 1976, PA AA, B83 Vol. 984.
11. Office 511: Criminal, Tax and Customs Law director Helmut Türk to Hans-Dietrich Genscher, memorandum, "Konvention gegen Geiselnahme," November 21, 1977, with attached convention draft, PA AA, B83 Vol. 989.
12. FRG Mission United Nations to Foreign Office, Telegram 3584, December 12, 1977, PA AA, B83 Vol. 989.

13. Office 502: Diplomatic and Consular Law, International Travel Law, Foreign Office, to Office 230: United Nations, "Unsere Geiselnahme-Initiative," October 19, 1976, PA AA, B83 Vol. 984.

14. Giovanni Mantilla, "The Political Origins of the Geneva Conventions of 1949 and the Additional Protocols of 1977," in *Do the Geneva Conventions Matter?*, ed. Matthew Evangelista and Nina Tannenwald (New York: Oxford University Press, 2017), 35–68.

15. FRG Mission United Nations to Foreign Office, Telegram 2465, October 8, 1976, PA AA, B83 Vol. 984; and FRG UN ambassador Rüdiger von Wechmar to Egyptian representative to the UN Ahmed Esmat Abdel Meguid, letter, October 8, 1976, PA AA, B83 Vol. 984.

16. FRG Embassy Paris to Foreign Office, Telegram 13, January 4, 1978, PA AA, B83 Vol. 1241; see also Blumenau, *The United Nations and Terrorism*, 181–82, 185–87. This stance was in line with prior French opposition to antiterrorism conventions, whether in the ICAO, UNGA, or Council of Europe.

17. See chapter 2, s.v. From Multilateralism to Unilateralism.

18. International Committee of the Red Cross, "Practice Relating to Rule 96. Hostage-Taking," *International Humanitarian Law Database: Customary International Humanitarian Law*, accessed April 5, 2018, https://ihl-databases.icrc.org/customary-ihl/eng /docs/v2_rul_rule96.

19. Foreign Office to FRG Embassies Abidjan, Algiers, et al., memorandum, "Massnahmen gegen den Terrorismus: Vorbereitung einer Initiative für die 31. GV," May 12, 1976, PA AA, B83 Vol. 983.

20. FRG Mission United Nations to Foreign Office, Telegram 2555, October 19, 1977, PA AA, B83 Vol. 989.

21. Blumenau, *The United Nations and Terrorism*, 178–79.

22. Good recent studies are Seth Anziska, *Preventing Palestine: A Political History from Camp David to Oslo* (Princeton, NJ: Princeton University Press, 2018); and Jørgen Jensehaugen, *Arab-Israeli Diplomacy Under Carter: The U.S., Israel, and the Palestinians* (New York: I. B. Tauris, 2018).

23. Blumenau, *The United Nations and Terrorism*, 179–81.

24. FRG Mission United Nations to Foreign Office, Telegram 3413, November 29, 1978, PA AA, B83 Vol. 1243.

25. Blumenau, *The United Nations and Terrorism*, 185–86.

26. Foreign Office to FRG Mission Geneva, Telegram 2726, February 9, 1979, PA AA, B83 Vol. 1243.

27. Mantilla, "The Political Origins of the Geneva Conventions of 1949," 59.

28. Harold H. Saunders, "Diplomacy and Pressure, November 1979–May 1980," in *American Hostages in Iran*, ed. Warren Christopher and Paul H. Kreisberg (New Haven, CT: Yale University Press, 1985), 72–143.

29. United Nations, "International Convention Against the Taking of Hostages," *United Nations Treaty Collection*, accessed November 5, 2019, https://treaties.un.org/doc /Treaties/1979/12/19791218%2003–20%20PM/Ch_XVIII_5p.pdf.

30. State Department, Bureau of International Security and Nonproliferation, "Convention on the Physical Protection of Nuclear Material," *U.S. Department of State Archive*, accessed September 13, 2019, https://2009-2017.state.gov/t/isn/5079.htm.

31. See Robert Brown, *Nuclear Authority: The IAEA and the Absolute Weapon* (Washington, DC: Georgetown University Press, 2015), 88–89; and International Atomic

Energy Agency, *The International Legal Framework for Nuclear Security* (Vienna: IAEA, 2011), 3.

32. Bureau of International Security and Nonproliferation, "Convention on the Physical Protection of Nuclear Material," articles 7–11.

33. U.S. House of Representatives, "Public Law 93–366," August 5, 1974, Office of the Law Revision Counsel, U.S. Code, accessed November 25, 2019, http://uscode.house.gov /statutes/pl/93/366.pdf.

34. "Japanese Hijackers Free Hostages, Surrender in Algiers," *Washington Post*, October 4, 1977, A19.

35. See chapter 2, s.v. From Multilateralism to Unilateralism.

36. See chapter 3, s.v. The Proliferation of Antiterrorism Tactical Units During the 1970s.

37. See Bernhard Blumenau, "The Group of 7 and International Terrorism: The Snowball Effect That Never Materialized," *Journal of Contemporary History* 51, no. 2 (April 2016): 316–34.

38. National security adviser Zbigniew Brzezinski to Vice President Mondale, Secretary of State Vance, and Secretary of Defense Brown, memorandum, "Terrorism," September 21, 1977, Jimmy Carter Presidential Library (CPL), national security adviser's files, General William Odom's files, Box 55, Terrorism SCC Working Group, 9/77–12/78.

39. Timothy J. Naftali, *Blind Spot: The Secret History of American Counterterrorism* (New York: Basic Books, 2005), 101.

40. "Agenda for Bonn," undated, CPL, national security adviser's files, General William Odom's files, Box 52, Terrorism Bonn Trip 10/77–2/78, p. 26.

41. Memorandum, "The NSC/SCC Working Group on Terrorism: Goals and Objectives," attachment to Anthony Quainton (Director, State Department Office for Combatting Terrorism) to members of the NSC/SCC Working Group to Combat Terrorism, memorandum, "Summary Minutes of the NSC/SCC Working Group to Combat Terrorism, August 30, 1978," August 31, 1978, CPL, national security adviser's files, General William Odom's files, Box 55, Terrorism SCC Working Group, 9/77–12/78.

42. An excellent bibliography on the G7 can be found at G7 Information Centre, "G7/G8 Bibliography: Scholarly Publications," University of Toronto, accessed April 2, 2018, http://www.g8.utoronto.ca/bibliography/biblio1.htm.

43. See the private secretary to the British prime minister, Bryan Cartledge, to the principal private secretary to the secretary of state for Foreign and Commonwealth Affairs, George Walden, memorandum, "Economic Summit, Bonn, 16/17 July 1978," July 19, 1978, with attached memorandums of conversation, "Second Plenary Session on Sunday 16 July at 15.15 in the Palais Schaumburg," and "Third Plenary Session on 17 July 1978 (opened 1040, closed 1300)," The National Archives of the United Kingdom (TNA), FCO 76/1867; and Edward Mickolus, "Multilateral Legal Efforts to Combat Terrorism: Diagnosis and Prognosis," *Ohio Northern University Law Review* 6 (1979): 13–51.

44. Anonymous, memorandum of conversation, "Third Plenary Session on 17 July 1978 (opened 1040, closed 1300)," TNA, FCO 76/1867, 2, 4–5.

45. U.S. Embassy Bonn to Department of State, Telegram 13070, July 17, 1978, JCL, Counsel's Office, Robert Lipshultz's subject files, Box 45, Terrorism, 7–78 [CF, O-A 714].

46. Secretary of Transportation Brock Adams to President Jimmy Carter, memorandum, "Bonn Summit Agreement on Hijacking," July 21, 1978, JCL, White House Central Files, Special Files—Foreign Affairs (FO), Box 44, Foreign Affairs 6–5 1/20/77–1/20/81.

47. Anonymous, memorandum of conversation, "Third Plenary Session on 17 July 1978 (opened 1040, closed 1300)," TNA, FCO 76/1867, 4.

48. Department of Trade, Foreign and Commonwealth Office, memorandum, "Report of the Implementation of the Bonn Statement on Air Hijacking," August 17, 1978, TNA, FCO 76/1868; and memorandum from William Odom to White House counsel Robert Lipshutz, "Bonn Statement on Terrorism," July 22, 1978, CPL, Counsel's Office, Robert Lipshultz's subject files, Box 45, Terrorism, 7–78 [CF, O-A 714].

49. Blumenau, *The United Nations and International Terrorism*, 187.

50. Blumenau, "The Group of 7 and International Terrorism," 328–31.

51. Blumenau, "The Group of 7 and International Terrorism," 331–32; and John S. Murphy, *State Support of International Terrorism: Legal, Political, and Economic Dimensions* (Boulder, CO: Westview, 1989), 71.

52. See chapter 4, s.v. Seeking a Double-Track EPC Compromise.

53. Philippa Drew (Home Office) to David Beattie (United Nations Department, Foreign and Commonwealth Office), memorandum, "German Draft of UN Convention on the Taking of Hostages," June 17, 1977, TNA, FCO 58/1131.

54. Bruce W. Warner, "Great Britain and the Response to International Terrorism," in *The Deadly Sin of Terrorism: Its Effect on Democracy and Civil Liberty in Six Countries*, ed. David A. Charters (Westport, CT: Greenwood, 1994), 13–42.

55. Markus Lammert, *Der Neue Terrorismus: Terrorismusbekämpfung in Frankreich in den 1980er Jahren* (Oldenbourg, Germany: De Gruyter, 2017), 157.

56. United Nations General Assembly, Ad Hoc Committee on International Terrorism Working Group, working paper, "Algeria, Barbados, India, Iran, Nigeria, Panama, Syrian Arab Republic, Tunisia, Venezuela, Yugoslavia and Zambia: Working Paper on Underlying Causes of International Terrorism," March 28, 1979, TNA, FCO 58/1631.

57. See Thomas Borstelmann, *The 1970s: A New Global History from Civil Rights to Economic Inequality* (Princeton, NJ: Princeton University Press, 2012).

58. See David Farber, *The Rise and Fall of Modern American Conservatism: A Short History* (Princeton, NJ: Princeton University Press, 2010).

59. See Laura Kalman, *Right Star Rising: A New Politics, 1974–1980* (New York: W. W. Norton, 2010), and Farber, *The Rise and Fall of Modern American Conservatism*.

60. Jeane Kirkpatrick, "Dictatorship and Double Standards," *Commentary* 68, no. 5 (November 1979): 34–45.

61. See Brian J. Auten, *Carter's Conversion: The Hardening of American Defense Policy* (Columbia: University of Missouri Press, 2010); Scott Kaufman, *Plans Unraveled: The Foreign Policy of the Carter Administration* (DeKalb: Northern Illinois University Press, 2008); and Robert H. Johnson, "Periods of Peril: The Window of Vulnerability and Other Myths," *Foreign Affairs* 61, no. 4 (Spring 1983): 950–70.

62. See Richard Pipes, "Team B: The Reality Behind the Myth," *Commentary* 82, no. 4 (October 1986): 25–40.

63. See Auten, *Carter's Conversion*; and Betty Glad, *An Outsider in the White House: Jimmy Carter, His Advisors, and the Making of American Foreign Policy* (Ithaca, NY: Cornell University Press, 2009).

64. See Kyle Burke, *Revolutionaries for the Right: Anticommunist Internationalism and Paramilitary Warfare in the Cold War* (Chapel Hill: University of North Carolina Press, 2018).

65. See Daniel Hummel, "Religious Pluralism, Domestic Politics, and American Evangelical Support for Israel," in *The Cold War at Home and Abroad: Domestic Politics and US Foreign Policy Since 1945*, ed. Andy Johns and Mitch Lerner (Lexington: University of Kentucky Press, 2018), 100–18; and Melani McAlister, *Epic Encounters: Culture, Media, and U.S. Interests in the Middle East Since 1945*, rev. ed. (Berkeley: University of California Press, 2005).

66. Stampnitzky, *Disciplining Terror*, 112.

67. Benjamin Netanyahu, "Foreword," in *International Terrorism: Challenge and Response; Proceedings of the Jerusalem Conference on International Terrorism*, ed. Benjamin Netanyahu (Jerusalem: Jonathan Institute, Transaction, 1981), xi–xii; see also Stampnitzky, *Disciplining Terror*, 112–13.

68. Conference reports include Benjamin Netanyahu, ed., *International Terrorism: Challenge and Response*; Benjamin Netanyahu, *International Terrorism: The Soviet Connection* (Jerusalem: Jonathan Institute, 1979); and Benjamin Netanyahu and Paul Johnson, *The Jerusalem Conference on International Terrorism* (Jerusalem: Jonathan Institute, 1979).

69. Stampnitzky, *Disciplining Terror*, 112–13; and Hänni, "Global Terror Networks," 67.

70. Netanyahu, *International Terrorism: Challenge and Response*, vii, 73, 343.

71. Netanyahu, *International Terrorism: Challenge and Response*, 49, 111, 162, 265.

72. Hänni, "Global Terror Networks," 60.

73. See for example Brian Crozier, *Strategy of Survival* (New York: Arlington House, 1978); and Robert Moss, "1979 Aims of Terror Inc." *Daily Telegraph*, January 2, 1979. For Moss and Crozier's CIA funding, see Bernard Nossiter, "CIA News Service Reported," *Washington Post*, July 3, 1975, A26; and Anthony Marro, "Congressman Says C.I.A. Pledges to Stop Sponsoring English-Language Books," *New York Times*, April 5, 1977, 30.

74. Netanyahu, *International Terrorism: Challenge and Response*, 172, 307, 350.

75. See Stampnitzky, *Disciplining Terror*, 114.

76. Edward S. Herman and Gerry O'Sullivan, *The "Terrorism" Industry: The Experts and Institutions That Shape Our View of Terror* (New York: Pantheon, 1989), 105.

77. Examples were Lord Alan Chalfont (a former British cabinet member), Hugh Fraser (a British MP), Jacques Soustelle (a member of the French National Assembly and ironically a previous leader of the terroristic Organisation de l'armée secrète), Manlio Brosio (former secretary general of NATO), Joop den Uyl (former prime minister of the Netherlands), Frank Cluskey (head of Ireland's Labour Party), and David Barrett (former premier of British Columbia). See Netanyahu, *International Terrorism: Challenge and Response*, 23, 79, 122, 165, 180, 250, 313.

78. Netanyahu, *International Terrorism: Challenge and Response*, 201.

79. Hänni, "Global Terror Networks," 61.

80. Stampnitzky, *Disciplining Terror*, 113–14.

81. Ray Cline, "The Strategic Framework," in *International Terrorism: Challenge and Response*, ed. Benjamin Netanyahu, 90–100.

82. A popular media example is Brian Crozier, "Anatomy of Terrorism," *The Nation* 188, no. 12 (March 12, 1959): 250–52; an academic one is Thomas Thornton, "Terror as a

Weapon of Political Agitation," in *Internal War: Problems and Approaches*, ed. Harry Eckstein (New York: The Free Press of Glencoe, 1964), 71–99; while a government example is Ray S. Cline (Bureau of Intelligence and Research), intelligence brief, "Latin America: The Growing Specter of Diplomatic Kidnappings," March 25, 1970, National Archives and Record Administration, Record Group 59: Records of the Department of State, Central Foreign Policy Files 1970–73, POL 23–8 LA, 1/1/1970. Lisa Stampnitzky, "From Insurgents to Terrorists: Experts, Rational Knowledge, and Irrational Subjects," in *Disciplining Terror*, 49–82, provides a detailed analysis of publications on terrorism before 1968.

83. Henry M. Jackson, "Terrorism as a Weapon in International Politics," in *International Terrorism: Challenge and Response*, ed. Benjamin Netanyahu, 33–38.

84. Brian Crozier, "Soviet Support for International Terrorism," in *International Terrorism: Challenge and Response*, ed. Benjamin Netanyahu, 64–72.

85. Ray Cline, "The Strategic Framework," 90–91.

86. George H. Bush, "The U.S. and the Fight Against International Terrorism," in *International Terrorism: Challenge and Response*, ed. Benjamin Netanyahu, 332–37. Bush added harsh criticism of the UN for its inability and unwillingness to address international terrorism.

87. See Bernhard Blumenau, "Unholy Alliance: The Connection Between the East German Stasi and the Right-Wing Terrorist Odfried Hepp," *Studies in Conflict and Terrorism* 43, no. 1 (January 2020): 47–68; Jeffrey Herf, *Undeclared Wars with Israel: East Germany and the West German Far Left, 1967–1989* (New York: Cambridge University Press, 2016); and Thomas Riegler, " 'Es muss ein gegenseitiges Geben und Nehmen sein': Warschauer-Pakt-Staaten und Terrorismusbekämpfung am Beispiel der DDR," in *Terrorismusbekämpfung in Westeuropa*, ed. Johannes Hürter (Oldenbourg, Germany: De Gruyter, 2015), 289–316. See also CIA, " 'Soviet Support for International Terrorism and Revolutionary Violence [Includes Annexes]': Top Secret Special National Intelligence Estimate (Sanitized Copy) SNIE 11/2-81," May 27, 1981, CIA Freedom of Information Act Electronic Reading Room (CREST), General CIA Records, CIA-RDP90T00155R000200010009-2.

88. Crozier, "Soviet Support for International Terrorism," 67–71; Cline, "The Strategic Framework," 94–95, "Questions and Answers: Fourth Session: Current Response of Democratic Societies," in *International Terrorism: Challenge and Response*, ed. Benjamin Netanyahu, 214–19, statement by Robert Moss, 216.

89. Robert Moss, "The Terrorist State," in *International Terrorism: Challenge and Response*, ed. Benjamin Netanyahu, 128–34.

90. Moss, "The Terrorist State," 128.

91. Moss, "The Terrorist State," 131.

92. Leslie H. Gelb, "Role of Moscow in Terror Doubted," *New York Times*, October 18, 1981, 9.

93. Bob Woodward, *Veil: The Secret Wars of the CIA 1981–1987* (London: Simon & Schuster, 1987), 131. Though pertinent CIA records are still classified, several recent studies have agreed that such propaganda efforts could have been possible. See Stampnitzky, *Disciplining Terror*, 119–20; and Hänni, "Global Terror Networks," 63–64.

94. A good example is Richard Pipes, "The Roots of the Involvement," in *International Terrorism: Challenge and Response*, ed. Benjamin Netanyahu, 58–63.

95. "Questions and Answers: Third Session: The Threat Posed by Terrorism to Democratic Societies," in *International Terrorism: Challenge and Response*, ed. Benjamin Netanyahu, 155–158; "Questions and Answers: Fourth Session," 217.

96. Hänni, "Global Terror Networks," 67.

97. Hugh Fraser, "The Tyranny of Terrorism," in *International Terrorism: Challenge and Response*, ed. Benjamin Netanyahu, 23–32; Cline, "The Strategic Framework," 99–100; and George Will, "Calculating the Public Interest," in *International Terrorism: Challenge and Response*, ed. Benjamin Netanyahu, 208–213.

98. Edward Teller, "The Spectre of Nuclear Terrorism," in *International Terrorism: Challenge and Response*, ed. Benjamin Netanyahu, 141–45.

99. Paul Johnson, "Preface: Fifth Session: The Role of the Media in the Struggle Against Terrorism," in *International Terrorism: Challenge and Response*, ed. Benjamin Netanyahu, 221–22.

100. Stampnitzky, *Disciplining Terror*, 109–10.

101. Mordecai Ben-Ari, "Protecting the Airways," in *International Terrorism: Challenge and Response*, ed. Benjamin Netanyahu, 289–93.

102. Shimon Peres, "The Threat and the Response," in *International Terrorism: Challenge and Response*, ed. Benjamin Netanyahu, 8–11; Fraser, "The Tyranny of Terrorism," 27; Alan Chalfont, "Our Main Problem: The Climate of Appeasement," in *International Terrorism: Challenge and Response*, ed. Benjamin Netanyahu, 79–89; and Cline, "The Strategic Framework," 100.

103. Johnson, "Preface: Fifth Session," 221–22; Michael Elkins, "Caging the Beasts," in *International Terrorism: Challenge and Response*, ed. Benjamin Netanyahu, 230–34; Norman Podhoretz, "The Subtle Collusion," in *International Terrorism: Challenge and Response*, ed. Benjamin Netanyahu, 235–41; Jacques Soustelle, "Liberty or License?," in *International Terrorism: Challenge and Response*, ed. Benjamin Netanyahu, 250–52; and "Questions and Answers: Fifth Session: The Role of the Media in the Struggle Against Terrorism," in *International Terrorism: Challenge and Response*, ed. Benjamin Netanyahu, 253–62.

104. See especially Bush, "The U.S. and the Fight Against International Terrorism," 333–34.

105. Netanyahu, "Conference Summary Statement," 361.

106. Prominent examples from the conference include Benjamin Netanyahu, "Foreword," xi–xii; Henry M. Jackson, "Terrorism as a Weapon in International Politics," 35–37; Annie Kriegel, "Public Opinion, Intellectuals and Terrorism in Western Europe," in *International Terrorism: Challenge and Response*, ed. Benjamin Netanyahu, 172–79; and Benjamin Netanyahu, "Conference Summary Statement," in *International Terrorism: Challenge and Response*, ed. Benjamin Netanyahu, 361–62.

107. Netanyahu, "Conference Summary Statement," 362.

108. Paul Johnson, "Spreading Fast: This World Conspiracy of Terror," *Evening Standard*, July 3, 1979.

109. U.S. Congress, "The Jerusalem Conference on International Terrorism Identifies the Soviet Union as the Primary Sponsor of Terrorism," July 10, 1979, *Congressional Record*, 96th Congress, 1st Session, Vol. 125, Part 14, pp. 17926–29.

110. Stampnitzky, *Disciplining Terror*, 116, Hänni, "Global Terror Networks," 78.

111. Hänni analyzes these articles in Hänni, "Global Terror Networks," 76–78. Examples include Robert Moss, "Moscow Backs Terror Inc.," *Daily Telegraph*, July 16, 1979; Brian Crozier, "The Soviets' Terror Tactics," *National Review*, August 3, 1979, 961; Hans-Josef Horchem, "Die Sowjetunion und der internationale Terrorismus: Eine Variante expansiver und erfolgreicher kommunistischer Politik," *Frankfurter Allgemeine Zeitung*, October 20, 1979, 11; and Robert Moss, "What Russia Wants," *The New Republic*, January 19, 1980, 23–25.

112. George F. Will, "Tracking Terror," *Washington Post*, August 9, 1979, A19.

113. John J. O'Connor, "TV Weekend: Jones as a Gentle Bear of Detectives," *New York Times*, September 28, 1979, C25.

114. Netanyahu, *International Terrorism: The Soviet Connection*; Netanyahu and Johnson, *The Jerusalem Conference on International Terrorism*; and Benjamin Netanyahu, *International Terrorism: Challenge and Response*.

115. The journalist Claire Sterling, for example, conducted significant interviews with Israeli, U.S., West German, and other antiterrorism officials, including intelligence representatives, for use in her book *The Terror Network*. See for example her notes in Claire Sterling, "Notebook Israel," 1978, Hoover Institution Archives (Hoover), Claire Sterling Papers (Sterling), Box 20, folder 10, "Israel undated;" and Claire Sterling, "Notebook Germany," undated, Hoover, Sterling, Box 20, folder 9, "Germany undated."

116. Moss, "What Russia Wants," 23.

117. O'Connor, "TV Weekend," C25.

118. Paul Nitze, "Strategy in the Decade of the 1980s," *Foreign Affairs* 59, no. 1 (Fall 1980), 82–101.

119. Nitze, "Strategy in the Decade of the 1980s," 90–91.

120. Nitze, "Strategy in the Decade of the 1980s," 91.

121. Nitze, "Strategy in the Decade of the 1980s," note 2.

122. Moss, "What Russia Wants," 25.

123. Robert Moss, "Terror: A Soviet Export," *New York Times*, November 2, 1980, SM11.

124. Moss, "Terror" and Shlomo Gazit, "The Myth and the Reality of the PLO," in *International Terrorism: Challenge and Response*, ed. Benjamin Netanyahu, 343–49.

125. See Charles Tyroler, *Alerting America: The Papers of the Committee on the Present Danger* (Washington: Pergamon-Brassey's, 1984), ix–xi.

126. Nancy Reagan to Brian Crozier, letter, June 5, 1980, Hoover, Brian Crozier Papers (Crozier), Box 3, folder 4, Correspondence Reagan, Ronald, 1980–1991.

127. See Richard Allen to Brian Crozier, letter, February 4, 1982; Brian Crozier to William Clark, letter, February 5, 1982; and Robert MacFarlane to Brian Crozier, letter, October 31, 1983; all in Hoover, Crozier, Box 3, folder 7, Correspondence White House, 1980–1986.

128. Don Oberdorfer, "Haig Calls Terrorism Top Priority," *Washington Post*, January 29, 1981, A1, A4. For Haig's views on terrorism more generally, see Naftali, *Blind Spot*, 117–18.

129. Stampnitzky, *Disciplining Terror*, 109–10.

130. U.S. Embassy Moscow to State Department, Telegram 2324, February 17, 1981, *Foreign Relations of the United States (FRUS)*, 1981–1988, Volume III: Soviet Union, January 1981–January 1983, Document 20, accessed April 26, 2018, https://history .state.gov/historicaldocuments/frus1981-88v03/d20; and memorandum from Richard

Pipes to Richard Allen, memorandum, "Weekly Report as of February 21," February 24, 1981, *FRUS, 1981–1988,* Volume III, Document 21, accessed April 26, 2018, https://history.state.gov/historicaldocuments/frus1981-88v03/d21.

131. National Foreign Assessment Center, " 'International Terrorism in 1979': Research Paper PA 80-100724," April 1, 1980, CREST, Argentina Declassification Project—The "Dirty War" (1976–83), C03291989.

132. Stampnitzky, *Disciplining Terror,* 130–31.

133. Richard Immerman, *The Hidden Hand: A Brief History of the CIA* (Chichester, UK: Wiley-Blackwell, 2014), 125–27.

134. Stampnitzky, *Disciplining Terror,* 120. Important CIA documents on the subject are still classified.

135. "Minutes of the Principals of the Department of State Staff Meeting," March 24, 1981, page 90, *FRUS, 1981–1988,* Volume III, Document 34, accessed June 14, 2018, https://history.state.gov/historicaldocuments/frus1981-88v03/d34.

136. RAND Corporation, *International Terrorism: Choosing the Right Target,* by Brian Jenkins, P-6597 (Santa Monica: RAND Corporation, 1981), accessed August 12, 2019, https://www.rand.org/pubs/papers/P6597.html, 1.

137. Philip Geyelin, "The Reigning White House Soviet Scholar," *Washington Post,* February 12, 1981, A19. This quotation was a cropped but direct excerpt from Pipes's presentation at the Jerusalem Conference. See Pipes, "The Roots of the Involvement," 62.

138. Ronald Reagan, "Excerpts From an Interview With Walter Cronkite of CBS News," March 3, 1981, *The American Presidency Project (APP),* ed. Gerhard Peters and John T. Woolley, accessed April 9, 2018, http://www.presidency.ucsb.edu/ws/?pid=43497, paragraphs 2–3.

139. Ronald Reagan, "The President's News Conference," March 6, 1981, *APP,* accessed April 9, 2018, http://www.presidency.ucsb.edu/ws/?pid=43505, El Salvador.

140. See for example Ronald Reagan, "Remarks at the National Legislative Conference of the Building and Construction Trades Department, AFL-CIO," April 5, 1982, *APP,* accessed August 12, 2019, https://www.presidency.ucsb.edu/node/244860; and Ronald Reagan, "Address to the Nation on United States Policy in Central America," May 9, 1984, *APP,* accessed August 12, 2019, https://www.presidency.ucsb.edu/node/261048.

141. Michael Ledeen and Claire Sterling, "Italy's Russian Sugar Daddies," *New Republic,* April 3, 1976, Hoover, Sterling, Box 9, folder 7, *New York Times* and other publications.

142. Claire Sterling, *The Terror Network: The Secret War of International Terrorism* (New York: Holt, Rinehart, and Winston, 1981), 2.

143. Sterling, *The Terror Network,* 292–93.

144. Sterling, *The Terror Network,* 3–4.

145. See the travel agendas in Sterling, Hoover, Box 10, folder 6, *The Terror Network: Correspondence and Itineraries 1979.* See also Sterling, *The Terror Network,* 14, 34, 221, 290–92.

146. Stampnitzky, *Disciplining Terror,* 117, 120; and Woodward, *Veil,* 125–31.

147. See for example Daniel Schorr, "Tracing the Thread of Terrorism," *New York Times,* May 17, 1981, BR4.

148. See Stampnitzky, *Disciplining Terror,* 119–20.

149. CIA, "SNIE 11/2-81," 1.

150. CIA, "SNIE 11/2-81," 7–8.

151. CIA, "SNIE 11/2-81," 2n5, 3n6, 6n8, 10n16.

152. CIA, "SNIE 11/2-81," 6n7.

153. Woodward, *Veil*, 131.

154. Stampnitzky, *Disciplining Terror*, 120.

155. Stampnitzky, *Disciplining Terror*, 110.

156. See Michael A. Reynolds, "The Wars' Entangled Roots: Regional Realities and Washington's Vision," in *Understanding the U.S. Wars in Iraq and Afghanistan*, ed. Beth Bailey and Richard H. Immerman (New York: New York University Press, 2015); and David Farber, *Taken Hostage: The Iran Hostage Crisis and America's First Encounter with Radical Islam* (Princeton, NJ: Princeton University Press, 2005).

157. White House, "National Security Decision Directive 138: Combatting Terrorism," April 3, 1984, Intelligence Resource Program, *Federation of American Scientists*, April 4, 2018, accessed April 26, 2018, https://fas.org/irp/offdocs/nsdd/nsdd-138 .pdf.

158. See Naftali, *Blind Spot*, 131–35; and David C. Wills, *The First War on Terrorism: Counter-Terrorism Policy During the Reagan Administration* (Lanham, MD: Rowman and Littlefield, 2003), 77–82.

159. Naftali, *Blind Spot*, 141–45.

160. See Reynolds, "The Wars' Entangled Roots" and Geoffrey Wawro, *Quicksand: America's Pursuit of Power in the Middle East* (New York: Penguin, 2010), 374–97.

161. Ronald Reagan, "Address to the Nation on Events in Lebanon and Grenada," October 27, 1983, *APP*, accessed April 9, 2018, http://www.presidency.ucsb.edu /ws/?pid=40696, paragraphs 50, 54.

162. "Contents," in *Terrorism: How the West Can Win*, ed. Benjamin Netanyahu (New York: Farrar, Strauss, Giroux, 1986), xiii–xv.

163. Suzanne Garment, "Terrorism Meeting Takes Temperature of the West," *Wall Street Journal*, June 29, 1984, 30.

164. Benjamin Netanyahu, "Preface," in *Terrorism: How the West Can Win*, ed. Benjamin Netanyahu (New York: Farrar, Straus and Giroux, 1986), ix–xi.

165. Stampnitzky, *Disciplining Terror*, 129–30.

166. Ray S. Cline and Yonah Alexander (CSIS) to Thomas H. Bushnell (Contracting Officer, Defense Supply Service Washington, Pentagon), letter, November 30, 1984, Library of Congress (LoC), Ray S. Cline Papers (Cline), 1945–1994, Box 33, folder 16 State-Sponsored Terrorism Study 1984–1985; and Colonel Karl F. Robinson (Chief, Strategic Plans and Policy Division, Pentagon) to Yonah Alexander (CSIS), memorandum, "Study Advisory Group Comments," with seven attachments, LoC, Cline, Box 33, folder 17, State-Sponsored Terrorism Study 1984–1985.

167. See Margaret I. Branick, "Extradition and the Conflict in Northern Ireland: The Past, Present and Future of an Intractable Problem," *Hastings International and Comparative Law Review* 25 (2002): 169–98; and Terry Richard Kane, "Prosecuting International Terrorists in United States Courts: Gaining the Jurisdictional Threshold," *Yale Journal of International Law* 12 (1987): 294–341.

168. Wills, *The First War on Terror*, 94–95, 101–3.

169. See chapter 2, s.v. From Multilateralism to Unilateralism.

170. Wills, *The First War on Terror*, 134.

171. Naftali, *Blind Spot*, 168.

172. Naftali, *Blind Spot*, 171–74.

173. International Maritime Organization, "Convention for the Suppression of Unlawful Acts Against the Safety of Maritime Navigation, Protocol for the Suppression of Unlawful Acts Against the Safety of Fixed Platforms Located on the Continental Shelf," *International Maritime Organization*, accessed August 13, 2019, http://www.imo.org/en/About/Conventions/ListOfConventions/Pages/SUA-Treaties.aspx.

174. Naftali, *Blind Spot*, 185.

175. Wills, *The First War on Terror*, 203, 205–7.

176. International Civil Aviation Organization, "Protocol for the Suppression of Unlawful Acts of Violence at Airports Serving International Civil Aviation, Supplementary to the Convention for the Suppression of Unlawful Acts against the Safety of Civil Aviation, done at Montreal, on 23 September 1971, done at Montreal on 24 February 1988," *ICAO*, accessed August 14, 2019, https://www.icao.int/secretariat/legal/Administrative%20Packages/via_en.pdf.

177. See Naftali, *Blind Spot*, 206–7, 219–21.

178. A detailed discussion of French counterterrorism is found in Markus Lammert, *Der Neue Terrorismus*.

179. Karrin Hanshew, *Terror and Democracy in West Germany* (New York: Cambridge University Press, 2012), 252–59.

180. Lammert, "Ein neues Analysemodell für die historische Terrorismusforschung?," in Hürter, *Terrorismusbekämpfung in Westeuropa*, 201–15, 208–9.

181. See for example the analysis of al Qaeda and associated movements in Mark E. Stout, Jessica M. Huckabey, and John R. Schindler, *The Terrorist Perspectives Project: Strategic and Operational Views of Al Qaida and Associated Movements* (Annapolis, MD: Naval Institute, 2008), 11–12, 90–92.

CONCLUSION

1. See Philippe Migaux, "Al Qaeda," in *The History of Terrorism: From Antiquity to Al Quaeda*, ed. Gérard Chaliand and Arnaud Blin (Berkeley: University of California Press, 2007), 314–48.

2. See Lisa Stampnitzky, *Disciplining Terror: How Experts Invented "Terrorism"* (Cambridge: Cambridge University Press, 2013), 144–45.

3. George W. Bush, military order, "Detention, Treatment, and Trial of Certain Non-Citizens in the War Against Terrorism," November 13, 2001, *President George W. Bush White House*, accessed November 25, 2019, https://georgewbush-whitehouse.archives.gov/news/releases/2001/11/print/20011113-27.html.

4. Ben Saul, "Terrorism as a Transnational Crime," in *Routledge Handbook of Transnational Criminal Law*, ed. Neil Boister and Robert Currie (New York: Routledge, 2015), 394–408.

BIBLIOGRAPHY

PRIMARY SOURCES

Archives

GERMANY

Archive of Social Democracy, Friedrich Ebert Foundation, Bad Godesberg
    Hans-Jürgen Wischnewski Papers
Federal Archives, Koblenz
    B106: Records of the Ministry of the Interior
    B108: Records of the Ministry of Transportation
    B136: Records of the Chancellery
    B140: Records of the Ministry of Justice
Political Archive of the Foreign Office, Berlin
    AVNA: Federal Republic of Germany: Records of the Diplomatic Missions
    B82: Federal Republic of Germany: Constitutional and Administrative Law
    B83: Federal Republic of Germany: Criminal, Tax, and Customs Law
    B150: Federal Republic of Germany: Records of the *Akten zur Auswärtigen Politik
    der Bundesrepublik Deutschland*
    ZA: Federal Republic of Germany: Temporary Archives

UNITED KINGDOM

The National Archives, Kew, Richmond, Surrey
    Records of the Board of Trade and of Successor and Related Bodies
    Records of the Cabinet Office

Records of the Ministry of Defense
Records of the Foreign and Commonwealth Office and Predecessors
Records Created or Inherited by the Home Office, Ministry of Home Security, and
Related Bodies
Records of the Prime Minister's Office

UNITED STATES

Archives of Labor and Urban Affairs, Walter P. Reuther Library, Wayne State University,
Detroit, Michigan
Air Line Pilots Association Collection
Central Intelligence Agency Freedom of Information Act Electronic Reading Room,
Washington, DC
Argentina Declassification Project—The "Dirty War" (1976–1983)
FOIA Collection
General CIA Records
Library of Congress
National Intelligence Council Collection
Digital National Security Archive, Washington, DC
The Soviet Estimate: U.S. Analysis of the Soviet Union, 1947–1991
Terrorism and U.S. Policy, 1968–2002
Gerald Ford Presidential Library, Ann Arbor, Michigan
Judith Hope Files
Bobbie Greene Kilberg Files
White House Central Files
Hoover Institution Archives, Stanford, California
James A. Arey Papers
William J. Casey Papers
Brian Crozier Papers
Robert A. Fearey Papers
Robert H. Kupperman Papers
Claire Sterling Papers
Jimmy Carter Presidential Library, Atlanta, Georgia
Counsel's Office: Robert Lipshutz's Subject File
National Security Adviser's Files: General William Odom's Files
White House Central Files
Library of Congress, Washington, DC
Ray S. Cline Papers
National Archives and Records Administration, College Park, Maryland
Record Group 59: Records of the Department of State
Record Group 237: Records of the Federal Aviation Administration
Nixon Presidential Library, Yorba Linda, California
National Security Council Files Collection
White House Central Files
White House Special Files, Staff Member and Office Files: John Dean Collection

White House Special Files, Staff Member and Office Files: Richard C. Tufaro Collection
White House Special Files, Staff Member and Office Files: David R. Young Collection

Edited Primary Source Collections

Akten zur Auswärtigen Politik der Bundesrepublik Deutschland (Files on the Foreign Relations of the Federal Republic of Germany)
American Presidency Project
Foreign Relations of the United States

Periodicals

Chicago Tribune
Daily Telegraph
Der Spiegel
Die Welt
Die Zeit
Evening Standard
Frankfurter Allgemeine Zeitung
Jewish Telegraph Agency
Libération
Le Monde
Nation
National Review
New York Times
Time
Times of Israel
U.S. News and World Report
Wall Street Journal
Washington Post

SECONDARY SOURCES

Books

Alexander, Martin S., and J. F. V. Keiger, eds. *France and the Algerian War, 1954–62: Strategy, Operations, and Diplomacy.* London: Frank Cass, 2002.
Alexander, Yonah, ed. *International Terrorism: National, Regional, and Global Perspectives.* New York: Prager, 1976.
Anderson, Benedict. *Imagined Communities: Reflection on the Origins and Spread of Nationalism.* Rev. ed. London: Verso, 2006.
Andreas, Peter, and Ethan Nadelmann. *Policing the Globe: Criminalization and Crime Control in International Relations.* New York: Oxford University Press, 2008.

Anziska, Seth. *Preventing Palestine: A Political History from Camp David to Oslo.* Princeton, NJ: Princeton University Press, 2018.

Aust, Stefan. *The Baader-Meinhof Complex.* Rev. ed. London: Bodley Head, 2008.

Auten, Brian J. *Carter's Conversion: The Hardening of American Defense Policy.* Columbia: University of Missouri Press, 2008.

Azani, Eitan. *Hezbollah: The Story of the Party of God.* New York: Palgrave Macmillan, 2009.

Bailey, Beth, and Richard H. Immerman, eds. *Understanding the U.S. Wars in Iraq and Afghanistan.* New York: New York University Press, 2015.

Bakker Schut, Pieter. *Stammheim: Der Prozess gegen die Rote Armee Fraktion.* Kiel, Germany: Neuer Malik, 1986.

Balzacq, Thierry, ed. *Securitization Theory: How Security Problems Emerge and Dissolve.* New York: Routledge, 2010.

Bassiouni, M. Cherif, and Edward Wise. *Aut Dedere Aut Judicare: The Duty to Extradite or Prosecute in International Law.* Dordrecht, The Netherlands: Martinus Nijhoff, 1995.

Bergstermann, Sabine. *Stammheim: Eine Moderne Haftanstalt als Ort der Auseinandersetzung zwischen Staat und RAF.* Oldenbourg, Germany: De Gruyter, 2016.

Bhimull, Chandra D. *Empire in the Air: Airline Travel and the African Diaspora.* New York: New York University Press, 2017.

Bjørgo, Tore, ed. *Root Causes of Terrorism: Myths, Reality, and Ways Forward.* London: Routledge, 2005.

Blumenau, Bernhard. *The United Nations and Terrorism: Germany, Multilateralism, and Antiterrorism Efforts in the 1970s.* Basingstoke, UK: Palgrave Macmillan, 2014.

Boister, Neil, and Robert Currie, eds. *Routledge Handbook of Transnational Criminal Law.* New York: Routledge, 2015.

Borstelmann, Thomas. *The 1970s: A New Global History from Civil Rights to Economic Inequality.* Princeton, NJ: Princeton University Press, 2012.

Boshoff, Henri, Anneli Botha, and Martin Schönteich. *Fear in the City: Urban Terrorism in South Africa.* Pretoria: Institute for Security Studies, 2001.

Bossong, Raphael. *The Evolution of EU Counter-Terrorism: European Security Policy After 9/11.* London: Routledge, 2012.

Bozo, Frédéric. *French Foreign Policy Since 1945: An Introduction.* New York: Berghahn, 2016.

Brands, Hal. *Latin America's Cold War.* Cambridge, MA: Harvard University Press, 2012.

Brennan, Ann Marie. *Transnational Terrorist Groups and International Criminal Law.* New York: Routledge, 2019.

Brighton, Mark Andrew. *The Sicarii in Josephus' Judean War: Rhetorical Analysis and Historical Observations.* Atlanta: Society of Biblical Literature, 2009.

Brown, Robert. *Nuclear Authority: The IAEA and the Absolute Weapon.* Washington, DC: Georgetown University Press, 2015.

Burke, Kyle. *Revolutionaries for the Right: Anticommunist Internationalism and Paramilitary Warfare in the Cold War.* Chapel Hill: University of North Carolina Press, 2018.

Burke, Roland. *Decolonization and the Evolution of International Human Rights.* Philadelphia: University of Pennsylvania Press, 2010.

Burleigh, Michael. *Blood and Rage: A Cultural History of Terrorism.* New York: Harper, 2009.

Burrough, Bryan. *Days of Rage: America's Radical Underground, the FBI, and the Forgotten Age of Revolutionary Violence*. New York: Penguin, 2015.

Buzan, Barry, Ole Waever, and Jaap de Wilde. *Security: A New Framework for Analysis*. London: Lynne Rienner, 1998.

Byrne, Jeffrey James. *Mecca of Revolution: Algeria, Decolonization, and the Third World Order*. Oxford: Oxford University Press, 2016.

Chaliand, Gérard, and Arnaud Blin, eds. *The History of Terrorism: From Antiquity to Al Qaeda*. Berkeley: University of California Press, 2007.

Chalk, Peter. *Western European Terrorism and Counter-Terrorism: The Evolving Dynamic*. New York: St. Martin's, 1996.

Chamberlin, Paul T. *The Global Offensive: The United States, the Palestine Liberation Organization, and the Making of the Post-Cold War Order*. New York: Oxford University Press, 2012.

Charters, David A. *The Deadly Sin of Terrorism: Its Effect on Democracy and Civil Liberty in Six Countries*. Westport, CT: Greenwood, 1994.

Choisel, Francis. *Comprendre le Gaullisme: A Propos de Quelques Contresens sur la Pensée et l'Action du Général de Gaulle*. Paris: Harmattan, 2016.

Christopher, Warren, and Paul H. Kreisberg, eds. *American Hostages in Iran*. New Haven, CT: Yale University Press, 1985.

Churchill, Lindsey. *Becoming the Tupamaros: Solidarity and Transnational Revolutionaries in Uruguay and the United States*. Nashville, TN: Vanderbilt University Press, 2014.

Clark, Nancy L., and William H. Worger. *South Africa: The Rise and Fall of Apartheid*. 2nd ed. New York: Routledge, 2011.

Coleman, Marie. *The Irish Revolution, 1916–1923*. Abingdon, UK: Routledge, 2014.

Connelly, Matthew. *A Diplomatic Revolution: Algeria's Fight for Independence and the Origins of the Post-Cold War Era*. Oxford: Oxford University Press, 2002.

Conze, Eckart. *Die Suche nach Sicherheit: Eine Geschichte der Bundesrepublik Deutschland von 1949 bis in die Gegenwart*. Munich: Siedler, 2009.

Costigliola, Frank and Michael J. Hogan, eds. *Explaining the History of American Foreign Relations*. 3rd ed. New York: Cambridge University Press, 2016.

Crelinsten, Ronald. *Counterterrorism*. Cambridge: Polity, 2009.

Crenshaw, Martha, ed. *The Consequences of Counterterrorism*. New York: Russell Sage Foundation, 2010.

——. *Terrorism and International Cooperation*. New York: Routledge, 1989.

Crenshaw, Martha, and Gary LaFree. *Countering Terrorism*. Washington, DC: Brookings Institution, 2017.

Crozier, Brian. *Strategy of Survival*. New York: Arlington House, 1978.

Dahlke, Matthias. *Der Anschlag auf Olympia '72: Die Politischen Reaktionen auf den Internationalen Terrorismus in Deutschland*. Munich: M Press, Martin Meidenbauer, 2006.

——. *Demokratischer Staat und Transnationaler Terrorismus: Drei Wege zur Unnachgiebigkeit in Westeuropa 1972–1975*. Munich: Oldenbourg, 2011.

Daigle, Craig. *The Limits of Detente: The United States, the Soviet Union, and the Arab-Israeli Conflict*. New Haven, CT: Yale University Press, 2012.

Dartnell, Michael York. *Action Directe: Ultra-Left Terrorism in France, 1979–1987*. Portland, OR: Frank Cass, 1995.

David, Saul. *Operation Thunderbolt: Flight 139 and the Raid on Entebbe Airport, the Most Audacious Hostage Rescue Mission in History.* New York: Little, Brown, 2015.

Deflem, Mathieu. *Policing World Society: Historical Foundations of International Police Cooperation.* New York: Oxford University Press, 2002.

Della Porta, Donatella. *Social Movements, Political Violence, and the State: A Comparative Analysis of Germany and Italy.* Cambridge: Cambridge University Press, 1995.

Dietrich, Christopher R. W. *Oil Revolution: Anticolonial Elites, Sovereign Rights, and the Economic Culture of Decolonization.* Cambridge: Cambridge University Press, 2017.

Ditrych, Ondrej. *Tracing the Discourses of Terrorism: Identity, Genealogy and State.* Central and Eastern European perspectives on international relations series. Basingstoke, UK: Palgrave MacMillan, 2014.

Dowty, Alan. *Israel/Palestine.* 3rd ed. Cambridge: Polity, 2012.

Eckstein, Harry, ed. *Internal War: Problems and Approaches.* New York: The Free Press of Glencoe, 1964.

Eder, Franz, and Martin Senn, eds. *Europe and Transnational Terrorism: Assessing Threats and Countermeasures.* Baden-Baden, Germany: Nomos, 2009.

Engel, Jeffrey. *Cold War at 30,000 Feet: The Anglo-American Fight for Aviation Supremacy.* Cambridge, MA: Harvard University Press, 2007.

English, Richard. *Irish Freedom: The History of Nationalism in Ireland.* Basingstoke, UK: Pan MacMillan, 2007.

Evangelista, Matthew and Nina Tannenwald, eds. *Do the Geneva Conventions Matter?* New York: Oxford University Press, 2017.

Evans, Martin. *Algeria: France's Undeclared War.* New York: Oxford University Press, 2012.

Elgindy, Khaled. *Blind Spot: America and the Palestinians, from Balfour to Trump.* Washington, DC: Brookings Institution, 2019.

Farber, David R. *The Rise and Fall of Modern American Conservatism: A Short History.* Princeton, NJ: Princeton University Press, 2010.

——. *Taken Hostage: The Iran Hostage Crisis and America's First Encounter with Radical Islam.* Princeton, NJ: Princeton University Press, 2005.

Ferguson, Niall, Charles S. Maier, Erez Manela, and Daniel J. Sargent, eds. *The Shock of the Global: The 1970s in Perspective.* Cambridge, MA: Belknap Press of Harvard University Press, 2010.

Finchelstein, Federico. *The Ideological Origins of the Dirty War: Fascism, Populism, and Dictatorship in Twentieth Century Argentina.* New York: Oxford University Press, 2014.

Flamm, Michael W. *Law and Order: Street Crime, Civil Unrest, and the Crisis of Liberalism in the 1960s.* New York: Columbia University Press, 2005.

French, David. *The British Way in Counter-Insurgency, 1945–1967.* New York: Oxford University Press, 2012.

Gage, Beverly. *The Day Wall Street Exploded: A Story of America in Its First Age of Terror.* New York: Oxford University Press, 2009.

Gaïduk, I. V. *Divided Together: The United States and the Soviet Union in the United Nations, 1945–1965.* Stanford, CA: Stanford University Press, 2012.

Galula, David. *Pacification in Algeria: 1956–1958.* New introduction by Bruce Hoffman. Santa Monica, CA: RAND Corporation, 2006.

Geifman, Anna. *Thou Shalt Kill: Revolutionary Terrorism in Russia, 1894–1917.* Princeton, NJ: Princeton University Press, 1993.

Germond, Basil, Jussi M. Hanhimäki, and Georges-Henri Soutou, eds. *The Routledge Handbook of Transatlantic Security*. New York: Routledge, 2010.

Glad, Betty. *An Outsider in the White House: Jimmy Carter, His Advisors, and the Making of American Foreign Policy*. Ithaca, NY: Cornell University Press, 2009.

Gleijeses, Piero. *Visions of Freedom: Havana, Washington, Pretoria, and the Struggle for Southern Africa, 1976–1991*. Chapel Hill: University of North Carolina Press, 2013.

Grandin, Greg. *The Last Colonial Massacre: Latin America in the Cold War*. 2nd ed. Chicago: University of Chicago Press, 2011.

Grandin, Greg, and Gilbert Joseph, eds. *A Century of Revolution: Insurgent and Counterinsurgent Violence During Latin America's Long Cold War*. Durham, NC: Duke University Press, 2010.

Grimm, Dieter. *Sovereignty: The Origin and Future of a Political and Legal Concept*. Trans. Belinda Cooper. New York: Columbia University Press, 2015.

Grob-Fitzgibbon, Benjamin. *Continental Drift: Britain and Europe from the End of Empire to the Rise of Euroscepticism*. Cambridge: Cambridge University Press, 2016.

Hanhimäki, Jussi M., and Bernhard Blumenau, eds. *An International History of Terrorism: Western and Non-Western Experiences*. London: Routledge, 2013.

Hanshew, Karrin. *Terror and Democracy in West Germany*. New York: Cambridge University Press, 2012.

Hellmuth, Dorle. *Counterterrorism and the State: A Comparative Analysis of European and American Responses to 9/11*. Philadelphia: University of Pennsylvania Press, 2016.

Herf, Jeffrey. *Undeclared Wars with Israel: East Germany and the West German Far Left 1967–1989*. New York: Cambridge University Press, 2016.

Herman, Edward S., and Gerry O'Sullivan. *The "Terrorism" Industry: The Experts and Institutions That Shape Our View of Terror*. New York: Pantheon, 1989.

Hirst, David. *The Gun and the Olive Branch: The Roots of Violence in the Middle East*. 3rd ed. London: Nation, 2003.

Hof, Tobias. *Staat und Terrorismus in Italien 1969–1982*. Oldenbourg, Germany: De Gruyter, 2011.

Hoffman, Bruce. *Inside Terrorism*. 3rd ed. New York: Columbia University Press, 2017.

Holland, Robert, ed. *Emergencies and Disorder in the European Empires After 1945*. London: Routledge, 2012.

Horchem, Hans-Josef. *Right-Wing Extremism in Western Germany*. London: Institute for the Study of Conflict, 1975.

——. *West Germany's Red Army Anarchists*. London: Institute for the Study of Conflict, 1974.

Hürter, Johannes, ed. *Terrorismusbekämpfung in Westeuropa: Demokratie und Sicherheit in den 1970er und 1980er Jahren*. Oldenbourg, Germany: De Gruyter, 2015.

Hürter, Johannes, and Gian Enrico Rusconi. *Die bleiernen Jahre: Staat und Terrorismus in der Bundesrepublik Deutschland und Italien, 1962–1982*. Munich: R. Oldenbourg, 2010.

Immerman, Richard. *The Hidden Hand: A Brief History of the CIA*. Chichester, UK: Wiley-Blackwell, 2014.

International Atomic Energy Agency. *The International Legal Framework for Nuclear Security*. Vienna: IAEA, 2011.

Iriye, Akira. *Global Community: The Role of International Organizations in the Making of the Contemporary World*. Berkeley: University of California Press, 2002.

——, ed. *Global Interdependence: The World After 1945*. Cambridge, MA: Belknap Press of Harvard University Press, 2014.

Iriye, Akira, Petra Goedde, and William I. Hitchcock, eds. *The Human Rights Revolution: An International History*. Oxford, New York: Oxford University Press, 2012.

Irwin, Ryan. *Gordian Knot: Apartheid and the Unmaking of the Liberal World Order*. Oxford: Oxford University Press, 2012.

Jackson, Richard, ed. *The Routledge Handbook of Critical Terrorism Studies*. New York: Routledge, 2016.

Jackson, Robert. *Sovereignty: The Evolution of an Idea*. Cambridge, MA: Polity, 2007.

Jarausch, Konrad. *After Hitler: Recivilizing Germans, 1945–1995*. Oxford: Oxford University Press, 2006.

Jenkins, Brian M. *Embassies Under Siege: A Review of 48 Embassy Takeovers, 1971–1980*. Santa Monica, CA: RAND Corporation, 1981.

——. *International Terrorism: A New Kind of Warfare*. Santa Monica, CA: RAND Corporation, 1974. https://www.rand.org/content/dam/rand/pubs/papers/2008/P5261.pdf.

——. *International Terrorism: Choosing the Right Target*. Santa Monica, CA: RAND Corporation, 1981. Accessed August 12, 2019. https://www.rand.org/pubs/papers/P6597.html.

Jensehaugen, Jørgen. *Arab-Israeli Diplomacy Under Carter: The U.S., Israel, and the Palestinians*. New York: I. B. Tauris, 2018.

Jensen, Richard Bach. *The Battle Against Anarchist Terrorism: An International History, 1878–1934*. Cambridge: Cambridge University Press, 2014.

Jensen, Steven L. B. *The Making of International Human Rights: The 1960s, Decolonization, and the Reconstruction of Global Values*. Cambridge: Cambridge University Press, 2016.

Johns, Andy, and Mitch Lerner, eds. *The Cold War at Home and Abroad: Domestic Politics and US Foreign Policy since 1945*. Lexington: University of Kentucky Press, 2018.

Kalman, Laura. *Right Star Rising: A New Politics, 1974–1980*. New York: W. W. Norton, 2010.

Kaufman, Scott. *Plans Unraveled: The Foreign Policy of the Carter Administration*. DeKalb: Northern Illinois University Press, 2008.

Khalidi, Rashid. *The Iron Cage: The Story of the Palestinian Struggle for Statehood*. Boston: Beacon, 2006.

Kittichaisaree, Kriangsak. *The Obligation to Extradite or Prosecute*. New York: Oxford University Press, 2018.

Klimke, Martin. *The Other Alliance: Student Protest in West Germany and the United States in the Global Sixties*. Princeton, NJ: Princeton University Press, 2010.

Klose, Fabian. *Human Rights in the Shadow of Colonial Violence: The Wars of Independence in Kenya and Algeria*. Trans. Dona Geyer. Philadelphia: University of Pennsylvania Press, 2013.

Krasner, Stephen, ed. *International Regimes*. Ithaca, NY: Cornell University Press, 1983.

Kraushaar, Wolfgang, ed. *Die RAF: Entmythologisierung einer Terroristischen Organisation*. Bonn: Bundeszentrale für Politische Bildung, 2008.

——, ed. *Die RAF und der linke Terrorismus*. 2 vols. Hamburg: Hamburger Editionen, 2006.

Krieken, Peter J. van. *Terrorism and the International Legal Order: With Special Reference to the UN, the EU and Cross-Border Aspects*. The Hague: T. M. C. Asser, 2002.

Ladd, James D. *SAS Operations*. London: Robert Hale, 1986.

Lambert, Joseph J. *Terrorism and Hostages in International Law: A Commentary on the Hostages Convention 1979*. Cambridge: Grotius, 1990.

Lammert, Markus. *Der Neue Terrorismus: Terrorismusbekämpfung in Frankreich in den 1980er Jahren*. Oldenbourg, Germany: De Gruyter, 2017.

Laqueur, Walter. *A History of Terrorism*. Rev. ed. New Brunswick, NJ: Transaction, 2001.

——. *The New Terrorism: Fanaticism and the Arms of Mass Destruction*. New York: Oxford University Press, 2000.

——. *Terrorism*. Boston: Little, Brown, 1977.

Large, David C. *Munich 1972: Tragedy, Terror, and Triumph at the Olympic Games*. Lanham, MD: Rowman and Littlefield Publishers, 2012.

Laschi, Giuliana, ed. *The European Community and the World: A Historical Perspective*. Bern, Switzerland: Peter Lang, 2014.

Latner, Teishan. *Cuban Revolution in America: Havana and the Making of a United States Left, 1968–1992*. Chapel Hill: University of North Carolina Press, 2018.

Leffler, Melvyn P., and Odd Arne Westad. *The Cambridge History of the Cold War, Volume II: Crises and Détente*. Cambridge: Cambridge University Press, 2010.

Lemler, Kai. *Die Entwicklung der RAF im Kontext des Internationalen Terrorismus*. Bonn, Germany: Bouvier, 2008.

LeoGrande, William M., and Peter Kornbluh. *Back Channel to Cuba: The Hidden History of Negotiations Between Washington and Havana*. Chapel Hill: University of North Carolina Press, 2015.

Levitt, Matthew. *Hezbollah: The Global Footprint of Lebanon's Party of God*. Washington, DC: Georgetown University Press, 2012.

Liang, His-Huey. *The Rise of the Modern Police and the European State System from Metternich to the Second World War*. New York: Cambridge University Press, 1992.

Loth, Wilfried. *Building Europe: A History of European Unification*. Berlin: De Gruyter Oldenbourg, 2015.

MacKenzie, David. *ICAO: A History of the International Civil Aviation Organization*. Toronto: University of Toronto Press, 2010.

Maier, Charles. *Once Within Borders: Territories of Wealth, Power, and Belonging Since 1500*. Cambridge, MA: Belknap Press of Harvard University Press, 2016.

März, Michael. *Die Machtprobe 1975: Wie RAF und Bewegung 2. Juni den Staat Erpressten*. Leipzig, Germany: Forum, 2007.

McAlister, Melani. *Epic Encounters: Culture, Media, and U.S. Interests in the Middle East Since 1945*. Updated ed., with a post-9/11 chapter. Berkeley: University of California Press, 2005.

McClintock, Michael. *Instruments of Statecraft: U.S. Guerilla Warfare, Counter-Insurgency, and Counter-Terrorism, 1940–1990*. New York: Pantheon, 1992.

McGrattan, Cilian. *Northern Ireland: The Politics of Entrenchment*. New York: Palgrave MacMillan, 2010.

McKearney, Tommy. *The Provisional IRA: From Insurrection to Parliament*. New York: Palgrave MacMillan, 2011.

McKenna, Joseph. *Guerrilla Warfare in the Irish War of Independence, 1919–1921*. Jefferson, NC: McFarland and Company, 2011.

Melzer, Patricia. *Death in the Shape of a Young Girl: Women's Political Violence in the Red Army Faction*. New York: New York University Press, 2015.

Milde, Michael. *International Air Law and ICAO*. 2nd ed. Gravenhage, The Netherlands: Eleven International Publishing, 2012.

Miller, Martin A. *The Foundations of Modern Terrorism: State, Society, and the Dynamics of Political Violence*. Cambridge: Cambridge University Press, 2013.

Milward, Alan S. *The European Rescue of the Nation-State*. 2nd ed. London: Routledge, 2000.

Mockli, Daniel. *European Foreign Policy During the Cold War: Heath, Brandt, Pompidou and the Dream of Political Unity*. London: I. B. Tauris, 2008.

Morris, Benny. *Righteous Victims: A History of the Zionist-Arab Conflict, 1881–1999*. New York: Knopf, 1999.

Moss, Richard. *Nixon's Back Channel to Moscow: Confidential Diplomacy and Détente*. Lexington University Press of Kentucky, 2017.

Moyn, Samuel. *The Last Utopia: Human Rights in History*. Cambridge, MA: Belknap Press of Harvard University Press, 2010.

——. *Not Enough: Human Rights in an Unequal World*. Cambridge, MA: Belknap Press of Harvard University Press, 2018.

Mueller, John, and Mark G. Stewart. *Chasing Ghosts: The Policing of Terrorism*. New York: Oxford University Press, 2016.

Murphy, John S. *State Support of International Terrorism: Legal, Political, and Economic Dimensions*. Boulder, CO: Westview, 1989.

Naftali, Timothy J. *Blind Spot: The Secret History of American Counterterrorism*. New York: Basic Books, 2005.

Neillands, Robin. *In the Combat Zone: Special Forces Since 1975*. New York: New York University Press, 1998.

Netanyahu, Benjamin, ed. *International Terrorism: Challenge and Response; Proceedings of the Jerusalem Conference on International Terrorism*. Jerusalem: Jonathan Institute; Transaction, 1981.

——. *International Terrorism: The Soviet Connection*. Jerusalem: Jonathan Institute, 1979.

——. *Terrorism: How the West Can Win*. New York: Farrar, Straus and Giroux, 1986.

Netanyahu, Benjamin, and Paul Johnson. *The Jerusalem Conference on International Terrorism*. Jerusalem: Jonathan Institute, 1979.

Newsinger, John. *British Counterinsurgency: From Palestine to Northern Ireland*. Basingstoke, UK: Palgrave MacMillan, 2016.

Nguyen, Lien-Hang T. *Hanoi's War: An International History of the War for Peace in Vietnam*. Chapel Hill: University of North Carolina Press, 2012.

Oberloskamp, Eva. *Codename TREVI: Terrorismusbekämpfung und die Anfänge einer europäischen Innenpolitik in den 1970er Jahren*. Oldenbourg, Germany: De Gruyter, 2017.

O'Neill, Bard E. *Insurgency & Terrorism: Inside Modern Revolutionary Warfare*. Washington, DC: Brassey's (US), 1990.

Pagès, Meriem. *From Martyr to Murderer: Representations of the Assassins in Twelfth- and Thirteenth-Century Europe*. Syracuse, NY: Syracuse University Press, 2014.

Passmore, Leith. *Ulrike Meinhof and the Red Army Faction: Performing Terrorism*. Basingstoke, UK: Palgrave MacMillan, 2011.

Patyk, Lynn. *Written in Blood: Revolutionary Terrorism and Russian Literary Culture, 1861–1881*. Madison: University of Wisconsin Press, 2017.

Pedahzur, Ami. *The Israeli Secret Services and the Struggle Against Terrorism*. New York: Columbia University Press, 2009.

Philpott, Daniel. *Revolutions in Sovereignty: How Ideas Shaped Modern International Relations*. Princeton, NJ: Princeton University Press. 2001.

Plummer, Brenda Gayle. *In Search of Power: African Americans in the Era of Decolonization, 1956–1974*. Cambridge: Cambridge University Press, 2013.

Porch, Douglas. *Counterinsurgency: Exposing the Myths of the New Way of War*. Cambridge: Cambridge University Press, 2013.

Przetacznik, Franciszek. *Protection of Officials of Foreign States According to International Law*. Boston: Martinus Nijhoff Publishers, 1983.

Pyle, Christopher H. *Extradition, Politics, and Human Rights*. Philadelphia: Temple University Press, 2001.

Reydams, Luc. *Universal Jurisdiction: International and Municipal Legal Perspectives*. Oxford: Oxford University Press, 2003.

Rabe, Stephen G. *The Killing Zone: The United States Wages Cold War in Latin America*. New York: Oxford University Press, 2012.

Rabert, Bernhard. *Links- und Rechtsterrorismus in der BRD von 1970 bis Heute*. Bonn, Germany: Bernard and Graefe, 1995.

Rapoport, David C., ed. *Terrorism: Critical Concepts in Political Science*. 4 vols. London: Routledge, 2006.

Rauh, Cornelia, and Dirk Schumann, eds. *Ausnahmezustände: Entgrenzungen und Regulierungen in Europa während des Kalten Krieges*. Göttingen, Germany: Wallstein, 2015.

Richards, Anthony. *Conceptualizing Terrorism*. Oxford: Oxford University Press, 2015.

Richardson, Louise. *What Terrorists Want: Understanding the Enemy, Containing the Threat*. New York: Random House, 2006.

Romaniuk, Peter. *Multilateral Counter-Terrorism: The Global Politics of Cooperation and Contestation*. London: Routledge, 2010.

Rote Armee Fraktion: Texte und Materialien zur Geschichte der RAF. Berlin: ID Verlag, 1997.

Royer, Aline. *Der Europarat*. Strasbourg: Council of Europe Publishing, 2010.

Ruggie, John Gerald, ed. *Multilateralism Matters: The Theory and Praxis of an Institutional Form*. New York: Columbia University Press, 1993.

Sageman, Marc. *Misunderstanding Terrorism*. Philadelphia: University of Pennsylvania Press, 2016.

Sanders, Andrew. *Inside the IRA: Dissident Republicans and the War for Legitimacy*. Edinburgh: Edinburgh University Press, 2011.

Sargent, Daniel J. *A Superpower Transformed: The Remaking of American Foreign Relations in the 1970s*. New York: Oxford University Press, 2015.

Saul, Ben. *Defining Terrorism in International Law*. Oxford: Oxford University Press, 2006.

Sayle, Timothy Andrews. *Enduring Alliance: A History of NATO and the Postwar Global Order*. Ithaca, NY: Cornell University Press, 2019.

Scheiper, Stephan. *Innere Sicherheit: Politische Anti-Terror-Konzepte in der Bundesrepublik Deutschland während der 1970er Jahre*. Paderborn, Germany: Ferdinand Schönign, 2010.

Schiller, Kay, and Christopher Young. *The 1972 Munich Olympics and the Making of Modern Germany*. Berkeley: University of California Press, 2010.

Schmahl, Stefanie, and Marten Breuer, eds. *The Council of Europe: Its Law and Policies*. New York: Oxford University Press, 2017.

Schmid, Alex P., ed. *The Routledge Handbook of Terrorism Research*. London: Routledge, 2011.

Schmidli, William Michael. *The Fate of Freedom Elsewhere: Human Rights and U.S. Cold War Policy Toward Argentina*. Ithaca, NY: Cornell University Press, 2013.

Schoultz, Lars. *That Infernal Little Cuban Republic: The United States and the Cuban Revolution*. Chapel Hill: University of North Carolina Press, 2009.

——. *In Their Own Best Interest: A History of the U.S. Effort to Improve Latin Americans*. Cambridge, MA: Harvard University Press, 2018.

Schrader, Stuart. *Badges Without Borders: How Global Counterinsurgency Transformed American Policing*. Oakland: University of California Press, 2019.

Silke, Andrew, ed. *The Routledge Handbook of Terrorism and Counterterrorism*. London: Routledge, 2018.

Slaughter, Anne-Marie. *A New World Order*. Princeton, NJ: Princeton University Press, 2004.

Snyder, Sarah B. *Human Rights Activism and the End of the Cold War: A Transnational History of the Helsinki Network*. New York: Cambridge University Press, 2011.

Spernol, Boris. *Notstand der Demokratie. Der Protest gegen die Notstandsgesetze und die Frage der NS-Vergangenheit*. Essen, Germany: Klartext, 2008.

Stampnitzky, Lisa. *Disciplining Terror: How Experts Invented 'Terrorism'*. Cambridge: Cambridge University Press, 2013.

Stein, Judith. *Pivotal Decade: How the United States Traded Factories for Finance in the Seventies*. New Haven, CT: Yale University Press, 2010.

Sterling, Claire. *The Terror Network: The Secret War of International Terrorism*. New York: Holt, Rinehart, and Winston, 1981.

Stout, Mark E., Jessica M. Huckabey, and John R. Schindler. *The Terrorist Perspectives Project: Strategic and Operational Views of Al Qaida and Associated Movements*. Annapolis, MD: Naval Institute, 2008.

Suri, Jeremi. *Power and Protest: Global Revolution and the Rise of Detente*. Cambridge, MA: Harvard University Press, 2003.

Taillon, J. Paul de B. *The Evolution of Special Forces in Counter-Terrorism: The British and American Experiences*. Westport, CT: Praeger, 2000.

Tellidis, Ioannis and Harmonie Toros, eds. *Researching Terrorism, Peace and Conflict Studies: Interaction, Synthesis, and Opposition*. New York: Routledge, 2015.

Thompson, Janice E. *Mercenaries, Pirates, and Sovereigns: State-Building and Extraterritorial Violence in Early Modern Europe*. Princeton, NJ: Princeton University Press, 1994.

Thorup, Mikkel. *An Intellectual History of Terror: War, Violence and the State*. London: Routledge, 2012.

Toaldo, Mattia. *The Origins of the US War on Terror: Lebanon, Libya and American Intervention in the Middle East*. New York: Routledge, 2012.

Travis, Philip. *Reagan's War on Terrorism in Nicaragua: The Outlaw State*. Lanham, MD: Lexington, 2017.

Tucker, David, and Christopher J. Lamb. *United States Special Operations Forces*. New York: Columbia University Press, 2007.

319

BIBLIOGRAPHY

Tyroler, Charles. *Alerting America: The Papers of the Committee on the Present Danger.* Washington, DC: Pergamon-Brassey's, 1984.

Unterman, Katherine. *Uncle Sam's Policemen: The Pursuit of Fugitives across Borders.* Cambridge, MA: Harvard University Press, 2015.

Van Vleck, Jenifer. *Empire of the Air: Aviation and the American Ascendancy.* Cambridge, MA: Harvard University Press, 2013.

Varon, Jeremy. *Bringing the War Home: The Weather Underground, the Red Army Faction, and Revolutionary Violence in the Sixties and Seventies.* Berkeley: University of California Press, 2004.

Verhoeven, Claudia. *The Odd Man Karakozov: Imperial Russia, Modernity, and the Birth of Terrorism.* Ithaca, NY: Cornell University Press, 2009.

Vowinckel, Annette. *Flugzeugentführungen: Eine Kulturgeschichte.* Göttingen, Germany: Wallstein, 2011.

Waldmann, Peter. *Terrorismus: Provokation der Macht.* 2nd ed. Hamburg, Germany: Murmann, 2005.

Wawro, Geoffrey. *Quicksand: America's Pursuit of Power in the Middle East.* New York: Penguin, 2010.

Weiss, Thomas G. and Rorden Wilkinson, eds. *International Organization and Global Governance: What Matters and Why.* London: Routledge, 2014.

Wilkinson, Paul. *Political Terrorism.* New York: Halsted, 1974.

Wills, David C. *The First War on Terrorism: Counter-Terrorism Policy During the Reagan Administration.* Lanham, MD: Rowman and Littlefield, 2003.

Wilson, Ray, and Ian Adams. *Special Branch: A History: 1883–2006.* London: Biteback 2015.

Wischnewski, Hans-Jürgen. *Mit Leidenschaft und Augenmass: In Mogadischu und Anderswo, Politische Memoiren.* Munich: C. Bertelsmann, 1989.

Woodward, Bob. *Veil: The Secret Wars of the CIA.* New York: Simon & Schuster, 1987.

Yaqub, Salim. *Imperfect Strangers: Americans, Arabs, and US Middle East Relations in the 1970s.* Ithaca, NY: Cornell University Press, 2016.

Zimmermann, Doron, and Andreas Wenger, eds. *How States Fight Terrorism: Policy Dynamics in the West.* Boulder, CO: Lynne Rienner, 2007.

Articles, Book Chapters, et al.

Abeyratne, Ruwantissa I. "Attempts at Ensuring Peace and Security in International Aviation." *Transportation Law Journal* 24, no. 1 (Fall 1996): 27–72.

Arendt, Hannah. "Ideology and Terror: A Novel Form of Government." *Review of Politics* 15, no. 3 (July 1953): 303–27.

Bakić, Dragan. "Apis's Men: The Black Hand Conspirators After the Great War." *Balcanica* 46 (2015): 219–39. doi:10.2298/balc1546219b.

Balzacq, Thierry. "The Three Faces of Securitization: Political Agency, Audience, and Context." *European Journal of International Relations* 11, no. 2 (June 2005): 171–201.

Barton, Mary S. "The British Empire and International Terrorism: India's Separate Path at the League of Nations, 1934–1937." *Journal of British Studies* 56, no. 2 (April 2017): 351–73.

——. "The Global War on Anarchism: The United States and International Anarchist Terrorism, 1898–1904." *Diplomatic History* 39, no. 2 (April 2015): 303–30.

Barton, Mary S., and David Wright, "The United States and International Terrorism." In *Oxford Research Encyclopedia of American History*, ed. Mark Lawrence. June 25, 2019. Accessed October 3, 2019, https://oxfordre.com/americanhistory/view/10.1093/acrefore/9780199329175.001.0001/acrefore-9780199329175-e-743.

Ben-Ari, Mordecai. "Protecting the Airways." In *International Terrorism: Challenge and Response; Proceedings of the Jerusalem Conference on International Terrorism*, ed. Benjamin Netanyahu, 289–93. Jerusalem: Jonathan Institute, 1981.

Blakesley, Christopher L. "The Practice of Extradition from Antiquity to Modern France and the United States: A Brief History." *Boston College International and Comparative Law Review* 4, no. 1 (Spring 1981): 39–60.

Blumenau, Bernhard. "The European Communities' Pyrrhic Victory: European Integration, Terrorism, and the Dublin Agreement of 1979." *Studies in Conflict & Terrorism* 37, no. 5 (May 2014): 405–21.

——. "The Group of 7 and International Terrorism: The Snowball Effect That Never Materialized." *Journal of Contemporary History* 51, no. 2 (April 2016): 316–34.

——. "The Other Battleground of the Cold War: The UN and the Struggle Against International Terrorism in the 1970s." *Journal of Cold War Studies* 16, no. 1 (Winter 2014): 61–84.

——. "Taming the Beast: West Germany, the Political Offence Exception and the Council of Europe Convention on the Suppression of Terrorism." *Terrorism and Political Violence* 27, no. 2 (March 2015): 310–30.

——. "Unholy Alliance: The Connection Between the East German Stasi and the Right-Wing Terrorist Odfried Hepp." *Studies in Conflict and Terrorism* 43, no. 1 (January 2020): 47–68.

Bozo, Frédéric. "France, Gaullism, and the Cold War." In *The Cambridge History of the Cold War, Volume II: Crises and Détente*, ed. Melvyn P. Leffler and Odd Arne Westad, 158–78. Cambridge: Cambridge University Press, 2010.

Boyle, Robert. "Recent Developments in Aerial Hijacking: The Role of International Negotiation." *Akron Law Review* 6, no. 2 (Spring 1973): 153–56.

Branick, Margaret I. "Extradition and the Conflict in Northern Ireland: The Past, Present and Future of an Intractable Problem." *Hastings International and Comparative Law Review* 25 (2002): 169–98.

Brasse, Marc, and Florian Huber, dir. *Vom Traum zum Terror—München 72*. Documentary. CITY: Spiegel TV, 2012.

Bush, George H. "The U.S. and the Fight Against International Terrorism." In *International Terrorism: Challenge and Response; Proceedings of the Jerusalem Conference on International Terrorism*, ed. Benjamin Netanyahu, 332–37. Jerusalem: Jonathan Institute, 1981.

Bush, George W. "Detention, Treatment, and Trial of Certain Non-Citizens in the War Against Terrorism." *President George W. Bush White House*. Published November 13, 2001. Accessed November 25, 2019. https://georgewbush-whitehouse.archives.gov/news/releases/2001/11/print/20011113-27.html.

Carbonneau, Thomas E. "The Provisional Arrest and Subsequent Release of Abu Daoud by French Authorities." *Virginia Journal of International Law* 17, no. 3 (Spring 1977): 495–513.

Cassese, Antonio. "The Multifaceted Criminal Notion of Terrorism in International Law." *Journal of International Criminal Justice* 4, no. 5 (November 2006): 933–58.

Chalfont, Alan. "Our Main Problem: The Climate of Appeasement." In *International Terrorism: Challenge and Response; Proceedings of the Jerusalem Conference on International Terrorism*, ed. Benjamin Netanyahu, 79–89. Jerusalem: Jonathan Institute, 1981.

Chaliand, Gérard, and Arnaud Blin. "From 1968 to Radical Islam." In *The History of Terrorism: From Antiquity to Al Qaeda*, ed. Gérard Chaliand and Arnaud Blin, 208–20. Berkeley: University of California Press, 2007.

——. "Terrorism in Time of War: From World War II to the Wars of National Liberation." In *The History of Terrorism: From Antiquity to Al Qaeda*, ed. Gérard Chaliand and Arnaud Blin, 221–54. Berkeley: University of California Press, 2007.

——. "Zealots and Assassins." In *The History of Terrorism: From Antiquity to Al Qaeda*, ed. Gérard Chaliand and Arnaud Blin, 55–78. Berkeley: University of California Press, 2007.

Cline, Ray. "The Strategic Framework." In *International Terrorism: Challenge and Response; Proceedings of the Jerusalem Conference on International Terrorism*, ed. Benjamin Netanyahu, 90–100. Jerusalem: Jonathan Institute, 1981.

Codification Division Publications. "Diplomatic Conferences." *Codification Division, Office of Legal Affairs, United Nations*. Accessed February 8, 2019. http://legal.un.org /diplomaticconferences/.

Cohen, William. "The Algerian War, the French State and Official Memory." *Réflexions Historiques* 28, no. 2 (Summer 2002): 219–39.

"Convention (IV) relative to the Protection of Civilian Persons in Time of War. Geneva, 12 August 1949." *International Committee of the Red Cross*. Accessed March 19, 2020. https://ihl-databases.icrc.org/applic/ihl/ihl.nsf/c525816bde96b7fd41256739003e636a /72728b6de56c7a68c1 2563cd0051bc40.

Conze, Eckart. "Securitisation: Gegenwartsdiagnose oder historischer Analyseansatz?" *Geschichte und Gesellschaft* 38, no. 3 (January 2013): 453–67.

Council of Europe. "European Convention on Extradition." Council of Europe. Accessed November 25, 2019. https://rm.coe.int/CoERMPublicCommonSearchServices/Displ ayDCTMContent?documentId=090000168006458̈7.

——. "European Convention on the Suppression of Terrorism." Council of Europe, January 1, 1977. Accessed November 25, 2019. https://rm.coe.int/16800771b2.

——. "Recommendation 684 (1972): International Terrorism." Council of Europe. Accessed November 25, 2019. http://assembly.coe.int/nw/xml/XRef/Xref-XML2HTML -en.asp?fileid=14718&lang=en.

Cross, Maïa K. Davis. "Rethinking Epistemic Communities Twenty Years Later." *Review of International Studies* 39, no. 1 (January 2013): 137–60.

Crozier, Brian. "Soviet Support for International Terrorism." In *International Terrorism: Challenge and Response; Proceedings of the Jerusalem Conference on International Terrorism*, ed. Benjamin Netanyahu, 64–72. Jerusalem: Jonathan Institute, 1981.

Daase, Christopher. "Die Historisierung der Sicherheit: Anmerkungen zur historischen Sicherheitsforschung aus politikwissenschaftlicher Sicht." *Geschichte und Gesellschaft* 38, no. 3 (January 2013): 387–405.

——. "Die RAF und der Internationale Terrorismus: Zur Transnationalen Kooperation Klandestiner Organisationen." In *Die RAF: Entmythologisierung einer Terroristischen Organisation*, ed. Wolfgang Kraushaar, 233–69. Bonn, Germany: Bundeszentrale für Politische Bildung, 2008.

Dahlke, Matthias. " 'Nur Eingeschränkte Krisenbereitschaft': Die staatliche Reaktion auf die Entführung des CDU-Politikers Peter Lorenz 1975." *Vierteljahrshefte für Zeitgeschichte* 55, no. 4 (October 2007): 641–78. doi:10.1524/VfZg.2007.55.4.641.

——. "Das Wischnewski-Protokoll: Zur Zusammenarbeit zwischen Westeuropäischen Regierungen und Transnationalen Terroristen 1977." *Vierteljahrshefte für Zeitgeschichte* 57, no. 2 (April 2009): 201–15. doi:10.1524/vfzg.2009.0041.

DeFabo, Vincent. "Terrorist or Revolutionary: The Development of the Political Offender Exception and Its Effects on Defining Terrorism in International Law." *American University National Security Law Brief* 2, no. 2 (Fall 2012): 69–104.

Diewald-Kerkmann, Gisela. "Justiz gegen Terrorismus: Terroristenprozesse in der Bundesrepublik, Italien und Großbritannien." In *Terrorismusbekämpfung in Westeuropa: Demokratie und Sicherheit in den 1970er und 1980er Jahren*, ed. Johannes Hürter, 35–62. Oldenbourg, Germany: De Gruyter, 2015.

——. "Die Rote Armee Fraktion im Original-Ton: Die Tonbandmitschnitte vom Stuttgarter Stammheim-Prozess," *Studies in Contemporary History*, 5 no. 2 (2008): 299–312, http://www.zeithistorische-forschungen.de/16126041-Diewald-Kerkmann-2-2008.

Dugard, John. "International Terrorism: Problems of Definition." *International Affairs* 50, no. 1 (January 1974): 67–81.

Easson, Joseph, and Alex P. Schmid. "Appendix 2.1: 250-plus Academic, Governmental, and Intergovernmental Definitions of Terrorism." In *The Routledge Handbook of Terrorism Research*, ed. Alex P. Schmid, 99–157. London: Routledge, 2011.

Eikel, Markus. "Keine Atempause: Das Krisenmanagement der Bundesregierung und die Flugzeugentführung von Entebbe 1976." *Vierteljahrshefte für Zeitgeschichte* 61, no. 2 (April 2013): 239–61.

Elkins, Michael. "Caging the Beasts." In *International Terrorism: Challenge and Response; Proceedings of the Jerusalem Conference on International Terrorism*, ed. Benjamin Netanyahu, 230–34. Jerusalem: Jonathan Institute, 1981.

Epps, Valerie. "The Development of the Conceptual Framework Supporting International Extradition." *Loyola of Los Angeles International and Comparative Law Review* 25 (2003): 369–88.

Erlenbusch, Verena. "Terrorism and Revolutionary Violence: The Emergence of Terrorism in the French Revolution." *Critical Studies on Terrorism* 8, no. 2 (June 2015): 193–210.

European Commission. "European Arrest Warrant." *European Commission: Policies, Information, and Services.* Accessed June 4, 2019. https://ec.europa.eu/info/law/cross-border-cases/judicial-cooperation/types-judicial-cooperation/european-arrest-warrant_en.

Ferrari, Lorenzo. "How the European Community Entered the United Nations, 1969–1976, and What It Meant for European Political Integration." *Diplomacy & Statecraft* 29 no. 2 (April 2018): 237–54, doi: 10.1080/09592296.2018.1452430.

Fischer, Frank. "Von der 'Regierung der Inneren Reformen' zum 'Krisenmanagement': Das Verhältnis zwischen Innen- und Aussenpolitik in der sozial-liberalen Ära 1969–1982." *Archiv für Sozialgeschichte* 44 (2004): 395–414.

Fischer von Weikersthal, Felicitas. "From Terrorists to Statesmen: Terrorism and Polish Independence." *Studies in Conflict and Terrorism* 43, no. 1 (January 2020): 5–23.

Fraser, Hugh. "The Tyranny of Terrorism." In *International Terrorism: Challenge and Response; Proceedings of the Jerusalem Conference on International Terrorism*, ed. Benjamin Netanyahu, 23–32. Jerusalem: Jonathan Institute, 1981.

G7 Information Centre. "G7/G8 Bibliography: Scholarly Publications." Accessed April 2, 2018. http://www.g8.utoronto.ca/bibliography/biblio1.htm.

Gage, Beverley. "Terrorism and the American Experience: A State of the Field." *Journal of American History* 98, no. 1 (June 2011): 73–94.

Gazit, Shlomo. "The Myth and the Reality of the PLO." In *International Terrorism: Challenge and Response; Proceedings of the Jerusalem Conference on International Terrorism*, ed. Benjamin Netanyahu, 343–49. Jerusalem: Jonathan Institute, 1981.

Geiger, Tim. "Die 'Landshut' in Mogadischu: Das Aussenpolitische Krisenmanagement der Bundesregierung angesichts der Terroristischen Herausforderung 1977." *Vierteljahrshefte für Zeitgeschichte* 57, no. 3 (July 2009): 413–56.

——. "Westliche Anti-Terrorismus-Diplomatie im Nahen Osten." In *Terrorismusbekämpfung in Westeuropa: Demokratie und Sicherheit in den 1970er und 1980er Jahren*, ed. Johannes Hürter, 259–88. Oldenbourg, Germany: De Gruyter, 2015.

Gilbert, Geoff. "The Irish Interpretation of the Political Offense Exception." *International and Comparative Law Quarterly* 41 (January 1992): 66–84.

Global Terrorism Database. National Consortium for the Study of Terrorism and Responses to Terrorism, 2009–2020. Accessed March 18, 2020. https://www.start.umd.edu/gtd/access/.

Graaf, Beatrice de. "Terrorismus als performativer Akt: Die Bundesrepublik, Italien und die Niederlande im Vergleich." In *Terrorismusbekämpfung in Westeuropa: Demokratie und Sicherheit in den 1970er und 1980er Jahren*, ed. Johannes Hürter, 93–116. Oldenbourg, Germany: De Gruyter, 2015.

Groupe d'Intervention de la Gendarmerie Nationale. "Historique." Accessed March 1, 2018. https://www.gendarmerie.interieur.gouv.fr/gign/Historique/Historique.

Guttmann, Aviva. "Combatting Terror in Europe: Euro-Israeli Counterterrorism Intelligence Cooperation in the Club de Berne (1971–1972)." *Intelligence and National Security* 33, no. 2 (Summer 2017): 158–75, doi: 10.1080/02684527.2017.1324591.

Haas, Peter. "Introduction: Epistemic Communities and International Policy Coordination." *International Organization* 46, no. 1 (Winter 1992): 1–35.

Hänni, Adrian. "Global Terror Networks: Die Diskursive Konstruktion der Terroristischen Bedrohung in den USA, 1886–1986." Dissertation, Institute of Social and Economic History, University of Zurich, 2013.

Hof, Tobias. "Anti-Terror-Gesetze und Sicherheitskräfte: Bundesrepublik Deutschland, Italien und Großbritannien in den 1970er und frühen 1980er Jahren." In *Terrorismusbekämpfung in Westeuropa: Demokratie und Sicherheit in den 1970er und 1980er Jahren*, ed. Johannes Hürter, 7–34. Oldenbourg, Germany: De Gruyter, 2015.

——. "The Moro Affair: Left-Wing Terrorism, Conspiracy and Security in Italy in the late 1970s." *Historical Social Research* 38, no. 1 (February 2013): 232–56.

Holden, Robert T. "The Contagiousness of Aircraft Hijacking." *American Journal of Sociology* 91, no. 4 (January 1968): 874–904.

Hürter, Johannes. "Regieren gegen Terrorismus: Die Beispiele Westminster, Bonn und Rom in den 1970er Jahre." In *Terrorismusbekämpfung in Westeuropa: Demokratie und Sicherheit in den 1970er und 1980er Jahren*, ed. Johannes Hürter, 63–80. Oldenbourg, Germany: De Gruyter, 2015.

Hummel, Daniel. "Religious Pluralism, Domestic Politics, and American Evangelical Support for Israel." In *The Cold War at Home and Abroad: Domestic Politics and*

US Foreign Policy since 1945, ed. Andy Johns and Mitch Lerner, 100–18. Lexington: University of Kentucky Press, 2018.

International Civil Aviation Organization. "Convention for the Suppression of Unlawful Acts Against the Safety of Civil Aviation (with Final Act of the International Conference on Air Law held under the Auspices of the International Civil Aviation Organization at Montreal in September 1971). Concluded at Montreal on 23 September 1971." *United Nations Treaty Series* 974, No. I-14118 (1975): 177–248. Accessed February 13, 2020. https://treaties.un.org/doc/Publication/UNTS/Volume%20974/volume -974-I-14118-English.pdf.

——. "Convention for the Suppression of Unlawful Seizure of Aircraft, signed at The Hague on 16 December 1970." *United Nations Treaty Series*, No. 12325 (1973): 106–111. Accessed November 25, 2019. https://treaties.un.org/doc/db/Terrorism/Conv2-english .pdf.

——. "The Convention on International Civil Aviation: Annexes 1 to 18: Annexes 1 to 18." *International Civil Aviation Organization*. Accessed November 25, 2019. http:// www.icao.int/safety/airnavigation/nationalitymarks/annexes_booklet_en.pdf.

——. "Convention on Offences and Certain Other Acts Committed on Board Aircraft, signed at Tokyo on 14 September 1963." *United Nations*. Accessed October 7, 2019. Accessed November 25, 2019. https://treaties.un.org/doc/db/Terrorism/Conv1-english .pdf.

——. "Protocol for the Suppression of Unlawful Acts of Violence at Airports Serving International Civil Aviation, Supplementary to the Convention for the Suppression of Unlawful Acts against the Safety of Civil Aviation, done at Montreal, on 23 September 1971, done at Montreal on 24 February 1988." *ICAO*. Accessed August 14, 2019. https://www.icao.int/secretariat/legal/Administrative%20Packages/via_en.pdf.

International Committee of the Red Cross. "Practice Relating to Rule 96: Hostage-Taking." *International Humanitarian Law Database: Customary International Humanitarian Law*. Accessed April 5, 2018. https://ihl-databases.icrc.org/customary-ihl/eng /docs/v2_rul_rule96.

International Maritime Organization. "Convention for the Suppression of Unlawful Acts Against the Safety of Maritime Navigation, Protocol for the Suppression of Unlawful Acts Against the Safety of Fixed Platforms Located on the Continental Shelf." *International Maritime Organization*. Accessed August 13, 2019. http://www .imo.org/en/About/Conventions/ListOfConventions/Pages/SUA-Treaties.aspx.

"Irish Republican Army (IRA) statement concerning a prisoner in Mountjoy Prison, Dublin (6 September 1971)." *Conflict Archive on the Internet*. Ulster University. Accessed February 20, 2020. https://cain.ulster.ac.uk/othelem/organ/ira/ira060971.htm.

Jackson, Henry M. "Terrorism as a Weapon in International Politics." In *International Terrorism: Challenge and Response; Proceedings of the Jerusalem Conference on International Terrorism*, ed. Benjamin Netanyahu, 33–38. Jerusalem: Jonathan Institute, 1981.

Jensen, Richard Bach. "The United States, International Policing and the War against Anarchist Terrorism, 1900–1914." In *Terrorism: Critical Concepts in Political Science*, vol. 1: *The First or Anarchist Wave*, ed. David C. Rapoport, 369–400. London: Routledge, 2006.

Johnson, Paul. "Preface: Fifth Session: The Role of the Media in the Struggle Against Terrorism." In *International Terrorism: Challenge and Response; Proceedings of the Jerusalem Conference on International Terrorism*, ed. Benjamin Netanyahu, 221–22. Jerusalem: Jonathan Institute, 1981.

Johnson, Robert H. "Periods of Peril: The Window of Vulnerability and Other Myths." *Foreign Affairs* 61, no. 4 (1983): 950–70.

Joyner, Christopher C. "International Extradition and Global Terrorism: Bringing International Criminals to Justice." *Loyola of Los Angeles International and Comparative Law Review* 25 (2003): 493–542.

Kane, Terry Richard. "Prosecuting International Terrorists in United States Courts: Gaining the Jurisdictional Threshold." *Yale Journal of International Law* 12 (1987): 294–341.

Keohane, Robert. "Multilateralism: An Agenda for Research." *International Journal* 45, no. 4 (Autumn 1990): 731–64.

Keohane, Robert O., and Joseph S. Nye. "Transgovernmental Relations and International Organizations." *World Politics* 27, no. 1 (October 1974): 39–62.

Kirkpatrick, Jeane. "Dictatorship and Double Standards." *Commentary* 68, no. 5 (November 1979): 34–45.

Kriegel, Annie. "Public Opinion, Intellectuals and Terrorism in Western Europe." In *International Terrorism: Challenge and Response; Proceedings of the Jerusalem Conference on International Terrorism*, ed. Benjamin Netanyahu, 172–79. Jerusalem: Jonathan Institute, 1981.

Kupperman, Robert. "Nuclear Terrorism: Armchair Pastime or Genuine Threat?" *Jerusalem Journal of International Relations* 3, no. 4 (Summer 1978): 19–26.

Lammert, Markus. "The Absent Terrorism: Leftist Political Violence and the French State, 1968–1974." In *An International History of Terrorism: Western and Non-Western Experiences*, ed. Jussi Hanhimäki and Bernhard Blumenau, 86–99. New York: Routledge, 2013.

——. "Ein neues Analysemodell für die historische Terrorismusforschung? Securitization-Prozesse in Frankreich und Deutschland in den 1970er und 1980er Jahren." In *Terrorismusbekämpfung in Westeuropa: Demokratie und Sicherheit in den 1970er und 1980er Jahren,* ed. Johannes Hürter, 201–15. Oldenbourg, Germany: De Gruyter, 2015.

Latner, Teishan A. "Take Me to Havana! Airline Hijacking, U.S.-Cuban Relations, and Political Protest in Late Sixties' America." *Diplomatic History* 39, no. 1 (January 2015): 16–44.

League of Nations. "Convention for the Prevention and Punishment of Terrorism." *World Digital Library*. Accessed November 25, 2019. https://www.wdl.org/en/item/11579/.

Lieberman, David M. "Sorting the Revolutionary from the Terrorist: The Delicate Application of the 'Political Offense Exception' in U.S. Extradition Cases." *Stanford Law Review* 59, no. 1 (October 2006): 181–212.

Ludlow, N. Piers. "More Than Just a Single Market: European Integration, Peace and Security in the 1980s." *British Journal of Politics and International Relations* 19, no. 1 (February 2017): 48–62.

Malik, Omar. "Aviation Security Before and After Lockerbie." *Terrorism and Political Violence* 10, no. 3 (September 1998): 112–33.

Mantilla, Giovanni. "The Political Origins of the Geneva Conventions of 1949 and the Additional Protocols of 1977." In *Do the Geneva Conventions Matter?*, ed. Matthew Evangelista and Nina Tannenwald, 35–68. New York: Oxford University Press, 2017.

Mazower, Mark. "Violence and the State in the Twentieth Century." *American Historical Review* 107, no. 4 (June 2002): 1158–78.

Meinhof, Ulrike. "Das Konzept Stadtguerilla." In *Rote Armee Fraktion: Texte und Materialien zur Geschichte der RAF*, 27–48. Berlin: ID Verlag, 1997.

Metzler, Gabriele. "Erzählen, Aufführen, Widerstehen: Westliche Terrorismusbekämp-fung in Politik, Gesellschaft und Kultur der 1970er Jahre." In *Terrorismusbekämp-fung in Westeuropa: Demokratie und Sicherheit in den 1970er und 1980er Jahren*, ed. Johannes Hürter, 117–36. Oldenbourg, Germany: De Gruyter, 2015.

Mickolus, Edward. "Multilateral Legal Efforts to Combat Terrorism: Diagnosis and Prognosis." *Ohio Northern University Law Review* 6 (1979): 13–51.

Migaux, Phillipe. "Al Qaeda." In *The History of Terrorism: From Antiquity to Al Qaeda*, ed. Gérard Chaliand and Arnaud Blin, 314–48. Berkeley: University of California Press, 2007.

Moss, Robert. "The Terrorist State." In *International Terrorism: Challenge and Response; Proceedings of the Jerusalem Conference on International Terrorism*, ed. Benjamin Netanyahu, 128–34. Jerusalem: Jonathan Institute, 1981.

Mujuzi, Jamil Ddamulira. "South Africa." In *Comparative Counter-Terrorism Law*, ed. Kent Roach. Cambridge: Cambridge University Press, 2015. https://doi.org/10.1017 /CBO9781107298002.019.

Netanyahu, Benjamin. "Conference Summary Statement." In *International Terrorism: Challenge and Response; Proceedings of the Jerusalem Conference on International Terrorism*, ed. Benjamin Netanyahu, 361–62. Jerusalem: Jonathan Institute, 1981.

——. "Foreword." In *International Terrorism: Challenge and Response; Proceedings of the Jerusalem Conference on International Terrorism*, ed. Benjamin Netanyahu, xi–ii. Jerusalem: Jonathan Institute, 1981.

——. "Preface." In *Terrorism: How the West Can Win*, ed. Benjamin Netanyahu, ix–xi. New York: Farrar, Straus and Giroux, 1986.

Neumann, Peter R. "The Myth of Ulsterization in British Security Policy in Northern Ireland." *Studies in Conflict and Terrorism* 26, no. 5 (May 2003): 365–77.

Nitze, Paul. "Strategy in the Decade of the 1980s." *Foreign Affairs* 59, no. 1 (Fall 1980): 82–101.

Oberloskamp, Eva. "Auf dem Weg in den Überwachungsstaat? Elektronische Daten-verarbeitung, Terrorismusbekämpfung und die Anfänge des bundesdeutschen Datenschutzes in den 1970er Jahren." In *Ausnahmezustände: Entgrenzungen und Regulierungen in Europa während des Kalten Krieges*, ed. Cornelia Rauh and Dirk Schumann, 158–76. Göttingen, Germany: Wallstein, 2015.

——. "Die Europäisierung der Terrorismusbekämpfung in den 1970er Jahren: Bundes-deutsche Akteure und Positionen." In *Terrorismusbekämpfung in Westeuropa: Demokratie und Sicherheit in den 1970er und 1980er Jahren*, ed. Johannes Hürter, 219–38. Oldenbourg: De Gruyter, 2015.

——. "Das Olympia-Attentat 1972: Politische Lernprozesse im Umgang mit dem transna-tionalen Terrorismus." *Vierteljahrshefte für Zeitgeschichte* 60, no. 3 (July 2012): 321–52.

Office of the Under Secretary for Global Affairs. "Frank E. Loy, Under Secretary of State for Global Affairs: Biography." *U.S. Department of State Archive: Information Released Online Prior to January 20, 2001*. Published November 2, 1998. Accessed January 25, 2019. https://1997-2001.state.gov/about_state/biography/loy.html.

Organization of American States. "Convention to Prevent and Punish the Acts of Ter-rorism Taking the Form of Crimes Against Persons and Related Extortion That are of International Significance, Signed at the Third Special Session of the General Assem-bly, in Washington, DC, February 2, 1971." *Organization of American States*. Accessed November 25, 2019. http://www.oas.org/juridico/english/treaties/a-49.html.

Passmore, Leith. "The Art of Hunger: Self-Starvation in the Red Army Faction." *German History* 21, no. 1 (January 2009): 32–59.

——. "International Law as an Extralegal Defense Strategy in West Germany's Stammheim Terror Trial." *Law, Culture and the Humanities* 9, no. 2 (June 2011): 375–94.

Peres, Shimon. "The Threat and the Response." In *International Terrorism: Challenge and Response; Proceedings of the Jerusalem Conference on International Terrorism*, ed. Benjamin Netanyahu, 8–11. Jerusalem: Jonathan Institute, 1981.

Pipes, Richard. "The Roots of the Involvement." In *International Terrorism: Challenge and Response; Proceedings of the Jerusalem Conference on International Terrorism*, ed. Benjamin Netanyahu, 58–63. Jerusalem: Jonathan Institute, 1981.

——. "Team B: The Reality Behind the Myth." *Commentary* 82, no. 4 (1986): 25–40.

Podhoretz, Norman. "The Subtle Collusion." In *International Terrorism: Challenge and Response; Proceedings of the Jerusalem Conference on International Terrorism*, ed. Benjamin Netanyahu, 235–41. Jerusalem: Jonathan Institute, 1981.

Police Fédérale. "CGSU: Unités spéciales de la police fédérale." *Police Haute Senne*. Accessed March 15, 2019. http://www.policelocale.be/5328/actualites/95-cgsu-unites-speciales -de-la-police-federale.

Pompidou Group. "History." Accessed March 5, 2018. https://www.coe.int/en/web /pompidou/about/history.

Press and Information Office, European Political Cooperation. "Introduction to EPC (European Political Cooperation)." Accessed March 10, 2020. http://aei.pitt.edu/1895 /1/EPC_intro.pdf.

"Questions and Answers: Fourth Session: Current Response of Democratic Societies." In *International Terrorism: Challenge and Response; Proceedings of the Jerusalem Conference on International Terrorism*, ed. Benjamin Netanyahu, 214–19. Jerusalem: Jonathan Institute, 1981.

"Questions and Answers: Fifth Session: The Role of the Media in the Struggle Against Terrorism." In *International Terrorism: Challenge and Response; Proceedings of the Jerusalem Conference on International Terrorism*, ed. Benjamin Netanyahu, 253–62. Jerusalem: Jonathan Institute, 1981.

"Questions and Answers: Third Session: The Threat Posed by Terrorism to Democratic Societies." In *International Terrorism: Challenge and Response; Proceedings of the Jerusalem Conference on International Terrorism*, ed. Benjamin Netanyahu, 155–58. Jerusalem: Jonathan Institute, 1981.

Raustiala, Kal. "The Architecture of International Cooperation: Transgovernmental Networks and the Future of International Law." *Virginia Journal of International Law* 43, no. 1 (Fall 2002): 1–92.

Re, Matteo. "The Red Brigades' Communiqués: An Analysis of the Terrorist Group's Propaganda." *Terrorism and Political Violence* (September 2017): doi:10.1080/09546 553.2017.1364639.

Republic of South Africa. "Terrorism Act 1967, Act No. 83 of 1967." In *Statutes of the Union of South Africa*. Pretoria: Government Printer, 1967, 1236–46.

Reynolds, Michael A. "The Wars' Entangled Roots: Regional Realities and Washington's Vision." In *Understanding the U.S. Wars in Iraq and Afghanistan*, ed. Beth Bailey and Richard H. Immerman, 21–53. New York: New York University Press, 2015.

Riegler, Thomas. " 'Es muss ein gegenseitiges Geben und Nehmen sein': Warschauer-Pakt-Staaten und Terrorismusbekämpfung am Beispiel der DDR." In *Terrorismusbekämpfung in Westeuropa*, ed. Johannes Hürter, 289–316. Oldenbourg, Germany: De Gruyter, 2015.

Romaniuk, Peter. "From 'Global War' to Global Governance: Counterterrorism Cooperation in World Politics." In *International Organization and Global Governance: What Matters and Why*, ed. Thomas G. Weiss and Rorden Wilkinson, 454–65. London: Routledge, 2014.

Saul, Ben. "The Legal Response of the League of Nations to Terrorism." *Journal of International Criminal Justice* 4, no. 1 (March 2006): 78–102.

——. "Terrorism as a Transnational Crime." In *Routledge Handbook of Transnational Criminal Law*, ed. Neil Boister and Robert Currie, 394–408. New York: Routledge, 2015.

Saunders, Harold H. "Diplomacy and Pressure, November 1979–May 1980." In *American Hostages in Iran*, ed. Warren Christopher and Paul H. Kreisberg, 72–143. New Haven, CT: Yale University Press, 1985.

Saupe, Achim. " 'Innere Sicherheit' und 'law and order': Die politische Semantik von Ordnung, Sicherheit und Freiheit in der bundesdeutschen Innenpolitik." In *Terrorismusbekämpfung in Westeuropa: Demokratie und Sicherheit in den 1970er und 1980er Jahren*, ed. Johannes Hürter, 171–200. Oldenbourg, Germany: De Gruyter, 2015.

Scott, Eric. "The Hijacking of Aeroflot 244: States and Statelessness in the Late Cold War." *Past and Present* 243 (May 2019): 213–45.

Soustelle, Jacques. "Liberty or License?" In *International Terrorism: Challenge and Response; Proceedings of the Jerusalem Conference on International Terrorism*, ed. Benjamin Netanyahu, 250–52. Jerusalem: Jonathan Institute, 1981.

State Department, Bureau of International Security and Nonproliferation. "Convention on the Physical Protection of Nuclear Material." *U.S. Department of State Archive*. Accessed September 13, 2019. https://2009-2017.state.gov/t/isn/5079.htm.

Steinhoff, Patricia G. "Kidnapped Japanese in North Korea: The New Left Connection." *Journal of Japanese Studies* 30, no. 1 (Winter 2004): 123–42.

——. "Portrait of a Terrorist: An Interview with Kozo Okamoto." *Asian Survey* 16, no. 9 (September 1976): 830–45.

Teller, Edward. "The Spectre of Nuclear Terrorism." In *International Terrorism: Challenge and Response; Proceedings of the Jerusalem Conference on International Terrorism*, ed. Benjamin Netanyahu, 141–45. Jerusalem: Jonathan Institute, 1981.

Thornton, Thomas. "Terror as a Weapon of Political Agitation." In *Internal War: Problems and Approaches*, ed. Harry Eckstein, 71–99. New York: The Free Press of Glencoe, 1964.

Townshend, Charles. " 'Methods Which All Civilized Opinion Must Condemn': The League of Nations and International Action against Terrorism." In *An International History of Terrorism: Western and Non-Western Experiences*, ed. Jussi M. Hanhimäki and Bernhard Blumenau, 34–50. New York: Routledge, 2013.

"Unit Interventie Mariniers." *Dutch Defense Press*. Accessed March 15, 2019. https://www.dutchdefencepress.com/unit-interventie-mariniers/.

United Nations. "Convention on the High Seas." *United Nations*. Accessed March 10, 2020. https://www.gc.noaa.gov/documents/8_1_1958_high_seas.pdf.

——. "Convention on the Prevention and Punishment of Crimes Against Internationally Protected Persons, Including Diplomatic Agents: General Assembly Resolution 3166 (XXVIII) of 14 December 1973." *International Law Commission*. Accessed November 25, 2019. http://legal.un.org/ilc/texts/instruments/english/conventions/9_4_1973_resolution .pdf.

——. "International Convention Against the Taking of Hostages." *United Nations Treaty Collection*. Accessed November 5, 2019. https://treaties.un.org/doc/Treaties /1979/12/19791218%2003–20%20PM/Ch_XVIII_5p.pdf.

——. "Legal Research Guide 6: Obligation to extradite or prosecute = Obligation d'extrader ou de poursuivre (aut dedere aut judicare): Bibliography (articles / books)." *United Nations Library and Archives at Geneva*. Accessed November 25, 2019. http://libraryresources.unog.ch/Legal/legal/ILC.

——. "Vienna Convention on Diplomatic Relations, Done at Vienna on 18 April 1961." *United Nations*. Accessed November 25, 2019. http://legal.un.org/ilc/texts/instruments /english/conventions/9_1_1961.pdf.

——. "Vienna Convention on the Law of Treaties (with Annex), Concluded at Vienna on 23 May 1969." *United Nations*. Accessed November 25, 2019. https://treaties.un .org/doc/publication/unts/volume%20l155/volume-1155-i-18232-english.pdf.

U.S. Congress. "The Jerusalem Conference on International Terrorism Identifies the Soviet Union as the Primary Sponsor of Terrorism." *Congressional Record*. 96th Congress, 1st Session, 1979. Vol. 125, pp. 17926–29.

U.S. House of Representatives. "Public Law 93–366." Office of the Law Revision Counsel, U.S. Code, August 5, 1974. Accessed November 25, 2019. http://uscode.house.gov /statutes/pl/93/366.pdf.

Walther, Rudolf. "Terror und Terrorismus: Eine Begriffs- und Sozialgeschichtliche Skizze." In *Die RAF: Entmythologisierung einer Terroristischen Organisation*, ed. Wolfgang Kraushaar, 50–70. Bonn, Germany: Bundeszentrale für Politische Bildung, 2008.

Warner, Bruce B. "Great Britain and the Response to International Terrorism." In *The Deadly Sin of Terrorism: Its Effect on Democracy and Civil Liberties in Six Countries*, ed. David Charters, 13–42. Westport, CT: Greenwood, 1996.

White House. "National Security Decision Directive 138: Combatting Terrorism." Intelligence Resource Program. *Federation of American Scientists*. Last edited April 4, 2018. Accessed April 26, 2018. https://fas.org/irp/offdocs/nsdd/nsdd-138.pdf.

Will, George. "Calculating the Public Interest." In *International Terrorism: Challenge and Response; Proceedings of the Jerusalem Conference on International Terrorism*, ed. Benjamin Netanyahu, 208–13. Jerusalem: Jonathan Institute, 1981.

Wunschik, Tobias. "Abwehr und Unterstützung des internationalen Terrorismus—Die Hauptabteilung XXII." In *Westarbeit des MfS: Das Zusammenspiel von "Aufklärung" und "Abwehr,"* ed. Hubertus Knabe, 263–73. Berlin: Ch. Links, 1999.

——. "Baader-Meinhof international?" *Aus Politik und Zeitgeschichte* 40–41 (2007): 23–29.

INDEX

Page numbers in *italics* indicate figures.

ARA. *See* Bureau of Inter-American Affairs
Arafat, Yasser, 18; PFLP expelled by, 59; PFLP opposition from, 36; UNGA speech by, 111, 134
Argentinean antiterrorism initiative, 52, 53
Arms Control and Disarmament Agency (ACDA), 135–36, 187
Austria: antiterrorism tactical units established in, 153; OPEC headquarters attack in Vienna, 1, 133–34, 174–75; Vienna Convention on Diplomatic Relations 1961, 48
Austrian Airlines flight bombing, 46–47

Baader, Andreas: arrest of, 120; RAF co-founded by, 119–20; suicide by, 149–50
Balcombe Street siege hostage situation, 139
Balkans, 16
Baroody, Jamil Murad, 98–99, 100–101
Begin, Menachem, 218
Beirut airport attack, 36
Belgium: antiterrorism tactical units established in, 145; convention suggestions of, 164; on European Convention addendum, 194
Belon, Christian, 46
Ben-Ari, Mordecai, 223
Bennett, W. Tapley, 96–97, 99, 101
Bettauer, Ronald, 77–79, 106–7
Birmingham, Alabama, 100
Black Panther Party, 23–24
bombings: of Austrian Airlines flight, 46–47; of Pan Am Flight 103, 236; suicide, 243; of SwissAir Flight SR330, 46–47, 55
Bonn Declaration, 212–14, *213*
Border Security Group 9. *See* Grenzschutzgruppe 9
Brandt, Willy: GSG 9 support from, 144; law enforcement reforms of, 120; Munich Olympic Games attack response of, 124–25
Brent, William Lee, 23–24
British government. *See* United Kingdom
British Special Air Services (SAS): antiterrorism tactical units based on, 143–44; counterinsurgency experience of, 121; GSG 9 cooperation with, 148, 152; training priorities of, 155–56; UK

Military Training Assistance Scheme participation of, 146
Brzezinski, Zbigniew, 212, 215
BSO. *See* Palestinian Black September Organization
Bundesamt für Verfassungsschutz. *See* Federal Office for the Protection of the Constitution
Bundeskriminalamt, 83, 120, 139–40, 154–55
Bureau of Inter-American Affairs (ARA), 29, 30
Bureau of Near Eastern Affairs (NEA), 26, 42
Bush, George H. W.: Diplomats Convention support from, 95, 96; at Jerusalem Conference, 219, 221, 223; on Libya, 236; on Lod Airport massacre, 86; on terrorism as surrogate warfare, 221; UNGA summarizing by, 99, 101, 104; of UN inability, 223, 300n86
Butler, Charles, 44–45, 61–62, 66–67

Cabinet Committee to Combat Terrorism (CCCT): Carter administration abolishing, 211; identification of terrorist groups, 170; Nixon administration founding, 90–91; studies by, 135
Camp David Accords, 207
Canada hostage crisis, 66, 83
Carlos the Jackal. *See* Ramírez Sánchez, Ilich
Carter administration: CCCT abolished by, 211; on Iran hostage crisis, 209; NSC Special Coordinating Committee Working Group on Terrorism created under, 212
Casey, William, 228, 230–31
CCCT. *See* Cabinet Committee to Combat Terrorism
Center for Strategic and International Studies (CSIS), 220, 233
Central Intelligence Agency (CIA): CPD on, 216; "International Terrorism in 1979" by, 228; media anticommunism funding from, 219; Munich Olympic Games attack report, 88; propaganda at Jerusalem Conference, 222, 231, 300n93; Ramírez Sánchez capture coordinated with, 2, 241; SNIE Soviet Union study

hostage situation (*continued*)
113–14, *114*, 132, 169–70, 289n38. *See also*
hijackings; Munich Olympic Games attack
human rights, 163
Hurwitch, Robert, 45, 48, 50–51, 53–54

IAEA. *See* International Atomic Energy
Agency
IATA. *See* International Air Transport
Association
ICAO. *See* International Civil Aviation
Organization
IDF. *See* Israeli Defense Forces
IFALPA. *See* International Federation of Air
Line Pilots Association
ILC. *See* International Law Commission
illegal combatants, 244, 245
Immigration Act (1903), 15
International Air Transport Association
(IATA), 31–32
International Atomic Energy Agency
(IAEA), 108–9, 209
International Civil Aviation Organization
(ICAO): Annex 17 of, 55, 108;
antihijacking subcommittee, 35–41,
43–44, 47; aviation security negotiations,
105–6; Committee on Unlawful
Interference with Aircraft, 35; Cuba as
founding member of, 37; establishment
and mission of, 32; European Convention
and repeating patterns from, 196–97;
hijacking prevention as focus of, 32–33;
technological security innovations for,
55–56; U.S. sanctions proposal to, 44–45,
61–62, 66–67, 105–6, 210. *See also* Hague
Convention; Montreal Convention;
Tokyo Convention
International Convention Against the
Taking of Hostages. *See* Hostages
Convention
International Convention for the
Suppression of Terrorist Bombings
(1997), 244
International Convention for the
Suppression of the Financing of
Terrorism (1999), 244
International Convention on the
Suppression of Acts of Nuclear
Terrorism (2005), 244

International Criminal Police Organization
(Interpol), 91, 104, 123, 127
International Federation of Air Line Pilots
Association (IFALPA), 40
international humanitarian law: hijacking,
extradite or prosecute principle and, 40;
prisoner-of-war status and demanding
rights under, 83–84; self-determination
under, 10; UN negotiating addendums
to, 205
international law: as border-spanning
tool, 5–6; over counterinsurgency,
8; European Convention changing
definition of terrorism in, 197; FRG
International Law Division, 162, 207–8;
laws of war, 10, 40, 205; militarized
counterterrorism over, 237–39;
normalization of conceptualizations
of terrorism in, 202–15; OAS, Hague,
and Montreal Conventions impacts to,
68–70; state sovereignty impacted by
approach to, 10; terrorism codified in,
201
International Law Commission (ILC):
Diplomats Convention draft, 79–80,
95–97; functions of, 78
international terrorism: Diplomats
Convention interconnected with, 95;
diversification of, 134–35; European
integration threatened by, 161–62; at
Jerusalem Conference, 215–24; media
adopting term of, 89; Munich Olympic
Games attack and concept of, 80–92;
NATO intelligence collaboration on,
91, 104; OLA working paper on, 94–95,
97–98, 99; origins of labeling attacks
as, 3; patterns emerging in, 4; Second
Conference on International Terrorism,
233; TREVI collaboration against
crime and, 125–42; UNGA debates in
1972 on, 72–74, 92–104, 111–12; UNGA
representatives discussing vote on, *93*;
UNGA Resolution 3034 On Measures
to Prevent International Terrorism,
102–4, *103*; UNGA submitting draft
resolutions on, 102; vagueness around
definition of, 94–95, 175–76. *See also*
specific topics
"International Terrorism in 1979," 228

kidnappings: of diplomats in Latin America, 50–51, 64; by Front de libération du Québec, 66, 83; by Italian Red Brigades, 139, 153, 191, *191*; similarities between hijacking and, 51; by 2 June Movement, 113–14, *114*, 132, 169–70, 289n38; two-pronged approach to addressing, 50–51. *See also* hostage situation/crisis
Kissinger, Henry, 35, 41, 42
Korean Airlines Flight Y-11, 46
Kröcher-Tiedemann, Gabriele, *114*, 134, 174, 189
Krosney, Herbert, 225
Kupperman, Robert, 135–36, 187

Laporte, Pierre, 66, 83
Laqueur, Walter, 89
Latin America: Argentinean antiterrorism initiative, 52, 53; counterinsurgency training in, 18–19, 49; diplomats as targets in, 48–55; as hotbed of violent activity, 48; kidnapping of diplomats in, 50–51, 64; National Security Doctrine adopted by, 49; Operation Condor in, 52, 82; Rebel Armed Forces in, 49–50; repression of political dissent in, 82; repression of population by governments of, 49; terrorist defined in, 49
laws of war: downplaying references to, 10; hijacking, extradite or prosecute principle and, 40; UN negotiating addendums to, 205. *See also* international humanitarian law
League of Nations, 16
Lebanese Civil War, 232
legal space convention draft, European, 191–95
Leonardo da Vinci-Fiumicino Airport attack, 121
Libya: Pan Am flight bombed by officials of, 236; Reagan administration on, 233, 235
Libyan Arab Airlines Flight 114, 105
Lod Airport massacre, 84–86, *85*
Lorenz, Peter, 113–14, *114*, 132, 169–70, 289n38
von Löwenich, Gerhard, 127–28, 137

Loy, Frank: allies of, 31–32, 34; antihijacking initiatives of, 30, 31–32, 33–35, 37, 39–41, 44–45; background as aviation expert, 29; State Department left by, 56
Lufthansa airlines: Flight 181 hijacking, 149–51, *150*, 207; Flight 615 hijacking, 71, 97

Maastrich Treaty (1992), 141
Macomber, William B., Jr., 50–51
Malmborg, Knute, 34, 37, 38–39, 40, 43, 44, 47
Marighella, Carlos, 18, 82, 83
media: antiterrorism tactical units gaining interest of, 151; CIA funding anticommunist, 219; Entebbe operation covered by, 147–48; hijackings downplayed by, 27–28; international terrorism term adopted by, 89; Jerusalem Conference referencing from, 224–25, 226–27; on Munich Olympic Games attack, 89; terrorism aided by, 223
Mein, John Gordon, 50
Meinhof, Ulrike, 119–20
Meins, Holger, 131–32
Meir, Golda, 71, 87, 89, 97
Méndez, Nicanor, 52, 53
militarized counterterrorism: advocacy of, 199, *200*, 201; Entebbe operation used for lobbying of, 199, *200*; Entebbe operation using, 198–99; over international law, 237–39; by Israel, 89–90; Jerusalem Conference adopting, 223–24; shift to, 4–5; U.S. beginnings in, 4–5, 199, 227–28. *See also* antiterrorism tactical units
Minimanual of the Urban Guerilla (Marighella), 18, 82
Mogadishu operation, 149–51, *150*, 207
Montreal Convention: adoption of, 67; extradite or prosecute principle and, 67; international law impacted by, 68–70; loopholes in, 75–76, 174; 1988 protocol added to, 236; as precedent for European Convention, 161; success of, 75; title of, formal, 286n4
Moro, Aldo, 139, 153, 191, *191*
Moss, Robert, 219, 221–22, 225, 226–27, 231
mujahideen, 229, 233